Comedy-Horror Films

Comedy-Horror Films
A Chronological History, 1914–2008

BRUCE G. HALLENBECK

McFarland & Company, Inc., Publishers
Jefferson, North Carolina, and London

LIBRARY OF CONGRESS CATALOGUING-IN-PUBLICATION DATA

Hallenbeck, Bruce G., 1952–
Comedy-horror films : a chronological
history, 1914–2008 / Bruce G. Hallenbeck.
p.   cm.
Includes bibliographical references and index.

ISBN 978-0-7864-3332-2
softcover : 50# alkaline paper ∞

1. Horror films—History and criticism.
2. Comedy films—History and criticism.
3. Motion pictures—History—20th century.
I. Title.
PN1995.9.H6H345   2009   791.43'6164—dc22   2009001825

British Library cataloguing data are available

©2009 Bruce G. Hallenbeck. All rights reserved

*No part of this book may be reproduced or transmitted in any form
or by any means, electronic or mechanical, including photocopying
or recording, or by any information storage and retrieval system,
without permission in writing from the publisher.*

On the cover: Poster art for the 1979 film *Love at First Bite* (AIP/Photofest)

Manufactured in the United States of America

*McFarland & Company, Inc., Publishers
Box 611, Jefferson, North Carolina 28640
www.mcfarlandpub.com*

To my wife Rosa, my life partner and best friend,
with whom I fully expect to die laughing

ACKNOWLEDGMENTS

Several people and institutions helped me in my research on this book. First and foremost, I'd like to thank the New York State Library, not just for employing me, but for being the fantastic facility that it is. One of the largest research libraries in the world, it supplied me with original film reviews and features from the *New York Times*. Thanks are also due to Steve Campbell at Video Visions in Chatham, New York, for providing me with some of the films reviewed herein; to Alpha Video; to Rodrigo at Kino; to Ed at Sue Procko Public Relations; to Movies Unlimited; and to Kip and Kimball Jenkins at The Missing Link (*www.missinglinkclassichorror.co.uk*) for the copy of *Sh! The Octopus*. Very special thanks to Larry Blamire, who allowed me to see his film *Trail of the Screaming Forehead* before it was even released. Can't wait to see the next one, Larry.

Table of Contents

Acknowledgments	vi
Preface	1
Introduction	3
1. The Silents: Unheard Punchlines and Subtitled Screams	5
2. The Thirties: Old Dark Houses and Gorilla Suits	15
3. The Forties: Killer Zombies and Comedy Teams	28
4. The Fifties: Elderly Monsters and Black Humor	52
5. The Sixties: Gothic Castles and Cleavage Galore	63
6. The Seventies: Naked Vampires and Young Frankensteins	88
7. The Eighties: American Werewolves and Toxic Avengers	118
8. The Nineties: Screams and Cemetery Men	167
9. Comedy-Horror in the New Millennium	193
Afterword	208
Appendix A: A Chronological Checklist of Films	209
Appendix B: Selected Short Subjects	231
Bibliography	235
Index	237

Preface

Comedy in the horror film? Horror in the comedy film? It seems like a strange combination; one moment a scream, the next moment a laugh. And yet comedy and horror are not strange bedfellows at all. They've been around almost as long as movies themselves.

As one who grew up reading such periodicals as *Famous Monsters of Filmland* (although its editor, the legendary Forrest J Ackerman, once admonished me to "never grow up"), I've subsequently read hundreds of tomes written about horror films as metaphors, full of dark sexual symbolism, of how they can be sexist and misogynistic and may make the viewer insensitive to violence. I've read endless treatises on how horror films can corrupt the young and, conversely, how they can be cathartic escape valves for our darkest impulses.

But I've never read a book that related the history of the comedy-horror film, that bastardization of unease and chuckles that has alternately delighted and frightened audiences from the days of silent films such as *The Bat* on up to such recent hits as *Scary Movie*. It seems as though film scholars love to get lofty about subtext, but the idea of humor combined with horror ... well, it seems to frighten them.

This book attempts to correct that oversight, and also attempts to explore just why we like gallows humor. What is it in the human condition that makes us want to laugh at the darkness around us, especially when things in the real world seem to be at their worst?

This book is a chronological look at comedy-horror films, a decade by decade examination of the best (and worst) examples of the genre. The (arguably) most important films are covered in-depth, and there are two appendices with credits, American release dates and other particulars of over 200 comedy-horror feature films from 1914 to 2008, as well as selected short subjects, including cartoons.

Needless to say, a tremendous amount of research has to go into a book of this kind, and there was much work involved, for over a year and a half, involving rifling through old newspaper clippings, reference books, taped radio interviews I conducted myself, and even perusals of old movie scripts at the New York State Archives. Websites, valuable tools for the researcher provided they're cross-referenced, were important too, especially the Internet Movie DataBase (*www.imdb.com*).

I hope this book will shed some light on the relationship between humor and horror as well as provide information to the reader about the films themselves and the people behind them. The intention was to write a serious—though hopefully entertaining—book about a topic that rarely receives serious attention.

Whether or not I've succeeded is up to the reader to decide.

INTRODUCTION

"There's a thin line between horror and hilarity."
—Robert Bloch, author of *Psycho*

Some people are born in one-horse towns. I was born in a Headless Horseman town.

For years now—centuries, even—there's been a feud going on between the tiny town of Kinderhook, New York (my birthplace and where I still reside), and the slightly larger town of Tarrytown, New York. It isn't a Hatfield-McCoy type of feud, but rather a literary one, and the gist of it is this: When the great American author Washington Irving wrote his classic story "The Legend of Sleepy Hollow," it was based on real places and real people. Did, in fact, the Headless Horseman ride through Kinderhook or Tarrytown?

In Kinderhook, the home team plays at Ichabod Crane Central School, which has a bas-relief in the school auditorium of the venerable schoolmaster being chased by the Headless Horseman. I live just down the road from the Sleepy Hollow Motel. And so on.

The truth of the matter is, Irving based his characters on actual citizens of Kinderhook and placed them in the Tarrytown setting. So both towns can claim the legend. The home of the real Ichabod Crane—one Jesse Merwin by name—still stands not far from where I live.

I write all this by way of introduction to explain my interest in all things both comic and horrific. "The Legend of Sleepy Hollow" was the first great comedy-horror story, and remains perhaps the best. Who could ever forget the poor lovesick schoolmaster pursued by that dreadful apparition on horseback—and who wouldn't chuckle at the fact that it was all just a Halloween prank? Irving's story contained the blueprint for all comedy-horror tales to follow: it made you laugh one moment and scream the next, and it was all tied neatly together with that Halloween sense of the mischievous.

The films covered in this book set out to do exactly what Irving did. Some of them succeed spectacularly and some fail miserably. Most of them fall somewhere in the middle. But all of them aim to hit you in the funny bone and at the small of your back, where your spine tingles.

Gallows humor, of course, goes back a long way. Whistling past the graveyard supposedly makes one feel safer. But safe from what? A good comedy-horror film knows what scares you: ghosts, zombies, vampires, werewolves, psycho killers, monsters of all shapes, sizes and descriptions. But comedy-horror films give you what straight dramatic horror films don't: the permission to laugh at your fears, to whistle past the cinematic graveyard and feel secure in the knowledge that the monsters can't get you. At least not until you stop whistling.

Psycho author Robert Bloch once told me: "Both horror and humor require the same distorted conception of reality to be effective." Who should know more about that subject than the creator of the very witty, but very dangerous, Norman Bates?

Of course, humor and horror are both in the eye (or empty eye socket) of the beholder.

Some people may think of Stanley Kubrick's film *The Shining* as a comedy. It certainly has some wonderfully black comedic moments ("Heeeere's Johnny!"), but the overall effect is one of impending doom, of a journey into the labyrinth of an insane and ghoulish mind. If you find that idea funny, then I don't want to have a beer with you.

Unintentionally humorous horror movies (and there are a lot of those) are also not under the purview of this book. Movies such as *Robot Monster*, for example, may make the viewer laugh at the sheer ineptitude of its special effects (a man in an ape suit with a deep sea diving helmet on his head, sometimes surrounded by soap bubbles), but it was made with such sincerity that it can't truly be called comedy-horror. This book will not concern itself with bad movies that have been roasted on *Mystery Science Theatre 3000*. For that kind of irony, you must go elsewhere. Any college campus will do.

And finally, there is one other sub-genre of the horror movie that won't find its way into these pages: the horror nudie, or T&A horror film. There's a New Jersey company called Pop Cinema that produces and distributes movies by the truckload with such titles as *Play-Mate of the Apes*, *Kinky Kong*, *Lord of the G-Strings* and *Spider-Babe*. They usually star young actresses who are willing to disrobe at regular and frequent intervals and get into compromising positions with each other. Although these parodies are frequently quite amusing, their intention is not to tickle your funny bone, but rather to elicit a completely different response from another part of your anatomy. I think you know what I mean.

Besides, writing about such films would actually be a conflict of interest. I'm perfectly willing to confess to being the author of such Pop Cinema movies as *Misty Mundae Mummy Raider*, *The Witches of Sappho Salon*, *Dr. Jekyll and Mistress Hyde* and *The Sexy Adventures of Van Helsing*. I'm certainly not about to review my own screenplays. Again, if you're looking for coverage on those particular films, you need to look elsewhere. An Internet search engine should be your first stop.

If, on the other hand, you like to travel through old dark houses to "have a po-*ta*-to" with Ernest Thesiger or visit Transylvanian castles full of gay Jewish vampires with Roman Polanski, or even spend a camping holiday in the woods with Bruce Campbell and some Deadites, then this could be the book for you.

It isn't all about horror and hilarity, however. Along the way, we'll take a look at the cultural and social significance of comedy-horror films in relation to the times in which they were produced. Not to be too lofty, but merely to peer under the surface to discover just why, at any given moment in history, we the audience love to be scared out of our wits while laughing out loud.

Some of the movies mentioned in this book may be the source of nostalgic memories for you. Perhaps descriptions of the ones you haven't seen will intrigue you enough to seek them out. But all of them, good, bad or indifferent, have one thing in common: they want to do what a good Halloween party does. You come into the spooky house, have a few laughs, a few scares, and then return to the real world refreshed. What could be more wonderful than that?

1

THE SILENTS
Unheard Punchlines and Subtitled Screams

When the movies were born in the late nineteenth century, there were no "art" films. There were really no film genres at all; they had yet to be invented. Motion pictures were merely a new invention, a source of amusement rather like computer games were a century later.

But fantasy quickly took hold of the infant cinema, and with it, darkness. It began with the films of Frenchman Georges Méliès. But it was too early in the game to throw truly horrifying images at fans of the Nickelodeon; they had to be eased into it.

As Phil Hardy points out in his groundbreaking book *The Encyclopedia of Horror Movies*: "Although Georges Méliès' *La Manoir du Diable* (1896), with its image of the Devil as a vampire bat, is undoubtedly the first horror film, in atmosphere and feeling the film is far closer to the tradition of comic fantasies in which smiling amazement, rather than terror, was the expected reaction."

Indeed, "smiling amazement" was the expected response to most fantasy-horror films of the era; even Thomas Edison's sixteen-minute version of *Frankenstein* (1910) softened its horrific impact, reassuring its patrons that the filmmakers "tried to eliminate all the actually repulsive situations and to concentrate on the mystic and psychological problems that are to be found in this weird tale."

Until the release of Robert Wiene's *The Cabinet of Dr. Caligari* in 1919, movie audiences seemed quite uncomfortable with horror. Although the genre had a long and even "respectable" history on the stage and in novels, it took filmgoers a while to warm up to it.

The comedy-horror film was, to a large extent, an American invention, which makes perfect sense since Irving's "The Legend of Sleepy Hollow" is a quintessential early American tale. But much of the material for silent comedy-horror films came from the stage rather than from literature.

In 1909, a play called *The Ghost Breaker* was written by Paul Dickey and Charles W. Goddard. It achieved considerable success, and by 1914 there was a film version, which is now lost, as are more than sixty percent of all silent films. In 1922, it was remade by producer Jesse L. Lasky and director Alfred Green. This version starred Wallace Reid, Lila Lee, Walter Hiers and Alfred Carewe. It too was a rather tepid affair, according to a review in *The New York Times* from September 11, 1922, in which the unnamed critic wrote:

> While sitting through *The Ghost Breaker* at the Rivoli this week you will probably be bothered by the intrusive and persistent reflection that it could have been a great deal better than

it is. And this is disturbing to anyone's enjoyment of a comedy.... For the fact is that the Dickey-Goddard play offered almost boundless opportunities for fun and thrills on the screen, and they have been taken advantage of only half-way and half-heartedly.... [W]hen the picture finally does to get the business of the ghosts and the treasure it picks up a little.... So it is not a complete failure.

And so our anonymous critic is telling us that the horror elements are much more interesting than the comedy elements in this version of *The Ghost Breaker*. By this time, of course, we had been through the real-life horrors of World War I and yet we, the collective audience, seemed to crave more horrors upon the screen. But we wanted them diluted with humor. We wanted to whistle past the graveyard of our loved ones, the soldiers, the victims of war. We wanted to laugh in the face of death.

One Exciting Night

During the Roaring Twenties, audiences were indeed roaring at some Broadway plays that combined screams with laughter. One of the earliest shows on the Great White Way to generate fright and titters was Mary Roberts Rinehart and Avery Hopwood's *The Bat*, first staged at the Morosco Theatre in 1920. Alexander Woollcott's review of August 24 that year was quite enthusiastic: "*The Bat* is a wild mystery melodrama, considerably wilder than any seen in these parts for a long time, and it is quite thoroughly interesting.... No end of fun if you let yourself go."

Apparently, a lot of people wanted to let themselves go in the twenties, as *The Bat* had a long and very successful run. Its success got the attention of legendary film director D. W. Griffith, who was, at this stage in his career, looking for a hit.

Although Griffith had made the hugely profitable *The Birth of a Nation* in 1915, he remained a controversial figure. A movie pioneer who perfected, among other things, the technique of cross-cutting to build suspense, Griffith was also very heavily criticized for the blatant racism in his 1915 epic, the first American feature-length film. Portraying the Ku Klux Klan as "heroes" who, in his view, restored order to the post–Reconstruction South, Griffith came under fire from the NAACP, who attempted (and failed) to have the film suppressed.

Griffith had been a child of the South; his father was a Confederate Army colonel and Civil War hero who told the young Griffith many romanticized tales of the war. These stories left a huge impression on him, and when he became a writer and director in the fledgling motion picture business, he used his father's stories as the basis for several of his films. By all accounts a rather humorless man, Griffith was also a staunch Republican, supporting Warren G. Harding, Calvin Coolidge and Herbert Hoover.

The Birth of a Nation, although highly impressive in technique, can be uncomfortable viewing today because of its derogatory depictions of black stereotypes, including scenes in which the white "heroes" kill black men to protect white women. Some say that Griffith attempted to "atone" for his bigotry in his next film, *Intolerance* (1916), but the damage had already been done. Although he continued to push the envelope of film technique in such films as *Broken Blossoms* (1919), *Way Down East* (1920) and *Orphans of the Storm* (1921), his films never again achieved the kind of financial success accorded to *The Birth of a Nation*.

In 1920, Griffith formed United Artists along with Charlie Chaplin, Mary Pickford and Douglas Fairbanks. Looking for a new concept that could give his finances a shot in the arm, Griffith felt that the stage success of *The Bat* and other "mystery melodramas" could be easily translated into big-screen box office. Under the nom de plume of "Irene Sinclair" he wrote a screenplay called *The Haunted Grande*. (He had at one time considered buying screen rights to *The Bat*, but ultimately decided to do a pastiche of it to save money.) It was intended to be a small film by Griffith's standards, a relatively low-budget affair that would hopefully turn a tidy profit.

The film's plot is a somewhat confusing hodgepodge of comedy, mystery and melodrama. An orphan girl (Carol Dempster) born in South Africa is adopted by a Southern society woman and brought to America. Her adoptive mother arranges for her to marry the rather smarmy J. Wilson Rockmaine (Morgan Wallace), with whom she is, of course, not in love. Her affections are given enthusiastically to John Fairfax (Henry Hull, who had just played the lead in the stage production of *The Cat and the Canary*), who invites her, her adoptive mother and Rockmaine to stay at his country estate. Bootleggers are secretly ensconced there, however, and shortly before the guests show up, the gang's leader is murdered. There's also a large sum of money hidden away somewhere on the estate, as well as strange noises, mysterious apparitions (wearing masks à la *The Bat*) and a police investigation that seems to center on Fairfax as the prime suspect.

Eventually retitled *One Exciting Night*, the film was previewed and got a less-than-overwhelming audience response. Griffith decided that the problem with the movie was that it lacked the usual spectacular climax that audiences had come to expect from his productions. He brought the actors back and shot a new and expensive ending involving a terrifying storm.

The climactic scene is pretty effective by the standards of the time. It just so happened that Griffith already had some actual hurricane footage that he had shot earlier, so he mixed it in with a storm that he created in the studio (the film was shot in Westchester, New York, and the Bronx). The real storm and the studio storm don't really match, but it is an exciting sequence that goes on for at least ten minutes. Pasteboard trees and outbuildings being "blown" about on wires look pretty phony today, but the entire sequence is so well-edited—a Griffith trademark—that you can almost forgive its artificiality.

The "comedy" elements are more difficult to forgive. There are three black characters, and all of them are played by white performers. The most offensive is Porter Strong as a cowardly servant who isn't above stealing someone's war medals and claiming them as his own. One of the most stereotypically "blackface" performances ever seen onscreen, Porter's blatantly racist portrayal is impossible to condone, either dramatically or morally.

The other actors are adequate, especially Hull, who would later achieve horror movie stardom as the *Werewolf of London* in (1935). When Rockmaine (Wallace) is discovered to be the murderer, it's really no surprise. He's all but twirled his moustache through the whole picture, and we just knew it couldn't be the charmingly upscale Fairfax.

Released on October 2, 1922, *One Exciting Night* was reasonably well received by audiences and critics of the time. *The New York Times* noted, "D. W. Griffith has given himself completely and frankly to old-fashioned, hair-raising melodrama and broad comedy in [this] hilarious thriller. And don't forget the storm. You won't, if you see it." However, the final cost of the movie—mainly because of Griffith's last-minute "hurricane"—only served to put the director even further into debt. His career continued its downward spiral, and by the time the talkies came in, he was more or less finished.

Nevertheless, *One Exciting Night* remains a pioneering comedy-horror film. While the tone of the movie veers wildly from maudlin romance to racist humor to arch symbolism, it is, like so many of Griffith's films, a grand experiment. Later comedy-horror films were better at balancing the humor and scares and were certainly more sophisticated in their approach. But once again, love him or hate him, Griffith paved the way.

The Headless Horseman

If you read my introduction to this book (and if you didn't, shame on you), you will know that one of my favorite stories is Washington Irving's "The Legend of Sleepy Hollow." What you may not know is that the most authentic filmed version of the story was made in 1922. Retitled *The Headless Horseman*, it starred no less an American luminary of the time than Oklahoma-born humorist and actor Will Rogers as Ichabod Crane.

The screenplay by its producer, Carl Stearns Clancy, is remarkably faithful to Irving's story. There are lines in the intertitles that are directly lifted from it (such as Katrina Van Tassel saying to Ichabod Crane, "I've heard that you've read several books quite through!"). Its brief running time (the prints that survive only run about 52 minutes, barely qualifying as a feature) ensures that padding is kept to a minimum.

But here's what makes it even more authentic: Instead of filming in some Hollywood studio, this early independent production directed by silent film veteran Edward Venturini was actually filmed on some of the real locations Irving used in his story, in and around Tarrytown, New York. The actual Dutch farmhouses, woodlands and covered bridges of the area, combined with convincing period costumes, bring Irving's story to life in a way that has never been done since. The fact that the production company called itself the Sleepy Hollow Corporation says a great deal about the filmmakers' intentions of staying true to the story's setting.

Crane, of course, is a rather unsympathetic character: he's a gawky nerd who wants Katrina not for her obvious charms but for her money. A great believer in ghosts, witches and goblins, he finally gets his comeuppance from town roughneck Brom Bones, who dresses up as the Headless Horseman and frightens Ichabod away from Sleepy Hollow forever. Even though Brom (Mr. Bones?) is a bully, he is at least honest about loving Katrina and we feel little compassion for the gangly and rather pompous schoolmaster.

The fact that Rogers, one of the most likable stars in movies at that time, was engaged to play such an unlikable character is a bit of irony that actually works for the film. Cast against type, Rogers is every inch the early 19th century schoolmaster, complete with a pigtail tied with a bow. He believes that "if you spare the rod, you spoil the child," and graphically demonstrates it in one scene in which he beats one of his students for causing a disruption in the class. Rogers is prissy and stern in the role, and while he may be a bit heavier than our usual image of the gangly Ichabod Crane, he plays the part sincerely and well. I have a feeling that Irving would have been thrilled with his performance.

The rest of the cast is good too, with Lois Meredith an appealing Katrina Van Tassel and Ben Hendricks Jr. a suitably beefy and athletic Brom Bones. The film is also beautifully shot by Ned Van Buren (a suitably early American Dutch name, that). An interesting bit of trivia is that it was the first feature photographed on panchromatic negative film, which was equally sensitive to every color of the spectrum. The early silents had all been shot on orthochromatic film, which had a tendency to make blue skies and blue eyes look flat white. The new panchromatic film was perfect for shooting on location, as *The Headless Horseman* was, capturing moody skies and moody eyes to equally good effect.

Speaking of effects, there are very few "special" ones in *The Headless Horseman*, but the ones that are used work very well. Director Venturini filmed the first sequence in which we see the Horseman (actually a fantasy of Crane's) in double exposure, making his appearance phantom-like, the way a true apparition might look. A simple effect, to be sure, and one that went all the way back to Melies, but quite effective all the same. There's another fantasy sequence (Crane imagines himself tarred and feathered by the villagers) that looks as though it may have been the only sequence actually filmed in a studio. As such, it doesn't really match the rest of the film, but as it's a dream sequence anyway, it doesn't detract from the movie either.

The high point of the story—the pursuit on horseback, with the Headless Horseman nipping at Crane's heels—is skillfully done. Rogers had been a rodeo cowboy, so his riding skills are put to perfect use in this climactic sequence. There are sweeping tracking shots (quite rare in films of this era) and close-ups that must have been filmed from the back of a moving vehicle, showing Crane in the foreground with the Horseman close behind.

The only false note is struck after Crane flees the scene when he is bopped on the head by the pumpkin that the "Horseman" has hurled at him. Satisfied that he has successfully routed the schoolmaster, Brom Bones pops his head out of his homemade Headless Horseman costume. While it is certainly implied in Irving's original story that the Horseman was, in fact, Brom Bones, the fact that the author really left it up to the reader to decide was a big part of the charm of the tale. Of course, American comedy-horror films of the period generally made it quite clear that whatever supernatural manifestations you thought you had seen actually had logical explanations, and this may have been why the filmmakers decided to show that the whole thing was really just a Halloween prank. It doesn't ruin the film by a long shot, but this nearly definitive *Headless Horseman* could have done without such an obvious bit of visual exposition.

Nevertheless, *The Headless Horseman*—released just after Halloween of 1922 by a company called the W.W. Hodkinson Corporation—remains the most faithful version of the story committed to film; *Ichabod and Mr. Toad*, the 1949 omnibus film which contains Disney's animated version is certainly more exciting, funnier and scarier. Tim Burton's 1999 *Sleepy Hollow* is much more elaborate and far more gruesome, but it's such a free adaptation of the story that it doesn't even qualify as comedy-horror. The Will Rogers version of *The Headless Horseman* is the one that Washington Irving himself would have loved, filmed as it was in his home town. And who knows? Perhaps the spirit of Irving watched the filming from the window of his house...

The Bat

The Bat finally reached the screen in 1926 courtesy of director Roland West, who had just filmed Lon Chaney in *The Monster*. Under the headline "Productions and Players" in the *New York Times* of February 15, 1925, was a "preview" of *The Monster*:

> The chief attraction at the Capitol this week is called *The Monster*. We hear that in it there are ghostly hands that stretch forth menacingly, sliding panels through which queer faces appear, and skeletons in closets. It is a story of a mysterious disappearance. Lon Chaney, who was seen in *The Hunchback of Notre Dame* and *He Who Gets Slapped*, appears in the title role. The Monster is a surgeon whose twisted brain delights in performing strange operations upon victims lured to his sanatorium....

The Monster was one of the first "mad doctor" movies, and again, it was based on a play (by Crane Wilbur) that had been well-received on Broadway. Although there are comedy elements in *The Monster*, and it's a beautifully directed film, West didn't really find his comedy-horror voice until he made the first film version of *The Bat*. Thought to be a lost film for decades, it was finally rediscovered in the eighties and is now available on DVD. Talk about discovering hidden gems; *The Bat* is a beauty.

Original poster for Alfred Green's *The Ghost Breaker* (1922).

First and foremost, it's a splendid looking film, with set design by none other than William Cameron Menzies, who would go on to design *Gone with the Wind*. West's direction keeps the 88-minute film moving at a brisk pace, and the balance between comedy and horror is perfectly summed up by the movie's tagline: "A laugh with every gasp!"

The plot sounds simple: Masked criminal in giant bat costume terrorizes guests at old Gothic mansion. But the story becomes more and more convoluted as it goes along, with $200,000 in hidden loot, characters thought to be dead who aren't, red herrings a-plenty, shocks wherever you turn and yocks galore. My favorite dialogue exchange is when Detective Moletti (Tullio Carminati) asks the maid (Louise Fazenda) what her full name is. She replies, "Lizzie Allen—whether I'm full or not." The title cards really nail home the point of "a laugh with every gasp."

But the gasps are good too, particularly the close-ups of the Bat in full costume moving in on Dale Ogden (Jewel Carmen). With huge pointed ears and nasty-looking fangs, he's a real "monster" before monster movies actually came into vogue, and his visage is one of the more memorable images of the silent era.

The players are all fun to watch, with Jack Pickford as the unlikely "hero," Eddie Gribbon as a Barney Fife–like detective, and Fazenda running all over the house screaming (silently) at every shadow. But the standout performer is Emily Fitzroy as Cornelia Van Gorder, the Agatha Christie–type mystery writer who is renting the mansion. Always calm, cool and collected, she is the one who is instrumental in finally subduing The Bat; she's a woman of real guts and intelligence.

There's no doubt that this is one of the films that inspired Bob Kane to create Batman (the other was the remake, *The Bat Whispers*, but more on that later). There's even a sort of "bat signal" when a moth shows up in a car's headlights, its shadow looking like a giant bat. And, of course, for better or worse, the idea of a masked killer knocking off people one by one in an old house is the basis of just about every slasher movie from *Halloween* (1978) to *Saw* (2003). Filmed almost entirely at night, *The Bat* has a spooky atmosphere that presages many of the Universal horrors that would come later, including *Frankenstein* and *Dracula*.

The review in the March 14, 1926, *New York Times* noted: "People in the theatre yesterday were distinctly affected by the spine-chilling episodes, and they were relieved by the comedy interludes."

That just about says it all.

The Cat and the Canary

One of the most popular of the "thriller" plays of the twenties was John Willard's 1922 comedy-horror play *The Cat and the Canary*. It incorporated all the classic ingredients of the "old dark house" mystery: the reading of a will, a family fortune, a haunted mansion and a homicidal maniac called The Cat who escapes from an asylum and takes refuge in the mansion, terrorizing all the guests.

New York Times theatre critic Alexander Woollcott reviewed the play on February 8, 1922, noting:

> The National Theatre has gone in for melodrama in the manner of Mary Roberts Rinehart— spooky melodrama, with a lot of quaking people cooped up in a shadowy old house, the while doors are opened by unseen hands, strangled cries are heard in the darkness and murdered men pitch headlong into the room from behind secret panels.... A creepy young thriller, nicely calculated to make every hair on the head rise and remain standing from 8:30 till nearly 11.

After the success of D. W. Griffith's horror spoof *One Exciting Night* in 1922, Carl Laemmle, the German-born president of Universal Pictures, sat up and took notice. Although no fan of Gothic horror, he wanted to capitalize on Griffith's success, and did so with such now-classic films as *The Hunchback of Notre Dame* (1923) and *The Phantom of the Opera* (1925), both starring the great Lon Chaney. But those were, of course, serious productions, and some might say *Hunchback* is more of an historical drama than a horror film.

When the Mary Roberts Rinehart-Avery Hopwood play *The Bat* became a successful film in 1926, Laemmle decided the time was right for Universal to enter the comedy-horror arena. He turned to Willard's hugely popular play because of its commercial potential as a film, with its plot centering on a beautiful heiress whose family attempts to drive her insane to collect her inheritance. At first, Willard was a bit hesitant to sell the play to Hollywood. As it was still being performed onstage, he feared that, according to film historian Douglas Brode, "that would have exposed to virtually everyone the trick ending ... destroying the play's potential as an ongoing moneymaker." Ultimately, Laemmle convinced Willard that the film would only increase the play's popularity, so the author relented. Willard was not asked to write the screenplay, which was assigned to Alfred A. Cohn and Robert F. Hill.

The next step was finding a director to take on the task of transforming play into motion picture. Laemmle was highly impressed by the film *Waxworks* (1924), directed by German filmmaker Paul Leni from a screenplay by *Nosferatu* screenwriter Henrik Galeen. Widely regarded as a masterpiece of German Expressionism, *Waxworks* is one of the first omnibus films, a trilogy of terror with a framing story that takes place at a wax museum. Highly influential, the film brought Leni international fame and Laemmle gave him a chance to work in Hollywood, which he readily accepted.

One of the things that impressed Laemmle about *Waxworks* was the director's penchant for humor that counterpointed the film's dark themes. Laemmle felt that Leni could combine his Expressionist background and Germanic feel for the Gothic with the humor of the Broadway production, giving it tremendous appeal for American audiences who were hungry for new sensations.

Lead actress Laura La Plante, who was chosen to portray heiress Annabelle West, was a veteran of some 50 films. Irish actor Creighton Hale, who had appeared in 64 silent films including the 1914 serial *The Exploits of Elaine* and D. W. Griffith's *Way Down East* (1920), accepted the comedic "hero" role of Annabelle's cousin, Paul Jones. The Cat, aka Charles Wilder, was played by Forrest Stanley, who had been in such films as *Through the Dark* (1924) and *Shadow of the Law* (1926).

To round out the cast, Leni and Laemmle cast Tully Marshall as lawyer Roger Crosby, Martha Mattox as housekeeper Mammy Pleasant, Gertrude Astor as Cecily Young, Flora Finch as Aunt Susan Sillsby and Lucien Littlefield as "crazy" psychiatrist (was there any other kind in silent films?) Dr. Ira Lazar.

In addition to his directing skills, Leni was also a painter and set designer. He did, in fact, design the sets for *The Cat and the Canary* along with Charles D. Hall, who would later design the unforgettable sets for *Dracula* and *Frankenstein* (both 1931). The sets reflected the aesthetics of German Expressionism, designed to represent in some subconscious way the emotions of the characters.

During the course of directing the film, Leni wanted to make sure his actors appeared to be sufficiently frightened. According to author Kevin Brownlow in his book *Annus Mirabilis: The Film in 1927*, *The Cat and the Canary* cinematographer, Gilbert Warrenton, told him that Leni used the sound of a gong to keep the actors on edge. "He beat that thing worse than the Salvation Army beat a drum," he told Brownlow.

The Cat and the Canary opened at New York City's Colony Theatre in September of 1927 and was an immediate hit. Mordaunt Hall's *New York Times* review of September 18 was headlined: "Mr. Leni's Clever Film: *Cat and Canary* an Exception to the Rule in Mystery Pictures." The review went on to note:

> Just as a painter gives character to his work by daubs from a knife or strokes with his brush, so with lights, shadows and the manipulation of the camera Mr. Leni goes forth and makes something really original with one interesting episode after another.... This is a film which ought to be exhibited before many other directors to show them how a story should be told....

Looking at *The Cat and the Canary* through modern eyes, it's important to remember that this type of movie—what has come to be called an "Old Dark House" film—was really a new genre at the time. Combining screams and scares had been hugely successful on Broadway, and as it turned out, the movies were an even better medium in which to experience sliding panels, thunderstorms, billowing curtains in darkened hallways and that cornerstone of the genre, clutching hands. The stage was one big master shot; in the film, Leni's camera prowled around the house, went in for close-ups, etc. The film probably generated more screams and chuckles than any movie before it.

The slapstick elements of the film may fail to captivate twenty-first century audiences, but Hale does a good job playing the reluctant hero, who is frequently wide-eyed with fright. The scene in which he hides under Cecily's bed is pretty risqué for its time. She strips down to her stockings and undergarments, and he wants to be the gentleman and avert his eyes, but of course he can't.

What still works in *The Cat and the Canary* just as well as it did in 1927 is the atmosphere. Much of the camerawork is reminiscent of Murnau and of Leni's own *Waxworks*. The usual look of silent films was achieved by placing a stationary camera in front of the actors. Leni obviously has no interest in that; his camera moves, lurks, even races down corridors where ghost-white curtains billow like wraiths and hairy hands lurk around doorways. This kind of virtuoso camerawork is still being used today in contemporary horror films, proving that Leni's style remains incredibly influential.

Critic Tony Rayns, in *The Time Out Film Guide*, called *The Cat and the Canary* "the definitive 'haunted house' movie.... Leni wisely plays it mainly for laughs ... hugely entertaining." John Calhoun, writing in *The Penguin Encyclopedia of Horror and the Supernatural* summed up the film's comedic-horrific aspects nicely, pointing out "Leni's uncanny ability to bring out the period's slapstick elements in the story's hackneyed conventions.... At the same time, Leni didn't short-circuit the horrific aspects..."

There's no question that *The Cat and the Canary* is one of the watershed moments of comedy-horror films, certainly in the silent era. Leni's skill at combining the two genres was unsurpassed at that time, and would remain so for the next several years. It remained for the talkies, with their ability to make us actually hear the screams and the funny lines, to beat Leni at his own game.

The Gorilla

The year 1927 also saw the release of Alfred Santell's *The Gorilla*, an adaptation of Ralph Spence's Broadway play. Interestingly enough, a young Walter Pidgeon turns out to be the gorilla (a costumed killer). The slapstick in the film didn't impress critics of the time, but apparently, it held the interest of actual apes. In a whimsical (but apparently factual) piece in *The New York Times* of November 17, 1927, headlined "Park Zoo Monkeys See a Gorilla Movie," it is noted:

> Bessie, the chimpanzee, and her caged companions in the monkey house at the Central Park Zoo saw their first motion picture last night. It was the screen version of *The Gorilla*, a stage melodrama of some seasons back, which will be shown in a local theatre next week.... Whenever the projection machine was stopped so that the reels could be changed, they raised an incessant racket, chattering and banging their trapeze bars about until the picture started again. Then they became quiet and watched until the next change of reels.... All present agreed that in one respect the monkeys were superior as an audience to some spectators in the movie houses. They didn't read the subtitles out loud.

The anonymous author of the piece didn't have to worry about that much longer; subtitles would soon be a thing of the past. The motion picture was about to find its voice, and often it would sound like a high-pitched scream, followed by nervous laughter.

2

THE THIRTIES
Old Dark Houses and Gorilla Suits

The stock market crash of October 1929 and the resultant human misery of the Great Depression coincided, ironically enough, with the true birth of the American horror film. The first film to really be identified as such was Tod Browning's *Dracula*, released in 1931 when the Depression was nearing its worst. Once again, human nature seemed to demand a safety valve for its anxieties, and the thirties saw the full flowering of the genre. Despite the fact that money was scarce and every penny in a family's budget was precious, people flocked to see "the talkies," especially horror films, in tremendous numbers.

The Bat Whispers

Roland West's gangster film *Alibi* (1929) was an early talkie starring Chester Morris as an unredeemed criminal. In 2005, the film was shown as part of a Roland West tribute at the American Cinematheque at the Egyptian Theatre in Los Angeles. The tribute noted that the film "illustrates [West's] innovative use of the then-new medium of sound, plus his baroque visuals that were as much influenced by German expressionism as avant-garde experimentation." *Alibi* also featured art direction by William Cameron Menzies.

It is, however, West's remake of his own silent film *The Bat*, retitled *The Bat Whispers* (to nail home the point that it's a "talkie"), that remains the director's best-remembered film. One of the reasons for this is that West shot two versions of the film simultaneously, one in the standard 1.33 aspect ratio, and the other in an early "widescreen" 65mm process. There was a short vogue in 1930 for various widescreen formats. *Happy Days* and *The Big Trail* were released in something called "Fox Grandeur"; Warner Bros. released *Kismet* in "Vistascope"; MGM's *Billy the Kid* went out in "Realife"; and RKO issued *Danger Lights* in "Natural Vision." The widescreen mini-trend was premature, however, as many theater managers found the process of converting to new equipment too costly, and filmgoers didn't want to pay increased prices to see the films, most of which weren't that wonderful to begin with. It wasn't until 1953 that the widescreen process started to become the cinema standard.

The Bat Whispers was available to theaters in both 35mm prints, photographed by Ray June, and in 65mm prints shot by Robert Planck. Aside from the formats themselves, there are minimal differences between the two versions. The 35mm version is the one most often seen, and it's stunning enough; it opens with a camera movement that suggests a bat in flight, swooping down at the stroke of midnight from a clock tower to soar through an open window. The use of miniatures combined with full-size sets completes the illusion; the filming was accomplished thanks to a lightweight camera dolly (created especially for the film by

Original poster art for Roland West's sound remake of *The Bat*, the 1930 "talkie" *The Bat Whispers*.

technician Charles Cline) which allowed the camera to be moved eighteen feet vertically in just a few seconds. Early sound films are not known for their fluid camera movements, as filmmakers were still getting used to the new technology and had a tendency to film from within enclosed glass booths, with microphones hidden somewhere on the sets (usually in the furniture, i.e., potted plants). But West liberated his camera, flying along with the Bat through windows and doorways. The first few minutes of *The Bat Whispers* are calculated to give the viewer vertigo, and in 1930, they must have succeeded.

Reuniting with his *Alibi* star Chester Morris, West gave the actor free rein to ham it up as the lead character, a "detective" who is—oh, let's just say it—actually The Bat. Of course, overacting was the order of the day in early talkie "melodramas," but Morris really takes flight, as it were, into realms of self-parody. But then again, *The Bat Whispers* doesn't take itself seriously for a moment.

Mordaunt Hall's review in the *New York Times* of January 16, 1931, exclaimed: "A bigger and better picture of *The Bat*, the old would-be spine-chiller, in which shrieks and giggles are mixed, is to be found at the Rivoli. It is bigger because it is shown on an enlarged screen and it is better because the characters have voices."

The review in Phil Hardy's *Encyclopedia of Horror Movies* is even more to the point: "If the material is the routine mixture of screams and laughs, West's direction is often truly startling, with scenes executed in shadow play, the camera performing stunning arabesques...."

Although *The Bat Whispers* may be dramatically creaky by today's standards, it's still fun to watch, and it's important to note that even in 1930 it was a deliberately "unrealistic" spoof. It has been stated that some of Morris' "squinting" in the film was a result of the exceptionally bright "underlighting" used for his closeups, which eventually burned his retinas and led to a condition that became known as "Klieg Eye."

The best performance in the film—and the most understated—is that of Grayce Hampton as Cornelia Van Gorder, the wealthy dowager who refuses to let The Bat frighten her out of her own house. An accomplished stage actress, she gives Van Gorder an excellent "don't mess with me" personality, stronger and more independent than most female characters you see in films today.

Some of the humor works and some of it doesn't, but *The Bat Whispers* is consistently entertaining from a comedy-horror standpoint, and extremely influential to this day: *Batman* creator Bob Kane has been quoted on the record as saying that he saw *The Bat Whispers* on its original release and it inspired him to create the character of Batman eight years later. Without realizing it, West is indirectly responsible for the whole *Batman* phenomenon. But then we should have guessed that from Morris' little speech at the end of the film: "The Bat always flies at night ... and always in a straight line!"

The Old Dark House

J.B. Priestley's 1927 novel *Benighted* appealed to director James Whale's mordant sense of humor, which was much in evidence in his *Frankenstein* (1931), possibly the most famous horror film of all time. Dwight Frye as Fritz is both a comic and tragic character, always lurking around the watchtower, pulling up his socks, muttering to himself—and of course bringing back a "criminal brain" to put into the skull of Frankenstein's creation, rather than the "normal brain" which he dropped on the floor after being startled by what sounds like somebody clashing a cymbal (an off-screen noise that is never explained). Aside from Frye's performance, though, *Frankenstein* is a fairly somber film. But you could sense an irony that Whale kept bottled up, just waiting to be released.

The following year, it was, in a film called *The Old Dark House*. According to *The Encyclopedia of Horror Movies*, Priestley later wrote about the title change, which he wasn't too crazy about: "My American publishers, presumably determined to make money out of one of my books or perish in the attempt, promptly abandoned my title, which has of course a double meaning and tells you almost everything about the novel, and with the title any pretensions the book might have to be a psychological or philosophical novel. They called it *The Old Dark House* and brought it out as a thriller. So disguised, it had a very good sale indeed."

Following up *Frankenstein* was going to be a difficult feat for Whale, but he engaged some very talented people to help him accomplish it. A February 14, 1932, *New York Times* column called "Projection Jottings" noted what was next for the star and director of *Frankenstein*: "Two Boris Karloff productions went into the hands of the adapters last week at the Universal plant. Benn W. Levy, author of *The Devil Passes* and *Mrs. Moonlight*, is in charge of *The Old Dark House*, a novel by J. B. Priestley. With this assignment *The Old Dark House* takes on a more or less British hue. Mr. Levy is an Englishman, and so is Mr. Priestley, and so is James Whale, who will direct the film. Mr. Karloff also hails from the other side of the pond."

Interestingly, the article went on to say that the second of Mr. Karloff's new productions would be *The Invisible Man*, to be adapted by Garrett Fort, who also adapted *Frankenstein* and *Dracula*, and to be directed by Robert Florey, who had just completed *Murders in the Rue Morgue* with Bela Lugosi. As any horror buff will tell you, *The Invisible Man* was ultimately directed by James Whale and starred Claude Rains in his screen debut.

The "Englishness" of *The Old Dark House* became even more prominent when its cast members were revealed in an April 24, 1932, *New York Times* article:

> Universal has collected an interesting cast for its production of *The Old Dark House*. Charles Laughton, the English actor who gave theatre-goers the shudders in *Payment Deferred* last Fall, has one of the leads. He was brought over by Paramount and loaned to Universal for this one film, his first picture in America. Gloria Stuart, the ingénue whose entrance into the films caused so much controversy that the Hays Office had to step in and adjudicate it, will have her first opportunity in *The Old Dark House*. Raymond Massey, who came over from England to play "Hamlet" and found his way into the pictures, has replaced Walter Byron in the cast.... In addition there are Boris Karloff, Melvyn Douglas and Lillian Bond.

A word about the Gloria Stuart "controversy": The article makes it sound as though the Hays Office had to step in to "adjudicate" because Stuart had done something risqué. But no, the future Oscar nominee for *Titanic* (1997) had apparently been signed to two separate movie contracts in 1932, one with Paramount and one with Universal. The former stage actress was much in demand, and apparently didn't consult an attorney before signing both contracts. A court arbitrator had to step in to ascertain which studio would be permitted to "introduce" Stuart to the filmgoing public, and Universal won.

Although it isn't mentioned in the *New York Times* piece, Douglas reportedly replaced actor Russell Hopton in the role of Roger Penderel. But undoubtedly the most interesting bit of casting in *The Old Dark House* is that of Elspeth Dudgeon, a woman, as the patriarch of the bizarre Femm clan. The story goes that Whale couldn't find a male actor who looked old enough to portray the 101-year-old character.

Production on *The Old Dark House* began in the third week of April, 1932, and was completed at the end of May, all at Universal Studios. Although no specific figures on the film's budget are available, based on the budget for other James Whale productions of the time, including *Frankenstein*, one can reasonably estimate that *The Old Dark House* cost around $250,000.

Ernest Thesiger was fifty-three when he appeared in the film as Roderick Femm, although he looks considerably older. He had known Whale from their stage work in England, where Whale had a great reputation as a theater director, particularly for *Journey's End*. Thesiger had made an impact there as the Dauphin in *Saint Joan*. Douglas, at the time an up-and-coming star, had been brought to Hollywood by Goldwyn, where he was supposed to have starred in a film called *Adventure Lady*. But the film was delayed and Douglas agreed to appear in Whale's film instead, as perhaps the closest role the film has to a "hero," Roger Penderel.

Eva Moore, who appeared as Roderick's sister Rebecca Femm, had been known in her younger days on the British stage as a great beauty, which comes as quite a surprise after seeing her in *The Old Dark House*. The 62-year-old actress' disturbingly witty portrayal of the Puritanical Rebecca, who looks as run-down as her house, is one of the more memorable in the film.

The Old Dark House was supposed to have been Laughton's debut for American audi-

Boris Karloff and Lillian Bond in James Whale's comedy-horror classic, ***The Old Dark House*** **(1932).**

ences, but Paramount's *Devil and the Deep* came out first. This was a legal necessity; Paramount had Laughton under contract and loaned him to Universal under the stipulation that *Devil and the Deep* would be released before *The Old Dark House*.

Screenwriter Benn Levy had written *Blackmail* (1929), the first English film in sound, for Alfred Hitchcock. He was asked to come over to the States to write *The Invisible Man*, but when that film was delayed, he accepted the job of writing *Devil and the Deep* and, eventually, *The Old Dark House*. He was a friend of Laughton's and was instrumental in getting the actor cast in both films.

Massey, an Oxford-educated Canadian, had recently appeared in the British film *The Speckled Band* as Sherlock Holmes. *The Old Dark House* was his first American film. He was cast as the other male lead, Philip Waverton, who is married to Stuart's character Margaret.

The cinematographer was Arthur Edeson, who had also photographed *Frankenstein*, and the art director was Charles D. Hall, who had also worked on Whale's previous shocker. With all these impressive pedigrees, the stage was set for another big money-maker for Universal.

For a number of reasons, however, this was not to be. *The Old Dark House* was released on October 20, 1932, and garnered mostly negative reviews from around the country. In New

Left to right: Raymond Massey (on floor), Lillian Bond, Gloria Stuart, Melvyn Douglas, Boris Karloff, Charles Laughton and Eva Moore in James Whale's ***The Old Dark House*** (1932).

York City, the critics seemed to appreciate Whale's very British humor. Mordaunt Hall wrote in the October 28, *New York Times*, "This current thriller, like *Frankenstein*, has the distinction of being directed by James Whale, who again proves his ability in this direction.... Mr. Karloff is, of course, thoroughly in his element as Morgan. He leaves no stone unturned to make this character thoroughly disturbing."

Karloff, in fact, doesn't have a great deal to do in the film. Mostly he gets drunk, makes some really weird vocalizations and chases Gloria Stuart around the house. His one bit of choice acting comes at the death of Saul Femm, memorably played by actor Brember Wills, another friend of Whale's who came to America just for the role. As Morgan the mute butler, Karloff grieves over Saul's death, a surprisingly tender moment from what Stuart's character calls "that brute Morgan."

The fact is that audiences in 1932 were disappointed with *The Old Dark House*. It didn't have the shock moments of *Frankenstein*, and its claustrophobic setting precluded it from having that film's scope. The humor went over the heads of most audiences, and state censor boards insisted on cutting bits out of the film, notably a few lines of dialogue uttered by Lillian Bond, in which she admits that her character, Gladys, is "kept" by Laughton's character, Porterhouse. A shot in which Wills bites Douglas on the throat was also frequently cut by the censors.

Ultimately, *The Old Dark House* did dismal box office outside of New York City. Interestingly enough, the only country where it really turned a profit was in England. It may be said that it's one of the most "British" American films ever made, for its gallows humor and straight-faced underplaying is distinctly British. It's set rather convincingly in the Welsh countryside, and the average viewer today might assume it to be a British-made movie.

Some of the film's dialogue was taken directly from the book. When the stranded travelers attempt to find refuge from the storm in the old dark house, the door is opened by Karloff, who sounds like he's trying to talk, but his vocal chords won't cooperate. Douglas quips, "Even Welsh ought not to sound like that."

Thesiger is absolutely indispensable to *The Old Dark House*. Prissy, effeminate yet controlled, his performance is one of the most memorable things about the film. The dinner scene is priceless, with Thesiger cajoling his guests to "Have a po-*ta*-to." Thesiger was perfectly in tune with Whale's sensibilities, his oddness and eccentricities punctuating the film at all the right moments.

Moore is equally as impressive, although in a different way. Stuart, as Margaret Waverton, decides to put on a flowing evening gown before dinner, for no apparent reason other than to give pre–Code audiences a bit of cheesecake. "That's fine stuff," Rebecca says, pointing to the gown, "but it'll rot..." Then she reaches out to poke Margaret right above her cleavage: "That's finer stuff still ... but it'll rot too, with time." A very uncomfortable scene, heightened tremendously by Edeson's camerawork in which we see various distorted reflections of Rebecca in the mirror.

Laughton, an inveterate scene-stealer, really whoops it up when he comes into the picture midway through, with Bond in tow. Bond is the one who turns out to have the more important role, though, for her character falls head over heels in love with Douglas'. The "love interest" seems a trifle out of place in this film, as everything else is so pitch perfect. But Bond's Gladys is a much livelier character than the rather stuffy Margaret, and she invests her role with a lot of good humor and vivacity.

The Old Dark House is one of the finest of all comedy-horror films because of Whale's penchant for the bizarre and because of the wonderful ensemble cast. As Phil Hardy wrote in *The Encyclopedia of Horror Movies*, "Allowed free rein for the first time in his career, Whale's black humor revels delightedly.... As much as anything, the delight of the film is the subtlety with which Whale shades comedy of manners into tragedy of horrors...."

Because of the poor reception afforded the film in 1932, the copyright was allowed to lapse and *The Old Dark House* probably would have become a lost film were it not for the heroic efforts of filmmaker (and Whale friend) Curtis Harrington, who eventually tracked down the negative in the Universal vaults and had it restored. We should all be very grateful to Harrington, because *The Old Dark House* is almost perfectly realized, both as a black comedy and as a classic horror film that has the power to disturb and thrill even today. Whale's most personal film survives, and we get to see his ultimate joke on the audience: that John Dudgeon is really Elspeth. That may have been Whale's little "gay" punchline to a film that reveled in characters that rebelled against the norms of the time.

Sh! The Octopus

Although there is certainly a lot of comedy in Whale's *Bride of Frankenstein* (1935), the film's ultimate theme of tragedy mitigates against it being a comedy-horror film. The next real comedy-horror film—and one of the weirdest Hollywood movies of the thirties—is a nearly-forgotten Warner Bros. picture called *Sh! The Octopus* (1937). The fact that it was made during a year when there were virtually no horror films released is only one of the odd things about this movie. Another is that, at a running time of only fifty-four minutes, it barely qualifies as a feature. It has been erroneously referred to as a remake of both *The Bat Whispers* and *The Gorilla*, but in fact it's yet another comedy-horror film based on a Broadway play of the twenties.

Sh! The Octopus, the play, debuted on Broadway on February 21, 1928. The following day, it was reviewed in the *New York Times* by an unnamed critic who noted, "Parts of the play are funny, parts of it actually do make a little flesh creep, and much of it is just noisy. But it never permits its spectators the luxury of a moment's slumber."

Written by Ralph Murphy (who also wrote *The Gorilla*) and Donald Gallaher, *Sh! The Octopus* is another old dark house thriller, except that this time it's set in a lighthouse. Perhaps, therefore, one might call it an old dark lighthouse thriller, if that isn't an oxymoron. The play was advertised as a "sneaky, snaky, slimy mystery," but it also had very strong horror elements, all of which were left intact when it was filmed by director William C. McGann.

The crazy plot involves Detectives Kelly (Hugh Herbert) and Dempsey (Allen Jenkins), who find themselves trapped on a stormy night (of course) in a lighthouse with a group of eccentric strangers. They include artist Paul Morgan (John Eldredge), who has just bought the lighthouse from the government; Vesta Vernoff (Marcia Ralston), who says her stepfather has been murdered; Captain Hook (George Rosener), the one-handed lighthouse caretaker; Captain Cobb (Brandon Tynan), a sailor who is a friend of the artist's; Polly Crane (Margaret Irving), a woman who claims to have escaped from her overly amorous boyfriend; and Nanny (Elspeth Dudgeon), housekeeper to Dr. Harriman, Vesta's scientist stepfather. Eventually, a character who calls himself Police Commissioner Patrick Aloysious Clancy (Eric Stanley) shows up, but no one in the lighthouse is above suspicion. After all, there's Dr. Harriman's body hanging from the ceiling, dripping blood on everybody. But the blood turns out to be chocolate syrup and the body is actually a dummy. Just what is going on here?

If the characters aren't strange enough, the story continues to get stranger as it goes along.

The police department has declared war on The Octopus, an arch-criminal who has his own submarine. Vesta eventually tells the detectives that the lair of the Octopus is beneath the lighthouse. Just to confuse the issue even further, there is apparently a real giant octopus lurking about in a sea cave nearby. Tentacles close and lock the lighthouse doors, preventing everyone from escaping; poison gas fills the place; and Kelly has an underwater battle with what looks like a man in a rubber octopus suit.

As you can see, the plot of *Sh! The Octopus* defies analysis. As the story continues, it makes less and less sense. There are also encounters with a turtle carrying a candle on its back, a barking seal, some frogs and a really terrific "unmasking" scene in which we discover that The Octopus is actually Nanny, our old friend Elspeth Dudgeon from *The Old Dark House*. Shortly after, however, we discover that the whole thing has been a dream; it turns out that Kelly has fainted at the hospital where his wife is giving birth and had to be revived with oxygen, which caused him to have a very weird dream indeed. One must wonder if there was more than oxygen going to his head, since *Sh! The Octopus* is perhaps the most surreal Hollywood comedy-horror film ever made. The plot makes no coherent sense; if there is no dead body, then there is no murder. So where is Vesta's stepfather? Who or what is The Octopus? Why are none of the characters what they seem to be?

The short running time of the film may indicate that certain plot points were cut out, but in reality the film is very close to the play. The *New York Times* review of the play pointed out, "It all turned out to be a dream at the Royale Theatre last night—not too bad a dream, perhaps, but a singularly crowded one." A *New York Times* film critic wrote of the movie version on December 24, 1937: "This is another of those scatter-brained spook comedies, with the fliberty-gibbet Hugh [Herbert] and his dead-pan team-mate, Allen Jenkins.... There is the usual assortment of corpses, disembodied voices and clutching hands (or rather, octopi tentacles), and a hopelessly confused shred of plot...."

Confused it certainly is, but *Sh! The Octopus* looks great, thanks to Arthur Todd's atmospheric monochrome cinematography. Ultimately, the film has the look and feel of a dream and the screenplay by George Bricker has its own interior dream logic. The fact is that what starts out as a fairly standard old dark house thriller ends up something like the famous "It May Look Like a Walnut" episode from the classic *Dick Van Dyke Show*, in which all of Rob Petrie's friends seemed to turn into aliens (including his wife), until it all turned out to have been a dream brought on by watching an old sci-fi movie on TV. If the humor in *Sh! The Octopus* had been, shall we say, more timeless, it may have become a classic. But its unorthodox running time and often lame jokes condemned it to semi-obscurity. Here's a typical exchange from the film:

> VESTA VERNOFF: Poor Nanny!
> DETECTIVE DEMPSEY: Who's Nanny?
> DETECTIVE HAROLD KELLY: Nanny's a goat! Hoo, hoo!

A word here about Herbert: Although not as broadly unfunny as the Ritz Brothers, he's certainly an acquired taste for modern audiences. He began his career in vaudeville and went to Hollywood after the advent of talking pictures. His trademark phrase in which he would flutter his hands and remark to himself, "Hoo, hoo, hoo, wonderful, wonderful, hoo, hoo, hoo!" makes it look a bit as if he's suffering from Tourette's Syndrome. His perpetually flustered persona carried him through a number of supporting roles, usually as an absent-minded professor and very occasionally, as in *Sh! The Octopus*, as the star.

The movie hasn't been completely forgotten, however. There's an independent rock band from Detroit, Michigan, that calls itself—you guessed it—Sh! The Octopus. Given the film's reputation for weirdness, the fact that its title lives on as the name of a rock band seems both ironic and appropriate.

The Cat and the Canary (1939)

In late 1938, the Universal horror cycle started all over again after the successful reissue of *Dracula* and *Frankenstein* as a double feature for Halloween. The new owners of Universal, who were looking for a hit, quickly rushed *Son of Frankenstein* with Karloff, Basil Rathbone and Bela Lugosi into production for a January 1939 release. Horror films had been floundering for a couple of years, partly because of a British ban placed upon them; the British government felt they were bad for public morale during Hitler's march to conquer the world. But the new life breathed into the classic monsters brought a succession of remakes and sequels.

On November 29, 1938, a headline in the *New York Times* read: "Paramount Plans to Remake *The Cat and the Canary*—Martha Raye in lead." The story went on to report: "Paramount today acquired remake rights to *The Cat and the Canary* from Universal and will film it on the Spring schedule with Bob Hope and Martha Raye in the leads. Arthur Hornblow Jr. will produce and writers will be assigned to prepare an adaptation this week."

For whatever reason, Raye ended up not being involved in the remake; the lead female role subsequently went to Shirley Ross, a vivacious singer-actress who is best remembered for singing a duet with Hope of "Thanks for the Memory" in the hugely successful musical feature *The Big Broadcast of 1938*. Ultimately, however, Ross was unceremoniously dropped from the film when a bigger star suddenly became available.

On March 2, 1939, the *New York Times* came out with this headline: "Delay in *The Dictator* Seen as Paulette Goddard Takes Role in Another Film." Goddard had been chosen by Charlie Chaplin (her husband) to co-star in his Hitler satire, which eventually became known as *The Great Dictator*. But the story in the *Times* revealed that Chaplin was having problems with the project: "Signaling postponement of *The Dictator*, which Charles Chaplin was to have started March 15, Paulette Goddard ... was engaged today by Paramount for the leading role opposite Bob Hope in *The Cat and the Canary*. Miss Goddard replaces Shirley Ross, who was originally cast. It is reported that Chaplin is having script trouble on his satire on European politics, and it is probable his film will not get under way before summer."

And so it was that Hope and Goddard teamed for what would be the first of three films. Producer Arthur Hornblow Jr. and Paramount chose Elliott Nugent to direct. He had been a stage actor and leading man in early talkies, but eventually became far better known as a writer, producer and director. The son of playwright-producer-actor J.C. Nugent, he had cut his teeth in vaudeville and got into film roles in 1929. He began directing some minor films in the early thirties, but his talent eventually got noticed and he graduated to bigger productions. Ultimately, he became one of Hope's favorite directors, helming such Hope hits as *My Favorite Brunette* (1947).

Other performers cast in *The Cat and the Canary* included John Beal and Douglass Montgomery as would-be heirs; Gale Sondergaard as Miss Lu, one of her patented "weird housekeeper" roles; and smoothly menacing George Zucco as attorney Crosby. Zucco played Moriarty to Basil Rathbone's Sherlock Holmes in that same year's *The Adventures of Sherlock Holmes* for 20th Century-Fox.

Released in November 1939, *The Cat and the Canary* was an instant smash. In the *New*

Bob Hope and Paulette Goddard find a clue in Elliot Nugent's *The Cat and the Canary* (1939).

York Times, Frank S. Nugent (no relation to the director) wrote: "Since mystery melodramas laid in old dark houses are mostly nonsense anyway, Paramount has had the wit and wisdom to produce a nonsense edition of John Willard's old shocker *The Cat and the Canary*. Streamlined, screamlined and played to the hilt for comedy, the new version ... is more harebrained than hair-raising, which is as it should be.... Good show."

Indeed, 1939's *The Cat and the Canary* raised the bar for all future comedy-horror films. Smoothly produced on impressive sets, the 74-minute film is fast-paced and consistently entertaining. It's the movie in which Hope created his "cowardly" hero role, the wisecracking man of the world who uses quips to fight off his fear. The story features all of the usual clichés: sliding panels, clutching hands, lights that turn themselves on and off, eerie wails and shadows galore. Beautifully shot in black and white, it has an elegant fog-bound atmosphere. The bayou settings don't look real for a moment, but the dreamlike quality of their appearance only adds to the overall effect of the film.

Hope has some good lines. When Cicily (Nydia Westman) asks him, "Do you believe people can come back from the dead?" he quips, "You mean like the Republicans?" He also has some bad lines, such as "Let's all drink Scotch and make wry faces." But as Nugent pointed out in his review, "Good and bad alike profit from Mr. Hope's comic style."

Hope has chemistry with Goddard from the start, and all of the other cast members are suitably creepy (especially Sondergaard) or intentionally annoying (Westman). There is really nothing new in the remake except for the approach. Whereas Leni's 1927 film treated the elements of the "old dark house" melodrama as if they were all new, the 1939 version takes an almost post-modern approach. Cast as a stage and radio actor, Hope continually comments on the action throughout the film as though he were performing it in a play. "Where's the leading lady?" he asks the assembled guests, and Goddard appears right on cue. Hope's winking performance assures us that, although we may have moments of fright and shock, everything will turn out just fine in the end. In a sense, Hope is the audience, just as scared as we are, blurting out his frequently lame jokes to keep from getting "goosepimples on my goosepimples," as he says at one point. And there's a certain bit of irony when Hope asks another character, "Where's Crosby?" Of course, this was a year before Bob and Bing went on the "Road" together.

Sadly, this *Cat and the Canary* is seldom seen today. But if you can find a copy of it, you'll see why audiences of that era were delighted with it. They were ready for something light and frothy, yet mixed skillfully with dark and scary. It was a perfect recipe, arriving as it did between the tragedy of the Great Depression and the upcoming horrors of World War II.

Left to right: The Ritz Brothers, Bela Lugosi, Anita Louise and Edward Norris in Allan Dwan's unfunny, un-scary 1939 remake of **The Gorilla**.

The Gorilla (1939)

The tagline for the 1939 remake of *The Gorilla* read: "Laughs plus Thrills = Entertainment." While that may be true in general, it certainly was not the case in this poorly conceived version of the Ralph Spence play, designed, in this instance, as a vehicle for the Ritz Brothers (Jimmy, Harry and Al). It was their contractual obligation movie, the last film they were assigned to do under their 20th Century–Fox agreement. Featured in the cast were Bela Lugosi and Lionel Atwill. Unfortunately, the presence of The Ritz Brothers—the film's *raison d'etre*—is also its biggest detriment.

As adapted by Rian James and Sid Silvers from the play, it's basically the same old convoluted story about Walter Stevens (Atwill) receiving a death threat from a murderer who calls himself "The Gorilla." He hires three extremely incompetent detectives (The Ritz Brothers) to protect him until midnight, the predicted hour of his doom. There's a creepy butler (Lugosi) and a carnival ape (Art Miles in a gorilla suit) lurking around. Patsy Kelly as a maid shrieks herself hoarse. Anita Louise as Atwill's niece screams herself silly. And the Ritz Brothers mug, grimace and pratfall their way through the movie.

A word here about the Ritz Brothers: although their version of *The Three Musketeers* (1939) isn't bad, in general they made the Three Stooges look like players in a drawing room comedy of manners. They're all but impossible to watch today, chewing every piece of scenery in *The Gorilla* as if they're playing to the last row in a crowded theater. Although the film is only 66 minutes long, their foolish antics make it seem interminable.

In other respects, *The Gorilla* has a lot going for it. Lugosi has an amusing scene or two and even saves the day at the end by sticking a gun in the villain's back. Atwill is his usual professional self. The direction by Hollywood veteran Allan Dwan is slick and fast-paced, while the camerawork of Edward Cronjager is fluid and crisp. The art direction by Lewis Creber and Richard Day is also first-rate, highlighting some lovely Gothic sets. All in all, it's a very well-produced motion picture.

As a comedy-horror film, though, it fails miserably. It is, in fact, an abject study in how not to make a comedy-horror film: Have an alleged comedy team express every conceivable reaction of shock, terror, disbelief and just plain stupidity, and have them menaced by a man in an ape suit. Stretch this concept—which the Stooges often did in about 20 minutes—to feature length. And wait for the audience to a) laugh, b) scream or c) leave the theater. Most audiences in 1939 opted for the latter.

Opening on May 26, 1939, *The Gorilla* was reviewed in the *New York Times* rather tersely by Thomas M. Pryor two days later: "It's all supposed to be either very funny or shockingly thrilling, depending how you look at it. We couldn't see it either way."

There is one funny line in the film, and it belongs to Patsy Kelly. It seems that the carnival gorilla is named Poe, for no particular reason. When the owner of said gorilla tells Kelly to beware, because Poe hates women, she replies, "So does Kipling!"

But one mildly amusing line in 66 minutes doesn't make a comedy-horror film.

3

THE FORTIES
Killer Zombies and Comedy Teams

By 1940, Hitler and his inhuman cronies were moving quickly in their quest for world domination. London was besieged by the Blitz and the world was becoming a very scary place indeed. By the time the U.S. was forced to enter World War II after Pearl Harbor, it almost seemed as though the apocalypse might be at hand.

Yet, as we have learned in the previous two chapters, the human taste for horror (and humor) only seems to be heightened when the world situation is at its most desperate. All through the forties, comedy-horror films would force us to face up to our worst fears and to laugh in the Devil's (i.e., Hitler's) face.

The Ghost Breakers

After the success of *The Cat and the Canary*, it was inevitable that Bob Hope and Paulette Goddard would be asked to star in another comedy-horror film by Paramount, and the offer arrived in 1940 as another remake of *The Ghost Breaker*, this time entitled *The Ghost Breakers*. Director George Marshall, who had just scored a major hit with the comedy-western *Destry Rides Again*, was signed to do something similar for the comedy-horror genre.

The supporting cast for *The Ghost Breakers* included Richard Carlson (later to become famous for such sci-fi classics as *It Came from Outer Space* and *Creature from the Black Lagoon*) as Geoff Montgomery, a suspicious character; the distinguished actor Paul Lukas as Parada, a Cuban real estate agent; Noble Johnson from *King Kong* as the zombie; and a young Anthony Quinn in a dual role as twin brothers Ramon and Francisco Mederes. There's also a don't-blink-or-you'll-miss-it screen debut by Robert Ryan as an intern in an early scene.

In many ways, though, the most interesting—and most controversial—support is provided by African-American actor Willie Best as Bob Hope's "boy" Alex Syracuse (a take-off on Jack Benny's second banana Eddie "Rochester" Anderson). Best was a victim of the racial stereotyping of the era; he often used the stage name "Sleep 'n' Eat." Some of his best-known screen appearances include Shirley Temple films such as *Little Miss Marker* (1934), as well as all-black musicals such as *Green Pastures* (1936). Despite the demeaning nature of some of these roles, Best performed them with consummate skill and impeccable comic timing, never seen to better effect than in *The Ghost Breakers*, in which he matches witticisms with Hope, barb for barb.

The Kentucky family feud subplot from the original play was jettisoned in favor of having Hope and Best escape from gangsters and head for Cuba, rather than Spain. Once in the Caribbean, the film's plot and style become considerably darker, although the laughs never stop flowing.

Particularly chilly are the scenes involving Johnson as the zombie, kept by his old voodoo-conjuring mother (Virginia Brissac) in a shack on the edge of a swamp. His pursuit of Goddard, who tries to escape him by running up a long staircase in the haunted castle she has inherited, is still one of the best zombie scenes on film, and one of the most stunningly photographed (by Charles Lang).

Hope was known as one of the best practitioners of rapid-fire one-liners in the business. A lot of it had to do with his radio experience, which by its very nature was fast and strictly verbal. A few examples of the non-stop *Ghost Breakers* banter include a discussion between Carlson, Goddard and Hope regarding zombies. Goddard notes that it must be horrible to be a zombie, prompting Carlson to continue: "It's worse than horrible, because a zombie has no will of his own. You see them sometimes, walking around blindly with dead eyes, following orders, not knowing what they do, not caring." Hope, apparently trying to be fair to both political parties, does a reverse take on his line from *The Cat and the Canary*, quipping, "You mean like Democrats?"

Politically incorrect or not, some of the funniest scenes involve Hope and Best. Early in the film, a thunderstorm causes the lights to go out and Hope says, "Basil Rathbone must be having a party." But when he says things to Best like, "You look like a blackout in a blackout. I'm gonna have to paint you white," that's the kind of humor that makes modern audiences a tad uncomfortable. However, there's nothing mean-spirited in the relationship between Hope and Best in the film, and part of the fun of it is seeing how these two comic masters top each other with verbal bon mots. One of the best examples of these comes when they're exploring the castle, and Hope says to Best: "Listen, you stay there, and if a couple of fellas come runnin' down the stairs in a few minutes, let the first one go. That'll be me."

Alex replies, "If somebody passes you, that'll be me."

This may be the old "Feets, don't fail me now" kind of routine, but it works because of the timing and the sheer likeability of the actors, especially Best. When they look at an old portrait that resembles Goddard, Best off-handedly says, "I'm befuddled." For whatever reason—probably his delivery, which sounds as if it's improvised—it turns into a very funny line.

According to Hal Erickson in *All Movie Guide*, Hope once said that Best was one of the finest actors he knew. They (and Goddard) appeared together again the following year in *Nothing but the Truth*, a non-horror comedy. But *The Ghost Breakers* may be the finest and funniest hour for each of them.

In the *New York Times* review of July 4, 1940, Bosley Crowther wrote:

> It looks as though Paramount has really discovered something: it has found the fabled formula for making an audience shriek with laughter and fright at one and (as the barkers say) the simultaneous time.... It worked out very nicely in *The Cat and the Canary* last year, and it is working quite as nicely—and even more amusingly, in fact—in *The Ghost Breakers*....

The Ghost Breakers is a high-water mark in comedy-horror films. Although most of the supernatural manifestations are explained away at the end, as was common with "old dark house" movies, the ghost itself is not. The scene in which we see it, as a white form of ectoplasm drifting out of a sarcophagus, remains one of the eeriest spectral scenes in a Hollywood movie.

Marshall remade *The Ghost Breakers* in 1953 as a Dean Martin–Jerry Lewis vehicle called *Scared Stiff*. Despite the presence of the always watchable Lizabeth Scott in the Paulette Goddard role, the movie falls flat mainly because of Lewis' mugging, in what is more or less the

Willie Best role. As is pointed out in *The Encyclopedia of Horror Movies*, the film turns into "a witless mess stretched very thin."

You'll Find Out

A less successful comedy-horror film was released later the same year as *The Ghost Busters*, but it had a blockbuster cast: Boris Karloff, Bela Lugosi and Peter Lorre. The starring role, however, went to big band leader Kay Kyser, a hugely popular radio star. His "Kay Kyser's Kollege of Musical Knowledge" ran for eleven years on NBC Radio, and his zany persona foreshadowed the acts of such future off-the-wall bandleaders as Spike Jones. Part quiz show, part big band concert, his program, which featured such loonies as Ish Kabibble (real name: Merwyn Bogue) and Harry Babbitt, was at the height of its popularity when his second film for RKO, *You'll Find Out*, went into production.

Its plot is pretty basic: Helen Parrish plays Janis Bellacrest, a young heiress who inherits the requisite old dark house. Unfortunately, there are those who would like to bump her off for that inheritance, and thereby hangs the rather slight tale. Karloff is a judge, Lugosi a swami complete with turban and Lorre is a scientist. As it turns out, however, they're all crooks trying to get at Parrish's fortune.

Somehow, Kyser and his band (all playing themselves) get mixed up in this situation and spend some scary times at the gloomy mansion. The result is a mildly amusing mixture, with the usual thunderstorms and apparent "ghosts." The three big horror stars are given very little to do but look menacing and are mostly wasted. There's plenty of time out for singer Ginny Simms to warble some tunes, and originally the three "boogie men" were supposed to have sung the final song in the movie, "The Bad Humor Man," but the final film has spared us that spectacle.

Nevertheless, Kyser is amiable enough onscreen, as is the film itself under the direction of David Butler. There are a lot of inside jokes and self-deprecating humor. At one point in the proceedings, Professor Karl Fenninger (Lorre) asks Judge Spencer Mainwaring (Karloff), "Who is this fellow, Kyser?" "Some bandleader," Mainwaring sniffs.

Some of the more interesting moments revolve around the use of a musical instrument called the Sonovox, which makes the human voice sound very weird indeed, almost as if it had been recorded in the grave. The device is something like what seventies rock star Peter Frampton used in his live album many years later, but much creepier.

One interesting note of trivia: This was the screen debut of actor Jeff Corey, who has a small role as a quiz show contestant. Corey was later a victim of the McCarthy-era blacklist, which forced him to go into teaching: among his acting students were Jack Nicholson, James Dean and Jane Fonda. When the blacklist was ended, he returned to acting and also went on to direct some of the better episodes of Rod Serling's *Night Gallery* in the seventies.

You'll Find Out never travels very far or very fast, but it does have a certain charm, as it's very much a time capsule of the early forties, featuring excellent examples of the musical and comedic styles of that bygone era. Kyser, almost forgotten now, made seven films, but *You'll Find Out* remains the best-remembered because of its iconic co-stars.

The Invisible Woman

Earlier in 1940, Universal had produced *The Invisible Man Returns* with Vincent Price in the starring role. James Whale had exploited the comic possibilities of invisibility in his adaptation of the Wells story in 1933, although for the most part *The Invisible Man* had been a rather serious study of the tragedy the abuse of such awesome power could bring to the scientist that Claude Rains portrayed. In the sequel, Price, in his first starring role in a horror film, played a character more sinned against than sinning. John P. Fulton's invisibility effects were just as good the second time around, and so Universal employed his expertise once again on *The Invisible Woman*, released on December 27, 1940. Universal's trust in Fulton was well founded: He received an Oscar nomination for his special effects.

The Invisible Woman is in no way a sequel to either *Invisible Man* movie before it. Although H.G. Wells gets screen credit for inspiration, the story concocted by Joe May (who had directed *The Invisible Man Returns*) and Curt Siodmak (creator of *The Wolf Man*), and the screenplay written by Robert Lees, Frederic I. Rinaldo and Gertrude Purcell, takes off in a completely different direction. The emphasis is on screwball comedy under the direction of A. Edward Sutherland, a specialist in both comedy and horror. In 1933, he had helmed the Lionel Atwill starrer *Murders in the Zoo* for Paramount; at the time he was asked to direct *The Invisible Woman*, he had just completed the comedy *One Night in the Tropics* for Universal.

The story revolves around classic absent-minded Professor Gibbs (John Barrymore), who invents a machine that can make living things invisible. Naturally, being a slightly mad scientist, he wants to make people invisible, so he advertises in a newspaper for a volunteer for the experiment. The ad catches the eye of lovely department store model Kitty Carroll (Virginia Bruce), who is the adventurous type and willing to try the experiment so she can get revenge on her former boss, Mr. Growley (Charles Lane), who had fired her. Unfortunately, her plans go awry when three gangsters (Oscar Homolka, Donald MacBride and Shemp Howard) steal the device.

As usual, Universal assembled an excellent cast. Margaret Sullavan had originally been scheduled to play the title role, but she backed out at the last minute and the part went to Bruce, a busy and talented actress who had just co-starred in Universal's sophisticated comedy *Hired Wife* with Rosalind Russell. Handsome leading man John Howard (who in 1942 would play a werewolf in *The Undying Monster* for Fox) played Dick Russell, a wealthy attorney who gives the professor financial backing for his machine; Charlie Ruggles, who had also been featured in *Murders in the Zoo* (1933), was cast as Russell's eternally befuddled butler; Margaret Hamilton, the Wicked Witch of the West herself from 1939's *The Wizard of Oz*, was given the fun role of Professor Gibbs' housekeeper, Mrs. Jackson; and Universal contract players Anne Nagel, Mary Gordon (Mrs. Hudson from the Sherlock Holmes films) and Maria Montez also appeared in small roles.

The aging Barrymore is charming as the slightly addled professor, a scientist who has never managed to produce anything of use to anyone before inventing his invisibility machine. His delight at his "astounding" discovery is palpable; he can be quite cranky too, as when he delivers a line to his car, admonishing it to "put yourself in the garage, lazy bones!" His performance is that of a great actor, past his prime, who's having a wonderful time playing a role that he never could have portrayed when he was younger. It's as if "The Great Profile" has felt a burden lifted and just lets himself go.

Howard and Bruce have a nice chemistry together and their scenes reveal why *The Invisible Woman* was considered to be quite risqué in its day. The strict Hays Code enforced by the Breen Office didn't allow for much eroticism on the screen, but Sutherland and company pushed the envelope as far as they could. The conceit, of course, is that you're only invisible when you're naked, and the fact that this time it's a shapely woman rather than Rains or Price puts a whole new spin on the idea. When Bruce sits in a chair next to Howard and starts putting on her stockings, her legs are revealed to Howard and the audience, and the temperature definitely goes up a bit. This kind of "naughtiness" appealed to audiences of the time, starved as they were for any "adult content" they could get on the screen, and it certainly didn't hurt the movie's box office.

The entire cast seems to be having a good time, which communicates to the viewer. Ruggles does some amusing pratfalls and double takes; Homolka wears a hideous toupee and overacts wildly, using his prodigious eyebrows expressively; and Shemp Howard is, well, Shemp Howard.

The Invisible Woman is not a great comedy-horror film for the simple reason that there are no truly scary moments. Everything is played for comedy to the extent that there's no real mood or atmosphere. There are some who might call it more of a comedy–science fiction movie rather than a comedy-horror film. But it is a part of Universal's great horror cycle and a gender-bending variation on one of their greatest continuing characters. As such, it was the last word on comic invisibility for a while, at least until Abbott and Costello got into the act. But more on that later.

King of the Zombies

After the extraordinary success of *The Ghost Breakers*, other studios tried to cash in on Paramount's box-office bonanza, including tiny Monogram Pictures, one of the oldest of the so-called "Poverty Row" production and distribution companies. In their press kit for the 1941 release *King of the Zombies,* they advised movie exhibitors to sell the movie "along the same lines as *The Ghost Breakers.*"

King of the Zombies was a low-budget affair, so the producers certainly couldn't afford the likes of Bob Hope. But this worked to the distinct advantage of African-American actor Mantan Moreland, who had been knocking around B-movies and "all-black" features for years. *King of the Zombies* became his greatest showcase, his only leading role in a "mainstream" feature.

Born in Monroe, Louisiana in 1902, Moreland reportedly ran away to join the circus when he was only twelve years old. He was brought back home several times, but his desire to be in show business would not abate and he ended up on the vaudeville stage. Moreland performed on Broadway and in Europe, where he honed his comedy skills.

Eventually, he drifted into the film business, initially appearing in bit parts playing shoeshine boys and waiters. Due to his superb comedy timing, he soon ended up with larger roles in all-black western parodies such as *Harlem on the Prairie* (1937) and other films that mainly played to segregated audiences, such as the 1942 comedy mysteries *Mr. Washington Goes to Town* and *Professor Creeps*, as well as mainstream studio movies in which he was usually cast as a terrified, cowardly manservant who inevitably ran away from ghosts, gangsters, monsters or whatever the script called for.

Servile roles were pretty much all that African-American actors could hope for in those days, at least for the major studios. But unlike Stepin' Fetchit and Sleep 'N' Eat (aka Willie Best), Moreland had higher comedic aspirations. His characters were often smarter than the white leads, and certainly more energetic.

Monogram was one of the few studios to see Moreland's potential as a comic actor. The studio executives put him under contract to appear opposite white actor Frankie Darro in a series of eight mystery comedies, starting with *Irish Luck* (1939). His character name, Jeff Jefferson, was a moniker that Moreland often used in his Monogram films.

Ultimately, Moreland became best known as Birmingham Brown, chauffeur to Sidney Toler's Charlie Chan in the long-running series that Monogram took over from 20th Century-Fox in 1944. He appeared in no less than fifteen films in the series, beginning with *Charlie Chan in the Secret Service* (1944). Toler's health gradually declined and he died midway through the series; the final six films starred Roland Winters as the Asian detective, who was never once portrayed by an Asian.

But it was *King of the Zombies* that allowed Moreland the opportunity to really show off his talent to an "integrated" audience. Third-billed in the movie after Dick Purcell and Joan Woodbury, Moreland this time played a character called Jefferson Jackson. It's his comic timing—and his character's intelligence—that helps to elevate *King of the Zombies* far above the usual Monogram fare.

Moreland's Jackson is a valet to two pilots (Purcell and John Archer) whose plane crashes on an uncharted island. When Jackson regains consciousness, he finds he's propped up against a tombstone upon which are engraved the words "Rest in Peace." Muttering to himself, "They sure don't waste no time around here!" he is happy to meet up with his comrades, who assure him that he isn't dead. "I thought I was a little off-color to be a ghost," he remarks.

"Off-color" is a pretty good description of the humor, but thanks to Moreland's smooth and perfectly timed delivery, even the politically incorrect lines seem innocent. One may wince at the stereotypes, but it's wise to bear in mind that white actors in comedy-horror films frequently played cowardly heroes as well.

The fact is, Jackson is in many respects the most intelligent character in *King of the Zombies*; he's the one who figures out what's going on once they take refuge in a mansion owned by one Dr. Sangre (Henry Victor). It soon becomes apparent to Jackson that the mansion is a hotbed of zombies and voodoo.

Although the film was released on May 14, 1941, months before America entered World War Two, *King of the Zombies* features an apparent Nazi villain. Victor, in a role originally intended for Bela Lugosi or Peter Lorre (neither of whom could commit to the film), speaks in German on his radio transmissions. He claims to be from Austria, but we know better. The presskit for the film describes Dr. Sangre as "a secret agent for a European government." A B-film it may be, but it was slightly ahead of its time.

Of course, director Jean Yarbrough and writer Edmond Kelso had no intention of making political commentary; they were just crafting entertainment for the masses. And it's safe to say that both black and white audiences got a kick out of *King of the Zombies*. It's the African-American character who saves the day here while the white characters remain pretty clueless. Once Jackson bonds with the pretty maid played by Marguerite Whitten, there's a lot of subtle (and not-so-subtle) subversion of white culture going on. When you consider the fact that a black character causes the downfall of a Nazi, well, the implications speak for themselves.

Along the way, the actors (and the audience) have a lot of fun. At one point, Jackson is apparently hypnotized by Sangre into becoming a zombie. But the subtext is that he may be merely pretending to be hypnotized. "Move over, boys," he says to the other zombies, "I'm one of the gang now."

By the end of the film, however, he has the situation well in hand and declares, "If there's one thing I don't want to be twice, zombies is both of 'em!"

Moreland did show up in another Monogram zombie film called *Revenge of the Zombies* in 1943, but it wasn't a comedy-horror film and it wasn't nearly as good as *King of the Zombies*. After all, *King of the Zombies* was Oscar-nominated for its music score! The music by Edward J. Kay is actually quite good, especially for a low-budget "quickie."

Moreland hit his cinematic peak with his recurring role in the Charlie Chan series, although the character wasn't what one would call three-dimensional. Birmingham Brown was forever warning his employer, Chan, not to venture into danger; but again, as in *King of the Zombies*, he was usually right.

By the fifties, audiences became uncomfortable with racial stereotypes in films, especially when the civil rights movement really got going in America beginning in the middle of the decade. Moreland, Stepin' Fetchit, Willie Best and others had a hard time finding employment and found themselves ostracized by Hollywood.

By the late sixties, Moreland made a minor comeback on television, even working with big-time celebrities such as Carl Reiner, Bill Cosby and Godfrey Cambridge. Alas, the timing was poor; by this time, Moreland was suffering from the after-effects of a stroke; he died of a cerebral hemorrhage in 1973. Mantan Moreland, a pioneering African-American performer, was buried in Valhalla Memorial Park Cemetery near Hollywood.

The Black Cat

In 1941, Universal, for no particular reason, decided to do another version of Edgar Allan Poe's *The Black Cat*, which they had already done in 1934 as a vehicle for Karloff and Lugosi. That film, directed by Edgar G. Ulmer, had been dark and moody, one of Universal's finest and most disturbing horror films, despite the fact that it had almost nothing to do with Poe's story.

This time around, they decided to film it as a comedy; amusingly, the writing credits for the film read: "Screenplay by Robert Lees, Robert Neville, Fredric I. Rinaldo and Eric Taylor ... Story by Edgar Allan Poe." Once again, however, it's doubtful that Poe would have recognized his tale in this creaky yarn of an old mansion, an inheritance and a house full of cats.

Director Albert S. Rogell assembled an all-star cast. Basil Rathbone, Broderick Crawford, Bela Lugosi, Gale Sondergaard, Gladys Cooper, Anne Gwynne and a very young Alan Ladd are among those trapped in the Winslow mansion on the night of a raging storm. Along for the ride is comic actor Hugh Herbert as a permanently befuddled antiques dealer named Mr. Penny.

The film's plot is fairly typical for an "old dark house" mystery. Cat fancier Henrietta Winslow, portrayed by vaudeville veteran Cecilia Loftus, is murdered by someone in her greedy clan. The family has gathered for the reading of the will and discovered that the dotty old lady has left everything to her feline friends. Not one of her relatives will receive a penny until all of the cats are dead. Despite that codicil, however, it's several of the humans who end up dying.

There are the usual suspects: Rathbone as Mr. Hartley, Abigail Doone as played by the ever-sinister Sondergaard, and of course Lugosi as yet another mysterious servant; Crawford is the over-eager real estate agent and Herbert his mind-numbingly foolish assistant. Herbert is very much the buffoon to Crawford's straight man, but his exaggerated mannerisms wear thin rather quickly.

There are some amusing moments here and there, such as when Crawford meets Ladd and says to him, "Oh, then you're the guy that slugged me." Ladd replies to the much larger Crawford, "Yeah, and I'll do it again any time you train down to my weight."

Most of *The Black Cat*, though, is a waste of formidable talent. Rathbone and Lugosi have very little to do, and the film is really carried by Crawford, Herbert, Sondergaard, Cooper and Gwynne, all of them doing what they're asked to do, which consists of screaming, acting befuddled and/or looking sinister. As with most Universal films of the period, it looks great and is fluidly photographed by Stanley Cortez, who also shot *The Magnificent Ambersons* (1942).

Hold That Ghost

Universal made a much better comedy-horror film in 1941, and it was the unofficial beginning of a whole new era. Their premier comedy team, Bud Abbott and Lou Costello, would later be known for meeting many of the Universal monsters starting with *Abbott and Costello Meet Frankenstein* (1948). But they had a flirtation with the genre in 1941 in a movie called *Hold That Ghost*, directed by Arthur Lubin, who would later direct Universal's 1943 remake *Phantom of the Opera*.

Hold That Ghost was co-written by two of the writers of *The Black Cat*, Robert Lees and Fred Rinaldo, along with John Grant. It was filmed beginning on January 21, 1941, and wrapped on February 24. Additional scenes were shot on May 13 (the nightclub scenes with Ted Lewis, who asks the musical question "Is everybody happy?" and also does a very politically incorrect version of "Me and My Shadow"). The Andrews Sisters were also brought in for these scenes.

Hold That Ghost was filmed before the Abbott and Costello comedy *In The Navy*, but release was held up so that Universal could cash in with the service-themed comedy to follow up their huge A&C hit, *Buck Privates*. Finally released on August 8, 1941, *Hold That Ghost* proved to be one of the boys' best comedies.

Bud and Lou are bumbling gas station attendants who somehow end up as the beneficiaries of a gangster's will. They attempt to claim their fortune so that they can become night club owners (their lifelong dream), but they end up stranded in a supposedly haunted tavern along with a number of other "guests," including Richard Carlson, Joan Davis, Evelyn Ankers and perpetual gangster Marc Lawrence. The latter is one of the dead gangster's cronies, and he's there to try and find a hidden cache of money. Things get spooky when a ghost ("with fangs," according to Davis) starts prowling around the dark corridors of the tavern.

Davis, a greatly underrated comedienne (her 1950s TV show *I Married Joan* rivaled *I Love Lucy*) has some of the best lines. It's obvious from the get-go that her character, Camille, finds Ferdie (Costello) strangely attractive. "Are you a married man?" she asks him. "No," he replies, and she states plainly, "Neither am I." Later, when they're in the tavern eating dinner, she takes one taste of the soup and remarks, "Just like mother used to make ... it stinks!"

There are, of course, the usual Abbott and Costello verbal exchanges. When Ferdie is frightened by a candle that moves by itself, he calls to Chuck (Abbott). When Chuck finally arrives, Ferdie admonishes him: "I called 42 'Oh Chucks' and you didn't come in." Chuck says defensively, 'I came in as soon as you hollered 'Oh Chuck.'" The very flustered Ferdie counters with, "From now on, don't wait for me to say, 'Oh Chuck!' Get in here on the 'Oh!'"

Ultimately, the "ghost" turns out to be a gangster, and the hidden loot is found in a stuffed moose head that hangs on the wall. All ends well for the boys, who use the money to open their nightclub. It's a pretty basic plot, but it was the blueprint for most of the *Abbott and Costello Meet...* pictures to follow in the late forties and the fifties. All the cast members are more than up to the job, especially Carlson, Ankers and Lawrence. And don't miss a cameo by "fourth Stooge" Shemp Howard as a soda jerk.

Hold That Ghost is a great introduction to the A&C "team," and an extremely entertaining harbinger of comedy-horror films to come.

Spooks Run Wild

Much has been written of the downward spiral of Bela Lugosi's career, of how he began in A pictures and ended up working for Poverty Row companies Monogram and PRC and, God help him, eventually for Ed Wood. It's important to remember, however, that some of these films were very popular in their day, particularly the East Side Kids series, which Lugosi entered in 1941.

The East Side Kids began as "The Dead End Kids" in the 1935 play *Dead End*. When the play was made into a film in 1937, the original "Kids" were retained, including Leo Gorcey, Huntz Hall, Bobby Jordan, Gabriel Dell, Billy Halop and Bernard Punsly. Several more films were made featuring "The Dead End Kids," the most famous being *Angels With Dirty Faces* (1938) with James Cagney and Humphrey Bogart and *They Made Me a Criminal* (1939) with John Garfield.

Universal borrowed the Dead End Kids (with the exception of Gorcey and Jordan) for a series of their own. Sam Katzman of Monogram produced a film called *East Side Kids* in 1940 featuring David Durand, Frankie Burke and Donald Haines from the Universal series. But the first time Katzman used the talents of Hall and Jordan was in the following feature, the spooky *The Ghost Creeps* (aka *Boys of the City*, 1940). Thus began Monogram's most popular series, ultimately totaling a whopping 21 films in just under six years. These were true Poverty Row productions, with budgets of around $33,000 per feature and shooting schedules of about a week each. This meant very little time for retakes, and it's easy to spot bloopers and ad-libs in most of the films.

Lugosi's entry into the series was in the seventh film, *Spooks Run Wild* (1941), which was originally filmed under the title of *Ghosts in the Night*. This was the second film in the series to feature Huntz Hall as Glimpy Williams, a real smart-aleck whose banter with Gorcey helped keep the films a step above total mediocrity.

The director of *Bowery Blitzkrieg*, Wallace Fox, was originally slated to direct but had to bow out due to an offer from Columbia to direct *The Lone Star Vigilantes*. Katzman quickly replaced him with Phil Rosen, a Russian-born director who had just completed filming *The Deadly Game* for Monogram.

Ghosts in the Night was filmed in August, 1941, on a shooting schedule of only a week and a half. By the time the movie was released to theaters on October 24, 1941, the title had been changed to *Spooks Run Wild*.

Lugosi's role is that of red herring. He plays a magician named Nardo who has a dwarf assistant (Angelo Rossito, who decades later would appear in *Mad Max: Beyond Thunderdome*). The two of them lurk around an old dark house and a graveyard for no particular reason, and the East Side Kids think Nardo is a homicidal maniac who has murdered several women in the neighborhood.

Lugosi looks impressive in the movie; he's dressed more or less like Dracula. He's given very little to do, however, and the film on the whole has little to recommend it. Interestingly enough, it was co-written by Carl Foreman, later to become a first-class screenwriter of such films as *High Noon* (1952) and a victim of the McCarthy blacklist. It may be impossible at this point to even ascertain which scenes Foreman was responsible for (the co-writer was Charles R. Marion), but one hopes it wasn't one of the film's typical examples of "wit," such as this one:

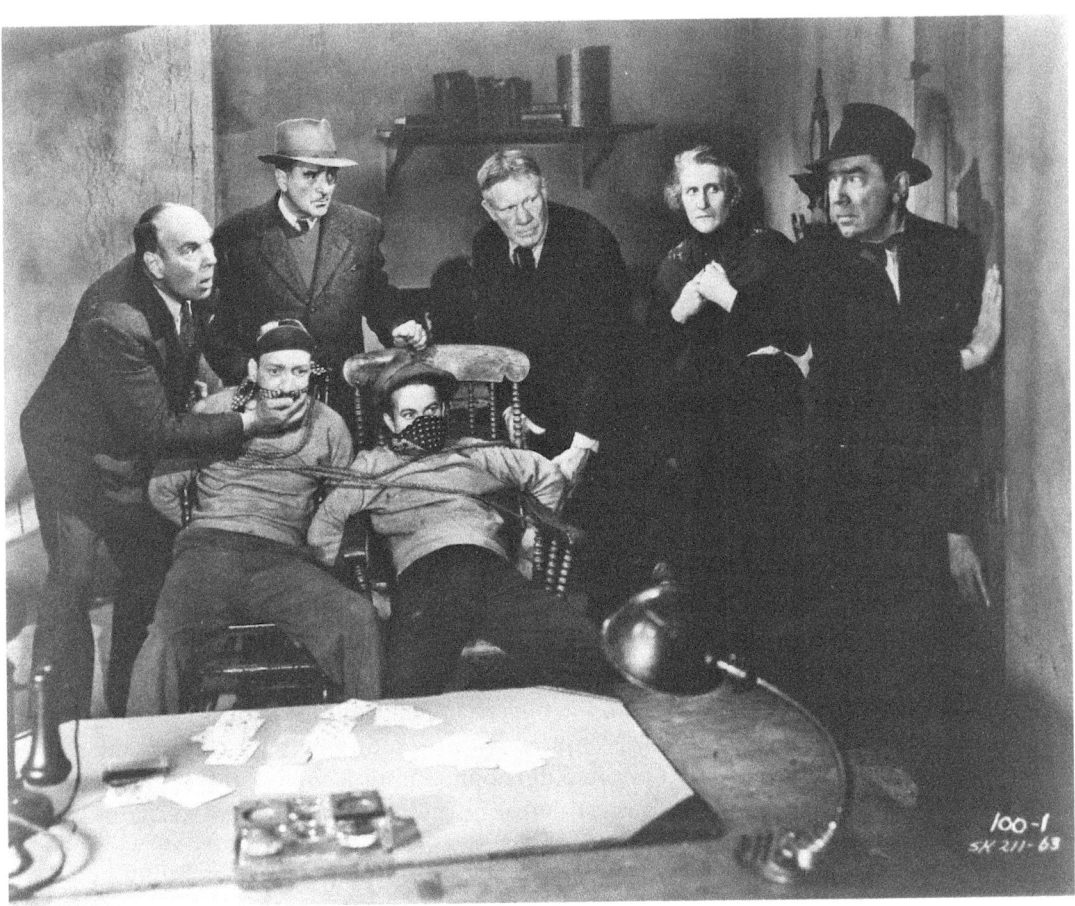

Huntz Hall and Leo Gorcey are held captive by thugs while Bela Lugosi (far right) checks the door in Lugosi's second East Side Kids movie, William "One Shot" Beaudine's *Ghosts on the Loose* (1943).

>   DANNY (BOBBY JORDAN): How can you read in the dark?
>   GLIMPY (LEO GORCEY): I went to night school.

As with most of the East Side Kids movies, there is little in *Spooks Run Wild* to interest a modern audience. The boys had already done the aforementioned film that touched on comedy-horror, 1940's *The Ghost Creeps*, but the two that they did with Lugosi are the only ones of real interest to fans these days, purely because of his presence.

Ghosts on the Loose

Lugosi's second East Side Kids movie was *Ghosts on the Loose* (1943), in which the boys try to fix up an old house for newlyweds but discover that the sinister-looking place next door is "haunted." In this case, the "ghosts" turn out to be Nazis, thereby giving the movie a timely edge during World War II. It was advertised with the tagline "The East Side Kids vs. The Man of a Thousand Horrors!" The screenplay by Kenneth Higgins was pretty much a rehash of both *Spooks Run Wild* and *The Ghost Creeps*, and once again Lugosi was given little screen time and was obviously there only to collect his probably minuscule paycheck.

As directed in a hurry by the infamous William "One Shot" Beaudine, *Ghosts on the Loose* is notable only for Lugosi's appearance and for one of the early performances of Ava Gardner, who plays the better-looking half of the just-married couple. Again, the humor is of the cornball variety, as when Mugs says to Glimpy, "Any normal person can get normal measles, but you gotta pick a fight with a Nazi and get German measles." The visual part of the joke is more amusing: Glimpy's face is covered with swastikas.

There's one especially funny gaffe in the film, but you have to listen carefully: at one point in the movie, Lugosi sneezes and, instead of *ah-choo*, utters a certain four-letter word. True to his nickname, "One Shot" Beaudine left it in.

One footnote: Gabriel Dell, who was part of the East Side Kids repertory company, did all the voices on a record album called "Famous Monsters Speak" in 1963. On side two, he did a dead-on impression of Lugosi as Dracula. Wonder where he picked that up?

The Boogie Man Will Get You

Starting in 1941, Boris Karloff was one of the stars of the hit Broadway play by Joseph Kesselring, *Arsenic and Old Lace*. At the height of the play's success that first year, Frank Capra made his film version, but without Karloff; the Broadway producers wanted him to continue in the stage production. After all, he played a character described as someone who "looked like Boris Karloff," so who better?

Capra made the film version with the understanding from the show's Broadway producers, Howard Lindsay and Russell Crouse, that it wouldn't be released until the show ended its Broadway run. It wasn't put into distribution until 1944, but in 1942 Lindsay and Crouse released Karloff from his contract so that he could go to Hollywood to star in a sort of *Arsenic and Old Lace* knock-off called *The Boogie Man Will Get You*.

The story was written by Hal Fimberg and Robert B. Hunt; Paul Gangelin and Edwin Blum were credited for the rather unoriginal screenplay, which borrows a great deal from *Arsenic and Old Lace*. There are a number of dead bodies in the basement, dotty relatives (including a shrieking ghost) and eccentric characters such as "Silvio the Human Bomb," an escaped POW from Italy by way of Canada. The casting of Karloff and Peter Lorre (their second film together) also had a kinship to *Arsenic*; Lorre had just appeared in the as-yet-unreleased film version.

The zany plot has something to do with a young divorcee named Winnie Jones (Jeff Donnell—not a man in drag, but billed as Miss Jeff Donnell) who buys an old New England inn from addled Professor Billings (Karloff). The judge currently lives there with his wacky housekeeper Amelia (Maude Eburne). Winnie, a free-spirited type and somewhat daffy herself, allows them to keep living in the place while she converts it into a "modern" hotel. She's blissfully unaware that Billings is conducting weird experiments on traveling salesmen, whom he keeps in the cellar after unsuccessfully attempting to turn them into "supermen." Lorre plays Dr. Lorenz, a quack who is also the town's sheriff, justice of the peace, undertaker and coroner, and who also holds the mortgage on the property. For no particular reason, he carries a Siamese kitten around in his coat pocket.

Winnie's ex-husband Bill (Larry Parks) also gets thrown into this eclectic mix, along with a slightly effeminate choreographer (Don Beddoe) and a moronic powder puff salesman (Max "Slapsie Maxie" Rosenbloom). As directed by Lew Landers, who had directed Karloff in 1935's *The Raven* under the name of Louis Friedlander, *The Boogie Man Will Get You* moves at a brisk pace throughout its brief sixty-six-minute running time, although the material is hardly up to the standard of *Arsenic and Old Lace*. It would, in fact, be quite forgettable were it not for Karloff and Lorre, who seem to be having a grand time. Their screen chemistry is the glue that holds the entire enterprise together.

The final movie in Karloff's contract with Columbia, *The Boogie Man Will Get You* throws so many ingredients into the brew that it sometimes feels as if the filmmakers are aware that the material isn't all that great, but that if they just keep things moving fast enough, the audience won't notice. Sometimes this works and sometimes it doesn't; aside from Karloff and Lorre, Rosenbloom comes off funniest, sort of a live-action version of one of those idiotic Warner Bros. cartoon dogs that keeps imploring, "Tell me about the rabbits, George." He actually has a moment in the film in which he says, "Am I unconscious yet?"

But Karloff, as the continuously befuddled and never evil "mad scientist," is a joy to watch; when Parks accuses him of murder, he protests: "Please! Please! The word is 'martyrized.'" Lorre is a constant delight, obviously improvising some of his material, especially with the kitten he keeps taking out of his pocket. Whether he's in his doctor mode ("Oh! Hardening of the skull!") or wearing his mortgage broker's hat ("Contractum sanctum putnam, which means done and dished up!"), he's a wonderfully likable and very funny rogue.

While *The Boogie Man Will Get You* is not remembered as a great classic, it remains a good example of the teaming of Lorre and Karloff; eventually they would make four films together, all of them comedy-horror films. And they took such obvious joy in spoofing their onscreen personas that it communicated directly to the audience. They winked, we smiled.

Arsenic and Old Lace

Meanwhile, Frank Capra's film of *Arsenic and Old Lace* remained unreleased until September 23, 1944. The play had been a sensation on Broadway, and one of the big reasons was Karloff. In a self-referential role written for him, he got to show off his comedic chops for audiences who had seen very little of that side of him. The play finally closed on June 17, 1944, after 1,444 performances. Warner Bros. was finally free to release the film version, and it too became a big hit.

One of the few flaws of Capra's film is that it doesn't feature Karloff, which, as we have noted, was not Capra's fault but rather due to Karloff's contractual commitment to the play. Replacing Karloff in the film version was his co-star from *The Old Dark House*, Raymond Massey.

Aside from that change, the film version is very faithful to the stage play. A few "hells," "damns" and other mild curse words had to be changed to appease the Production Code people, but other than that, Kesselring's macabre black comedy made it to the screen intact.

The story is fast and crazy. A drama critic named Mortimer Brewster (Cary Grant) is forced to deal with the fact that his two maiden aunts (Jean Adair and Josephine Hull) have taken to murdering lonely old men—thirteen, at last count—by poisoning them with homemade wine seasoned with arsenic, strychnine and "just a pinch" of cyanide. Brewster has a brother who thinks he's Teddy Roosevelt, and who digs "locks for the Panama Canal" in the aunts' basement that are actually graves for the victims. Just to round things off, Mortimer has another brother named Jonathan (Massey) who has murdered a number of people on his own and who has received plastic surgery from one Dr. Einstein (Peter Lorre) to conceal his identity; unfortunately, the alcoholic doctor had watched a movie starring Boris Karloff just before performing the operation, and subconsciously made Jonathan's face a replica of

Cary Grant and Priscilla Lane in Frank Capra's uproarious 1944 film version of Joseph Kesselring's Broadway hit *Arsenic and Old Lace*.

Karloff's. Meanwhile, Mortimer has just been married to Elaine (Priscilla Lane) and is afraid to tell her that insanity runs in his family.

Capra retained all of the incidents and most of the dialogue from the play, only adding a couple of exterior shots early in the film. The lead role of Mortimer was originally planned for Bob Hope, fresh off his successes in *The Cat and the Canary* and *The Ghost Breakers*, but

Jonathan Brewster (Raymond Massey) is questioned by his brother Mortimer (Cary Grant) in Frank Capra's *Arsenic and Old Lace* (1944).

Paramount wouldn't release him from his contract. Capra had also considered Jack Benny and, of all people, Ronald Reagan, for the role, but finally settled on Cary Grant. Adair, Hull and John Alexander as Teddy all reprised their roles from the Broadway production.

Clocking in at 118 minutes, a fairly long feature for those days, *Arsenic and Old Lace* starts off at a frantic pace and never lets up for a second. It's hilarious, raucous and very, very irreverent, everything a farcical black comedy should be. The dialogue (by Kesselring, Julius J. Epstein and Philip G. Epstein) sparkles. Fortunately, all of the cast members are up to the task, with Grant at high energy throughout, sometimes breaking the "fourth wall" and looking in exasperation at the camera, as if to say, "Can you believe this?" As Mortimer, he's stuck in the middle of a very bizarre situation: his bride waits for him next door (it's their wedding night) as he tries to alert the local police to the threat posed by Jonathan, without wanting to turn in his aunts, while at the same time trying to get Teddy committed to the "Happydale Rest Home." He fears that he will go crazy like the rest of his family. At one point he says to Elaine, "Insanity runs in my family. It practically gallops." Finally, after many loopy incidents, he discovers that he is not really a Brewster at all, but was in fact adopted. In the original play, he happily tells his bride that he's a bastard; in the film, he tells her that he's "the son of a sea-cook."

Lorre gives a smooth and frequently uproarious performance as Dr. Einstein, a character loosely based on gangland surgeon Joseph Moran. His debate with Jonathan as to whether or not "the old ladies" have killed as many people as he has is absolutely first-rate in its timing and delivery. Jonathan insists he has killed thirteen people, one more than the old ladies. "You cannot count the one in South Bend!" Einstein insists. "He died of pneumonia!" Jonathan counters with: "He wouldn't have died of pneumonia if I hadn't shot him!" But Einstein stands firm: "No, no, Johnny. You cannot count him. You got twelve, they got twelve. The old ladies is just as good as you are!"

While one wishes that Karloff had been allowed to reprise the role that was written for him, Massey acquits himself admirably as Jonathan. He's made up to look something like Karloff (on a bad day, perhaps) and bristles every time someone says to him, "You look like Boris Karloff!" Massey also provides the film with its creepiest moments, enhanced by Sol Polito's shadow-laden cinematography. He's good, but one can't help but wonder how much better Karloff would have been.

The "old ladies" are wonderful. Their matter-of-fact attitudes toward their "mercy killings" are as droll as can be. "Aunt Abby, how can I believe you?" Mortimer asks her at one point. "There are twelve bodies in the cellar and you admit you poisoned them." Abby (Hull) replies: "Yes, I did. But you don't think I'd stoop to telling a fib!"

There are also nice comic turns by Jack Carson as a police officer who's a wannabe playwright; the venerable Edward Everett Horton as the head of Happydale; and James Gleason as perpetually exasperated Police Lieutenant Rooney. As Mortimer's long-suffering bride, Lane doesn't have a great deal to do, but she looks very good doing it.

Truly one of the first and still one of the best of all cinematic black comedies, *Arsenic and Old Lace* is just as funny (and as spooky) today as it was in 1944.

The Canterville Ghost

Many critics consider Jules Dassin's 1944 version of Oscar Wilde's *The Canterville Ghost* to be a comedy-fantasy rather than a comedy-horror film. The opening of the film, however, is pretty grim and owes as much to Poe as to Wilde. In the seventeenth century, cowardly Sir Simon de Canterville (Charles Laughton) flees a duel and seeks refuge in his family castle. His stern father (Reginald Owen) is so ashamed of Sir Simon that he walls him up in his room, burying him alive. As if that weren't enough, Lord Canterville curses his unfortunate son, admonishing him to find no spiritual rest until one of his descendants redeems him with an act of bravery. Now if that isn't horrific, what is?

Flash forward to 1944, when a group of American soldiers are billeted in Canterville Castle. It's now the property of a young child, Lady Jessica de Canterville (Margaret O'Brien). One of the soldiers stationed there, Cuffy Williams (Robert Young), just happens to be a descendant of the Cantervilles. You can probably guess the ending at this point, but the fun is in getting there.

Laughton has a wonderful time as Sir Simon, especially when he's a ghost. Walking around on "special" occasions with his head tucked underneath his arm, he chews all the scenery in sight. But there's a great sadness to the character as well. "I have roamed these halls for three centuries and I am so tired. If I could only rest," Sir Simon laments.

Needless to say, the film ends happily for all when Cuffy overcomes his natural "Canterville" ways and performs a heroic act against the invading Nazis. Sir Simon gets to "rest" in a plot on the estate he's been yearning for, Cuffy feels like a new (and brave) man and Lady de Canterville no longer fears the ghost. It's a charming tale well told, all the more surprising when one considers that the film was what Hollywood euphemistically terms a "troubled production."

Dassin was not brought in as director until the film had been in production for thirty-eight days under the supervision of Norman Z. McLeod. News items at the time cited the usual "creative differences," but those in the know said that McLeod was replaced at the insistence of Laughton. Whatever the case, Dassin brought his own personality to the production, and was probably responsible for what "darkness" there is in the movie's style. In 1941, Dassin had directed a highly regarded 20-minute version of Poe's *The Tell Tale Heart* starring Joseph Schildkraut. And so perhaps the allusions to Poe in the opening sequence, and Sir Simon's longing for death, are Dassin's contributions. At this stage of the game, we'll probably never know for sure.

All the players are amiable enough, with Young delivering an especially relaxed and likable performance as a man who has to work very hard to overcome his natural cowardice. As Lady de Canterville, O'Brien's British accent is inconsistent, to say the least, but there are certain things one can forgive a child actress. She's really quite delightful in the role.

The Canterville Ghost is Laughton's show, however, and he runs with it. When he delivers lines such as "Excuse me, I really must gibber at the oriole window," he's very funny, but also very winsome. What a terrible fate to have to wander darkened halls for centuries when your only "work" is to scare tourists. A fate worse than death, indeed.

Ghost Catchers

The comedy team of Olsen and Johnson is barely remembered today, but in their time they had a following to rival that of Monty Python or Spike Jones. Chic Johnson and Ole Olsen began as vaudeville musicians, eventually abandoning the quartet they were in to appear as a two-man musical comedy act. They added more performers to the mix and by 1918 their brand of zany, anarchic comedy mixed with music was a huge success with audiences around the country.

After making a few film and radio appearances in the early thirties, the duo hit it big with their Broadway production of *Hellzapoppin* in 1938. The mixture of comedy blackouts and music became one of the longest-running Broadway shows in history, eventually spawning a movie version in 1941. Although the film version was a bit more "Hollywood" in its somewhat more linear storyline, it was successful enough to get the team contracts with Universal Pictures. Their first followup to *Hellzapoppin* was another wacky musical comedy film

Gloria Jean and Walter Catlett in a tight spot in the Olsen and Johnson comedy-horror film *Ghost Catchers* (1944), directed by Edward F. Cline.

called *Crazy House* (1943), after which they decided to enter the "old dark house" sweepstakes with *Ghost Catchers* (1944).

Directed by Edward F. Cline (who also co-wrote the story with Milt Gross), *Ghost Catchers* owes its existence as much to *Hold That Ghost* as to *Hellzapoppin*. In fact, the famous "moving candle" scene from *Hold That Ghost* is parodied in *Ghost Catchers*. The plot is quite similar too: Colonel Breckinridge Marshall (Walter Catlett), an impoverished but ambitious Southern gentleman, rents a townhouse just down the block from Carnegie Hall in New York, hoping that his two daughters (Gloria Jean and Martha O'Driscoll) will hit it big in the music world. But their first night in the old house is filled with ghostly noises, including the sound of somebody tap dancing.

Susannah (O'Driscoll) runs to the adjoining building for help, but, in a very odd scene indeed, finds herself in the middle of an Olsen and Johnson sketch. The duo, who use their real names in the film, own a nightclub (called, not surprisingly, "Olsen and Johnson's") where they perform what used to be called "nut humor." They decide to help the young woman discover what's going on in her new abode, and eventually discover that the house was once owned by Wilbur Duffington (Jack Norton), a wealthy alcoholic whose two biggest hobbies were tap dancing and drinking plum brandy.

One of the stranger ideas in the film concerns the assumption by Olsen and Johnson

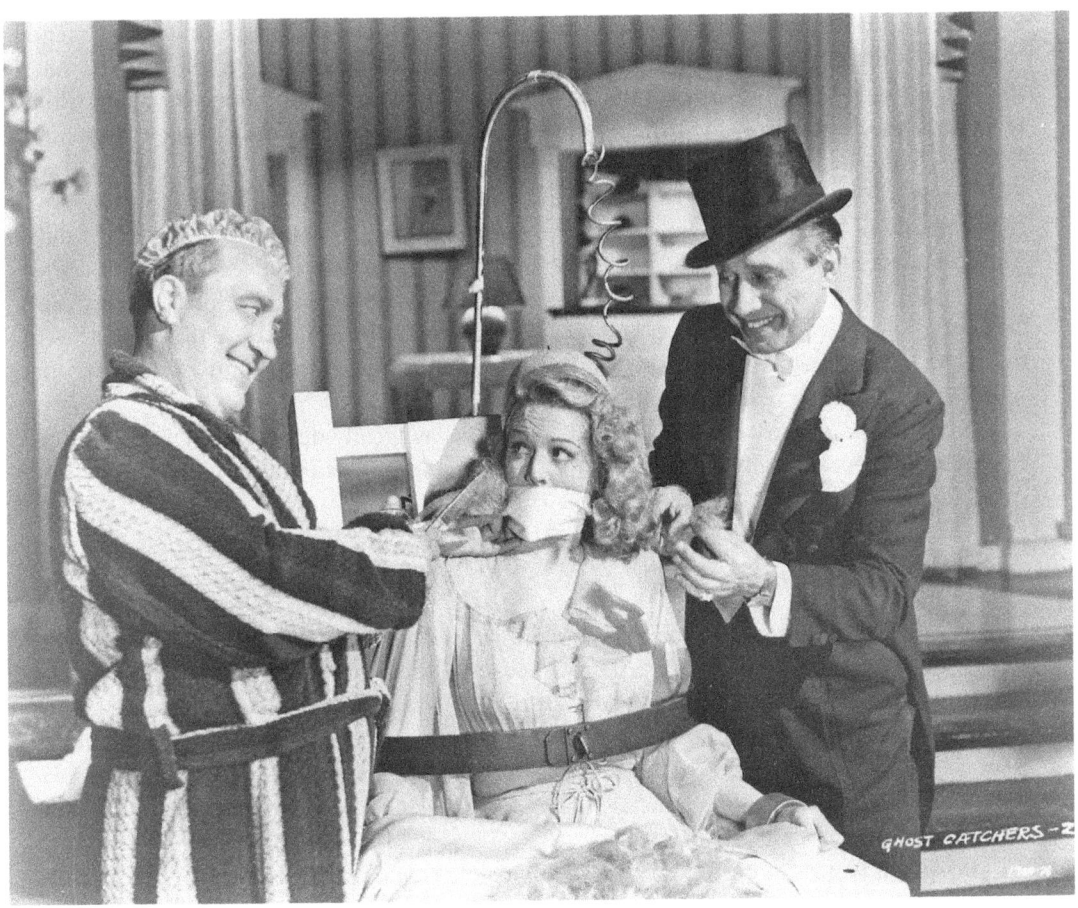

Ole Olsen (left), Gloria Jean and Chic Johnson in Edward F. Cline's "nut humor" classic *Ghost Catchers* (1944).

that, as Duffington shuffled off his mortal coil in 1900, he would be appalled by swing music. Following up on this reasoning, the boys bring in a swing band to exorcise the ghost. This ploy actually seems to work, but shortly after the exorcism, there are more strange goings-on in the house.

It turns out that, in addition to the ghost, there is also a gang of criminals inhabiting the mansion, much in the manner of *Hold That Ghost*. The gangsters include Lon Chaney Jr. in a bear costume, Andy Devine dressed as a horse and Leo Carrillo as a zombie-mummy. Obviously, this doesn't make a whole lot of sense, but the story is really just a clothesline upon which to hang all the gags.

The gags include a grown man who cries like a baby, a pair of midgets dressed like two of Disney's Seven Dwarfs and the conceit that the only way to get the ghost to appear is to offer him a bottle of his favorite booze. The fact that the ghost is played by Norton, a specialist in what used to be called "dipsomaniac" roles, adds a kind of delicious irony to the casting.

The dwarfs are especially funny because they're so unexpected. They bristle when Snow White is mentioned ("We hear that all the time," one of them sniffs) and stand in marked contrast to some of the other gangsters, one of whom is so tall he bumps his head on the top of the door frame.

Cline keeps the proceedings moving at a rapid pace, although the musical numbers tend to interrupt the action a bit too much. A couple of interesting notes of trivia: The conductor of the swing band is Kirby Grant, later to find fame on television as *Sky King*, while O'Driscoll would star in 1945 as the heroine of Universal's monster rally *House of Dracula*.

Olsen and Johnson are not nearly as famous today as Abbott and Costello or the Marx Brothers. Although they did more Broadway shows and television well into the fifties, their special brand of "nut humor" poked satirical fun at many movies and celebrities of the day. Their pointed spoofery of Abbott and Costello in *Ghost Catchers* (especially as both teams were then under contract to Universal) is priceless to movie buffs, but a lot of mainstream audiences won't get the references today. The only pop culture reference that really holds up in the twenty-first century is the gag involving Snow White; most of the others are too much of their time to really resonate now.

Nonetheless, Olsen and Johnson and *Ghost Catchers* really deserve to be rediscovered. It's a film that occasionally goes beyond *Sh! The Octopus* in its surreal sense of humor, and that's saying a lot.

Zombies on Broadway

Another comedy team virtually unknown today, Wally Brown and Alan Carney were RKO's answer to Abbott and Costello. Brown was a vaudevillian who came to Hollywood in 1942 and made his movie debut in 1943's *Petticoat Larceny*. Someone at RKO got the idea to emulate the success of Universal's Abbott and Costello and teamed Carney with short, chubby Alan Carney, a Costello "type." Their debut as a comedy team was in *Adventures of a Rookie* (1943). They used the same character names—Brown as Jerry Miles and Carney as Mike Strager—in each of their B-movie vehicles.

Brown and Carney's best movie is arguably 1945's *Zombies on Broadway* (originally titled *Loonies on Broadway* before its release), which admittedly isn't saying much. Their films are more or less indistinguishable from one another and their attempts to imitate Abbott and Costello are all too obvious. The humor is generally lame and forced, but at least *Zombies* is nicely produced and features an interesting supporting cast including Bela Lugosi, Anne Jeffreys and Darby Jones, the memorable seven-foot-tall zombie from Jacques Tourneur's classic film for Val Lewton, 1943's *I Walked With a Zombie*.

The rather silly plot concerns Jerry and Mike's attempt to obtain a "real live zombie" to promote the opening of a new nightclub called "The Zombie Hut." The owner of the club is a gangster named Ace Miller (Sheldon Leonard, future producer of *The Danny Thomas Show*, among others) who lets the two press agents know that if they don't produce the real thing by opening night, they're toast.

The boys are shipped off by the gangsters on a banana boat to the Caribbean, where they meet up with one Dr. Renault (Lugosi), who just happens to be turning people into zombies on a little island called San Sebastian. They also meet beautiful nightclub singer Jean LaDance (Jeffreys), who sees them as her ticket to get off the island. Hijinks ensue, Renault ends up getting killed by his own zombie, and Mike, Jerry, Jean and a monkey head back for New York, with Ace himself ending up saving the show by being transformed into a zombie thanks to a hypodermic injection of Renault's "zombie fluid."

This could have been an interesting, almost blackly comic ending, but it ends up being just routine under the direction of Gordon Douglas, who would do a much better job nine years later as director of the fifties sci-fi classic *Them!* Then again, there wasn't much anyone could do with the material written by Lawrence Kimble and Robert E. Kent from a story by Robert Faber. The jokes are corny and the sight gags—especially when Carney is temporarily transformed into a zombie, complete with ping-pong ball eyes—fall flat. Although they made eight films together, Carney and Brown never got past being sub-par Abbott and Costello clones.

The best things about *Zombies on Broadway* are the cinematography by Jack Mackenzie, the performances of Jeffreys (who has an elegant sex appeal) and Lugosi (essentially reprising his zombie-maker role from 1932's *White Zombie*) and the nods to *I Walked With a Zombie* (the imposing Jones is joined by his co-star from that film, Sir Lancelot). But any film in which a monkey gets the best jokes is in serious trouble indeed.

Released on May 1, 1945, the film's reception is pretty much summed up by "A. W.'s" review in the *New York Times*: "Despite all the mystic charades and scientific claptrap, this minor comedy item ... comes up with very few laughs.... RKO's scenarists were trying real hard but *Zombies on Broadway* is no laughing matter."

Carney and Brown's next film was their last, an even weaker film than *Zombies on Broadway*. Entitled *Genius at Work*, it reunited the team with Lugosi and Jeffreys, and even threw in Lionel Atwill, all to little effect. It has the distinction of being Atwill's last film; other than that, and the fact that RKO dropped Carney and Brown's contract after its dismal reception, *Genius at Work* has no distinction at all.

Abbott and Costello Meet Frankenstein

It was up to the most popular comedy team of the forties to bring comedy-horror films to their finest hour of the decade. By 1946, Universal had pretty much exhausted their classic monster franchises with such monster rallies as *House of Frankenstein* (1944) and *House of Dracula* (1945), each featuring Dracula, Frankenstein's Monster and the Wolf Man. The timing was right to pair their monsters, which had brought Universal so much money and publicity, with their comics, who had done likewise.

That year of 1946 was a pivotal one for Universal. With the end of World War II, the British uber-producer J. Arthur Rank was looking to expand his horizons. Peacetime brought a return to filmmaking in Great Britain, and Rank wanted to ensure that American audiences had the opportunity to see such British films as David Lean's *Great Expectations* (1946) that had been produced by his company. Rank bought a one-quarter interest in Universal and instigated a merger with an American independent production company called International Pictures. The founder of International, William Goetz, was named head of production at the newly named Universal-International Pictures, Inc. Due to Rank's association, Universal-International received American distribution rights for Rank's films, including Laurence Olivier's *Hamlet* (1948). Rank had hoped to improve the quality of Universal's output, and Goetz presided over the production of such films as *The Naked City* (1948), but the studio still struggled financially.

By the late forties, Goetz was no longer in charge, and the studio heads decided they had been a bit hasty to abandon their old cash cows. On March 14, 1948, in the "Hollywood Digest" column of the *New York Times*, the headline read, in part, "Old Ghoulish Friends Roam the Sets at Universal...."

The story by Thomas F. Brady continued:

> Universal-International, long the home of spectral entertainment, has attained a chimerical crescendo in recent weeks with ... Frankenstein's monster, Dracula, the Wolf Man and the

Invisible Man all working at once. The majority of these lovable characters are concentrated in *Abbott and Costello Meet Frankenstein*, a film described by the studio as a comedy. Glenn Strange is playing ... the monster.... Lon Chaney Jr. has resumed his old mantle as the studio's lycanthrope.... Bela Lugosi, the perpetual Dracula, disclosed last week that he will be revived by one of the unwary comedians.... Mr. Lugosi, who was scrambling on the floor of his dressing room for a missing shirt stud at the time, commented that he was relieved that Universal had not asked him to do anything unbecoming to Count Dracula's dignity in the association with Abbott and Costello. "There is no burlesque for me," he said. "All I have to do is frighten the boys, a perfectly appropriate activity. My trademark will be unblemished."

Actually, the road to what is now considered to be one of the all-time great comedy-horror films was not always a smooth one. The screenplay by Robert Lees, Frederic I. Rinaldo and John Grant was originally titled *The Brain of Frankenstein*, but was changed to *Abbott and Costello Meet Frankenstein* during production. The producers decided that the original title sounded too much like a straight horror film, and they wanted audiences to know from the outset that this was an Abbott and Costello romp, but with a difference.

Initially, Costello hated the script, complaining that his five-year-old-daughter could write a better one. Two things changed his mind: a $50,000 advance on his salary and the hiring of veteran Abbott and Costello director Charles T. Barton to helm the project. The team considered him to be their best director; he had previously guided the boys through their paces in such films as *Buck Privates Come Home* and *The Wistful Widow of Wagon Gap* (both 1947) and they were good friends with him as well.

Karloff was originally approached to play a role in the film, but respectfully declined. He felt that the comedy approach would be an insult to the monster, whom he considered his "baby." As a courtesy to Universal, Karloff did eventually help to promote the film upon its release.

One bit of off-screen irony involved the studio considering Ian Keith to play Dracula. Keith had been one of the original choices for the role in Tod Browning's original *Dracula* (1931), but had not been available. At that time, they chose Lugosi only after a number of actors had either been unavailable or had turned it down. The reason they considered Keith for the role in *Abbott and Costello Meet Frankenstein* was because, incredibly, the studio heads thought Lugosi was dead. Acting in films for Monogram and PRC had kept him under their radar for the past several years. When they did indeed discover he was alive, Lugosi's agent stormed into the studio and told him they owed him the role. Lugosi, who had not done a major studio film in some time, jumped at the chance to play the count once more.

Abbott and Costello Meet Frankenstein went into production on February 5, 1948, on a budget of $760,000. One of the first changes that Universal-International made was to fire their veteran makeup genius Jack Pierce, who had created all of the classic monsters from Karloff's Frankenstein Monster to Chaney's Wolf Man. Their reason? Pierce's makeup effects were not cost-effective. After unceremoniously sacking Pierce, they hired young makeup artists Bud Westmore and Jack Kevan, who used Pierce's designs to create rubber appliances that saved hours of time in application and thousands of dollars in cost. Westmore and Kevan would stay with the company for many years, eventually creating monsters for such now-classic movies as *Creature from the Black Lagoon* (1954) and *This Island Earth* (1955).

Glenn Strange was brought back to play the Monster, having done so for the firm's previous two monster rallies. The new rubber head appliance that he wore reportedly was so tightly fitted to his head that when he removed it, sweat poured out in rivulets from underneath.

Strange also had moments of mirth on the set, though. The scene in which Wilbur Grey (Costello) is sitting on the monster's lap (without realizing it) required multiple takes because Costello kept improvising bits of business that cracked up Strange. The interested viewer can witness the rare sight of the Monster laughing uncontrollably in a made-for-DVD documentary called *Abbott and Costello Meet the Monsters*, which is included on the box set *The Best of Abbott and Costello Volume Four*, released by Universal in 2005.

Apparently, Abbott and Costello presided over several pie fights on the set as well, keeping everyone in stitches except perhaps Lugosi, who considered all the clowning around "undignified" and chose not to be included. In any case, the boys were careful not to throw pies at any of the "monsters" when they were in makeup.

At one point during the shooting of the laboratory scene, Strange tripped over a camera cable and broke his ankle. Chaney wasn't playing the Wolf Man that day, so he stepped in to put on the Frankenstein Monster makeup and filled in for Strange in a scene in which Dr. Mornay (Lenore Aubert) gets thrown through a window. Chaney, of course, had previously played the Monster in *The Ghost of Frankenstein* (1942).

Studio animator Walter Lantz, who created the cartoon character Woody Woodpecker, provided the animation for Dracula's transformations into a bat and back again. Production on *Abbott and Costello Meet Frankenstein* was completed on March 20, 1948.

It's interesting to note that films that are now considered classics were often not well-received by critics of the time. A case in point: The *New York Times* review of *Abbott and Costello Meet Frankenstein* by Bosley Crowther in the July 29, 1948, issue, headlined, "That One Laugh." Crowther didn't have much good to say about the film: "Most of the comic invention in *Abbott and Costello Meet Frankenstein* is embraced in the idea and the title. The notion of having these two clowns run afoul of the famous screen monster is a good laugh in itself. But take this gentle warning: get the most out of that one laugh while you can, because the picture ... does not contain many more."

Well, that's a matter of opinion. Most critics now consider *Abbott and Costello Meet Frankenstein* (or, as the onscreen title reads, *Bud Abbott Lou Costello Meet Frankenstein*) to be the comedy duo's best movie. It's also one of the quintessential comedy-horror films; the comedy scenes are genuinely funny and the horror scenes genuinely spooky. Let's face it, when it comes to comedy-horror, the classic Universal monsters outclass gorillas and octopi any day.

And the monsters are well used. Lugosi gets some great lines ("You young people, making the most of life ... while it lasts") and swoops around in grand style as Dracula, aka "Dr. Lajos." The only misstep, and one he should have protested, was the mirror shot of him putting the bite on Aubert. Vampires, of course, do not cast reflections, something the director either knew about but didn't care or perhaps was unaware of, in which case Lugosi should have informed him that such a shot would go against the vampire mythology. In either case, it's a mistake that many fans have complained about, hardly enough to ruin the film but enough to get under the skin of true aficionados.

Nevertheless, Lugosi lives up to his promise that he made to the *New York Times* about keeping his trademark unblemished; he never burlesques himself, and always essays his most famous role with the dignity it deserves. And, as Dracula, he really carries the plot, for it is he who wants the brain of Wilbur (Costello) to be put into the skull of the Frankenstein Monster, who will then "obey him like a trained dog."

Chaney is as good as ever as the doomed Lawrence Talbot. There's no attempt at continuity from the previous film, *House of Dracula*, in which he was "cured" of his lycanthropy.

Bud Abbott, Glenn Strange and Lou Costello in a posed publicity shot for Charles T. Barton's *Abbott and Costello Meet Frankenstein* (1948).

In fact, there's no continuity from *House of Dracula* for any of the characters. In *House*, Dracula (John Carradine in this case) is once more reduced to a skeleton by sunlight and the Monster is again burned alive. Then again, by 1945, continuity had gone astray in the whole series and the monsters just started returning from their various horrible deaths with no explanation. Like Mount Everest, they were there.

Such was the case in *Abbott and Costello Meet Frankenstein*; the monsters just "were." Chaney delivers all of his lines with utmost sincerity, even when Costello gave him some real zingers in return. At one point in the proceedings, Talbot says to Wilbur, "You don't understand. Every night when the moon is full, I turn into a wolf." Wilbur, ever oblivious, retorts, "You and twenty million other guys."

Chaney, like Lugosi, maintains his dignity, remaining straight-faced and classically tragic throughout. He is, in a sense, one of the heroes of the film, for it is he who leaps onto Dracula after the count has transformed into a bat and falls with him into the sea. Whether drowning kills werewolves or vampires is another matter, but it's one of the last great moments of Universal horror.

Glenn Strange actually has more screen time as the Monster in this film than in either of the other two "serious" movies in which he played the part. Although he never gave the character much soul, he certainly looks imposing (he was in fact six feet six inches tall) and

Lou Costello, Bela Lugosi and Glenn Strange have some laughs behind the scenes of Charles T. Barton's *Abbott and Costello Meet Frankenstein* (1948).

his craggy features are perfect for the role. His one comic moment—when he bumps into Wilbur and is frightened by him, complete with Dracula telling him, "Don't be afraid!"—is priceless.

And the comic duo are, indeed, at their best in their first "meet the monsters" adventure. True to form, they have a lot of verbal byplay, such as when Wilbur and Chick (Abbott) find a crate supposedly containing Count Dracula's remains in the wax museum, which leads to the following exchange:

> CHICK: You know there's no such person as Dracula. I know there's no such person as Dracula.
> WILBUR: But does Dracula know it?

Later, after Wilbur sees Dracula lying in the crate, he says to Chick: "You know that person you said there's no such person? I think he's in there ... in person."

The classic "moving candle" routine from *Hold That Ghost* is recreated, with a twist, in this scene. When Dracula actually rises from the crate, Wilbur calls for Chick, but when he arrives, he doesn't see the count, who is hiding in a dark corner. This happens several times, a new take on one of their most famous running jokes.

The film's final gag occurs when Vincent Price makes an "appearance" as the Invisible

Man. It's an interesting foreshadowing of another film to come, *Abbott and Costello Meet the Invisible Man* (1951), in which Arthur Franz played the role. And it's a great coda to *Meet Frankenstein*. After the Monster has burned to death (again), Wilbur and Chick escape on a rowboat. Chick says, "Now that we've seen the last of Dracula, the Wolf Man and the Monster, there's nobody to frighten us any more." A disembodied voice—the unmistakable silken tones of Vincent Price—pipes up. "Oh, that's too bad, I was hoping to get in on the excitement." Chick, startled, queries: "Who said that?" to which the voice responds, "Allow me to introduce myself. I'm the Invisible Man." As if to prove it, he lights a cigarette, which seems to float in thin air. The boys jump into the sea.

Abbott and Costello Meet Frankenstein is now an acknowledged classic, one of the most beautifully produced comedy-horror films of all time, featuring two iconic comedians meeting three (or four, if you count the *Invisible Man*) iconic screen monsters. It's an unbeatable combination, and one that resonates with baby boomers to this day.

For me, it was the first film I ever owned. I received a ten-minute silent digest version of it in 8mm for my eighth birthday. Life doesn't get any better than that.

Abbott and Costello Meet the Killer, Boris Karloff

The success of *Abbott and Costello Meet Frankenstein* gave new life to Abbott and Costello's career, and they followed it up with, ironically, a movie that had originally been written for Bob Hope. The original script, *Easy Does It*, had never gotten past the screenplay stage, so Universal-International purchased the rights and reworked it for their number one comedy team.

Originally announced in early 1949 as *Abbott and Costello Meet the Killers*, it ended up being called, rather strangely, *Abbott and Costello Meet the Killer, Boris Karloff*. While all three performers were used to getting their name above the title, this was the first film in which they all had their names *in* the title.

Oddly enough, the role that Karloff ended up playing had been written for a woman. Called "Madame Switzer" originally, the character was changed for Karloff to "Swami Talpur." Karloff was hired only five days before shooting began. The studio wanted him back, and since he had refused to appear in the previous romp, perhaps he felt that he owed them a favor. Whatever the case, his role in the new film, despite its prominence in the title and advertising, amounted to little more than a red herring.

The final screenplay was written by frequent A&C writer John Grant from a story by Hugh Wedlock, Jr. and Howard Snyder. Costello plays hotel bellboy Freddie Phillips, who is the main suspect in the murder of attorney Amos Strickland (Nicholas Joy). Abbott plays Casey Edwards, the hotel detective who tries to clear Freddie of the crime.

Several of Strickland's former clients just happen to be at the hotel, and they're all pretty eccentric. Not only do we have Karloff as the sinister swami, there's sultry femme fatale Lenore Aubert from *Meet Frankenstein* as his associate Angela Gordon, and other odd characters played by Victoria Horne, Roland Winters, Harry Hayden, Claire DuBrey, Vincent Renno and veteran character actor Alan Mowbray as the hotel manager.

The film went into production on February 10, 1949, and wrapped on March 26. After completion of filming, Costello suffered a relapse of rheumatic fever, which he had first come down with in 1943. Plagued by health problems all his life, Costello was bedridden for several months in 1949.

Although not as consistently funny as *Meet Frankenstein*, *Abbott and Costello Meet the*

Killer, Boris Karloff has a lot going for it and is generally underrated by fans and critics alike. Audiences were bound to be a bit disappointed; how do you follow the classic Universal monsters? But Karloff was on hand, looking as sinister as ever, albeit in an underwritten part. He does have some good bits of business with Costello, waving his hands and using his best hypnotic voice to convince him, "You didn't see me ... I wasn't here." Then, of course, Costello says to Abbott, "I didn't see him." "You didn't see who?" Abbott inquires. "The man who wasn't there," replies Costello.

The real surprise is that there's a lot of genuine black humor in the film, a kind of ghoulishness that we hadn't seen in many comedy films before. Black comedy was only just coming into vogue in British films such as *Kind Hearts and Coronets* (also 1949). In *Meet the Killer*, corpses are everywhere throughout the hotel, and they keep popping up in the most unexpected places. They're in closets, bedrooms, hallways ... and in one scene, Bud and Lou play cards with two of them, trying to convince another rather dim-witted character that the corpses are just two very tired poker players. It's the kind of humor that was exemplified much later by Alfred Hitchcock in *The Trouble With Harry* (1955) and, ultimately, in *Weekend at Bernie's* (1989). One doesn't often think of Abbott and Costello as "cutting edge," but in this case, they were ahead of their time. All of the scenes featuring the dead bodies were cut out of the film when it was released in Australia and New Zealand, and in Denmark—because of the "corpses playing cards" scene—the film was banned outright.

Toward the end, *Meet the Killer* loses some of its steam when the action is transferred to an underground cavern, at which point there's yet another "moving candle" scene, this time with the candle sitting atop the back of a tortoise. The actual killer (spoiler alert!) turns out to be the hotel manager, who has been trying to frame Strickland's former clients and blackmail them. So Karloff, despite the film's title, is not the killer after all.

New York Times film critic Bosley Crowther was obviously no fan of Abbott and Costello—or of black comedy—as witness his review published on September 19, 1949, which read in part: "[M]ost of the humor—if that's what you'd call it—is derived from the slapstick display of the two comedians juggling a couple of very stiff corpses in a hotel.... [Costello] has quite a gay old time lugging these two extinct persons hither and yon, stuffing them into linen closets and making other sport with them. 'This ain't funny,' says the fat comedian at one point—and, believe us, he is right."

Despite Crowther's objections, the film went on to be another money-maker for Universal-International, assuring us that the series of "Meet the Monsters" films would continue. But as the forties drew to a close, times were changing. Abbott and Costello themselves predicted it with the gallows humor of *Meet the Killer*. After the real-life horrors of World War II, the world was becoming a darker place. And comedy-horror films would ultimately journey to dangerous countries of the mind, to pitch-black places where they had never dared go before.

4

THE FIFTIES
Elderly Monsters and Black Humor

There was more prosperity in America during the fifties than at any other time in history. The postwar baby boom was in full swing, people saw the U.S.A. in their Chevrolets and everyone should have been high on optimism. But life is rarely so simple.

There was also more anxiety in the fifties than ever before, not just in the U.S., but throughout the world. The unleashing of the real-life horrors of World War II, from uncovering the Nazi concentration camps to the unparalleled destruction caused by the atomic bombs dropped on Hiroshima and Nagasaki, generated new fears about what kind of evil was abroad in the world. Added to that devil's brew was a paranoid fear that communists were hiding behind every bush (or under every bed); a new witch hunt, McCarthyism, was born in America.

Abbott and Costello Meet the Invisible Man

As far as comedy-horror films were concerned, though, the fifties started out innocuously enough. Although Abbott and Costello had flirted with cutting-edge black comedy in *Meet the Killer*, they'd had a few problems with international censors over it, so they decided to go the safe route with their next "Meet" movie.

One might expect *Abbott and Costello Meet the Invisible Man* (1951) to co-star Vincent Price, as the boys had encountered Price in his invisible guise at the end of *Meet Frankenstein*. Alas, it was not to be. Although, plotwise, *Meet the Invisible Man* was very similar to *The Invisible Man Returns* (1940), which had starred Price, the new movie, which was advertised as "It's all NEW and a RIOT too!" would feature Arthur Franz as the duo's mostly unseen co-star.

Originally, the film had been intended as a "straight" horror film in Universal's profitable Invisible Man series. But after the huge success of *Meet Frankenstein* and *Meet the Killer*, the script was rewritten to make it another horror-comedy with Bud and Lou. In fact, Universal's classic monster series was now officially dead except for the comedy duo's spoofs.

In *Abbott and Costello Meet the Invisible Man* (on screen title: *Bud Abbott Lou Costello Meet the Invisible Man*), the boys' character names are their real-life first and middle names: Bud Alexander and Lou Francis. They play two bumbling private detectives who investigate the murder of a boxing promoter. The crime is pinned on Tommy Nelson (Franz), a boxer whose girlfriend's (Nancy Guild) uncle (Gavin Muir) has developed an invisibility serum. The good doctor has a photograph of Claude Rains on his wall, referring to him as "Dr. Griffin," which makes this film an official sequel to James Whale's *The Invisible Man* (1933).

The doctor refuses to inject Nelson, claiming that the serum is too unstable and may cause madness. But Nelson wants to become invisible to investigate the murder of his former manager and prove that he is innocent of the crime, so he injects himself. He asks Bud and Lou to help him on his quest.

As directed by Charles Lamont, a Russian-born industry veteran who had worked with The Three Stooges and Charley Chase, *Abbott and Costello Meet the Invisible Man* is one of the better entries in the series. It's fast-paced and often quite funny, and the invisibility effects by David Horsley are every bit as good as those he did for T*he Invisible Man Returns, The Invisible Woman* and *Invisible Agent*.

The screenplay by Frederic I. Rinaldo, John Grant, Robert Lees, Hugh Wedlock Jr. and Howard Snyder makes the most of the comic possibilities of invisibility. When Nelson first makes himself invisible, Detective Roberts (William Frawley, soon to become Fred Mertz on *I Love Lucy*) asks Lou, "How did he get out?" Lou replies, "Installments.... He did a Gypsy Rose Lee ... I went to shake his hand, his hand was gone. I looked up to speak to him, his head was gone. Then he took off his shirt, his body was gone. He took off his pants, his legs were gone. Then he spoke to me. *I* was gone."

The climactic set piece is a match in which Lou boxes Rocky Hanlon (John Day), one of Nelson's arch-enemies in the ring. The invisible Nelson gets into the ring with them, giving the crowd the idea that Lou is beating the stuffing out of Hanlon when it's actually his invisible punches that are doing it. This sequence is wonderfully handled and is a perfect example of Costello's gift for physical comedy. His timing in this long and excitingly filmed scene is absolute perfection, as he pulls his punches while Nelson, unseen, completes them for him. "His punches just come out of nowhere," Hanlon tells his manager.

Abbott and Costello Meet the Invisible Man went into production on October 3, 1950 and was completed on November 6. It was released on March 19, 1951, and was another hit for the studio. Even some of the critics seemed to like it this time. Thomas M. Pryor's *New York Times* review enthused about the boxing scene: "For sheer slapstick tomfoolery this fight is one of the funniest things Abbott and Costello have had to offer in a long, long while."

The studio was so pleased with the film that Lamont was hired to do the remaining "Meet" films with A&C. Shortly after the filming of *Meet the Invisible Man* was completed, Bud and Lou made their first of nineteen appearances on *The Colgate Comedy Hour*, thereby conquering that most fantastic monster of them all, television.

Abbott and Costello Meet Dr. Jekyll and Mr. Hyde

"All new! All wild! All fun!" was the tagline for Universal-International's *Abbott and Costello Meet Dr. Jekyll and Mr. Hyde*, an unwieldy title if ever there was one. Filmed between January 26 and February 20, 1953, the

Boris Karloff as Mr. Hyde in Charles Lamont's *Abbott and Costello Meet Dr. Jekyll and Mr. Hyde* **(1953).**

movie benefits from Lamont's smooth direction. There were no less than five screenwriters: Howard Dimsdale, Sid Fields, Grant Garett, John Grant and Lee Loeb. With all those scribes, you might have thought they would have given the boys more to do, but *Abbott and Costello Meet Dr. Jekyll and Mr. Hyde* succeeds in spite of the duo, not because of them.

By this time, Bud and Lou were getting tired, and it shows. Slim (Abbott) and Tubby

Mr. Hyde (stuntman Eddie Parker) meets Dr. Jekyll (Boris Karloff) in a posed publicity shot for Charles Lamont's *Abbott and Costello Meet Dr. Jekyll and Mr. Hyde* (1953).

(Costello) are American policemen who have been sent to London to study British police techniques. There, they encounter Dr. Jekyll (Boris Karloff), who, needless to say, is a part-time Mr. Hyde.

It's safe to say that Robert Louis Stevenson would have found his Jekyll and Hyde concept nearly unrecognizable here. Karloff, who was in his sixties by then, is certainly the oldest actor to play Dr. Jekyll, and when he becomes Mr. Hyde he looks more like the Wolf Man than anything else. Add to that the fact that Costello is also transformed into a werewolf-like monster who can turn other people into monsters by biting them, and you have a very confused movie. Perhaps there were, after all, too many cooks spoiling this cinematic broth.

There is, of course, a romantic subplot, this time involving a newspaper reporter (Craig Stevens) and a fetching suffragette named Vicky (Helen Westcott). Jekyll has eyes for Vicky, and when he sees the reporter moving in on what he considers his territory, he reverts to Hyde to do his dirty work.

Actually, the idea that Jekyll is evil to begin with and just needs Hyde to carry out his murders—with the implication that he wouldn't have the nerve to do them himself—is a thematically interesting one. But the script never develops it, and it's all too obvious that when Jekyll becomes Hyde, the stunt man takes over, running over rooftops and leaping about like a hirsute gnome. The character is never referred to as "Hyde" at any time, and is just as mute and ferocious as any werewolf.

The film falls rather flat where Abbott and Costello are concerned; there is virtually none of the usual banter between them, as this is more of a slapstick farce than most of their other "Meet" movies. One of the things that separated the duo from other comedy teams was their verbal byplay, and it's sorely missed here. Instead, there are visual gags such as the shot of a very large hypodermic impaling Costello's derriere (several times); Costello being temporarily transformed into a man-sized, two-legged mouse; and the final scene in which he bites the police inspector (Reginald Denny) and several officers, transforming them all into monsters. Although these slapstick routines are mildly amusing, they offer none of the carefully constructed wordplay ("Who's on First?," etc.) that the boys were known for.

The film's high points include Karloff's usual urbane performance, a pleasing Victorian atmosphere and better-than-average romantic players in Stevens and Westcott. The Hyde makeup is also very good, a sort of cross between Fredric March's Hyde in Rouben Mamoulian's classic 1932 version of Stevenson's story with Chaney's famous werewolf.

Released on August 10, 1953, *Abbott and Costello Meet Dr. Jekyll and Mr. Hyde* was a big hit, much bigger than A&C's previous couple of films. As usual, the critics panned it, but that never prevented audiences from seeing an Abbott and Costello movie before. The team had one more monster to meet before they called it quits.

Abbott and Costello Meet the Mummy

Abbott and Costello Meet the Mummy went into production on October 28, 1954, with a budget of $738,000. Again directed by Charles Lamont, it was the first Universal "Mummy" film since 1944's *The Mummy's Curse*. It was also the 28th—and last—Abbott and Costello film produced by the company.

The comedy team of Dean Martin and Jerry Lewis had long since eclipsed Abbott and Costello at the box office, even invading their horror-comedy turf with *Scared Stiff*. Abbott and Costello were suffering from over-exposure; their television show was still in syndication and their old movies were in nearly constant re-release, while at the same time their performances on *The Colgate Comedy Hour* had consisted mostly of stale rehashes of their old material.

Abbott and Costello Meet the Mummy plays like an extended version of their TV series, complete with phony-looking sets and TV actors such as Richard Deacon and Michael Ansara looking very uncomfortable (and unconvincing) as Egyptians.

The plot has something to do with a mummy named Klaris, an obvious take-off on the name "Kharis" that was used in the four previous Mummy films. Klaris is the guardian of Princess Ara's tomb and has a sacred medallion that reveals where a treasure may be found. Somehow, Costello ends up swallowing the medallion (in a hamburger, no less) and he becomes, shall we say, very important to a cult called the Followers of Klaris, led by the extremely sultry yet tough Madame Rontru (Marie Windsor) and the high priest Semu (Deacon).

The story is, of course, nonsense, but that had never stopped the boys from being funny before. It did this time, however. Abbott looks tired—he was nearly sixty years old at the time. Most of the routines fall flat because his timing is off, and Costello, although giving it the old school try, looks as though he'd rather be in Philadelphia.

The film isn't helped by its shoddy look. The mummy's costume looks like a rubber suit

Bud Abbott, Edwin Parker and Lou Costello in the final A&C movie for Universal-International, Charles Lamont's *Abbott and Costello Meet the Mummy* (1955).

with a bandage motif, which is probably exactly what it was. At one point, for no particular reason, there are three mummies running around; two fake ones (Abbott and Ansara) and one real one (stunt man Edwin Parker).

Windsor gives by far the most interesting performance in the film; Madame Rontru is a take-no-prisoners villainess, what they used to call "a pushy broad" in the fifties. She seems to be the only one having fun in the whole movie.

Shooting on the film wrapped November 24, 1954, and it was released on May 23, 1955 to lackluster reviews and so-so business. The Abbott and Costello era had clearly come to an end. The movie played kiddie matinees; once the most popular comedy team in America, the "boys" were no longer young, and their time had passed.

Universal-International decided not to renew A&C's contract, and in 1956, the IRS pursued the duo for back taxes, which forced them to sell all their assets. Their partnership was dissolved, and Costello made one film on his own, *The 30 Foot Bride of Candy Rock*, before dying of a heart attack on March 3, 1959.

Abbott struggled for a few more years, attempting a comeback in 1960 with another comic, Candy Candido. "The best straight man in the business" didn't stay with the act for long, however, and made a few solo television appearances, eventually voicing his own character in a series of Abbott and Costello cartoons made by Hanna-Barbera in 1966. Costello's character was voiced by Stan Irwin. Shortly afterward, Abbott retired, and he died of cancer on April 24, 1974. There would never be another comedy team like Abbott and Costello; the mold had been broken and the American sense of humor was taking a different—and somewhat darker—turn.

The Bat (1959)

"When it flies ... someone dies!" screamed the ads for the 1959 remake of *The Bat*. The film was written and directed by Crane Wilbur, from the Avery Hopwood–Mary Roberts Rinehart play. Wilbur was a triple threat, a writer-director-actor who had made his mark in such silent films as *The Perils of Pauline* (1914), the famous cliffhanger with Pearl White. As a writer, he had written the play *The Monster*, which was adapted for the 1925 Roland West film with Lon Chaney. He had also written the screenplay for *House of Wax* (1953), the sensational 3-D film starring Vincent Price. It was that movie, more than any other, that made Price a horror star, and Wilbur wisely cast the ubiquitous actor in his version of *The Bat*.

Wilbur's screenplay is much the same mixture as before: An insane murderer called "The Bat" is on the loose in a mansion full of people, most of whom are searching for stolen loot that is somewhere in the house. This time around, The Bat is said to be "a man with no face" who murders women by tearing out their throats with his "claws." In other words, Wilbur made the tale a bit more gruesome to appeal to changing audience tastes.

Another thing that Wilbur did, though, was accent the horror over the comedy, making his version the most "serious" one yet. The great character actress Agnes Moorehead is well cast as Cornelia van Gorder, the mystery writer. Her maid, Lizzie Allen (Lenita Lane), gets the best lines and the most laughs, as in the other versions. Early in the proceedings, The Bat is creeping around van Gorder's mansion and releases a real bat, which promptly bites Lizzie. The high-strung maid gets into a panic; you might say Lizzie's in a tizzy, fearing that she will get "the rabies." You know everyone's in trouble when van Gorder calls the doctor and he turns out to be Vincent Price.

Interestingly enough, though—and here comes a spoiler—Price does not turn out to be

The Bat, although he is a cold-blooded murderer who guns down a friend to get his hands on the hidden money. The doctor himself is later killed by The Bat as he is working in his lab—ironically enough, with bats.

Audiences unfamiliar with the play may have been tempted to believe that the butler (John Sutton) actually "did it" and was indeed The Bat. But as in the other versions, it turns out to be Anderson, the policeman—in this case Lt. Andy Anderson, played by the rather dour Gavin Gordon.

By 1959, *The Bat* was a throwback to another era, and had it not been for the presence of Price (who at the time was the hottest horror actor in Hollywood) it probably wouldn't have been as well-received as it was. When released on August 9 of that year, it did okay business and even garnered a few decent reviews; incredibly, the *New York Times* considered it to be superior to its co-feature, *The Mummy*, now considered to be one of the all-time classics from Hammer Films. The years haven't been especially kind to Wilbur's film, however; his direction is rather pedestrian, downright creaky at times. It isn't helped by Louis Forbes' "jazzy" score.

There are some good things going for this version, however. Moorehead, who had started her career in Orson Welles' Mercury Theatre on radio, is an appropriately tough and resourceful van Gorder. At times she's a bit pompous; she admonishes Lizzie not to call her "Corny." And when Lizzie points out that one of her books "scared hell out of me," she makes a disapproving face. But she acquits herself well in dangerous situations, throwing a poker at The Bat at one point and, needless to say, unmasking him at the end. She gives a very enjoyable and exuberant performance, never quite going over the top into self-parody.

Price, of course, is the perfect red herring, delivering his lines with his usual urbane gusto. By this time in his career, after appearing in such films as *The Mad Magician* (1954) and *House on Haunted Hill* (1959), audiences were expecting him to play the villain, so it must have been a bit of a surprise in those days when he turned out to be a lesser character, a mere cold-hearted thug rather than The Bat himself.

The other cast members seem to be having a reasonably good time, with former child star Darla Hood (of the Our Gang/Little Rascals comedies) making her final appearance in a feature film. It was perhaps prophetic; Hood had been a child star in the thirties, and *The Bat* was of a similar vintage. The times were indeed changing, and old dark house mysteries started to look like relics of an earlier and more innocent era. It was up to younger filmmakers to tap into the fears—and the humor—of hipper, more cynical teenage audiences.

A Bucket of Blood

Ubiquitous young director Roger Corman had already made a number of "straight" horror films for AIP in the fifties, but many of them had contained a touch of dark humor. With his 1959 release for the company, *A Bucket of Blood*, he erased the line between comedy and horror altogether. Much later, in his book *How I Made a Hundred Movies in Hollywood and Never Lost a Dime*, he pretty much gave himself credit for creating a new genre, as witness this quote: "I was, as I believed at the time, virtually creating a new genre—the black-comedy horror film. Whereas I had mixed a little humor and science fiction in films like *Not of This Earth*, now I was out to create a different kind of film—more cynical, darker, more wickedly funny."

As we have seen, Corman certainly didn't create the comedy-horror film, but it might be said that he took the genre to a new level. *A Bucket of Blood* is, as its title suggests, quite gruesome, but its poster screamed, "You'll be sick—from laughing!"

Corman insists to this day that he made *Bucket* on a bet. As he recounts in his 1990 book, "In the middle of 1959, when AIP wanted me to make a horror film but had only $50,000 available, I felt it was time to take a risk, do something fairly outrageous. I shot *Bucket* on a few sets in only five days."

Ever creatively restless, Corman by this point wanted to do something different. In his book, he continues: "My fastest shoot until *Bucket* had been six days. I accepted AIP's challenge, but I was tired of horror. I wanted to have some fun and change the equation. I decided to do a horror-type film with a hip, cutting edge. I called Chuck [Griffith, Corman's main screenwriter] and we decided to create a comedy-horror-satire about the trendy beat coffeehouse scene. For research, we spent a long evening drifting in and out of coffeehouses along Sunset Strip. We kicked around story ideas as we wandered and, by evening's end, we had a plot structure."

Actually, the plot of *A Bucket of Blood* owes a great deal to that of *Mystery of the Wax Museum* (1933) and its remake *House of Wax* (1953). As with those films, an artist (Corman regular Dick Miller) uses real corpses upon which to mold his sculptures. The big difference is that *Bucket* is set very firmly in the contemporary (1959) "art world," with all its pretensions. After he accidentally kills a cat, Walter Paisley (Miller) panics and covers the cat's dead body with clay. A frustrated sculptor, he shows it to some of his beatnik friends and they rave over its "anatomical correctness" and dark beauty. He calls the sculpture, simply enough, "Dead Cat."

Walter produces another "masterpiece" after he is confronted in his apartment by a narcotics agent (Bert Convy) who informs him that he has just unwittingly been given heroin by someone at the coffeehouse where he works as a busboy. Once again, Walter panics and whacks the young man with a frying pan, killing him instantly. He presents this sculpture as "Murdered Man."

By this time, his greed and need for acceptance from the coffeehouse crowd has unhinged his mind, and he next kills a model (Judy Bamber) who had posed nude for him. Eventually, he even attempts to murder Carla (Barboura Morris), the woman he's had a crush on for years. The police and Walter's friends from the coffeehouse pursue him to his apartment, and there they find his ultimate "masterpiece": his own corpse, hanging from the ceiling. The beat poet Maxwell H. Brock (Julian Burton) quips, "I suppose he would have called it 'Hanging Man.'"

A Bucket of Blood really is a five-day wonder. The speed at which it was filmed probably contributes to its comic intensity, and the cast seems game for just about anything. Miller, a character actor who usually appears in small roles, shines here in his only starring vehicle. Walter Paisley is a sad, lonely little man who lives by himself in a dingy apartment. Night after night, he sees the "artists" in the trendy coffeehouse The Yellow Door perform their poetry and present their works. He longs to be accepted by them, which is what ultimately drives him to murder. But he never really comes across as a villain and always has our sympathy. He has, after all, done most of it for love, but when Carla spurns him ... well, he just doesn't dig life any more, baby.

A Bucket of Blood is at its most satiric when it's deflating the pomposity and pretentiousness of the "artists" at The Yellow Door. First and foremost is the poet Maxwell, who recites such stream-of-consciousness drivel as, "Where are John, Joe, Jake, Jim, Jerk? Dead, dead, dead! They were not born, before they were born, they were not born. Where are Leonardo, Rembrandt, Ludwig? Alive, alive, alive! They were born!" The fact that Maxwell's audience seems to find every word he utters of vast importance only makes the satirical knife sharper.

In his book, Corman recalled that a lot of improvisation went into *Bucket*: "This was truly a fast-paced romp from the start, almost like a party. It didn't feel like work; we were all laughing throughout the shoot. The spirit on the set was very loose among my 'family' of players ... everyone was coming up with ideas as we went and we just tossed them in."

Corman knew that the fun they had making the film communicated to the audience at the first sneak preview in Hollywood. I'll let him have the last word on *A Bucket of Blood*: "The audience at the sneak laughed throughout the film and applauded at the end. I had made a successful comedy that also commented on the ambitions and pretensions of the art world. When a critic wrote that the art world was a metaphor for the movie world, I didn't deny it."

5

THE SIXTIES
Gothic Castles and Cleavage Galore

The fifties, never the staid times they have often been portrayed as being, actually heralded the decline of censorship and Hollywood's dominance of the international film scene. Motion pictures from Great Britain, France, Italy, Sweden and even Japan opened the eyes of moviegoers to other cultures, and frequently those imports were allowed to get away with more in the areas of sex and violence than American films were. Hollywood was forced to compete with other markets for the first time in its history.

Sex symbols such as Marilyn Monroe, Brigitte Bardot and Sophia Loren had been allowed to glide suggestively across the screen in various states of undress, and there was no turning back. The advent of the birth control pill in 1960 showed the way forward: sex, both on the screen and off, would be more explicitly in the public eye than it ever had been before.

What most people think of as the sixties wasn't a revolution so much as an evolution. The movies did a slow striptease through the whole decade until, by 1969, full frontal nudity and simulated sex acts were allowed in mainstream movies. The entire culture was changing, although it really was just a matter of degree as far as films were concerned. Before the Hays Code had been enforced in 1934, there had been a lot of risqué movies as well.

But the sixties were different. It wasn't just the movies that were changing, it was the entire culture, from inside and out. Beatniks made way for hippies, booze made way for drugs, and monogamy was out. There was a new freedom, not only in cinema, but in literature, music, theater and fine arts.

Horror films were deadly serious business in the early sixties. Hammer continued its domination of the international market with such Gothic feasts for the eyes as *The Brides of Dracula* (1960), with Peter Cushing reprising his role of Van Helsing, which he had played to consummate effect in *Horror of Dracula* (1958). The genre had become such big business that even Alfred Hitchcock took a stab at it with a little film called *Psycho*.

Hitchcock has been quoted as referring to *Psycho* as "a comedy." There is certainly a great deal of black humor in Joseph Stefano's screenplay. "A boy's best friend is his mother," says Norman Bates (Anthony Perkins) to Marion Crane (Janet Leigh). Later on, when his mother makes her "appearance," he threatens to carry her down to the fruit cellar. "You think I'm fruity, huh?" "she" says to him.

Nevertheless, *Psycho* is not really a comedy-horror film. It's a very witty, stylish and intelligent movie, but no more of a comedy than Hitchcock's *Rear Window* (1954), which also features a lot of humor. The laughs in both films are there to relieve the tension; but each movie (*Psycho* in particular) goes for the jugular, not the funny bone. And they succeed wildly in their goals.

Psycho may have been a comedy to Hitchcock, but for the general public it was a scream fest like no other. The legendary trailer that Hitchcock did for the film, in which he wanders gleefully about the Bates Motel, even pointing out the toilet as containing "an important clue," is very amusing indeed. But while the trailer for *Psycho* may be a mini-comedy, the film itself is not.

The Little Shop of Horrors

It was up to Roger Corman to make the first real comedy-horror film of the sixties: *The Little Shop of Horrors* (1960). Much has been written about this crazy little film. Its production is the stuff of myth, and much misinformation has been written about it over the years.

The Little Shop of Horrors is often called "the best film that was ever shot in two days." Corman has always denied this, noting that even he couldn't shoot a film that fast. Years later, screenwriter Charles B. Griffith recalled how the whole project came about. It was intended to be a follow-up to *A Bucket of Blood* (1959).

"After *Bucket*," Griffith said, "we went out on the town and started throwing our ideas around. Roger and I talked over a bunch of ideas, including gluttony. The hero would be a salad chef in a restaurant who would wind up cooking customers and stuff like that, you know? We couldn't do that, though, because of the [Production Code]. So I said, 'How about a man-eating plant?' And Roger said, 'Okay.' By that time, we were both drunk."

The legend behind the film's production goes something like this: The manager of Producers Studio, where American-International Pictures shot most of their films at the time, had informed Corman that another film (nobody seems to recall which one) was about to wrap. The leftover sets included a large office. Corman's brother Gene, a producer in his own right (*Night of the Blood Beast*, 1958, among others) supposedly made a wager with him that he couldn't make a film with that set. In typical Corman fashion, he simply had the set redone as a flower shop.

The real reason that Corman shot the film so fast was pretty much the same reason that Corman did everything: to save money. On January 1, 1960, new industry rules were scheduled to go into effect that would allow all actors to be paid residuals for any future releases of films that they appeared in. This new ruling would have an effect on the way Corman, and every producer in Hollywood, would produce their films. Residuals would now be split up between producers and actors. And so it was that Corman decided to shoot *The Little Shop of Horrors* during the final week of December, 1959, before these rules went into effect. So the shoot had to be cheap and fast.

The budget was $30,000, low even by Corman's and AIP's standards. Corman cast several actors he had worked with in the past, performers he knew he could count on to deliver the goods in a professional manner during a fast shooting schedule. He recruited Jonathan Haze (*Not of This Earth*, *It Conquered the World*) as nerdy flower shop employee Seymour Krelboyne; Jackie Joseph (*Speed Crazy*) as sweet, well-endowed but ditzy Audrey Fulquard; Mel Welles (*The Undead*, *Attack of the Crab Monsters*) as tightwad flower shop owner Gravis Mushnick; and the ubiquitous Dick Miller (*A Bucket of Blood*'s Walter Paisley) as regular customer Burson Fouch, who has a habit of eating carnations. Oh, yes, and one other actor of note: a young man named Jack Nicholson, who had just starred in Corman's *The Cry Baby Killer*, was cast as Wilbur Force, the masochistic dental patient.

Corman rehearsed the actors for three days before shooting. Principal photography was completed in two days and one night (over the weekend), but the part of the story you don't usually hear is that the actors were brought back for re-shoots and additional scenes for the following two weekends. So the film's reputation as "the best movie ever shot in two days" is quite an exaggeration. It may, however, be the best film ever made in three weekends.

The film was shot television-style, with three cameras rolling simultaneously. Supposedly, every scene was shot with only one take, but as it was captured on three cameras, there was enough material from which to edit. The actors had to be good, though, as there wasn't much money or time for retakes.

Corman embraced the cheapness of the budget by making the most of his "Skid Row" sets. The Yiddish humor of the script is emphasized by the signs in the flower shop: "Lots plants cheap," etc. The deadpan narration by Wally Campo as Detective Joe Fink is straight out of *Dragnet*, but as if Jack Webb were on some kind of mind-altering drug. The film wouldn't be the same without it.

It's safe to say that the off-the-wall humor of *The Little Shop of Horrors* was, like the humor in *A Bucket of Blood*, way ahead of its time. Audiences in the early sixties weren't used to seeing severed limbs used as comedy props, and the idea of people being eaten by a large plant—which has a name, Audrey Jr.—was certainly innovative. The plant even speaks, demanding, "Feed me!" of the hapless Krelboyne. The voice was supplied by writer Griffith.

And who could forget the scene in the dentist's office, in which we see Nicholson's character reading *Pain* magazine? Sadomasochism was not exactly the topic of polite dinner table conversation in 1960, but there it is out in the open when Force begs Krelboyne (who is in disguise as a dentist) to take care of his "three or four abscesses and nine or ten cavities" and pleads with him to not use an anesthetic. ("No novocaine. It dulls the senses.") When Krelboyne lets up on the drill, fearing that he's causing Force too much pain, the willing patient shouts out, "Oh my God, don't stop now!" with all the "force" of a lover in the throes of passion. Finally, the actor now known for his "killer smile" walks out of the office proudly displaying his very noticeable lack of front teeth.

In the film's ending, when all the faces of Audrey Jr.'s victims show up as buds on the plant, we see that poor Krelboyne is in there too, as the plant has swallowed him as well. "I didn't mean it!" he cries, as his crimes become visible to all.

The Little Shop of Horrors is one of Corman's gems, an idea that was born on "a night out on the town" that's every bit as looney as it sounds. Corman has always been at his most brilliant when working on the cheap, and the hilarious performances he gets out of his ensemble cast prove how good he was at working under this kind of self-imposed pressure. Although it was passed off as just another drive-in picture at the time, *The Little Shop of Horrors* has grown in cult status over the years, ultimately transformed into an unlikely stage musical hit which was turned into a successful 1986 film called simply *Little Shop of Horrors* (*The* was dropped from the title), a movie that lacked all the low-budget charm of the original. What a long and winding road of success for such a tiny, "insignificant" comedy-horror film.

Creature from the Haunted Sea

The final film in Corman's unofficial comedy-horror trilogy didn't fare quite as well, but it's certainly an interesting and unusual production. *Creature from the Haunted Sea* (1961) was part of a three-picture deal that Corman filmed in Puerto Rico. The other two, *The Last Woman on Earth* and *Battle of Blood Island*, are non-comedy movies, but *Creature from the Haunted Sea* is one of Corman's most outrageous parodies.

As so often happened with Corman, the movie came about because of economics. Through his company, Filmgroup (which had also produced *The Little Shop of Horrors*), Corman discovered that tax incentives would be available if he filmed in Puerto Rico. The World War II yarn *Battle of Blood Island* was first to go before the cameras, followed by *The Last Woman on Earth*.

In his wildly entertaining book *How I Made a Hundred Movies in Hollywood and Never Lost a Dime* Corman related how *Creature from the Haunted Sea* came about: "*Last Woman* was a two-week shoot. It was going so well and we were having such a good time that I decided to do another movie. I called Chuck Griffith in L.A. and woke him up. 'Chuck, I need another comedy-horror film and you've got a week to write it,' I said. 'There's no time for rewrites. I've got a small cast so write for them. If you need more actors write small roles for Beach Dickerson and me as well.' He was very sleepy and I wasn't certain he understood completely the story line we discussed, but he agreed. I would use the same three main leads from the first movie, plus pick up some local Puerto Rican actors.... We called it *Creature from the Haunted Sea*."

Essentially a remake of the Humphrey Bogart movie *To Have and Have Not* (1944), but with a monster, *Creature from the Haunted Sea* features an excellent cast of crazies. Antony Carbone (who was also in Corman's *Pit and the Pendulum* that year) stars as Renzo Capetto, alias Capo Rosetto, alias Ratto Pazetti, alias Zeppo Staccato, alias Shirley Lamour(!), an American gangster who steals money from the Cuban treasury shortly before Castro comes into power. He's accompanied on his yacht by several Cuban nationals (including a general) and his girlfriend Mary-Belle Monahan, alias Mary Monahan Belle, alias Belle Mary Monahan, alias Monahan Mary Belle, as played by Betsy Jones-Moreland. What he is not aware of, however, is that one of his crew members is a secret agent known as Sparks Moran. (As the narrator of the film, Moran points out that his real name is "Agent XK150.") The inept spy is played by none other than Robert Towne, the screenwriter who would later write *The Tomb of Ligeia* (1964), the last of Corman's Poe films. In 1974, Towne hit the A-list big time with his Oscar-winning screenplay for Roman Polanski's *Chinatown*. In *Creature from the Haunted Sea*, Towne acts under the name of Edward Wain.

Other members of this very odd crew include Happy Jack Monahan, Mary Belle's brother (Robert Bean); and one of the weirdest characters in the history of comedy-horror films, Pete Peterson Jr. (Beach Dickerson), "son of Pete Peterson Sr., vaudeville animal impersonator." It seems that Peterson Jr. does very little but make animal noises, imitating Himalayan yaks, lions, bears and birds with little or no provocation. Eventually, he meets and falls in love with a Cuban woman with the same strange talent.

On the way to this happy ending, however, the crew members encounter the title creature, a pop-eyed monster that looks like a giant hairball. It certainly isn't very frightening, although it does kill a fair number of people. In the end, the creature ends up with the treasure, not that it does the beast very much good.

The plot summary gives you some idea of the madness of Griffith's screenplay, which foreshadowed television spy shows such as *Get Smart* in its spoofery of secret agents. The movie often trips over into the truly surreal, such as when Moran finds a telephone booth in the jungle and discovers that "the phone service is excellent." Another man, smiling like a moron, waits to use the phone, while a third man (who is wearing a three-piece suit) deliberately walks through a stream on his way to the phone booth.

Mary Belle sings a truly weird song called "Kiss Me Baby" which features a nonsense lyric about "The Creature from the Haunted Sea." When the yacht capsizes and they're forced to row the lifeboat to shore, she warbles another little ditty: "Row, row, row your boat, gently down the crick. Merrily, merrily, merrily, merrily, I think I'm gonna be sick."

Carbone maintains his ersatz Bogart character throughout the film, and Towne is actually very funny as Sparks Moran. The movie isn't as slick as *The Little Shop of Horrors*, with both sound and continuity problems, but you have to give Corman credit: He knew how to make three movies back to back with the same actors and the same locations, and he knew how to sell them when they were completed.

In his book, Corman remembered: "The craziness of the shoot showed in the finished film. The audience at the sneak preview laughed and applauded just as they had with *Little Shop*. Nobody was making movies like these."

What a Carve-Up!

As Great Britain was such a hotbed of horror movies in the early sixties, it was inevitable that they would, sooner or later, make some horror parodies. One of the first was *What a Carve-Up!* (1961), known in the U.S. as *No Place Like Homicide*. It's actually a remake of an earlier British horror film, *The Ghoul* (1933), which starred Boris Karloff in the title role. Produced by the team of Monty Berman and Robert S. Baker, who had already made the Hammer-inspired films *Blood of the Vampire* (1858), *The Trollenberg Terror* (aka *The Crawling Eye*, 1958), *The Flesh and the Fiends* (1959) and *The Hellfire Club* (1960), *What a Carve-Up!* is one of the better horror spoofs of the decade. Starring Sydney James and Kenneth Connor, two veterans of the long-running *Carry On* series, the film also features a treasure trove of British character actors: Donald Pleasence as a sinister and mysterious character; Michael Gough as a club-footed butler; and Dennis Price, Michael Gwynn and George Woodbridge in supporting roles. The leading lady was the lovely Shirley Eaton, who three years later would become a sixties icon when she was painted gold in the James Bond classic *Goldfinger*.

Connor plays a proofreader of horror fiction who, with his friend Syd (James), gets mixed up in the strange goings-on in his ancestral manor house. There are the usual (for this type of film) weirdos creeping around the Yorkshire Moors, including a masked murderer and a whole family of, shall we say, eccentric Brits.

The mixture of *Carry On*–style comedy and old dark house movie clichés proves to be a potent and effective one. As directed by Pat Jackson, *What a Carve-Up!* feels a lot like an Abbott and Costello movie with British accents. Beautifully photographed in black and white by co-producer Berman, the film has a creepy atmosphere that ranks with some of the best serious horror films. Rarely seen today, this charming movie perfectly evokes the time and place in which it was made, and it deserves to be rediscovered.

The Old Dark House (1963)

Another comedy remake of the era is the Hammer–William Castle version of *The Old Dark House*. Although it features plenty of oddball characters and has some amusing moments, it doesn't compare favorably with James Whale's 1932 version. For one thing, the plot has been drastically changed. Castle, known for his gimmicky horror films such as *House on Haunted Hill* and *The Tingler* (both 1959), had just made a comedy-fantasy with American actor Tom Poston called *Zotz!* Poston was brought over to Hammer's Bray Studios to star in *The Old Dark House* as a man who is visiting his distant relatives at the imposing Femm Manor.

The entire crew of Hammer's *The Old Dark House* (1963) surrounds director William Castle and star Tom Poston (second row center). Courtesy www.horrorconnection.com.

As with *What a Carve-Up!* there are some wonderful actors on hand: the husky-voiced Fenella Fielding as Morgana (the name was taken from Karloff's character in the original, Morgan the butler); Peter Bull in two roles, as the twins Casper and Jasper; Robert Morley as one of Poston's uncles, whose obsession with guns leads to his death; Joyce Grenfell as the mother of the twins, whose interest in knitting leads to her death; Mervyn Johns as another uncle who is convinced the world will soon end and is building an ark; and Janette Scott as the lovely Cecily, who turns out to be ... well, not a nice person.

Poston, always a droll comic actor, does well in his role as the befuddled American, and all of the performers have their moments to shine. They do what they can with Robert Dillon's uninspired screenplay and Castle's routine direction. As an adaptation of the J.B. Priestley novel *Benighted*, though, this version falls pretty flat. As with all Hammer Films, it's smoothly produced, but Castle's ham-fisted ideas about comedy don't really meld with Hammer's more serious and classical approach to the genre.

In a way, though, *The Old Dark House* comes across as a warm-up for the TV series *The Addams Family*, which premiered on American television the following year. Sure enough, the main title backgrounds are by Charles Addams himself. Unfortunately, and inexplicably, the effective color photography by Arthur Grant was lost on American audiences: The film was released in color in England, but stateside Columbia Pictures decided to release it in black and white. This was not an uncommon practice in those days; the British shocker *Dotor Blood's Coffin* (1961) had suffered the same fate. It was really just a matter of economics; it was cheaper to strike black and white prints for exhibition than it was to strike color prints. Those who are horrified by the colorization of old films should take note; back in the sixties, some films were "monochromized."

The Horror of It All

At least Terence Fisher's *The Horror of It All* (1963) was shot in black and white to begin with, so it had nothing to lose when it was released in the U.S. The plot is very similar to that of Castle's *Old Dark House*: another American, in this case a salesman played by, of all people, Pat Boone, develops a crush on a British bird named Cynthia (Erica Rogers) and basically stalks her all the way to her ancestral home, which is, of course, an old dark house. Once again, it's a household of eccentric Brits: Andree Melly from Fisher's masterly *The Brides of Dracula* plays Cynthia's sister, who seems to be a vampire; Valentine Dyall (*City of the Dead* aka *Horror Hotel*, 1960) is the deep-voiced head of the household; Archie Duncan is the family looney who, in this case, is locked in the basement instead of the attic; Jack Bligh is a mad scientist-inventor; and Dennis Price is an actor who may not be what he seems to be.

There's no question that Fisher was one of the greatest horror directors who ever lived. His contribution to Hammer Horror is beyond doubt and beyond measure. But *The Horror of It All*, despite a screenplay by Ray Russell (*Mr. Sardonicus*), doesn't work very well, largely due to the casting of the wooden Boone in the leading role. The fact that Boone also sings the title song really doesn't help. No film that Fisher directed is without interest to the British horror fan, and *The Horror of It All* has some nice moments from Melly, who is obviously having a lot of fun spoofing her *Brides of Dracula* vampiress character. The film is, however, a pretty routine effort by all those involved. It isn't a bad movie to see on television at three in the morning, but you'll probably forget most of it the next day.

The Raven

One of the most successful comedy-horror films of the sixties was Roger Corman's *The Raven* (1963), which came about because of one of the episodes in Corman's 1962 omnibus Poe film, *Tales of Terror*. Since 1960, Corman had been specializing in Poe adaptations starring Vincent Price, after pleading with James H. Nicholson and Samuel Z. Arkoff to give him bigger budgets and the chance to make period horror movies in color, as Hammer had been doing so successfully since 1957. His first was *House of Usher* (1960), which was almost as big a hit that year as *Psycho*. The follow-up *Pit and the Pendulum* (1961) was perhaps even more floridly Gothic than the first. By the time he got around to the third, *Tales of Terror*, Corman's restless mind was getting a little bored, so he asked screenwriter Richard Matheson to turn Poe's "The Black Cat" (mixed with a bit of "The Cask of Amontillado") into a comedy. The casting of Peter Lorre opposite Price in that segment proved to be a terrific choice. Lorre ad-libbed his way through the role as the drunken lout Montressor who walls up his adulterous wife (Joyce Jameson) and her lover (Price) in the cellar. Unfortunately for him, he walls up his black cat as well, and it gives the game away to the police with its yowling.

Lorre's performance is comedic from the word go. His exchanges with his wife are con-

Peter Lorre, Vincent Price and Joyce Jameson in "The Black Cat," a segment of Roger Corman's *Tales of Terror* (1962).

sistently funny (when she reaches into her cleavage to give him money, he says, "Thank you for looking into your heart"), and his walling-up of Price, who says to him, "What are you doing?" to which he replies, "I'll give you three guesses," is, well, priceless.

Corman next commissioned Matheson to write an all-out comedy version of *The Raven*, co-starring Price, Lorre, Boris Karloff and the luscious Hazel Court (*The Curse of Frankenstein, The Man Who Could Cheat Death*). Also in the cast was Jack Nicholson.

Karloff had turned down an offer to appear in the new *Old Dark House* because "the new version ... was not to my liking." But he did like Matheson's screenplay for *The Raven*, even though to some extent it burlesqued another of his old films, Universal's *The Raven* (1935). Matheson noted, "*The Raven* had to be a comedy because it's totally comic to take a poem and expect a horror film to come out of it."

Although the film begins with Price reciting Poe's poem, we quickly discover that this Poe picture is going to be a romp when a raven flies into his window and Price asks the raven, "Will I ever see my lost Lenore again?" to which it replies, "How the hell should I know? What am I, a fortune teller?" in Lorre's voice. It turns out that Lorre has been transformed into a raven by the evil sorcerer Scarabus (Karloff) and he requests that Price, another wizard, change him back. Traveling through Price's Gothic, cobwebbed basement ("I don't get down here very often," Price comments), they find some interesting ingredients to go into the transformation spell. Price picks up a jar of eyeballs and quickly puts it back. "What was that?" Lorre asks. "I'd rather not discuss it, if you don't mind," Price replies. Another jar is labeled "Entrails of trouble horse."

Much has been said of how Lorre constantly improvised his lines. Corman himself pointed out, "Peter kept everyone on their toes, myself included. He would just begin to improvise unexpectedly. Vincent was always willing to play along with it, but Boris, who was very methodical about his craft, was befuddled. Amused, but befuddled."

My favorite Lorre line in the film comes when he attempts to cast a spell on Karloff with his magic wand. With one wave of his hand, Karloff causes the wand to droop like a flaccid member. "Oh, you, you dirty old man!" Lorre shouts.

Original poster art for Roger Corman's 1963 parody of Edgar Allan Poe's poem *The Raven*.

Peter Lorre, Vincent Price and Olive Sturgess are all tied up in Roger Corman's witty *The Raven* (1963), one of the most successful comedy-horror films of the sixties.

Apparently, Karloff was quite pleased that he got to dally a bit with Hazel Court in the film. One of her best roles, the saucy Lenore allowed Court free rein to show off her comic delivery, as well as her charms. The favorable review in *Time* magazine pointed out, "She is a lusty redhead with a cleavage that could comfortably accommodate the collected works of Edgar Allan Poe and a bottle of his favorite booze besides."

When I interviewed her for *Little Shoppe of Horrors* magazine in 1990, Court told me what it was like to work with the horror veterans: "Boris Karloff. He was like a pussycat. A gentle, very sweet man. Peter Lorre wouldn't always know his lines. Boris always would. But the others would come on and kind of make it up a little. But it was always all right. Peter was very, very funny. He would be telling stories and intellectualizing in between takes. It was fascinating. You'd just sit back and try to listen to them all. They'd all try and top each other with their stories."

Court was less impressed with future superstar Jack Nicholson: "I always remember him saying, 'I'm going home to write tonight.' He was always talking about this great writing talent he thought he had.... I never suspected he would become a great movie star. It was strange; he was this little person who popped around on the set. He popped around in a funny costume, with knee-breeches and a funny hat! He looked rather like one of those little stone statues you can buy to put in your garden!"

Corman related to Victoria Price in the book *Vincent Price: A Daughter's Biography*: "I said to Jack, who was a young actor, 'You're good. I've seen you do improvisation in class. You are good with comedy. You can learn from Vincent and Peter and Boris because these are professional actors. They are good and they are funny and you can use your youthful vitality and your natural humor and combine it with them and learn to work with them.'"

The interesting thing is, future Oscar winner Nicholson is the weak link in *The Raven*. He's quite wooden and looks uncomfortable in his period costumes. The only moment he really comes alive is when he is suddenly possessed by an evil spirit and we see that killer smile. For one brief shining moment, he becomes the Jack Nicholson we've come to know and love.

All in all, though, *The Raven* is a comedy-horror triumph, complete with beautiful Gothic sets by Corman's favorite art director Daniel Haller, lush cinematography from Poe film regular Floyd Crosby, excellent comedic performances and an all-around sense of fun, as though the actors are enjoying making the film as much as we enjoy watching it. It remains one of the best movies that AIP ever released.

The Comedy of Terrors

The Raven was such a hit that Price, Lorre and Karloff got together a year later for another horror spoof, *The Comedy of Terrors*. This time, though, Corman was not to direct. The job went instead to veteran horror specialist Jacques Tourneur (*Cat People, Night of the Demon*). Corman was busy wrapping up his Poe masterpiece, *The Masque of the Red Death* at the time.

Once again, Richard Matheson turned in a very funny screenplay that cast Price and Lorre as two desperate undertakers who try to drum up business by killing their "clients" themselves. It's a classic black comedy plot and once again features Floyd Crosby's splendid widescreen cinematography and Daniel Haller's expert art direction.

Originally, Karloff was signed on to play Shakespearean actor John F. Black, but his arthritis (which was becoming more and more debilitating by this time) precluded him from doing all the running around that would be required. Karloff was re-cast as Mr. Hinchley, the senile father-in-law of Price's character, Waldo Trumbull. The role of Black went to former Sherlock Holmes Basil Rathbone, who literally ran with it. Busty blonde Joyce Jameson from *Tales of Terror* was back as Trumbull's annoying wife Amaryllis, who fancies herself a singer but whose warbling is so off-key it shatters every glass in the house. And just for fun, comedy veteran Joe E. Brown was brought in for an amusing cameo as a cemetery caretaker.

Tourneur's hand at comedy isn't as subtle as Corman's, and *The Comedy of Terrors* is much more of an all-out farce than *The Raven*. Price and Lorre really become a comedy team here, much like Laurel and Hardy, with Lorre the constant bungler to Price's straight man. Hopelessly in love with Amaryllis, Lorre's Felix Gillie always seems to be a day late and a dollar short. The mischievous actor proves himself, once again, a master of the ad-lib and the pratfall; Gillie is by far the most endearing character in a film full of oddballs, blackmailers and murderers.

Although the film had nothing to do with Poe, it certainly looks like part of the cycle and even features Price reciting a line from *The Raven*, albeit drunkenly and with his own additions: "...I dreamed of gently, gently rapping ... rapping gently with a hammer on a baby's skull."

Karloff had a rare (and rarely used) gift for comedy, as witness the scene in which he

The original poster for Jacques Tourneur's all-star comedy-horror film *The Comedy of Terrors* (1964).

delivers a completely doddering and befuddled eulogy for Black: "And so, my friends, we find ourselves gathered around the bier of Mrs. ... eh ... Mr. ... You know whom ... this litter of sorrows, this cairn, this cromlech, this dread dochma, this gart, this mastaba, this sorrowing tope, this unhappy tumulus, this ... this ... *what is the word*? This ... er, *coffin*! Never could think of that word! Requiescat in Pace, Mr. ... um ... Mr. ... the memory of your good deeds will not perish with your untimely sepulchre." Karloff's delivery of these lines is spot-on, drop-dead funny, reminding us of the fact that he did, after all, star on Broadway in *Arsenic and Old Lace* and *Peter Pan*, and was an actor who was just as adept at generating laughs as he was at generating screams.

The Comedy of Terrors, however, is all but stolen by Rathbone, supposedly one of Trumbull and Gillie's victims, but who is (unbeknownst to them) subject to cataleptic trances. He has an annoying (to them) habit of coming back to life, all the while reciting a scene from Macbeth ("What place is this...?"), which provides for some hilarious moments in the last third of the film.

While *The Comedy of Terrors* may not be as well-remembered as *The Raven*, it's a consistently entertaining and often laugh-out-loud funny comedy-horror film, with a first-rate cast firing on all cylinders. The *Los Angeles Herald Examiner* wrote of the film: "Boris Karloff, Peter Lorre, Vincent Price and Basil Rathbone ... score in every reel. [AIP] ought to plan a series with them."

AIP did, in fact, plan a follow-up with all four actors to be entitled *Sweethearts and Horrors*, also written by Matheson. It was not to be, however, as Lorre died from a cerebral hemorrhage on March 23, 1964. Delivering Lorre's eulogy, Price said: "This was a man to be aware of at all times, for he was well aware of who shared the stage with him and working with him never failed to fulfill the seventh and perhaps most sacred sense—the sense of fun."

Dr. Terror's House of Horrors

In February, 1965, a film called *Dr. Terror's House of Horrors* was released in Britain by Regal Film Distributors. It was picked up by Paramount that June in the U.S. and the poster billed it as "The Fear of the Year." The film was the very first in the Amicus series of anthology films, in this case a five-story omnibus starring two of rival company Hammer's biggest stars, Peter Cushing and Christopher Lee. Producer Milton Subotsky also "borrowed" Hammer director Freddie Francis (*The Evil of Frankenstein, Nightmare*) and cinematographer Alan Hume (*The Kiss of the Vampire*).

Determined to beat Hammer at their own game, Subotsky himself wrote the screenplay, which was based on five half-hour scripts he had written for television back in 1948, when he had worked as a scriptwriter on NBC's *Lights Out* series. The stories had never been used, so Subotsky dusted them off and put them into the portmanteau film, tied together by a framing story in which five passengers meet on a train and are "entertained" by a man with Tarot cards who calls himself Dr. Schreck (Cushing). Schreck tells each man his "fortune," which inevitably turns out to have a horrific ending.

Never one to pretend to false modesty, Subotsky once boasted that "the script was a wonderful package of entertainment," and he wasn't far wrong in this case. It's pretty much everything a horror fan could hope for: a story about a werewolf, another about a creeping vine, a voodoo story, a crawling hand thriller and finally a vampire tale.

In the States, *Creepy* magazine had made its debut on newsstands a few months previously, a black and white comic book filled with beautifully illustrated Gothic horror tales

Peter Cushing as the mysterious Dr. Schreck in Freddie Francis's *Dr. Terror's House of Horrors* (1964).

that usually had surprise endings. It seemed as though Subotsky's timing was just right on *Dr. Terror*. Young audiences, in particular, were looking for just the combination of thrills and laughs that *Dr. Terror* would provide them.

Although not completely a comedy-horror film, *Dr. Terror* certainly has a lot of humor, and the segment entitled *Voodoo* is pretty much played for laughs. The story stars British comic actor Roy Castle, who had his own variety show on the BBC at the time. Castle plays a jazz trumpeter who hears a voodoo chant in the Haitian jungle at night. He finds the music irresistible and starts to write it down when he's discovered by the voodoo cult members. They warn him not to write down the music or perform it lest he incur the wrath of the voodoo god Damballah.

Needless to say, he ignores their warning, returns to London and performs the music in a night club with his band. A supernatural wind suddenly blows through the nightclub, causing havoc, and he runs out into the night.

One of the film's in-jokes involves Castle's character running smack dab into a wall upon which hangs the poster for *Dr. Terror's House of Horrors*—with all of the character names listed as the stars. It is, perhaps, one of the first "post-modern" moments in a genre film.

Eventually, Damballah shows up in Castle's apartment, looking a bit less scary than one might have hoped; for one thing, he wears what looks like a diaper. He takes the written music from Castle's trembling hands and walks out into the darkness.

Voodoo, the third segment in the film, is a clever story, combining Subotsky's interest in jazz with his interest in horror. Castle is obviously having a fine time in the role as a sort of British lounge lizard, leering at the female voodoo dancers and just being generally irreverent. He also has one of the most memorable lines in the film's framing story, when he mentions to the other passengers, "There might just be something to this occult business. I once met a gypsy fortune teller who told me that I would receive an unexpected surprise, and that very day I walked under a pigeon."

Dr. Terror's House of Horrors veers from comedy to horror quite seamlessly. Although the other stories are not as light-hearted as *Voodoo*, they all have a twist in the tale which can either cause amusement or unease. The last scene in *Creeping Vine*, for instance, causes both: When it has been established that the only thing that will prevent the creeping vines from taking over the world is fire, we see a shot of the vine putting out the fire by whacking at it with a newspaper. You smile, but you get creeped out at the same time.

The first story, *Werewolf*, is the most atmospheric and serious of the bunch. The surprise comes when the werewolf turns out to be a woman, the person we least suspected. *Disembodied Hand*, which stars Christopher Lee, starts out with a big laugh when Lee, who plays snooty art critic Franklyn Marsh, dismisses the work of an artist named Eric Landor (Michael Gough) during a show at an art gallery. Then he goes on to praise another painting, a sort of modern art mess which he says "shows the work of a master." He asks to meet the artist, and a very amused Landor introduces him—to a chimpanzee. Landor has made a fool out of Marsh, who won't let him forget it.

From here, the story takes a much darker turn when Marsh runs over Landor with his car, severing his hand. The embittered painter takes his own life, but then his disembodied hand starts turning up in the most unexpected places, terrorizing Marsh in his office, his home—and ultimately, in his car, causing him to have an accident that leaves him blind. He will be an art critic no more.

Again, a nice sting at the end of the story helps to make *Disembodied Hand* the one tale in *Dr. Terror's House of Horrors* that everybody remembers. Beautifully acted by Lee, who has a real knack for playing pompous upper-class twits, and Gough, sympathetic and desperate as the artist, this tale is a real classic.

The final story in the film, *Vampire*, stars a very young Donald Sutherland as a small-town doctor who marries a mysterious woman (Jennifer Jayne) he has met in Europe. Unfortunately for him, she turns out to be a vampire, albeit an unusual one who can walk around in daylight and who doesn't sleep in a coffin. She does, however, turn into a red-eyed bat at night and flies around biting children until she's discovered by a local doctor (Max Adrian), who urges Sutherland to drive a stake through her heart. Eventually, he does, and after he's carted away by the police for murdering his wife, Adrian turns to the camera and says, "There wasn't room in this town for two doctors ... or two vampires!" At that, he turns into a bat and flies toward the audience.

At the end of the film we find that all five of our protagonists have been killed in a train wreck. Apparently, Schreck (whose name means "terror" in German) has quite a sense of humor. He is, in fact, Death with a capital D, and the whole movie has been one big practical joke on the five passengers. They won't be killed by strangling vines, werewolves, vampires, voodoo gods or crawling hands. Their entwined fate is a mundane train crash. But what fun we, the audience, have had on the way.

Dr. Terror's House of Horrors remains one of the very best Amicus films, setting the tone for all the rest. Many of the later omnibus films were written by Robert Bloch, combining his comedy ideas with horror concepts quite effortlessly in such stories as *The Cloak* in *The House that Dripped Blood*. And when Amicus got around to adapting William M. Gaines' wonderful EC Comics in *Tales from the Crypt* (1972) and *The Vault of Horror* (1973), they combined humor, horror and retribution quite effectively. Although none of their films was total comedy-horror, they offered many memorable, darkly humorous moments.

The excellent cast in *Dr. Terror's House of Horrors* makes even the preposterous elements seem quite believable. Francis's direction is solid and professional, as is Hume's fluid camerawork. It was a big hit in 1965, is rarely seen today, and deserves to be restored on DVD, at the very least. Few films combine amusement, irony and scares so effectively. But then, with a title like that, how could it fail?

Carry on Screaming!

The next big British comedy-horror film was part of a long-running franchise. Since 1958, the *Carry On* films had become a British institution. The first film, *Carry on Sergeant*, had been filmed for £74,000 and had gone on to become the third highest-grossing British film of 1958. As Steven Paul Davies wrote in 2002 in the liner notes for Anchor Bay's *The Carry On Collection* DVD box set: "Forget sharp satire. The *Carry On* series began and continued with vulgar, but never crude, humor and jokes which could be seen a mile off. This predictability was and still is part of the fun. The early films were always suggestive and never explicit. Peter Rogers, producer of every film in the series, himself commented: 'We talk a lot about sex in our films. But nothing ever happens....'"

With British horror films at the peak of their popularity in the mid-sixties, it was inevitable that the *Carry On* films would reflect the trend. They had already spoofed *Cleopatra* (1963) in *Carry On Cleo* (1964) and the secret agent craze in *Carry On Spying* (also 1964). The twelfth *Carry On* movie was *Carry On Screaming!* (1966), an affectionate parody of the Hammer horror films that combines elements of various horror motifs: Frankenstein's monster, a mummy, a voluptuous "vampire" and a kind-of werewolf. Much of the series' regular cast was featured, including Kenneth Williams as the undead Dr. Watt, Joan Sims as a policeman's shrewish wife, Charles Hawtrey as Daniel Dan, aka "Dan Dan the Gardening Man," and Bernard Bresslaw as a Lurch-like butler. Guest stars included Harry H. Corbett as Detective Sergeant Sidney Bung and Fenella Fielding from William Castle's *The Old Dark House* as the seductively vampiric Valaria.

The *House of Wax*–like plot involves Dr. Watt and Valaria kidnapping women and turning them into mannequins. They do this with the aid of a monster they've brought to life called Oddbod (Tom Clegg), a sort of cross between the Frankenstein Monster and a werewolf. The bizarre case is investigated by Bung and his assistant, Detective Constable Slobatham (Peter Butterworth).

The *Carry On* series used the same personnel from film to film, and *Carry On Screaming!* was no exception: It was produced by Peter Rogers and directed by Gerald Thomas, as all the others had been. One of the few regular actors not to appear in *Carry On Screaming!* was Sidney James, who had a previous stage commitment; he was replaced by Corbett. Fans of the series will note that his character's first name is Sidney, indicating that the role was originally written for James, who always played characters with his real first name.

Carry On Screaming! is one of the better films in the series for a number of reasons. First and foremost, it looks a lot like a Hammer horror film thanks to the fog-shrouded but colorful cinematography of series regular Alan Hume, who had also photographed Hammer's *The Kiss of the Vampire* (1963) and Amicus' *Dr. Terror's House of Horrors*. It was filmed at Pinewood Studios and on location in Berkshire and Buckinghamshire from January 10, 1966, to February 25 of that year. Shot on many of the same locations as some of the Hammer horrors, it perfectly captures the look and feel of British horror films of the period.

Talbot Rothwell's screenplay contains the usual bad puns one associates with the *Carry On* films, not to mention the sexual innuendo. At one point, Valaria asks Bung if she can "blow his whistle." During a succeeding bout of lovemaking, she asks if he minds if she smokes. When he assents, she does, of course, start smoking from every orifice in her body until the room is totally engulfed in smoke. Subtlety was never the strong suit of these films.

Still, *Carry On Screaming!* is a romp thanks to the actors, Fielding in particular. In addition to the fact that she has that Hammer cleavage thing down in a little Gothic number obviously inspired by TV horror host Vampira's gown, she once again showcases her comedic abilities by doing a spot-on impression of Joan Greenwood, the British actress featured in such films as *Kind Hearts and Coronets* (1949) and *Mysterious Island* (1961). Her voice and mannerisms are pitch-perfect parodies of Greenwood's, but encased in a sexy exterior that Greenwood never quite possessed.

Also very funny is series regular Jim Dale as Albert Potter, a "nice young man" who is quite bewildered by the fact that his girlfriend Doris (Angela Douglas) has been transformed into a mannequin. When Bung taps Doris's body with his pipe and hears a metallic sound, he asks Potter, "Does that sound like Doris?" Potter replies, "I don't know. I've never hit her with a pipe before."

Williams does his usual mugging as the re-animated Dr. Watt, whose name of course becomes the butt of several "Who's on First?" Abbott and Costello–type jokes. Williams' effeminate mannerisms and over-acting are an acquired taste, but he can be quite amusing, especially when he plays the sort of leering, ambisexual type of character that he plays here. You get the impression that no one is safe around him, male or female.

Carry On Screaming! is not the type of film to win festival awards or Oscars. There's a perfectly awful theme song warbled by the ever-popular "Anon" (short for "Anonymous"?) over the opening credits that nails that point home. But as part of one of the longest-running series in film history, it more than lives up to expectations. The best way to enjoy a *Carry On* movie is to pretend you're twelve years old and just discovering all that stuff about the birds and the bees. In this case, off-color jokes and horror combine, and what twelve-year-old could resist that?

The Ghost and Mr. Chicken

By the time *The Ghost and Mr. Chicken* was released in 1966, it seemed like a throwback to another era. Don Knotts, Barney Fife himself from *The Andy Griffith Show*, had also played the popular "Nervous Man" character on *The Steve Allen Show* in the fifties, and it seemed inevitable that Knotts, who was usually the "second banana," would get his own starring vehicle. *The Ghost and Mr. Chicken* was the first of five features in which he would star.

The movie plays like an extended version of *The Andy Griffith Show*, which is not surprising, considering that Griffith himself was consulted on story ideas for it. He suggested expanding on a plot from the TV series that had to do with a spooky old house.

The film takes place in and around the Simmons Mansion somewhere in Kansas, called "the murder house" by the locals due to the fact that Mr. Simmons supposedly murdered his wife there and then committed suicide. The oldsters say that you can still hear Simmons' ghost playing the organ at midnight.

Knotts plays Luther Heggs, a typesetter for the town newspaper who dreams of becoming a reporter. He gets his chance when he's assigned by his editor (Dick Sargent, the second Darrin on TV's *Bewitched*) to spend the night in the mansion on the fiftieth anniversary of the murder-suicide. Sure enough, the organ starts to play at midnight and Heggs, after much mugging, flees the house.

Heggs' story in the next day's newspaper ("The horribleness and awfulness of it will never be forgotten") gets the attention of everyone in town, including Nicholas Simmons, nephew of the mansion's former owner. He sues Heggs for libel, and much of the rest of the film takes place in the courtroom, until the jury is asked to accompany Heggs to the mansion to see if his story is true.

The Ghost and Mr. Chicken features many old dark house clichés: An organ-playing "ghost" was old hat in the thirties, but then the screenplay by James Fritzell and Everett Greenbaum could hardly be called "cutting edge," despite the garden shears that end up in the throat of a portrait of Simmons' wife, which then drips blood. There's nothing remotely original about the story, and the resolution of the "mystery" should surprise no one who's been paying attention.

That said, the film is an ideal vehicle for Knotts, who stutters, stammers and shakes his way through the movie. He seems to be so afraid at times, especially when he's in the old mansion alone at night, that when he starts running, his feet barely touch the ground. There are moments when you're afraid he may literally take flight.

Heggs is really just Barney Fife in disguise. Like Fife, he's full of bluster ("That's right, karate made my whole body a weapon") but in reality he is, indeed, "Mr. Chicken." Despite this, a beautiful woman named Alma Parker (one-time *Playboy* centerfold Joan Staley) is, somewhat improbably, drawn to him romantically.

As directed by Alan Rafkin, the movie has both the look and feel of a sixties television show, right down to the casting of Hal Smith (Otis the town drunk in *The Andy Griffith*

Show) as Calver Weems, another town drunk who gets bashed on the head in the first scene. Other familiar faces from television include Liam Redmond as the janitor Kelsey, Lurene Tuttle as Mrs. Natalie Miller, Robert Cornthwaite (who also appeared in *The Thing from Another World*, 1951) as attorney Springer, Skip Homeier as the reporter Ollie Weaver, Reta Shaw as spiritualist Mrs. Halcyon Maxwell, Ellen Corby as Miss Neva Tremaine and veteran character actor Burt Mustin as Mr. Dellagondo.

The cinematography, full of bright colors even in the old dark mansion, also suggests vintage television. Indeed, Knotts' G-rated antics were geared toward TV fans, and nothing was put into the film that would have shocked or offended them. The "horror" is tame, as is the "sex" (an old lady at the boarding house whispering the word "bosoms" is about as naughty as it gets), to the point that a lot of viewers today may think it's a Disney picture.

There are a couple of interesting touches. The Simmons Mansion is actually a revamped version of the Bates house from *Psycho*. Vic Mizzy, the film's composer, composed the theme for the TV series *The Munsters*, also produced by Universal. And there's a running gag in the movie that has become something of a legend. Whenever Heggs attempts to speak in public (one of Knotts' best "Nervous Man" routines) a voice from the crowd yells out, "Attaboy, Luther!" It happens at several points in the movie, including the courtroom scene, and most amusingly at the ending when Heggs gets married to Alma and is just about to kiss her. The phrase was uttered by the film's co-screenwriter Everett Greenbaum and is one of the funniest bits in the movie. As a kind of homage, it was also heard many years later during the bowling championship scene in the movie *Kingpin* (1996).

The Ghost and Mr. Chicken is certainly no classic, but it's an amiable and rather sweet movie that's fondly remembered by many baby boomers. The old-fashioned story takes place in a picture-perfect Norman Rockwell America that probably never really existed. The film already had the sheen of nostalgia when it was originally released, and its warm, good-natured and rustic humor has only grown more charming and quaint with the passage of time. It harks back to an era when even comedy-horror films didn't have to be hard-edged.

The Fearless Vampire Killers

In the mid-sixties, young Polish director Roman Polanski was having trouble getting his second feature film produced, despite the critical acclaim afforded to his first feature, *Knife in the Water* (1962). The film had been a big success at the Cannes Film Festival that year, but Hollywood showed little interest in the director's work, feeling that he was strictly an "art-house" filmmaker.

When he went to London, Polanski tried to get a project going with Hammer, and, interestingly enough, was turned down. But just down the road from Hammer near London's Wardour Street were the offices of Compton-Cameo, a small production company run by exploitation king Tony Tenser, producer of such films as *That Kind of Girl* (1963) and *The Black Torment* (1964). Many years later, Tenser recalled his first meeting with Polanski: "My secretary phoned upstairs to say there is a Mr. Gutowski and a Mr. Polanski here to see me. I had heard of Polanski because he made *Knife in the Water*, which got excellent critical reviews. What it had done at the box office I don't know. I guessed that if they were coming to see me they had gone to everybody else. But Polanski was a name, he is a director that draws the press, a brilliant director but a difficult personality to understand."

Polanski and his production partner, Gene Gutowski, attempted to pitch a black comedy project called *When Katelbach Comes*, but Tenser pointed out that they would only be interested in something blatantly commercial. He suggested a contemporary horror film, and Polanski went to his home in Paris to work on it with his usual writing partner, Gerard Brach.

The result was *Repulsion* (1965), a breakthrough for Polanski and for horror films in general. Its blunt combination of brutal murders and sex couldn't have been more commercial, but in Polanski's hands the film attained heights of artistry that Tenser's films had never been known for previously. Starring beautiful French actress Catherine Deneuve as a sexually repressed woman going slowly mad, *Repulsion* went on to become a sensation, garnering such reviews as "the stuff of which films are made" (*The Evening Standard*) and "brilliantly executed, stark and absorbing ... a remarkable shocker of a film" (*Saturday Review*). The box office matched the reviews and Polanski became a bankable director.

Thanks to the success of *Repulsion*, Tenser agreed to let Polanski direct the project he had originally pitched to him, *When Katelbach Comes*. Eventually, the film was released as *Cul-de-Sac*, starring Donald Pleasence, Lionel Stander and Françoise Dorleac, and, in a small role, Jacqueline Bisset. The budget this time was £120,000, more than twice the budget of *Repulsion*.

Despite the extra cash flow, Polanski gave Tenser a hard time on *Cul-de-Sac*, as the producer noted later: "He had no idea about money at all; it was a means to an end for him. All our problems came over the budget.... [W]e simply didn't want to go over the budget. We couldn't afford it, we didn't have the money."

A deeply personal and quite bizarre film, *Cul-de-Sac* wasn't as well received as *Repulsion*, but that didn't stop Polanski from pursuing other avenues to finance his next feature. Tenser took a look at a synopsis and didn't think much of it: "[I]n my opinion the subject matter wouldn't sell seats. I thought if Polanski directed, it would be a good film but to me it didn't seem a great premise. Probably his least appealing movie, from my perspective anyway."

The synopsis that Tenser turned down eventually became *The Fearless Vampire Killers*, and much to Polanski's delight (and later regret) Martin Ransohoff at MGM agreed to back the project as a co-production between Cadre Films (Gutowski's production company) and Filmways for presentation by MGM—to the tune of two million pounds, a substantial budget in those days. Polanski was "going Hollywood" and would now be able to choose the cast and crew of his dreams.

There were still hurdles to overcome, however. As *The Fearless Vampire Killers* was intended to be a parody of Hammer's vampire cycle, Polanski originally wanted to film it in Transylvania, a province of Romania. But Romania was a communist country then, and it turned out to be unfeasible to film there. It was decided to film interiors at MGM's Borehamwood Studios in England, with location filming in the Alps.

Polanski cast character actor Jack MacGowran (who had also appeared in *Cul-de-Sac*) in the lead role of Professor Abronsius, an old and somewhat feeble vampire hunter traveling Europe in search of his prey. As Alfred, Abronsius' bumbling assistant, Polanski cast himself, something he had done before in his early short films. For the lead female role of Sarah, the director chose lovely young Sharon Tate, who had just appeared in the occult thriller *Eye of the Devil* for Filmways. Another actor from *Cul-de-Sac*, Iain Quarrier, was chosen for the role of a vampire of questionable sexuality.

To round out the cast, Polanski hand-picked several British actors: Alfie Bass as the Yiddish-sounding innkeeper (and Sarah's father) Yoine Shagal; Fiona Lewis, who would later appear in *Dr. Phibes Rises Again* (1971), as a bosomy tavern wench; Ferdy Mayne, who would later appear in Hammer's *The Vampire Lovers*, as Count Von Krolock, the villain of the piece; and ex-boxer Terry Downes (*A Study in Terror*, 1965) as a slightly lecherous hunchback. Also in a small role was Ronald Lacey, who would memorably play the Peter Lorre–type villain in *Raiders of the Lost Ark* (1981).

The crew Polanski chose was also absolutely first-rate. Director of photography Douglas Slocombe would later go on to photograph all three Indiana Jones films among many others. Production designer Wilfrid Shingleton had worked in that capacity on numerous episodes of TV's *The Avengers*. Choreographer Tutte Lemkow from *Fiddler on the Roof* arranged the "Dance of the Vampires" for the film's climactic scene.

Although there were production problems on the film, it has been said that Polanski really enjoyed making it. In his book *The Cinema of Roman Polanski*, Ivan Butler quoted Slocombe as saying, "I think [Roman] put more of himself into *Dance of the Vampires* [the British title] than into any other film. It brought to light the fairy-tale interest that he has. One was conscious all along when making the picture of a Central European background to the story. Very few of the crew could see anything in it—they thought it old-fashioned nonsense. But I could see this background.... I have a French background myself, and could sense the Central European atmosphere that surrounds it. The figure of Alfred is very much like Roman himself—a slight figure, young and a little defenseless—a touch of Kafka. It is very much a personal statement of his own humor. He used to chuckle all the way through."

One of the production problems occurred when Polanski decided to switch film formats during the shooting, from flat to anamorphic (widescreen). Scenes that had already been filmed flat were later optically converted to anamorphic.

In his autobiography, Polanski recalled: "Our first month's outdoor filming became a series of ingenious improvisations, mainly because the last-minute switch from one location [Austria] to another [Ortisei, an Italian ski resort in the Dolomites] had left us so little time to revise our shooting schedules. The fact that we were filming in Italy entailed the employment of a certain number of Italian technicians, and that, in turn, bred some international friction. Gene Gutowski rightly suspected that the Italians were robbing us blind."

But a funny thing happened on the way to the film's release in 1967. The day after the opening at the Baronet Theatre in New York City, this headline appeared in the November 14, 1967, *New York Times*: "Polanski Disavows *Vampire* Film Cuts."

The article went on to say that Polanski had requested MGM and Filmways to remove his name from the movie's credits and advertising. When he was reached in Hollywood, where he was filming *Rosemary's Baby*, Polanski said, "I've called them and asked to have my name removed because I don't want credit for a film I didn't really make. The one now showing is far from the one I filmed."

Gutowski was also quoted in the piece as saying that the version currently playing "has been so radically changed by reasons of recutting, redubbing, revoicing, altered dialogue, altered sound track and altered sound effects that it no longer represents the motion picture created, written and directed by Roman Polanski."

The article concluded by noting that neither Polanski nor Gutowski planned any legal action, so it's safe to say that they just wanted to point out that the film as released was not the film that they envisioned. Indeed, the *Times* review that appeared that day was not kind. Critic Bosley Crowther opined, "It's no wonder Roman Polanski would prefer to repudiate the cut of his new film.... [T]his beautifully produced, superbly scenic and excitingly photographed spoof of old-fashioned horror movies is as dismal and dead as a blood-drained corpse."

In a Crowther article appearing in the *Times* a few weeks later ("The Melting Pot Boils Over"), he declared that Polanski had been ruined by Hollywood: "Mr. Polanski is the Polish director whose *Knife in the Water* was a brilliant display of incisive dramatic exploration with a cast of three aboard a boat on a Polish lake, and whose *Repulsion* was a shattering comprehension of the deterioration of a mind. Now, with generous backing and loose encouragement from an Anglo-American company, he has turned out this spoof of monster pictures which is also a travesty of cinematic artistry."

So what exactly happened between production and release of *The Fearless Vampire Killers*? It seems that Martin Ransohoff got it into his head that the film was too long and too odd for American audiences, so he cut out between sixteen and twenty minutes, redubbed some of the actors' voices and tacked on an animated credit sequence that featured the MGM lion turning into a ghoulish-looking vampire. He also added the subtitle *Pardon Me But Your Teeth Are in my Neck*. Polanski was not amused, nor were very many American audiences of the time.

Critics and audiences in Europe, however, were a different matter, because they got to see Polanski's original version of *Dance of the Vampires*, as it was known in England and on the Continent. It gradually became a cult film in Europe, but we Yanks weren't able to see it in its original cut until it was released on video in the U.S. in 1990.

For those accustomed to seeing the film on CBS late night showings back in the seventies, the uncut version is something of a revelation. The first thing that jumps out at you (especially on the DVD release of 2004) is the look of the film. Styled exactly like a Hammer Gothic (if Hammer had had this kind of budget), it's a visual feast from the first frame to the last. From the stunning snow-capped Alps locations to Count Von Krolock's moldering yet beautiful castle, the film is an overwhelming visual experience. The costumes, particularly those in the masquerade ball, are works of art in themselves. Who can ever forget Sharon Tate in that ball gown, as red as her flowing hair?

The intense visual style of the film is complemented by the fact that Polanski uses techniques from silent films. Long stretches are dialogue-free, allowing Polanski plenty of opportunity to give the movie the feeling of a silent, from under-cranking some footage—a style often used in older films for comic effect, and rarely for eerie effect, as in F.W. Murnau's 1922 *Nosferatu* ("The dead travel fast")—and with his liberal use of sight gags, such as Shagal frozen in an odd position after being set upon by vampires. If you can imagine Murnau combined with Charlie Chaplin, you'll have a very good idea of what Polanski achieves in *The Fearless Vampire Killers*.

The performers, too, are a joy to watch. Jack MacGowran is a hoot as Professor Abronsius, whether he's getting frozen in the snow or stuck in a castle window. He's a bit like an older, more doddering version of Inspector Clouseau. My personal favorite line of his is when he says of Count Von Krolock: "Takes me for a nincompoop, that necrophile!"

Polanski is extremely likable as Alfred, a well-meaning but blundering vampire killer wannabe who just happens to be an incurable romantic. Falling in love with Sarah at first sight (and who could blame him?), Alfred comes across as a shy young man who dearly wants to please Abronsius, but who at the same time desires the beautiful Sarah. The fact that he also makes a few grabs at the tavern serving girl (Lewis) indicates that there's a ladies man inside him just waiting to come out.

Speaking of "coming out," the scene in which Count Von Krolock's son Herbert (Quarrier) tries to seduce Alfred with his vampire ways is one of the funniest in the film. Taking off on Hammer's penchant for lesbian vampires (à la Andree Melly in *The Brides of Dracula*, who seems to want more than blood from Yvonne Monlaur), Polanski imagines what "undeath" might be like for a gay male vampire. Herbert ends up chasing Alfred like a spurned lover all through the castle in one of the film's more uproarious scenes. But Polanski never really allows the film to become too broad, a point that Ransohoff completely missed when he attempted to turn it into a farce. Polanski's intention was to inject his unique brand of Central European humor into a classic Gothic horror story. After Alfred escapes from Herbert, Abronsius says, "He went berserk. Did you provoke him or what?" Alfred replies, "No, he got excited all on his own." This is very odd—and for Polanski, very personal—humor, and you either get it or you don't.

Another interesting fact about the film is that there are moments when it's very creepy indeed, such as the scene in which the graveyard gives up its dead and all the vampires rise for the masquerade ball. It's a sequence worthy of Hammer at its most atmospheric, as beautifully shot and staged as any "serious" vampire set piece.

Mayne as Count Von Krolock is obviously having a wonderful time; he sometimes looks more like Christopher Lee than Lee himself. His most effective scene is probably when he gives his little speech at the masquerade ball to the assembled vampires: "A year ago, exactly on this same night, we were assembled here in this very room; I your pastor, and you my beloved flock. With hopefulness in my heart I told you then that with Lucifer's aid we might look forward to a more succulent occasion. Cast back your minds. There we were, gathered together, gloomy and despondent, around a single meager woodcutter."

Of course, the occasion on this night is to taste the blood of Sarah (which wouldn't be a bad Hammer title). And Sarah, as played by Tate, is heartbreakingly beautiful. It's impossible to watch this film now without thinking about the tragic—and truly horrible—end that came to Sharon Tate, and the nightmare of the Manson murders that, to this day, must haunt Polanski. It brings an extra note of doom—one that was never intended—to the movie. Tate is breathtaking to look at, as fresh-faced a heroine as ever there was in a vampire film, and extremely capable as an actress as well. It makes one wonder what kind of a superstar she might have been had she been given more time on this planet.

But that's all part of the spell cast by *The Fearless Vampire Killers*. It's funny, yes, in a weird and quirky way, but it's also eerie and dreamlike. At the end of the film, Alfred gets his wish after a fashion: He is bitten by Sarah, who is now a vampire, and destined to spread the curse of the undead throughout the world. Perhaps that sums up Polanski's philosophy: No matter how much good you try to do, evil always wins out. The fact that he can still find such an idea amusing is a tribute to his survival skills; after all, both of his parents died in concentration camps. If you can live with that, you can live with anything.

Perhaps Phil Hardy's *Encyclopedia of Horror Movies* sums it up best: "The film is an astounding tour de force that is funny, chilling and intensely lyrical at the same time and shows that the generally accepted wisdom that horror shall either be played straight or become a comedy is false, since both jokes and anxiety are rooted in the same soil of unconscious desires and combine to generate the sense of the uncanny."

From the Jewish jokes, such as when the vampirized innkeeper reacts to a character brandishing a cross by saying, "Oy, have you got the wrong vampire!" to the beautiful music score by Krzysztof Komeda (who would later score *Rosemary's Baby*) to the magnificent ballroom scene inspired by Hammer's *The Kiss of the Vampire*, *The Fearless Vampire Killers* is a fever dream of Gothic sensuality, florid and nightmarish imagery, and it contains perhaps the most perfectly realized dark humor in any comedy-horror film. Polanski was really whistling past the graveyard with this film, facing up to the past horrors of his life—and, sadly, foreshadowing his own horrors yet to come.

If *Abbott and Costello Meet Frankenstein* is the Cadillac of comedy-horror films, then *The Fearless Vampire Killers* is the Rolls-Royce.

Spider Baby

Jack Hill's *Spider Baby* is a deeply weird comedy-horror film; in a very real sense ahead of its time, it was filmed over a week or so in 1964 and not released until 1968. By that time, its star, Lon Chaney, Jr., had been dead for two years, a victim of liver failure. The fact that he had been ill for years, suffering from alcoholism, hadn't prevented the venerable actor from talk-singing the movie's title song, a charming little ditty subtitled *"The Maddest Story Ever Told."*

Chaney plays the chauffeur/guardian of the Merrye family who are afflicted by a disease called "Merrye's Syndrome," a chronic condition that causes them to degenerate mentally and physically, beginning at around the time they hit puberty. The children are hardly a "merry" bunch: Ralph (Sid Haig) looks like a leftover from Tod Browning's *Freaks* (1932); Virginia (Jill Banner) is fascinated by spiders to the extent that she moves like one; and Elizabeth (Beverly Washburn) seems childlike, but harbors a kind of feral brutality hidden just beneath the surface.

The first victim of the family is Mantan Moreland as an ill-fated postman who ends up with his ear sliced off and his body fed to ... well, whatever lurks in the basement. Moreland, who was attempting a career comeback in the sixties, lasts all of five minutes, but as he's in the opening scene (which happens to be quite gruesome), his screen time is highly memorable.

Bruno (Chaney) looks over the bizarre brood, tolerant of their eccentricities, until Peter (Quinn Redeker) and Emily (Carol Ohmart from William Castle's *House on Haunted Hill*, 1958), distant relatives of the Merryes, arrive to ascertain if they have a legal right to take possession of the property. An interesting dinner party takes place in which all of the family are present, along with an attorney (Karl Schanzer) and his young, attractive assistant (Mary Mitchel). Ralph has just killed a cat, which is served as part of the dinner, along with a salad made of weeds, some mushrooms and a few deceased insects.

Things get stranger and stranger; Ralph travels through the house by using a dumb-waiter and gets quite aroused by the two good-looking women visiting the rundown place. Unable to speak, he manages to say a lot with his leers. Bruno makes the mistake of leaving the house to run an errand and the "children" seize upon the opportunity of the mouse being away to instigate some very violent "play:" The attorney is murdered, his corpse thrown into the basement where some sort of inbred relations eat him for dinner. Ralph sexually attacks Emily, apparently causing her to have a rather abrupt personality change in which she becomes just as violent as the rest of the Merrye clan.

Finally, Bruno returns and discovers that everything he has tried to hold together is falling apart; unable to deal with the fact that the secrets regarding the family will be revealed to the world, he blows up the house with a fistful of dynamite. All may or may not be over, however; Peter's young daughter seems to have a fascination with spiders. The film ends with the most dreaded words in B-movies: "The End ... or is it?"

Spider Baby has a diseased, sickly atmosphere that anticipates that of David Lynch's *Eraserhead* (1976), with Alfred Taylor's black and white cinematography contributing images of death and decay that are still disturbing today. Hill, a Corman protégé who had been among the many directors (Francis Ford Coppola and Monte Hellman among them) contributing to T*he Terror* (1963) pulled out all the stops he could get past the censors for this independent production. Shot in late summer of '64, the film seems to have been cursed: its producers went bankrupt, which was why it didn't see the light of day until 1968. When it finally was released, it went unnoticed. The distributor changed the title to *The Liver Eaters* (an especially sick joke considering that Chaney had died of liver disease in the interim) and it still didn't catch on. It wasn't until years later, when perhaps the public had become more attuned to Hill's vision—and when midnight shows and bootleg videos entered the marketplace—that *Spider Baby* finally found an audience.

It's a shame it hadn't happened sooner, because Chaney's performance in the film ranks with his very best. Reportedly "on the wagon" during the shooting, Chaney portrays Bruno as a likable but misguided character, the ultimate "enabler" who indulges every whim and fantasy of his weird wards. This, of course, leads to disaster, but when Bruno finally sees the error of his ways he atones in the only way he knows how: he destroys everything and everyone, including himself.

There are a number of knowing in-jokes; the attorney and his assistant note that they're big fans of horror films, especially of *The Wolf Man*. Bruno intones, "There's a full moon tonight," in his best Lawrence Talbot voice. But the great thing about Chaney's performance is that it's poignant, not just jokey. When he turns to look at the camera before setting off the dynamite, the look on his face is a winsome, reflective one. Perhaps Chaney knew he was dying at that point; in any case, he just seems to shrug it off as of no consequence.

Hill never really lived up to the promise of *Spider Baby*; he became an exploitation director with an erratic career, turning out everything from blaxpoitation (*Coffy*, 1973) to R-rated "T&A" fare (*The Swinging Cheerleaders*, 1974). But if he never makes another film, he made his mark with *Spider Baby*. As Schlocker the attorney notes in the film, "This has gone well beyond the boundaries of prudence and good taste."

6

THE SEVENTIES
Naked Vampires and Young Frankensteins

If the sixties had indeed sown the seeds of free love and the breaking down of old barriers, the seventies illustrated what the flower children were like in full bloom. For the first time, mainstream movies not only reveled in nudity but in explicit sex. Hardcore and mainstream merged, beginning with a phenomenon called *Deep Throat* in 1972. The raincoat crowd now wore leisure suits.

But the taboos had been broken before the sixties had ended, not only with love fests like Woodstock, but with movies such as Sam Peckinpah's *The Wild Bunch* (1969) and its ballet of slow-motion violence. It was a new era of both frankness and gore on the screen. Now that the Motion Picture Code had been abolished in the U.S. and replaced with a rating system, it seemed as though just about anything could be shown at your local bijou.

The Horror of Frankenstein

By 1970, film censorship had relaxed to the point where movies such as Robert Altman's *MASH* were allowed to poke fun at such institutions as the military, complete with full frontal nudity and the use of the "F" word (the first time the now over-used word was uttered in an R-rated film). But the really shocking thing about *MASH* was the fact that much of the humor was based on the horrors of war. Blood flowed freely throughout the operating rooms in the film, yet audiences were encouraged to laugh at the absurdity of it all.

It was in this climate that Hammer Films decided to re-work their first Gothic blockbuster, *The Curse of Frankenstein* (1957), for a "modern" audience. The result, Jimmy Sangster's *The Horror of Frankenstein* (1970), was not financially successful and has been much maligned over the years. Perhaps it is time for a re-evaluation, for Sangster's film is truly one of the better horror parodies ever made. Its wit is subtle, almost Oscar Wildean, and filled with irony.

Sangster was one of the original architects of Hammer horror, having written the screenplay for *Curse* and most of the first wave of the Hammer Gothics. As time wore on, however, he made no secret of the fact that he was bored with the Gothics and preferred to work on more personal projects that he initiated himself, such as the Bette Davis suspense thriller *The Nanny* (1965), which he both wrote and produced.

Sangster had left the confines of Hammer to work in Hollywood during the late sixties. He recalled the genesis of *The Horror of Frankenstein* in his witty memoir *Do You Want it Good or Tuesday? From Hammer Films to Hollywood! A Life in the Movies.* According to Sangster, "I was enjoying myself in Hollywood when I got a call from Hammer. They were going to do yet another Frankenstein movie. They'd had a script written by a man named Jeremy Burnham but it needed some work done on it, would I be interested in doing the rewrite? I told them I wasn't. What if they let me produce it? Still not interested. Then I had an idea. I'd rewrite the script and produce it—providing they'd let me direct as well. Short pause over the phone. They'd call me back. This they did about an hour later. Deal! The script's in the mail."

Sangster went on to describe his misgivings about the project: "Three days later the script arrived. I read it and my heart sank. It was virtually identical to the script I had written for Hammer umpty years ago, the first Frankenstein movie they made. As far as I could see they needn't have bothered paying a writer to come up with something they as good as owned already. All of a sudden I didn't want to do it anymore."

Too much of a professional to go back on his word, Sangster went about rewriting the script, "trying to bring something different to it." He continued, "I packed my bags, moved out of my apartment, and went back to London where I eventually delivered my rewrites. They were pronounced acceptable to Hammer. I honestly don't think anyone read the final script.... As far as they were concerned, Sangster was making a *Frankenstein* movie. Let him get on with it."

And get on with it he did. As for the casting: "There was no question of using Peter Cushing again because I'd written the part much younger. [Hammer chief] James Carreras wanted me to cast the actor they'd just used in *Taste the Blood of Dracula*, Ralph Bates. I didn't think he was right and told him so. At least meet the man, said Sir James, who was grooming Ralph to take over the Peter Cushing parts in any number of upcoming movies. Not, I hasten to say, because they wanted to break with Peter, it was just that he was getting a little old to carry off the sex symbol image that Hammer was selling by now. So I duly met Ralph, was suitably impressed, and he got the part. A couple of days later I cast David Prowse as the Monster and we were off and running."

After that shaky start, Sangster and Bates actually became very good friends. I got to know Ralph Bates before his untimely death of pancreatic cancer at the age of fifty-one. He was one of the nicest people I ever knew: charming, witty, an expert on food and wine, and a loving husband to his wife, actress Virginia Wetherell, whom he met on the set of Roy Ward Baker's *Dr. Jekyll and Sister Hyde* (1971), a movie that could have been comedy-horror, but ended up being straight horror with a very blackly comic subtext.

Bates had been spotted by Carreras in a BBC miniseries called *The Caesars* in which he played the infamous Caligula. Carreras immediately cast him as Lord Courtley, disciple of Christopher Lee's Count Dracula, in *Taste the Blood of Dracula* (1969).

Bates and Sangster hit it off from the start, and by all accounts, the fun began. As Sangster wrote, "I have to admit here that I have never had such an enjoyable time as I did during the six weeks we were shooting *Horror of Frankenstein*. I loved every minute of it. Ralph Bates became a very good friend and later asked me to be godfather to his son William. The crew were wonderful. We kept to schedule and budget and we never stopped laughing."

That fact was seconded by Bates in a radio interview I did with him in 1984. "Listen, we had so much fun making that," he said. "I think it showed. We just had a ball. I don't know if it's a great film. I don't think Jim is all that proud of it. But we had such a good time."

In his book, Sangster expanded on the experience: "Some directors believe that unless the set is rife with fear and tension the end result won't be any good. Personally, I think that's a load of bullshit. But to each his own. Nevertheless, happy set or not, I am forced to admit that I didn't make a very good movie. I meant it to be lighthearted. It was so lighthearted its feet never touched the ground."

Bates told me that he felt "it fell slightly between two stools and it didn't go far enough with the comedy. And I don't think it went far enough with the Gothic horror."

Be that as it may—and Bates was a very humble fellow—many critics got the joke when *Horror of Frankenstein* was originally released, even if audiences didn't. As Sangster recalled, "At least they understood what I was trying to get at…"

One of the problems the fans may have had with the film was that they may have felt Hammer was trying to put the beloved Cushing out to pasture. But according to Bates, that wasn't their intention at all. "I'd met him," he told me, "because publicity-wise, with me doing *Frankenstein*, it was him handing over the role [to me], which was rubbish anyway, because that was never the intention. I was just playing him young and he would have gone on playing Frankenstein quite rightly … and he did afterwards anyway. Such a kind, good man."

Although there have been stories told over the years that indicated Hammer was planning a series of six films starring Bates as Baron Frankenstein, nothing said by Sangster or Bates has ever indicated this. Sangster continued to "apologize" for the film in his book: "I think one of the reasons the movie wasn't as good as it could have been was that there was nobody to keep me in check. I was the writer-producer-director, the closest thing you can get to being God. Nobody was around to say 'you can't do this' or 'that doesn't work.' James Carreras never saw the dailies and never visited the studio."

Veronica Carlson, who plays Elizabeth (the role originated by Hazel Court in *Curse*), told me about the "schoolboy humor" that Sangster and Bates reveled in during production, and that she didn't quite feel part of "the club," but that she also had a great time. As for Bates, although he thoroughly enjoyed "cutting up" (in more ways than one) on the set, when the cameras rolled he took his work seriously. "I had seen the Hammer original when I was a kid," he said, "but I don't think I was really influenced by Peter when I played the role. I think I was influenced by the way they shoot them, really. There was a particular Hammer style. A lot of it had to do with speed and organization."

Whatever his influences may have been, Bates makes the role of Baron Frankenstein his own in *The Horror of Frankenstein*. His performance is urbane, charming and icy, all at the same time. There's a telling scene when the baron's assistant Wilhelm (Graham James) says to him, "You're a strange one, Victor … one moment you can be kind and charming, the next you're as cold as the grave. I sometimes wonder which is the real Baron Frankenstein." The baron offhandedly replies, "You must let me know when you find out." Wilhelm does find out, the hard way, when Frankenstein murders him in cold blood after he's threatened to reveal his work to the authorities.

Indeed, as with the Cushing Frankenstein films, the baron is the monster here. During the course of the film, he murders his father, his maid, Elizabeth's father, his assistant Wilhelm, and a graverobber (Dennis Price), and is ready to let his childhood friend (Stephen Turner) go to the gallows for the crimes he (Frankenstein) has committed.

And like Cushing's Frankenstein, he's a misogynist as well. Although his tastes run to the carnal as well as the scientific, his cruel mistreatment of the women in his life is completely amoral. His callous indifference to their feelings is reminiscent of the way Lord Byron allegedly treated women. Bates's baron was an antihero just made for the "anti-establishment" early seventies.

And while there may indeed be "schoolboy humor" in the film (such as in the scene where a dismembered hand is shocked by the current of a galvanic battery to give the "up yours" sign), there's also a great deal of caustic wit. Price has a great time in his scenes with Bates; when the baron reminds him to deliver to him only "undamaged goods," he smiles wryly and says, "Of course, you have to understand that they're all damaged in a little way, or they wouldn't be dead, now would they?"

Price's scenes with his wife (Joan Rice) are priceless. On one of their grave-robbing expeditions, he sits by the side of the grave, eating and drinking, while his wife performs the hard work of digging. When she reads him a newspaper story about a terrible accident that has killed dozens of people, he gives that wry smile again and says, "The good Lord has been kind to us, lovey. We have plenty of work to do."

The other cast members all seem as though they're in on the fun. Although Carlson doesn't have a great deal to do as Elizabeth, she looks absolutely gorgeous doing it in a variety of low-cut gowns and extravagant hairdos. Jon Finch, who would go on to star in Roman Polanski's *Macbeth* (1971) and Alfred Hitchcock's *Frenzy* (1972) acquits himself admirably as a stalwart police lieutenant. And Kate O'Mara shines as Alys, the beautiful but scheming maid, who gives "satisfaction" to the baron, as she did to his father before him.

The Horror of Frankenstein has been attacked from many angles over the years. In his book *English Gothic: A Century of Horror Cinema*, author Jonathan Rigby opined, "Ralph Bates is a smarmy and charisma-free Baron.... The Monster is a bald, muscle-bound nonentity."

I actually find the Monster to be quite enjoyable; as played by David Prowse, who would later become famous as the body (but not the voice) of Darth Vader, he looks like a giant, hairless baby—which makes perfect sense, since he's just been born. When the baron walks over to his new creation to say, "How do you do? I'm Baron Frankenstein," he knocks him to the floor with one sweep of his arm.

That sums up the approach of *The Horror of Frankenstein*: classic British understatement. Whereas *The Curse of Frankenstein* was full of sound, fury, sensationalism and blood, *Horror* is subtle, even gentle, by comparison. Even the ending is underplayed: A little girl accidentally (and unknowingly) destroys the Monster in an acid vat during a police interrogation. After everyone leaves, Bates looks down at the vat and the Monster's boots float to the surface, all that's left of his creation. He turns to the camera with a sort of "Que Sera Sera" expression and that's the end of the film.

The Bates baron is notable for his unflappable ability to just carry on with things. He's so single-minded that nothing will stop his experiments, and if anyone gets in his way, he'll eliminate them as emotionlessly as possible. To him, killing people is no worse than swatting flies. "You're beginning to bore me, Alys," he says to his maid, and shortly afterward, she's dead.

Howard Thompson in the *New York Times* proved that mainstream critics "got" the film better than most fans did: "It's not only painless but also fun. Hammer Productions has finally spared the hammer and applied some deft needlework and snug embroidery.... Imagine a kind of *Kind Hearts and Coronets* detour. Instead of a sly blade gently murdering legacy obstacles, there's a personable young baron, Ralph Bates, crisply dispatching friends and relatives while setting up a laboratory for you-know-what.... The wry, pointed dialogue is nicely clipped off by a game cast..."

On a personal note, I first saw *The Horror of Frankenstein* at a "dusk to dawn" drive-in show in 1974. It didn't start until three in the morning. Any movie that can make you laugh—indeed, keep you in stitches—at that hour must have something going for it.

The Vampire Happening

In the early seventies, Italian producer Pier A. Caminnecci was looking for a star vehicle for his lovely Scandinavian wife Pia Degermark. She had made a big splash as the lead in *Elvira Madigan* (1967), which had its world premiere at the Cannes Film Festival and garnered great critical acclaim, and went on to box office success. Offers came pouring in for Degermark, who was only eighteen when the film was released. Unfortunately, her tender age led to some poor choices, among them marriage to Caminnecci.

Her producer husband set up an international production for her in Germany. He hired British director and Oscar-winning cinematographer Freddie Francis (*Dr. Terror's House of Horrors*) to direct a screenplay by German writers Karl-Heinz Hummel and August Rieger. The script, entitled *Gebissen Wird Nur Nachts*, was a sort of ripoff of Polanski's *The Fearless Vampire Killers*. Degermark was slated to play Hollywood actress Betty Williams, who inherits a Transylvanian castle that (needless to say) is haunted by a vampire. It turns out that one of her ancestors was Clarimonde, a blood-sucking countess, who crawls out of her tomb to terrify the local populace. The film ends with a very debauched vampire's ball at the castle, featuring Ferdy Mayne (here billed as Ferdie Mayne), Count Krolock from *The Fearless Vampire Killers*, as Count Dracula himself.

It's obvious that producer Caminnecci wanted to go Polanski one better and throw a lot of sex and nudity into his vampire comedy. Director Francis, who rarely featured those elements in his films, was willing to go along with the producer's wishes. The result? The fact that *The Vampire Happening* (the film's English title) is watchable at all is due almost entirely to Dagermark's presence and the reliable professionalism of Francis.

There is an interesting subplot in the film: The castle happens to be next door to a monastery, and a monk named Martin (Joachim Kemmer) is having problems with his vows of chastity. Wherever he goes, he seems to see sex, whether it's in the shape of a tree, or in the sight of Betty Williams undressing at her castle window. And this is where the film takes on new meaning for fans of literary vampires: *The Vampire Happening* is to date the only feature film version of French writer Theophile Gautier's "Clarimonde," an 1836 short story that influenced everything from L. Sheridan Le Fanu's *Carmilla* to the romantic vampire yarns of *Weird Tales* author Clark Ashton Smith.

"Clarimonde," known by a host of other titles including "The Dead Leman" and "The Beautiful Vampire," virtually invented the theme of the gorgeous vampire who partakes of her lover's blood to stay alive, and whose love for him transcends even death. Gautier was one of the great French writers of the Romantic movement and filled his tales with exotic imagery and a great deal of erotic power. "Clarimonde" is his most famous tale, and its theme of the young man who is about to take his vows but cannot get the image of the magnificent Clarimonde out of his mind, is unexpectedly reflected in *The Vampire Happening*. The only other filmed version of the story, a serious hour-long adaptation, was made for the Canadian-produced vampire television series *The Hunger* in 1998. Needless to say, the comedic approach of *The Vampire Happening* hardly does the story justice, but it gives the film a special place in vampire movie history.

As is the case with every film directed by Francis, *The Vampire Happening* looks great; the director's keen eye for visuals elevates moments of the film to something like art, and Degermark's beauty and acting ability are both vividly on display. Although she spends a good deal of the film either topless or in the nude, Degermark gives not one, but two very relaxed and amiable performances, as the vampire and the American actress. The English dubbing, of course, robs the film of what comic timing it may have had in its original language, but most of the humor is of the slapstick variety anyway.

There are acres of exposed flesh in *The Vampire Happening*, but one should bear in mind that at the time of the film's production, sex and nudity were all the rage. Caminnecci apparently knew a commercial idea when he saw one, and at least he had the good taste to put Francis behind the camera so that it didn't devolve into total sexploitation.

That said, *The Vampire Happening* doesn't come within light years of Polanski's vision, despite Mayne's presence. Advertised as "The Adult Vampire Sex Comedy," the film has a leering, juvenile tone that is nothing like Francis' usual work. One can only assume that, professional that he was, he gave the producer what he wanted.

So there you have it: a vampire sex comedy filmed in Germany by an Italian producer and a British director starring a Swedish actress. An international co-production of that type can only result in a mishmash, and *The Vampire Happening* is no exception. There's an occasional witty line or two, such as when Mayne's Dracula tells an associate, "Call me Christopher. I'm sure he won't mind," in reference to that era's reigning screen Dracula, Christopher Lee. But much of the humor in *The Vampire Happening* is, shall we say, lost in translation.

The film was not well-received, and Degermark divorced Caminnacci two years later. What happened afterwards is sadder still: She emigrated to America, then returned to her native Sweden a few years later, suffering from anorexia nervosa. Seriously ill, she gave up her acting career to found an organization to aid other anorexics. Eventually, she ran into trouble with the law, was accused of passing false checks, and was finally sent to Stockholm's state prison. The young actress who had been hailed as "the next Ingrid Bergman" had fallen from a great height to an even greater depth. The story behind the story is not always a pretty one.

Psychomania

One of the more obscure comedy-horror movies of the seventies, but one which has a small yet devoted cult of fans, Don Sharp's *Psychomania* (1971) stays with you over the years, despite—or perhaps because of—its low budget. Sharp cut his teeth (so to speak) on Hammer horrors in the sixties, helming some of their better Gothics such as *The Kiss of the Vampire* (1963) and *Rasputin the Mad Monk* (1965). Australian-born, Sharp dabbled in a number of different genres for other British companies, including action-adventure (*The Face of Fu Manchu*, 1965) and science fiction (*Curse of the Fly*, 1965); he even directed one of the first British rock 'n' roll movies, *The Golden Disc* (1958). This eclectic background came in very handy when he tackled *Psychomania*, a bizarre black comedy written by Julian Zimet (who wrote the screenplay for the 1965 sci-fi film *Crack in the World* under the name of Julian Halevy) and Arnaud d'Usseau, who later co-wrote the screenplay for the 1972 Spanish movie *Horror Express* with Zimet.

The plot is an outrageous combination of biker movie and supernatural horror film, while at the same time a parody of both. Tom Latham (Nicky Henson from Michael Reeves' classic *Witchfinder General*, 1968) is a member of a British motorcycle gang called The Living Dead. His mother (Beryl Reid, who had just appeared in Tigon's *The Beast in the Cellar*, 1971) and her rather odd butler (the great actor George Sanders in the twilight of his career) hold séances in their home, and Tom's deceased father is spoken of in hushed tones. Tom discovers that his father had made some sort of pact with the Devil, and Tom decides to carry on the family tradition by making his own deal with Satan (who may just be the butler) to return from the dead. During a police chase, Tom sails off a bridge on his motorcycle to his apparent death. But not so fast: When his friends gather at the grave site, an old stone circle called "The Seven Witches," singing a song called "Riding Free," Tom (who has been buried sitting on his bike) bursts out of his grave, alive and well.

Tom now realizes that death is not final at all; in fact, it's fun! Because you can only be killed once, you can commit the most heinous crimes and get away with them because you've become indestructible. Tom urges his biker pals to join him in death, and they are only too eager to do so, in various colorful ways. One jumps out of a plane without a parachute, another leaps into a river weighted down with chains. One biker climbs to the top of a building, getting the attention of a policeman down below. The policeman orders him to come down, to which the biker replies cheerily, "I'll be right down!" and leaps to his (temporary) death.

This brief synopsis gives only a hint of the taboos broken by *Psychomania*. If it hadn't been passed off as just another horror film in an era full of them, perhaps it would have caused more outrage. Or perhaps the very British black humor sailed over the heads of American audiences. Whatever the case, the film pokes fun at mass suicide, Satanism, biker violence and anarchy. In many ways, it predates the whole punk rock movement in England in its totally irreverent approach to serious topics. In one scene, the undead gang runs over a baby in a carriage just for fun; that's about as nasty as it gets. And the film was rated PG in America!

The performances are wonderfully droll and straight-faced, with Henson a standout as a biker who just wants to have as much undead fun as he can. When he first returns from the dead, he calls his mother from a pub to let her know that he's fine. "Well, apart from being dead, that is," he explains.

Reid and Sanders seem to be having quite a lot of fun, and the always excellent Robert Hardy (Hammer's *Vampire Circus*, 1971) is on hand as Chief Inspector Hesseltine to ground the whole thing in some kind of reality.

Make no mistake, *Psychomania* is in poor taste. But the nature of comedy-horror films is to break taboos, and *Psychomania* was released at a time when the flower power movement, with its message of peace and love, was at its cultural zenith. It was a movie that dared to laugh at violence, death and suicide, dared even to suggest that the afterlife could be a "gas." It's also a movie that deserves to be much better known than it is.

Sharp went on to direct such big-budget films as the 1978 remake of *The 39 Steps* and the Alastair MacLean film *Bear Island* (1979), but his work has never been more assured—nor more over the top—than it was on *Psychomania*. It is ripe for rediscovery.

The Abominable Dr. Phibes

By 1971, the fun-loving folks at American-International Pictures had pretty much exhausted the Edgar Allan Poe source material for their biggest star, Vincent Price. There was definitely a need for new blood. This arrived in the form of a screenplay by American writers James Whiton and William Goldstein called *The Abominable Dr. Phibes*. The story centered on Dr. Anton Phibes, a scientist, musician, doctor and Bible scholar. After a car crash in which his face is horribly burned and his wife Victoria receives serious injuries, Phibes seeks revenge on the nine doctors who tried but failed to save her. His vengeance takes the form of the ten plagues of Egypt: One doctor is stung to death by bees, another bitten to death by bats, another eaten by locusts and so on.

When AIP brought in Robert Fuest to direct the film, he rewrote most of the script, turning it into what is now considered a camp classic. As Price was often accused of over-the-top performances in some of the Poe films, Fuest felt that this time he would add more deliberate humor to the script. In the original screenplay, Phibes was more "abominable," abusing his assistant Vulnavia (Virginia North) and being generally very unpleasant. Fuest decided to make the character more sympathetic, despite the fact that he goes around killing people in nasty ways. The director also changed some of the murder scenes, including the death of Dr. Kitaj (Peter Gilmore), who is bitten to death by rats. The original script had him killed on a boat, but Fuest felt that he could have escaped just by jumping into the water. He decided to have him blown up in a rat-infested plane instead.

Fuest, who had cut his directorial teeth on the cult classic British television show *The Avengers* in the sixties, turned *The Abominable Dr. Phibes* into a stylish visual feast. The setting of the story in the thirties made it a natural for an art deco look, most effectively used in Dr. Phibes' mansion, where he performs at the organ with his "Clockwork Wizards," a band of automatons. He frequently dances in the ballroom with Vulnavia, a mysterious and coldly beautiful woman whose background is never explained. When he shares a toast with her, he pours the wine into a hole in the back of his throat, as he has no usable mouth. It's one of the film's best visual jokes, and the punchline is when he hiccups.

The outlandish plot combined with Fuest's flamboyant visual style made *Dr. Phibes* one of AIP's biggest hits. Falsely advertised as Vincent Price's 100th film, it was released in America on May 18, 1971, to better-than-average reviews and played the drive-in circuits for most of that summer.

Price, who never really took himself too seriously, apparently had a wonderful time making the movie. The makeup that he wore took hours to apply, and word has it that it had to be reapplied often because he kept laughing, which ruined it. Caroline Munro, later to become a fantasy icon in such films as *The Golden Voyage of Sinbad* (1973) and *The Spy Who Loved Me* (1977), was at that time a model turned actress who played the small but pivotal role of Phibes' dead wife Victoria. All she had to do was lie in a glass coffin; she told me in a 1984 radio interview that Price kept her entertained and well-fed, as he was a noted gourmet cook. "He brought me lots of quiche," Munro said, "and he kept me fat and happy."

Price was also a well-known collector of fine art, and there's an amusing in-joke in the film after he kills Dr. Longstreet (Terry-Thomas) by relieving him of his blood. Phibes happens to look up at the painting over Longstreet's head, a rather tasteless and poorly executed piece of art. He turns toward the camera and shakes his head disdainfully, then walks out of the shot.

The Abominable Dr. Phibes also benefits from an extremely fine supporting cast, including Joseph Cotten as one of the doctors. Originally, the venerable Peter Cushing had been slated for the role, but he had to bow out due to the illness of his wife, who died later that year. Cotten is excellent as the doctor whose son (Sean Bury) is abducted by Phibes, who hopes to fulfill the Biblical curse of "death of the first born" on the boy.

The police, who always seem to arrive a day late and a dollar short, are wonderfully played by Peter Jeffrey (as Inspector Trout), Derek Godfrey (Crow), Norman Jones (Sergeant Schenley) and John Cater (Waverly). The latter character is a self-important police chief who can never remember Trout's name, and calls him by various "fish" names—Pike, Breen, etc.—in a running joke throughout the film.

Dr. Phibes's victims also acquit themselves admirably: Susan Travers, David Hutcheson, Edward Burnham, Alex Scott, Peter Gilmore, Maurice Kaufmann and the aforementioned Terry-Thomas, who has a wonderful turn as a doctor who likes to watch stag movies in private. The only weak link in the cast is Bury as Lem Vesalius, whose voice is all too obviously dubbed. Speaking of voices, ubiquitous voice-over artist Paul Frees, who among other things voiced Boris Badenov in *Rocky and Bullwinkle* on American TV, sings the song "Darktown Strutter's Ball" in the rather amazing scene in which Dr. Hargreaves (Scott) has his head crushed by the mechanical frog mask that he's wearing at a fancy dress ball.

The most original death in the film, though, has to be the murder of Dr. Whitcombe (Kaufman), who is impaled on the horn of a brass unicorn head. An exasperated Waverly exclaims, "A brass unicorn head is catapulted across a London street and impales an eminent surgeon. Words fail me, gentlemen."

There are so many songs in *The Abominable Dr. Phibes* that the film almost qualifies as a musical. Many of the murders are accompanied by songs from the period, including "Charmaine," "You Stepped Out of a Dream," "Close Your Eyes" and "Elmer's Tune." And just to give the audience a final wink, "Over the Rainbow" is played over the end credits.

The Abominable Dr. Phibes remains one of Price's most entertaining films, and it succeeds both as horror and as comedy. It paved the way for an onslaught of comedy-horror films to come.

Dr. Phibes Rises Again

The financial success of *The Abominable Dr. Phibes* ensured that Price would return as the character, so AIP rushed a sequel into production. *Dr. Phibes Rises Again* benefited from a slightly higher budget than the first film, allowing for some location filming in Spain. The new screenplay was co-written by Robert Blees and Robert Fuest and had a distinctly Egyptian air about it. When Phibes awakens from his death-like sleep three years later, he finds that his house has been ransacked and his papyrus scrolls have been stolen. He needs these scrolls to find a pharaoh's tomb where the River of Life flows so that he can return his beloved wife Victoria to life. Phibes is pursued to Egypt by Inspectors Waverly and Trout (John Cater and Peter Jeffrey returning from the first film) and by Beiderbeck (Robert Quarry, who had just played the vampire Count Yorga in two AIP films). Beiderbeck wants to find the River of Life so that he can stay young forever (he's already several hundred years old) and preserve his lover Diana (Fiona Lewis, the buxom servant girl from *The Fearless Vampire Killers*).

The convoluted plot is at times confusing, not helped by some last-minute changes such as the return of Vulnavia, who had her face burned off by acid in the original film. The intention was to have Phibes' assistant in the sequel be a new character, but AIP wanted to retain the name of Vulnavia. It became even more of a continuity problem, since the actress who created the role, Virginia North, was now pregnant. Young actress Valli Kemp was cast in the role instead, and no explanation was given for her return from death; it could be said, though, that she wasn't quite herself.

Despite these discrepancies, however, the production team was much the same as before. Production designer Brian Eatwell returned to create more eye-popping art deco settings and John Gale contributed a fine original music score, this time including some classical pieces.

There are some especially amusing cameos, with Terry-Thomas returning in a new role as Lombardo, a stuffy shipping agent; Hugh Griffith, also in a new role, as Harry Ambrose, who ends up being stuffed into a gigantic gin bottle and thrown into the sea; and veteran character actress Beryl Reid as Harry's dotty old cousin.

Several Hammer veterans have good roles in the film. Gerald Sim and Lewis Fiander, who had just appeared together in Hammer's *Dr. Jekyll and Sister Hyde* (1971), play Phibes victims; Sim is sand-blasted to death and Fiander is crushed in his own bed. The venerable Peter Cushing has a brief role as a ship's captain, and Milton Reid, a heavy in such Hammer horrors as *The Terror of the Tongs* (1960) and *Night Creatures* (1962), has a memorable but dialogue-free role as Biederbeck's manservant, who is killed when a golden snake pierces his skull.

Other colorful deaths include a man clawed to death by an eagle and then eaten; a man stung to death by scorpions; and Beiderbeck aging like Dorian Gray in the matter of a few seconds after failing to find the River of Life. Some of the murders are a bit gruesome, especially in the British version, which features some scenes that are a few seconds longer than in the PG-rated American edition.

Despite the fact that a little more money was allocated to the production, there were some production problems. New lines of dialogue were given to Phibes to cover the fact that some scripted features were cut for budgetary reasons. Apparently, the original screenplay featured some set-pieces that were beyond AIP's reach, such as the Pyramid at the climax of the film, which was originally planned to consist of several levels filled with traps and then overrun with boiling oil. This too had to be altered for budgetary reasons. Add to this the fact that Price and Quarry didn't get along on the set (rumors were abounding that Quarry was to be AIP's new horror star, replacing Price) and you might have thought that *Dr. Phibes Rises Again* would be a disaster.

But the classy group of actors assembled assured audiences that they would get their money's worth. Price is as droll as he was in the first film, delivering lines such as, "So once more I have been forced to kill for you, Victoria. Only that you may live again, my noble wife," without a touch of irony. But his trademark humor is there, especially when he sits down to a fine fish dinner that Vulnavia has prepared. "I see that you have done wonders with the local fish," he says after stuffing some into the hole in his neck. Then he begins to choke, until finally he pulls a fishbone from his throat. The look that he gives Vulnavia is classic Price.

Waverly and Trout are on the verge of becoming a true comedy team in this edition, with exchanges such as this one:

> TROUT: I'm a bit apprehensive about finding the others, sir. Do you think you know where we are?
> WAVERLY: Trout, I don't think; I know.
> TROUT: I don't think you know either, sir.

Waverly gets the best line, though, after the discovery of a body that is completely mutilated, with only the head intact. Trout says, "What about Baker? Should we dispose of his body?"

Waverly replies, "I don't know about his body, but I think we should give his head a decent burial."

Quarry is very good as the obsessed, doomed Biederbeck, a sort of Flying Dutchman fated to wander the earth for eternity. As the object of his affections, Lewis — she of the bee-stung lips and deep cleavage — is a delight, especially when she tells Beiderbeck, "Don't worry, darling, it isn't the end of the world," as he ages to death before our eyes.

Everyone involved in *Dr. Phibes Rises Again* is more than up to the task. It's one of those rare sequels that's just as good as — if not a bit better than — the original film. Even Caroline

Munro returns as the dead Victoria, still looking quite content in her glass coffin. Must have been all those quiches Price prepared for her.

Dr. Phibes Rises Again was to have been the second film in a trilogy. The third film, which was proposed by original writer James Whiton, has alternately been titled *Phibes Resurrectus, The Brides of Dr. Phibes* or *The Seven Fates of Dr. Phibes*. It was never filmed under any title. AIP co-founder James H. Nicholson was soon to leave the company, handing it over to his partner, Samuel Z. Arkoff. The company moved away from Gothic comedy-horror films to produce blaxploitation movies and straight action films. An era was coming to an end.

Theater of Blood

Theater of Blood is considered by many critics to be one of Vincent Price's greatest performances in a horror movie, allowing the actor a tour-de-force as Shakespearean actor Edward Lionheart, who avenges himself by grotesquely murdering the critics who wronged him. He does this by re-enacting scenes from various Shakespeare plays; the first victim is stabbed to death on the Ides of March à la *Julius Caesar*, the second speared and dragged behind a horse à la *Troilus and Cressida* and so on.

Theater of Blood is a class act all the way. The cast is remarkable, virtually a "Who's Who" of distinguished British actors. The doomed critics are played by Harry Andrews (*Man of La Mancha, The Ruling Class*, many others), Coral Browne (*The Killing of Sister George* and soon to become Mrs. Vincent Price), Robert Coote (*Scaramouche*, many others), Jack Hawkins (*The Bridge on the River Kwai*), Ian Hendry (original star of *The Avengers*), Michael Hordern (*Anne of the Thousand Days*, many others), Arthur Lowe (*This Sporting Life*, many others), Robert Morley (*Oscar Wilde*, Hammer's *The Old Dark House*) and Dennis Price (*Kind Hearts and Coronets*, Hammer's *The Horror of Frankenstein*). There are also excellent supporting turns by Diana Dors, Milo O'Shea, Madeline Smith (Roger Moore's first Bond girl in *Live and Let Die*, 1973) and Diana Rigg as Lionheart's faithful daughter Edwina.

Theater of Blood is one of Price's goriest films, and one of its best conceits is pointing out the violence inherent in Shakespeare's plays. There's a heart torn out and weighed on a scale (Shylock's "pound of flesh" from *The Merchant of Venice*), a man drowned in a butt of wine (*Richard III*), a decapitation (*Cymbeline*), a man forced to eat his "babies" (actually poodles) as in *Titus Andronicus*, a man forced to murder his wife (*Othello*) and a woman electrocuted by hair curlers, à la Joan of Arc in *Henry VI Part 1*.

But in addition to all that blood, *Theater of Blood* is also one of Price's wittiest films. Gruesome though the murders may be, Price accomplishes them with a lot of style, portraying a different character for each killing. He gets to deliver a lot of Shakespeare's most famous speeches, including Marc Antony's eulogy from *Julius Caesar* ("Friends, Romans, countrymen...") and the "To be or not to be" monologue from *Hamlet*. The inside joke, of course, is that many critics over the years found Price to be a bit of a ham actor, especially in Roger Corman's Poe films. So, in a sense, Price was really getting his own revenge on the critics. Devastated that he doesn't win the Best Actor Award from the Critic's Circle, he berates them: "You deliberately humiliated me in front of my press, my public and my peers. It was the culmination of your determined denial of my genius! For thirty years the public has acknowledged that I am the master.... But you, with your overwhelming malice, give the award to a twitching, mumbling boy who can barely grunt his way through an incomprehensible performance!"

The original American poster for Douglas Hickox's *Theatre of Blood* (1974)(using the British spelling), featuring one of Vincent Price's best film performances.

The screenplay by Anthony Greville-Bell, based on an idea by Stanley Mann and John Kohn, is as clever as can be, and makes the most of the Price vs. Critics motif. Before he dispatches Larding (Coote), he admonishes, "So, this critic slept through my Richard, did he? No doubt because you supped too much, you drunken hog. You may know that in *Richard III*, Clarence—and I do want you to try out for that part, Larding—was drowned in a vat of wine!" As his assistants, all drunken tramps, dutifully drown Larding, Lionheart smiles and says, "Excellent, Larding. I'll make an actor of you yet!"

Douglas Hickox proved to be the perfect director for the project. Known for his wit and style, he had made his mark in such films as *Entertaining Mr. Sloane* (1968). He also knew how to keep stories moving at a cracking pace, never more in evidence than in *Theater of Blood*. He brought out the irony of the tale in such sequences as the infamous "poodle pie" scene in which effeminate critic Meredith Merridew (Morley) is forced to eat his poodles baked in a pie, just as Queen Tamora was fed the flesh of her children in *Titus Andronicus*. Merridew is thus "the old queen" from Shakespeare's text—sort of.

More gay humor is in evidence when Chloe Moon (Browne) comes to visit "Butch," her new hairdresser, actually Lionheart in an outrageous Afro wig. Lionheart looks at the police officer who has been sent to protect her and says, "Who's this great big beautiful thing with you? Is he yours?" She replies tiredly, "Only just."

As Lionheart adjusts the rollers in her hair, she notes that they're very odd-looking. "Naughty, naughty!" he says. "Don't touch. Butch knows best. They're something new from Gay Paree."

Later, Miss Moon tells him, "You know, Butch, I'm very uncomfortable." This is when Butch has a slight change in tone and starts quoting the Bard, a sure sign that the end is near: "'Bring forth that sorceress condemned to burn.' That's from Henry VI, ducky, Part 1. It's a very interesting play, don't you agree, Miss Moon? Particularly that scene where Joan of Arc gets burnt at the stake." At that point, Lionheart removes his disguise and his victim becomes, quite literally, toast.

There's also a lot of exciting action in *Theater of Blood*, such as the fencing scene between Lionheart and Devlin (Hendry), the closest character to a hero in this movie. They (or at least the stunt men) fight all the way through a gymnasium, even fencing while jumping on trampolines. There are also a couple of thrilling car chases and a fiery ending in which Lionheart's "Theater of Blood" burns down.

Diana Rigg has a wonderful time as Lionheart's beautiful but, shall we say, misguided daughter, appearing in several different disguises. Sometimes she appears as herself, usually to seduce one of the critics back to the theatre, but she also shows up as a policeman and a chef, actually a disguise within a disguise since she's already made up as a male hippie. She also seems to relish being included in several of the Shakespearean lines; Rigg is, after all, a Shakespearean herself, having appeared many times with the Royal Shakespeare Company throughout the world.

Everyone in the ensemble cast has their "turn" in their individual death scenes, and only Hendry's character survives to the end. Edwina ends up being accidentally killed by the drunken tramps, and Lionheart, insane with grief, sets fire to the theatre. "Burn! Burn!" he shouts. "Come, fire, consume this petty world. And in its ashes, let my memory lie!"

Lionheart carries Edwina's body to the roof and jumps just before the roof caves in. Devlin comments to Inspector Boot (Milo O'Shea), "He was overacting as usual, but he knew how to make an exit."

Originally titled *Much Ado About Murder*, *Theater of Blood* is a high mark in Vincent

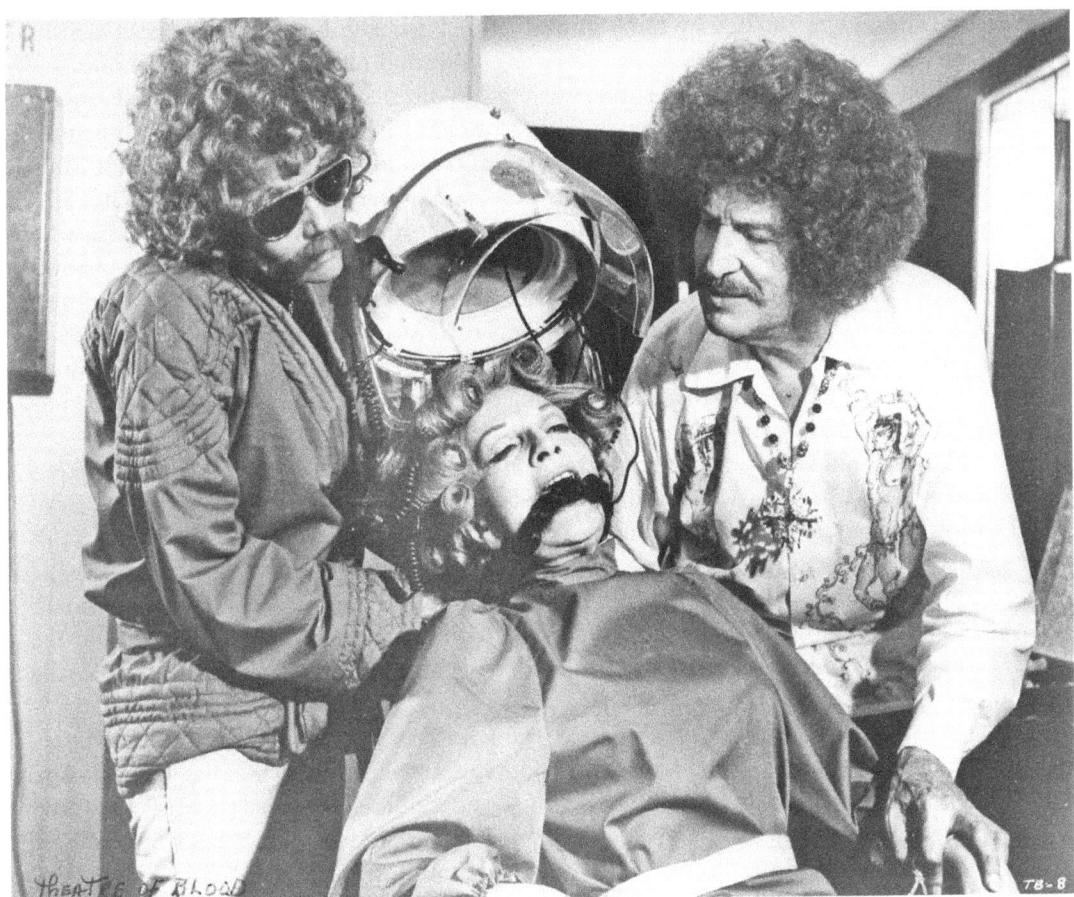

Diana Rigg (in male drag), Coral Browne and Vincent Price in Douglas Hickox's *Theater of Blood* (1973), a high-water mark in Price's career.

Price's film career. His performance is both intentionally over the top—as befits the character—and affecting. The remarkable thing about Price's Lionheart is that, by the end of the film, despite all the carnage he's wrought, we feel pity for him. He never really comes across as evil; he's just an actor who has been wounded one too many times by the critics, who feels that he's been wronged and this is the only way he can strike back. It's one of Price's best performances, not just in a horror film, but in any film.

Theater of Blood never strikes a false note, from the opening titles under which we see various murders from silent Shakespeare films, to the superb music by Michael J. Lewis to the excellent cinematography by Wolfgang Suschitzky. It's one of the finest, most literate, most intelligent comedy-horror movies ever made and it remains a triumphant example of its type to this day.

Flesh for Frankenstein

One of the most bizarre comedy-horror films ever made—indeed, one of the most bizarre films of any type ever made—is *Flesh for Frankenstein* (1973), known in the U.S. at the time of its theatrical release as *Andy Warhol's Frankenstein*. Originally filmed in a 3-D process called

Space Vision, it was rated X by the Motion Picture Association of America because of its extreme sex and violence. Then again, nearly every Warhol film suffered the same fate.

Although many people may assume the film was directed by Warhol, *Flesh for Frankenstein* was actually directed by Warhol's "house" director Paul Morrissey, who also helmed the Warhol-produced movies *Flesh* (1968), *Trash* (1970) and *Heat* (1972). The Warhol-Morrissey esthetic is well reflected in *Frankenstein*. Filmed in Italy at the famous Cinecitta Studios by a crew of Italian veterans—including assistant director Antonio Margheriti, who directed the Barbara Steele classic *Castle of Blood* (1964)—it's a lovingly photographed homage to Italian Gothic horror films, as well as to Hammer horror, while at the same time a parody of both. The irony inherent in the screenplay by Morrissey and Tonino Guerra (who, amazingly enough, also co-wrote Federico Fellini's *Amarcord*, 1974, and Michelangelo Antonioni's *Blow-Up*, 1966) gives the film a winking detachment, so that you find yourself convulsed with laughter during some of the goriest scenes ever filmed.

In its own unique way, *Flesh for Frankenstein* is also a political statement. Baron Frankenstein, played by Udo Kier, who had just starred in the notoriously violent *Mark of the Devil* (1970), is a degenerate aristocrat who has a Nazi-like vision of creating the perfect race of humans. These beings will, of course, obey his every command, or so he hopes.

Frankenstein has children by his own sister (Monique van Vooren), a creepy woman who has no love for the baron and instead dallies with her handyman (Warhol superstar Joe Dallesandro). Among other things, she enjoys having him suck her armpits ... rather noisily too.

There's very little one can say about *Flesh for Frankenstein* without veering off into tasteless territory. The film has something to say about the sexual perversions of the upper classes. Frankenstein, in addition to being a mad scientist who spouts all the usual clichés ("The medical profession would love to claim my achievement as part of their own..."), is what can only be referred to as an "intestinophile." In one of the most disgusting but perversely funny scenes ever filmed, he gets so excited bringing life to his beautiful female creation (Dalila Di Lazzaro) that he opens her stomach and has, shall we say, "relations" with her insides. "To know death, Otto," he says to his moronic assistant, "you must fuck life ... in the gall bladder." Words to live by?

Kier, who had already been knocking around European films for years, achieved a kind of cult stardom as Baron Frankenstein. Those who revere "seventies Eurotrash" consider him to be a kind of god. His intentionally flat, heavily accented delivery of lines such as, "Make him unconscious, but don't kill him, or damage his head in any way!" are just plain hilarious.

Almost as funny is Arno Juerging as Otto, a lab assistant so dim he makes Dwight Frye's Fritz in James Whale's *Frankenstein* look like Einstein by comparison. After witnessing his master's fondling of female intestines, he tries the same thing with the maid, with disastrous results. Indeed, people's stomachs are opened at an alarming rate in the film; Morrissey makes disembowelment look as easy as unzipping a pair of pants.

By the end of the film, when Baron Frankenstein delivers a lengthy monologue while his heart or liver or something equally revolting dangles at the end of a spear (having been impaled by Dallesandro), you almost feel as though you've spent amateur night at the butcher shop. There are more entrails per square foot in *Flesh for Frankenstein* than in all of George Romero's *Dead* films put together. The fact that the gore is all mixed up with perverted sex just makes the whole experience that much more unforgettable, especially in its original 3-D. It seems as though various fleshy and bloody organs are dangling right in front of your face.

Of course, Morrissey takes every opportunity to use the 3-D camera to its tackiest advantage. When Dallesandro dallies with a couple of overripe whores in a bordello, a lizard starts crawling on the three of them. Where the lizard came from is unclear, but Dallesandro picks it up and shoves it at the camera so we can get the full 3-D effect. Among the film's many parodic targets is the 3-D process itself, made bigger, bolder and stupider by Morrisey.

Flesh for Frankenstein was a big hit upon its release in 1974. Only in the seventies could such a politically incorrect, extremely distasteful, sexually bizarre film become a commercial success. They sure don't make them like this any more, which some people may feel is just as well.

In his essay for the Criterion Collection DVD release of *Flesh for Frankenstein*, Maurice Yacowar wrote: "As Alfred Hitchcock often demonstrated, in rather different tones, comedy and horror, laughter and fear, are closely related experiences. In few films are they yoked as exuberantly as in Paul Morrissey's *Flesh for Frankenstein*."

Blood for Dracula

But there was more outrage to come from the Warhol factory. Morrissey was in Italy to shoot not one, but two pictures. The filming of *Frankenstein* had gone more quickly and less expensively than expected, so the followup, *Blood for Dracula*, was rushed into production

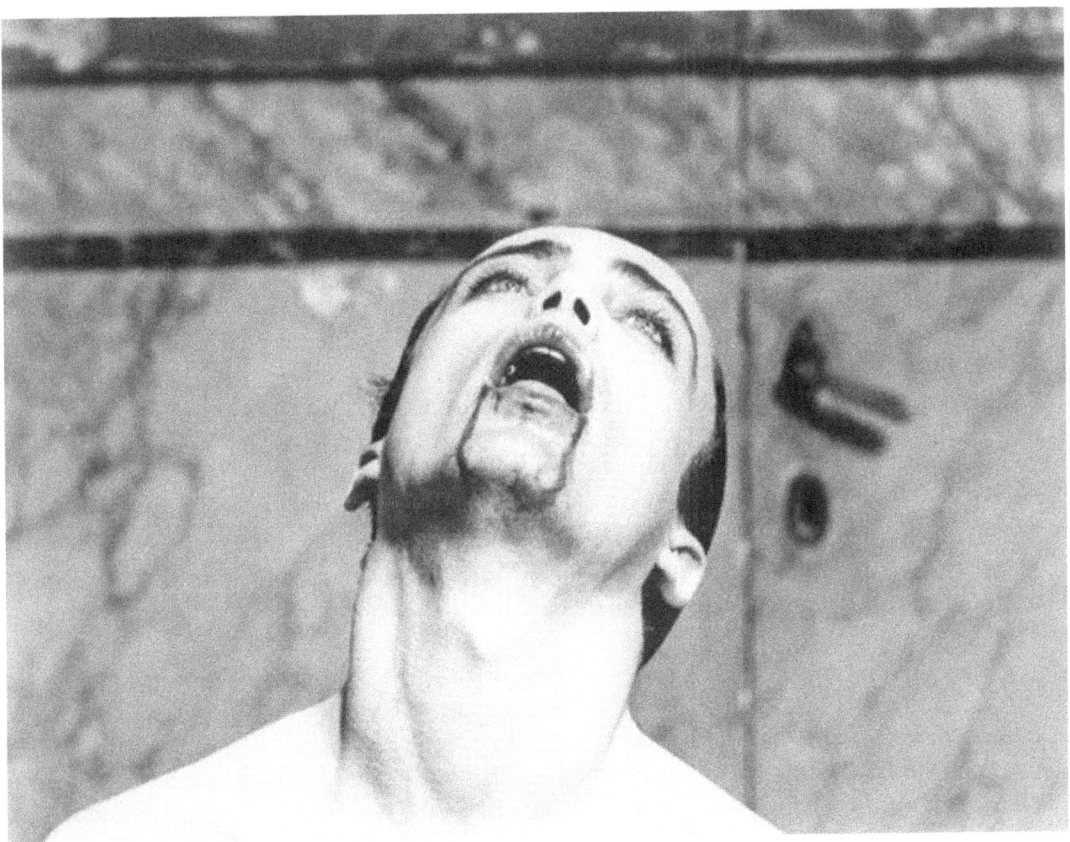

Udo Kier as Dracula has a bad reaction to "impure" blood in Paul Morrissey's outrageous *Blood for Dracula* (1974).

with the same crew and much of the same cast. The film is partly improvised, again on beautiful Italian locations, and in many respects is superior to *Frankenstein* in both style and subtext.

Udo Kier is the sickest Dracula ever seen, in more ways than one. It seems that Romania is running out of virgins, and, in Morrissey's vision, only virgin blood will keep Dracula alive. With his rather odd assistant Anton (Arno Juerging again) he travels to Italy, thinking that he is more likely to find virgins in a Catholic country. The unintentional irony, of course, is that Rumania is also a Catholic country in actual fact, but never mind that. It's safe to say that *Blood for Dracula* is not concerned with facts. It is concerned with ideas, however, and more than you might expect.

In Italy, the pale, pasty-looking count befriends impoverished aristocrat Marchese di Fiori (the great Italian film director Vittorio de Sica), who happens to have four daughters of marriageable age. Interested in marrying off his daughters to a wealthy landowner, he's more than happy to offer them to Dracula.

What neither di Fiore nor Dracula knows, however, is that two of his daughters have regular dalliances with Mario, (Joe Dallesandro), a hunky Marxist who's always spouting off about the evils of capitalism. The other two daughters are still virgins, but the eldest is considered to be too plain and the youngest is only fourteen.

Assured that all the daughters are virgins, Dracula dines on the necks of the two who are considered to be the best catches. Needless to say, the non-virginal blood doesn't work and Dracula becomes violently ill, vomiting blood into the camera over and over again. If *Dracula* had been filmed in 3-D as *Frankenstein* had, this scene may have been too disgusting to bear.

One of the sickest jokes in the movie comes about when Mario realizes that the only way he can save the youngest daughter from the clutches of the count is by deflowering her. He does so up against the murals on the wall of the beautiful but decaying old mansion in a scene that is both exquisitely photographed and repulsive, not to mention wildly politically incorrect.

At the film's climax, Mario takes his favorite handyman weapon, an axe, and chops off Dracula's arms and legs, after which he impales him. The aristocracy is symbolically destroyed by Marxism. One form of repression replaces another.

Blood for Dracula may have a lot of subtext, but it also has a lot of funny lines. Kier is every bit as droll as he was in *Frankenstein* and a lot more sickly looking. His face actually turns green after he drinks the blood of the "impure" daughters. "The blood of these whores is killing me!" he cries. There are times when you almost feel that Kier, the actor, might just keel over at any moment. It's really one of his best performances; you can't help but feel sorry for such a pathetic individual. Forget any idea you may have of Count Dracula being a commanding figure; this symbol of a dying aristocracy is a whimpering, emaciated wretch on the verge of total collapse.

Perhaps the most revolting scene in the movie concerns the rape of the youngest daughter. Her virginal blood spills onto the castle floor, and when she and Mario leave, Dracula crawls in to lap it up. Beyond the symbolism, it's a scene guaranteed to inspire revulsion.

"*Blood for Dracula* is not a film for the squeamish," wrote Maurice Yacowar upon the occasion of the Criterion DVD release. "It has obvious appeal for the lover of Grand Guignol—but it equally addresses the thoughtful." To which one might add: yes, but what a way to get the audience to think!

As in *Frankenstein*, Dallesandro comes across as a big dumb guy from the Bronx. It's hilarious to hear his deadpan delivery on such lines as, "That's the way it is with all that rich trash. They're sick and rotten. The only future's in socialism."

When one of the two daughters he services tells him that Dracula needs virgin blood (which Kier pronounces as "wirgin blood"), Mario replies, "Oh, well, you didn't tell me this. So what's he doin' with you two whores?" Dallesandro pronounces the word as "hoors." Obviously, there's a lot of wordplay going on here, not to mention a fair number of anachronisms.

Yacowar wrote, "Morrissey obviously has a lark with the vampire film conventions. He seems to be both in and outside the genre, utilizing it and satirizing it at the same time. So no explanation is given for why the Italian peasant Mario speaks New York colloquial; a modern character is simply forced onto the period. His Marxist clichés also satirize the political pretensions of the European art cinema."

Whatever the case, *Blood for Dracula* is the perfect companion piece to *Flesh for Frankenstein*. It's even more post-modern in its approach, as witness the casting of de Sica, a long way from directing *The Bicycle Thieves* (1948) here. His attempts at pronouncing the word "Dracula" in his heavy Italian accent are quite amusing. De Sica died less than a year after appearing in the film; it's too bad he didn't do more acting. He's really enjoyable to watch.

Equally fun is Roman Polanski's improvised cameo. He was directing his film *What?* on a soundstage nearby when he was asked to do a pub scene in *Dracula*, an entertaining bit of business in which he comes across as a sort of con man-card shark. Alert Polanski fans will note that he wears the same moustache in *What?* as he does in *Dracula*.

As with Morrissey's previous film, *Blood for Dracula* sounds indefensible on the face of it. Yet for all of its outrageous excesses, Morrissey is attempting to point out that humanity's collective lust spoils everything. We end up feeling sorry for the count and disliking Mario. As Yacowar put it, "In front of his hammer and sickle, Mario brutalizes his women. When he supplants di Fiore and dispatches Dracula, Mario represents not the triumph of the people but the replacement of one tyranny with another, less dignified."

It's easy to get lofty about Morrissey's artistic pretensions. But the simple fact is, both his *Frankenstein* and *Dracula* gross us out and make us laugh at the same time, the way a child might do at the dinner table when he opens his mouth and shows you what he's eating. It may not be high art, but it makes us giggle in spite of ourselves. If making comedy-horror films is, in some respects, about breaking taboos, then Morrissey may just be the master of the sick joke. It's comedy-horror at its most visceral. Morrissey must have been one of those kids who liked to show his friends road kill because it was "funny." We don't want to laugh, we don't even want to smile at such things—but we can't help it. God save us all.

Young Frankenstein

What can be said about Mel Brooks' *Young Frankenstein* that hasn't been said before? It's virtually guaranteed to make you smile, if not laugh out loud, at every scene. The performers are obviously having such a good time that it's infectiously transferred to the audience. In fact, it's rumored that they were having so much fun on the set that additional scenes were shot so they could put off having to wrap the production.

Whatever the case, *Young Frankenstein* is a bona fide classic. After Brooks' western movie parody *Blazing Saddles* became a smash hit in early 1974, audiences wondered what the comedy genius would do next. When he announced that his next film would be an affectionate

Marty Feldman is Igor ("Pronounced Eye-Gor") in Mel Brooks's masterpiece *Young Frankenstein* (1974).

parody of the old Universal monster movies, a lot of people scratched their heads. And when he further announced that it would be filmed in black and white, studio executives got a bit nervous. It turned out they had no reason to be. Brooks knew exactly what he was doing.

That should have come as no surprise to anyone who knew him. Brooks, who was born Melvin Kaminsky in Brooklyn, had started out in show business as a stand-up comic in the Catskills, and in the fifties became a comedy television writer for *Your Show of Shows*, along with Sid Caesar and Carl Reiner. In the early sixties, he performed on a series of comedy records as "The 2,000-Year-Old Man" along with Reiner. In 1965, with Buck Henry, he created the hit TV series *Get Smart*, starring Don Adams as bumbling secret agent Maxwell Smart.

His first feature film, *The Producers*, was not well received by critics upon its initial release in 1968. The black comedy about two theatrical business partners (Gene Wilder and Zero Mostel) who conspire to create the worst conceivable Broadway show so they can use it as a tax write-off, was considered to be utterly tasteless—especially the theme song of the show, "Springtime for Hitler." Nevertheless, the film became a hit on college campuses and received an Oscar for Best Original Screenplay.

Brooks liked Wilder's performance so much that he cast him again in *Blazing Saddles*. And here's the interesting little secret about *Young Frankenstein*: It's as much his film as Brooks'. Wilder, in fact, wrote the original screenplay himself before Brooks took on the task of directing it. When Brooks came on board, he rewrote much of the script, but the entire concept remained. Wilder reveals in a documentary that was made for *Young Frankenstein's* DVD release that he had to fight Brooks for what turned out to be one of the movie's signature scenes, the "Puttin' on the Ritz" routine. Originally, Brooks thought it would be too silly, but Wilder was so passionate in his defense of it that Brooks finally agreed it should stay in. The rest, as they say, is history.

Wilder essayed the title role of the original Dr. Frankenstein's grandson, Frederick Frankenstein. ("It's pronounced Fronkensteen.") The other actors assembled for *Young Frankenstein* couldn't have been bettered. British comic actor Marty Feldman, who had appeared on American television on *The Dean Martin Show* and his own short-lived series *Marty Feldman's Comedy Machine*, turned out to be a brilliant choice for Igor ("It's pronounced Eye-gor"), the inevitable hunchbacked lab assistant. With his bug-eyes (actually the result of a thyroid condition called Grave's Disease) and impeccable comic timing, Feldman is one of the greatest delights of the film.

Madeline Kahn had just made a huge impression in *Blazing Saddles* as a dance hall girl à la Marlene Dietrich in *Destry Rides Again* (1939). Just prior to that, she had been nominated for a Best Supporting Actress Oscar for her performance in *Paper Moon*. In *Young Frankenstein*, she was cast as Elizabeth, Frankenstein's fiancée, and became one of the few characters from Mary Shelley's original novel to be included in the film—albeit a very different Elizabeth from the one Shelley created. For one thing, she doesn't want Frankenstein to embrace her at the railway station because her taffeta dress "wrinkles so easily," she says coldly.

Cloris Leachman (Frau Blucher in the film) had made her feature film debut in Robert Aldrich's classic film noir movie *Kiss Me Deadly* (1955) and had done a lot of notable television work, including appearing in the classic *Twilight Zone* episode "It's a Good Life" (1962). Her portrayal in *Young Frankenstein* (offscreen horses whinny every time her name is mentioned) was such a hit that she quickly became a member of Brooks' unofficial stock company.

Teri Garr had been bouncing around Hollywood for about ten years before *Young Frankenstein* shot her to stardom. Her film debut had been as an extra in *A Swingin' Affair* (1963) and she appeared in several Elvis Presley movies as an uncredited background dancer. She also had a small but significant role in the psychedelic movie *Head* (1968), starring The Monkees. Her comedic timing in *Young Frankenstein* is every bit as good as that of her older co-stars. Who could ever forget the introduction of her character, Inga, when she asks

Frankenstein if he would like a roll in the hay? Frankenstein raises his eyebrow and makes a stuttering sound, whereupon Inga smiles and says, "It's fun!" and then proceeds to literally roll in the hay. "Roll, roll, roll in zee hay!" she sings in her ersatz German accent.

Peter Boyle, the Monster, had starred opposite a very young Susan Sarandon in the controversial 1970 film *Joe*, in which he had played a bigoted (and ultimately violent) New York City blue-collar worker. His impressive height was one of the reasons he was cast as the Monster, but it turned out that he was also very, very funny. All one needs to do is view the "Puttin' on the Ritz" scene to see that this excellent dramatic actor is also a gifted comedic performer, who of course went on to win an Emmy or two for his comedy work on TV's *Everybody Loves Raymond*.

Speaking of "serious" actors doing comedy, one of the funniest scenes in *Young Frankenstein* is the one in which the Monster comes to the cottage of an old blind man, who is played by Gene Hackman. Hackman had previously won a Best Actor Oscar for his unforgettable portrayal of cop Popeye Doyle in *The French Connection* (1971) and perhaps wouldn't have been the first person one might have thought of to play a cameo in a movie parody. But apparently Brooks knew something the rest of us didn't about Hackman's comic abilities, because the scene between him and Boyle is a gem. Based directly on the similar scene in *Bride of Frankenstein* (1935) featuring Boris Karloff and character actor O.P. Heggie, it's a delight from start (when the blind man realizes that the Monster is "an incredibly big mute") to finish (when he lights the Monster's thumb on fire, thinking it's a cigar).

Kenneth Mars, who had appeared in *The Producers* as the Nazi playwright, was cast as Inspector Kemp, a character similar to Lionel Atwill's in *Son of Frankenstein* (1939). As in *Son*, the inspector has a wooden arm, which in this case is ultimately used as a battering ram by the villagers when they storm the castle. The scene in which he plays darts with Frankenstein is a pitch-perfect parody of a nearly identical scene in *Son* in which Atwill plays darts with Basil Rathbone.

What makes this film such an affectionate homage to its source material is the fact that Brooks went to the trouble of recreating the monochrome look of the old Universal horrors, right down to the usage of Kenneth Strickfaden's actual lab equipment from the original *Frankenstein*. Brooks also employed old-styled opening credits and scene transitions that would have been at home in early thirties films, such as wipes, irises and numerous fades to black. The photography by Gerald Hirschfeld also evokes the period, as does the musical score by Brooks' favorite composer, John Morris.

It's this type of attention to detail that makes *Young Frankenstein* soar above most other horror parodies. While some parody filmmakers deride their source material, Brooks and Wilder obviously love it. They've seen the films they're parodying hundreds of times and know their every nuance. Ultimately, *Young Frankenstein* is a movie for film buffs, but written, directed and performed in such a way that average Joes and Josephines can enjoy it just as much for its outrageous and wacky humor.

Everyone has a favorite line from *Young Frankenstein*, whether it's "What knockers!" (delivered by Wilder) or "Say it! He vas my *boyfriend*!" (delivered by Leachman). And everyone has a favorite sight gag, whether it's Igor's constantly shifting hump (ad-libbed by Feldman) or the ravishing of Elizabeth by the Monster (he has an "enormous schwanzstucker" which transforms her into a sex-crazed "bride of Frankenstein"). It's safe to say that just about everyone loves *Young Frankenstein*, which in 2003 was selected for preservation by the Library of Congress National Film Registry and was remolded into a successful Broadway musical, also produced by Brooks.

The movie is best described with a word that is rarely used in conjunction with any type of film, much less a comedy-horror film. But *Young Frankenstein* is about as close to perfect as a comedy-horror film gets. Simply put, it's a masterpiece.

The Rocky Horror Picture Show

"I would like, if I may, to take you on a strange journey," says The Criminologist (Charles Gray) early in the proceedings of *The Rocky Horror Picture Show* (1975). He isn't kidding. A movie that could only have been made in the spaced-out seventies, *The Rocky Horror Picture Show* went from being a flop to a phenomenon thanks to special "Midnight Movie" showings.

The film was based on *The Rocky Horror Show*, a stage musical that opened in London on June 19, 1973. Written by Richard O'Brien, an Englishman who had grown up in New Zealand, the musical (originally titled *They Came from Denton High*) was developed by O'Brien with the help of Australian theatre director Jim Sharman. It became a sensation almost immediately. In the feature-length documentary *Midnight Movies: From Margin to Mainstream* (2005), O'Brien recalled that on opening night, there was a thunderstorm and a flash of lightning revealed that Vincent Price was sitting in the audience. "Talk about a good omen!" O'Brien enthused.

Actress Britt Ekland, a fan of the production, was instrumental in bringing the show to the attention of Hollywood producers, and 20th Century-Fox put the film version into production on October 21, 1974. Many of the people who made the stage show a success were brought onto the film, including director Sharman, production designer Brian Thomson and costume designer Sue Blane. Young actor-singer-dancer Tim Curry reprised his role of Dr. Frank N. Furter, O'Brien returned as Riff Raff, the role he created, and Little Nell (aka Nell Campbell) came back as groupie Columbia, with Patricia Quinn returning as Riff Raff's sister, Magenta.

The story is an insane combination of horror–sci-fi parody and bisexuality, inspired by both Hammer horror films and "Glam Rock" that was popularized in the early seventies by performers such as David Bowie, whose ambiguous sexuality and over-the-top costumes flaunted convention like a slap in the face. In the film, as in the stage show, newly engaged young couple Brad (Barry Bostwick) and Janet (Susan Sarandon) have a flat tire on a rainy night and take shelter at a nearby manor house. The place just happens to be "peopled" by bizarre Transylvanians, who quickly show the couple how to do "The Time Warp," the best-remembered song from the movie.

But Brad and Janet end up learning much more when Dr. Frank N. Furter appears. The self-described "sweet transvestite from Transsexual, Transylvania" has discovered "the secret to life itself." This turns out to be his hunky creation Rocky (Peter Hinwood), whom he brings to life in classic Frankenstein fashion. As Frank chases his newly minted man all over the mansion, biker Eddie (Meat Loaf) bursts onto the scene, motorcycle and all. In one of the few gory moments in the film, Eddie is killed by Frank, but all the guests seem to take it in stride.

Brad and Janet are shown to their separate bedrooms, and Frank sneaks into both rooms to seduce each one (using identical dialogue). Janet, feeling a bit guilty, wanders off looking for Brad but instead runs into Rocky. After she discovers that Brad has been just as unfaithful as she has, she decides to throw caution to the wind and seduce Rocky.

Meanwhile, Brad and Janet's old high school science teacher Dr. Everett Scott (Jonathan

Adams) has come to the mansion looking for his nephew Eddie. All the guests are invited for dinner, but after dining, they discover that what they've been eating is actually Eddie, whose remains are lying underneath the table. Understandably, they run away in horror and Frank captures them, somehow turning them into statues and then ordering them to perform in—horrors!—a cabaret show. But Riff Raff and Magenta suddenly appear in their true forms, as aliens from the planet Transsexual, in the galaxy of Transylvania. They dispose of Frank, Rocky and Columbia but let the Earthlings go. And the mansion, apparently a disguised starship, takes off into space.

Obviously, the story is daft by any definition, but after such films as *Flesh for Frankenstein* and *Blood for Dracula*, perhaps it didn't seem all that strange to audiences of the seventies. Many things about it hark back to a kinder, gentler and perhaps less sexually confused time.

For example, the film's opening song, "Science Fiction Double Feature," references a number of classic sci-fi and horror films, including *The Day the Earth Stood Still* (1951), *Flash Gordon* (1936), *The Invisible Man* (1933), *It Came from Outer Space* (1953), *Doctor X* (1932), *Forbidden Planet* (1956), *Tarantula* (1955), *The Day of the Triffids* (1962), *Night of the Demon* (aka *Curse of the Demon*, 1957) and *When Worlds Collide* (1951).

The look of the movie also recalls many of the old Hammer films, as it was filmed at Bray Studios in Berkshire, England, the home of Hammer for most of the company's reign. Adjacent Oakley Court, which was seen in such Hammer classics as *The Brides of Dracula* (1960) and *The Reptile* (1965), was used as Dr. Frank N. Furter's "castle." Although IMDB.com claims that the tank and bandaged dummy used in the film's creation scene are from Hammer's *The Revenge of Frankenstein* (1958), to this trained eye, they look much more like the props from Hammer's seminal *The Curse of Frankenstein* (1957).

In any case, the location and props used do give the film a sort of Hammer horror "look." The casting of Gray as the film's narrator also reminds one of Hammer, as he was their villain in Terence Fisher's masterly *The Devil Rides Out* (1967).

Neither Bray Studios nor Oakley Court were in very good condition by this time, and with filming taking place during an English autumn and winter, some of the actors became very uncomfortable indeed. Sarandon, who along with Bostwick was cast by Fox because they wanted two American stars, came down with pneumonia after shooting the pool scene from the end of the film. The fact that she spent most of the filming in her underwear certainly didn't help.

The Rocky Horror Picture Show wrapped production on December 19, 1974. There were a number of concepts that had been dropped during production, including usage of clips in the opening song from the various films mentioned (rights to the clips were deemed too costly) and the idea to do an homage to *The Wizard of Oz* (1939) by shooting the first twenty minutes of the film in black and white and then switching to color when "The Time Warp" gets underway. Unfortunately, the B&W and color processes (not to mention the widescreen and "normal" film ratios) didn't match, and again it would have been expensive and difficult to pull off.

After a few post-production problems, including the fact that Hinwood couldn't sing and had to be dubbed by Trevor White, the film was released on September 26, 1975, at the UA Theatre in Westwood, California. It did fairly well at that venue but bombed everywhere else. It wasn't well received by critics or audiences at the time and was pulled from circulation quickly.

But *The Rocky Horror Picture Show*, like a Hammer vampire, wouldn't die. Although it was withdrawn from its eight opening engagements due to lack of attendance and its planned Halloween opening in New York City was cancelled, Fox re-released it on college campuses a few months later on a double bill with Brian De Palma's *Phantom of the Paradise* (1974), another film that had failed to engage mainstream audiences. But the double feature didn't perform much better than either picture had done on its own.

The popularity of "midnight movies" such as Alejandro Jodorowsky's *El Topo* (1970) and John Waters' *Pink Flamingos* (1972) inspired Fox to issue it as a midnight movie. It opened at midnight on April Fool's Day, 1976, in New York City. Word of mouth began to build, and by Halloween, the phenomenon of "audience participation" was in full swing: People were dressing in costumes based on those in the movie and they were shouting lines from the film at the screen.

Thus began *Rocky Horror*'s second life. By the middle of 1978, it was playing in over fifty theaters nationwide on Friday and Saturday midnight screenings. Across the country, fans began to gather at conventions, local performance groups were formed and, improbably, *The Rocky Horror Picture Show* became a belated sensation.

"A different set of Jaws," shouted the newly created poster art for the film, highlighting the close-up of the red lips that open the movie. What is it that made *Rocky Horror* the biggest midnight movie of all time? In a word, it was the seventies, a decade that consolidated the social, and more specifically, sexual changes of the sixties. Rock stars such as David Bowie, Mick Jagger and Elton John were rumored to be bisexual. Actress Maria Schneider, who co-starred in *Last Tango in Paris* (1972) with Marlon Brando, admitted to the press that she liked women sexually as well as men. It was a time of free-thinking hedonism and rampant sexual experimentation.

It's safe to say that *The Rocky Horror Picture Show* could never have been made, let alone released, ten years earlier. Even in 1975, it failed to achieve mainstream acceptance. But it appealed to a core audience of people who were, perhaps, not the most popular at school or the most sexually experienced. It appealed to young audiences on the verge of adulthood who were open to new ideas about gender, music and sexual mores. In short, it appealed to "outsiders."

It's easy to see why. Brad and Janet represent the children of the Eisenhower era, straight-laced, puritanical types who don't believe in sex before marriage. When they're introduced to Frank, all of that changes. Frank is the sixties and seventies, male and female, all rolled into one. He is the harbinger of dangerous ideas, of a new sexual freedom that can only destroy the safe, white-bread way of living represented by the fifties. He is carnal lust personified. "Give yourself over to absolute pleasure," he tells both of them. "Don't dream it, be it."

A first viewing of *The Rocky Horror Picture Show* tends to be a bit overwhelming in its strangeness: you get the impression that the only thing the movie has to say is that it's really fun to dress up in garters and fishnet stockings. But there's a subtext that makes it worth more than one viewing, albeit perhaps not the hundred-odd screenings some of its more fervent fans have attended.

There's a certain sadness to the film. When Riff Raff and Magenta show up at the climax to end Frank's fun, they're really the morals police arriving on the scene. "It's not easy having a good time!" Frank says at one point. Dr. Scott puts it another way: "You saw what became of Eddie. Society must be protected." So the result of having too much "fun" is death, according to mainstream society.

When Brad and Janet are seduced by Frank into his "extreme" lifestyle, all of their pent-up fifties frustrations are let loose. Janet, looking fetching in her white bra, loses her inhibitions as she sings to Rocky about her wish "to be dirty!"

Rocky Horror gathers up all of society's "outsiders" in one fell swoop: Horror fans, geeks, nerds, transvestites, gays and bisexuals all jump into the pool at the end. Janet kisses Columbia, Brad kisses Frank, and they seem to live in total bliss ... until those in charge of society's morals arrive to end their Woodstock moment.

When Riff Raff kills them, Magenta cries, "But I thought you liked them. They liked you!"

"They didn't like me! They never liked me!" screams the uptight Riff Raff. He has destroyed the "evil," and restored society to its "normal" state. And it may just be because he was jealous of all the fun they were having.

Attempting to get any of this from The *Rocky Horror Picture Show* at a midnight screening is futile. The audience is too busy throwing rice at the screen, dancing around in costume and yelling out all the lines. To really understand the film, it's best to watch it in the privacy of your own home. Once you get past the over-the-top performances, the bizarre costumes and the seventies rock songs (some of which are very good), you'll find that there is a wistful, bittersweet tale behind it all. Oscar material? No. A time capsule of what it was like to be on the fringe of "normality" in the seventies? Absolutely.

The *Rocky Horror Picture Show* still plays in theaters over thirty years after its release. It's made more than $140 million in that time. It's the longest-running film of all time thanks to those fans, once outcasts, who are now part of the mainstream.

Murder by Death

Although *Murder by Death* (1976) is usually referred to as a spoof of mystery movies, it also qualifies as a comedy-horror film because of its old dark house atmosphere and its surreal ending. The tagline for the movie was: "By the time the world's greatest detectives figure out whodunit.... You could die laughing!"

The screenplay was certainly a departure for Neil Simon, famous for such Broadway hits as *The Odd Couple*. Instead of relying on reality-based humor, his script plays more like an extended Monty Python sketch, complete with shameless puns and non sequiturs. The cast was a virtual "who's who" of great British and American actors of the time, not all of whom specialized in comedy. Just to make things even weirder, famous *In Cold Blood* author Truman Capote was cast as millionaire Lionel Twain, who of course lists his address as "Two Two Twain."

The plot is a parody of any number of Agatha Christie mysteries, with a special kinship to *And Then There Were None*. But Christie never wrote such eccentric characters as Twain, who has a blind butler (Alec Guinness) and a deaf cook (Nancy Walker), making communication between the two of them virtually impossible. Twain has invited "the world's greatest detectives," all of whom are pastiches of famous literary models, to come to his mansion and attempt to solve a murder that will happen at midnight. One million dollars will be paid to the sleuth who solves the crime. And what sleuths they are.

Inspector Sidney Wang (Peter Sellers) is based on Charlie Chan, and constantly murders the English language with his faulty grammar and syntax. He travels with an adopted Japanese son named Willie (Richard Narita). Dick and Dora Charleston (David Niven and Maggie Smith) are urbane upper-class Brits obviously modeled after Nick and Nora Charles, the *Thin Man* couple. Milo Perrier (James Coco), based on Christie's Belgian detective Hercule Poirot, arrives at the mansion accompanied by his chauffeur Marcel (James Cromwell, in his first film role). Sam Diamond is there to represent the American contingent, a hard-boiled gumshoe played to perfection (and with a Humphrey Bogart–like accent) by Peter Falk. With him is his secretary Tess Skeffington (Eileen Brennan). And finally, Christie's Miss Marple is skewered as Jessica Marbles, played all in tweed by Elsa Lanchester, accompanied by her wheelchair-bound and very ancient "nurse," Miss Withers (Estelle Winwood in her final film role).

It's an odd cast of characters indeed, and as played by such wonderful performers, a great deal of fun. As directed by Robert Moore, it moves along with high energy to its improbable — and baffling — conclusion. There are some delicious touches along the way, such as the caricatures of the actors (beneath the opening credits) drawn by Charles Addams. Alert viewers will note that the scream used as the sound of the doorbell on Twain's house is actually Fay Wray's scream from the 1933 *King Kong*.

The film went through a number of changes during shooting, and Simon was on the set to do whatever rewrites were deemed necessary. Orson Welles had originally been considered for the role of Sidney Wang, but was unable to accept the part due to a previous commitment. Myrna Loy had been offered the role of Dora Charleston, a parody of the character she played in the *Thin Man* movies, but declined, claiming that she would have just been parodying herself, so what would be the point?

Katharine Hepburn was originally asked to play a character called Dame Abigail Christian, but left the project after finding out that Loy had dropped out. The character was eventually re-written to become the part that Winwood played, Nurse Withers, and Lanchester's Jessie Marbles was added as the Christie homage.

Murder by Death never makes a great deal of sense, especially toward the end when the "mystery" spirals completely out of control. After near-deaths by such methods as snake, scorpion, poison gas and bombs, all the detectives come up with their own ideas on who murdered Twain, the first victim. The butler, another victim, turns out to be alive, but then rips off his "butler" mask to reveal that he is actually Twain. All of the detectives were wrong; it seems as though there was no murder at all. When his adopted son asks him if there was indeed a murder, Wang replies: "Yes; killed good weekend."

The final twist is revealed after all the guests have left. "Twain" pulls off "his" second mask to reveal that "he" is none other than Yetta, the deaf cook. She laughs maniacally.

It's impossible to figure out what has or hasn't happened at the end of *Murder by Death*, but it has been an awful lot of fun to watch such seasoned actors delivering such silly one-liners. Twain admonishes Wang to "say your goddamn pronouns," while Wang has some of the best lines, such as "Room filled with empty people," and "Observe strange sounds."

But it's Twain who sums up the movie when all is said and done, speaking to the literary detectives grouped around him: "You've tricked and fooled your readers for years. You've tortured us all with surprise endings that make no sense. You've introduced characters in the last five pages that were never in the book before. You've withheld clues and information that made it impossible for us to guess who did it. But now, the tables are turned. Millions of angry mystery readers are getting their revenge."

The point of the film? You can't solve a murder when you're not even sure if there was one, not even if you're a great "literary detective." Silliness reigns, and the mystery is turned upside down.

Sellers, never a really good judge of his own films, was convinced that *Murder by Death* was going to be a critical and commercial disaster. He got the producers to buy back his percentage share of the movie's profits. Then the film went on to garner an enthusiastic response at the 1976 Venice Film Festival and became a box office hit, as well as receiving a fair amount of critical acclaim. It even spawned a sequel of sorts, *The Cheap Detective* (1978), with Falk reprising his role of Sam Diamond. And Sellers, by his own actions, received none of the profits.

Attack of the Killer Tomatoes!

A movie with one of the most memorable titles of all time, *Attack of the Killer Tomatoes!* (1978) is a hit-and-miss, low-budget (under $100,000) takeoff on such fifties B-movies as *Attack of the Giant Leeches* (1959) and *Beginning of the End* (1957). Instead of giant worms or bugs, immense tomatoes are running rampant through the countryside, spreading terror. There seems to be no particular reason for this sudden vegetable mutation, except for the fact that they're rebelling against humankind in much the same fashion as our avian friends in Alfred Hitchcock's *The Birds* (1963). In fact, the film opens with titles announcing that "people laughed" at Hitchcock's film, and implies that no one will laugh at killer tomatoes.

Well, mainstream critics didn't find the film very funny, but they may have been missing the point. *Attack of the Killer Tomatoes!* is in reality a very clever parody of fifties monster movie clichés. Written by John De Bello, Costa Dillon (as C.J. Dillon) and J. Stephen Peace (as Steve Peace), it was directed by De Bello in deadpan fashion. An audience unused to such parodies may be unsure of where to laugh, but it's safe to say that not one moment of the film is intended to be serious. With a pre-credit sequence involving a large tomato rising up out of a woman's garbage disposal and backing her into a corner (much in the style of the fifties B-movies in which cowering victims scream into the camera), it's hard to imagine anyone finding this movie to be "unintentionally" funny. But some people apparently did, at least initially.

De Bello and company were actually experimenting with the same sort of aesthetic that Corman had perfected with his trilogy *A Bucket of Blood*, *Little Shop of Horrors*, and *Creature from the Haunted Sea*. Instead of aspiring to make a large-scale film on a minuscule budget, both Corman and De Bello made the conscious decision to celebrate their low budgets by using intentionally silly special effects (the ping-pong ball eyes of the *Creature from the Haunted Sea* monster, for example) and absurd storylines punctuated with non sequiturs and "campy" acting styles.

De Bello's actors are all unknowns. Credited as Rock Peace, co-writer Peace has the pivotal role of Wilbur Finletter, a government agent under the command of Mason Dixon (David Miller), who is determined to defeat the tomato rebellion. The team also includes Sam Smith (Gary Smith), an African-American agent who is a master of disguise; Greg Colburn (Steve Cates), a Navy scuba diver; and Gretta Attenbaum (Benita Barton), a Russian Olympic swimmer.

Smith is assigned to infiltrate the tomatoes, but he makes a lousy undercover agent: He blows his cover when he asks one of the tomatoes to "pass the ketchup." A breakthrough occurs, however, when the song "Puberty Love" happens to play on the car radio at the moment that Dixon is being surrounded by huge tomatoes. The fearsome fruits roll away, terrified by the insipid pop song warbled by "Ronny Desmond."

The tomato revolt has actually been engineered by the president's press secretary Jim Richardson (George Wilson). Dixon is kidnapped by Richardson, but manages to escape, bearing with him a vinyl copy of "Puberty Love." The tomatoes are somehow corralled into a stadium where the ghastly song is played over loudspeakers. The violent vegetables shrink down to normal size and the stadium-goers squash them under their shoes. But our heroine, Lois Fairchild (Sharon Taylor), is cornered by an extremely clever tomato wearing earmuffs (actually very large toilet seat covers). Dixon arrives in the nick of time and shows the tomato the music and lyric sheet to "Puberty Love" that he carries with him. Apparently the tomato can read music and is destroyed. Then Dixon sings a love song to Fairchild, and it seems as though we have our happy ending at last.

But wait: In true B-movie fashion, there is more to come. The last shot of the film features a carrot rising from the ground and saying to its fellow carrots: "All right, you guys, they're gone now." A carrot revolt has begun.

Attack of the Killer Tomatoes! is a movie that sets out to be as outrageous as possible. Some gags work and some don't, but De Bello and company succeed in creating some truly surreal moments in spite of, or because of, the film's low budget. The scene in which the military and the scientists meet for the first time is both a raucous take-off on any fifties sci-fi movie you care to name and a nod to the famous "stateroom scene" in the Marx Brothers' *A Night at the Opera* (1935). The meeting room is so tiny and cramped that even the more elderly generals are forced to crawl over the table (which takes up all but a few inches of the room) to get to their seats. Meanwhile, a Japanese scientist (Paul Ova) babbles incoherently in a dubbed-in voice that doesn't match his lip movements, à la *Godzilla*. Some of the dialogue is of the politically incorrect kind, such as when the scientist, whose command of English is not perfect, deadpans, "Technically, sir, tomatoes are fags." An American doctor corrects him by saying, "He means fruits."

More humor of the peculiarly seventies tasteless type ensues when Smith actually convinces the rather dim Wilbur that he's Adolf Hitler, despite the fact that he's African-American. One of the film's truly priceless lines is uttered in another scene in which Wilbur finds Gretta's mutilated corpse in the woods where she had been ordered to go on a reconnaissance mission. He reports to the other team members: "I just wanted to warn you, there's been tomato activity reported in your area. Carry on."

It may be the case that *Attack of the Killer Tomatoes!* does its job too well. Some critics and audiences consider it to be the worst film in history because they apparently believe it's just one of those low-budget movies that's so ineptly made that it's unintentionally hilarious. They're just not paying attention. Everything in the movie is intended to make you laugh, from the scene in which tomatoes attack swimmers at the beach in a *Jaws* parody, to the looks of terror on people's faces when they see giant tomatoes rolling towards them.

Those who got the joke turned *Attack of the Killer Tomatoes!* into a cult film. In fact, it spawned three low-budget sequels: *Return of the Killer Tomatoes!* (1988), *Killer Tomatoes Strike Back!* (1990) and my personal favorite title, *Killer Tomatoes Eat France!* They were all directed by De Bello and all share the same B-movie sensibility, although they're not as clever or charming as the original. It remains a classic of "camp," and it's a title that's now familiar to almost everyone, even though relatively few have actually seen the movie itself.

The film was saluted by A-movie director Tim Burton in his big-budget sci-fi spoof *Mars Attacks!* (1995). The ending of Burton's film shows the Martians being defeated by a song warbled by country music yodeler Slim Whitman. Parody is parodied, perhaps the greatest compliment one filmmaker can give to another.

Love at First Bite

The funniest thing about *Love at First Bite* (1979) is the casting of George Hamilton as Count Dracula. The man with the world's most famous tan playing a vampire who can never see the light of day is irony personified. But the joke pretty much ends there.

By the mid-seventies, the Hammer vampire cycle had run out of steam with such updates as *Dracula A.D. 1972* (1972) and *The Satanic Rites of Dracula* (1973), the latter of which was the last Dracula film Christopher Lee did for Hammer. By the time that *The Legend of the Seven Golden Vampires*, a kung fu vampire film co-produced with Hong Kong's Shaw Brothers, was released in 1974, the genre had begun to fall into self-parody.

But there was an unexpected return of the count in 1977, when a Broadway revival of the original play *Dracula* became a big hit with handsome Frank Langella in the lead. He turned the fearsome count into an unlikely matinee idol, and by 1979, no less than three major Dracula films were released: Werner Herzog's obsessive remake of F.W. Murnau's *Nosferatu* (with the new title of *Nosferatu the Vampyre*) starring Klaus Kinski; an adaptation of the stage version starring Langella; and Stan Dragoti's comedy, *Love at First Bite*.

Released on April 27, 1979, *Love at First Bite* was the first of the new wave of Dracula films to be seen by the public. It was also the most successful financially, and one of the last films to be released by American-International Pictures before they were absorbed by Orion Pictures.

A good cast was assembled: Hamilton as the suave Count Vladimir Dracula (one of the only times the character's first name was used in a film); Susan St. James as Cindy Sondheim, a New York City model who is the object of his affections; Richard Benjamin as Dr. Jeffrey Rosenberg, who changed his name from Van Helsing; Dick Shawn as NYPD Lt. Ferguson; and *Laugh-In*'s Arte Johnson as Renfield.

The plot has potential: Dracula is languishing in his castle, mooning over pictures of Sondheim that he encounters in fashion magazines. Why he's reading such magazines is never explained, but never mind. He and his assistant Renfield take off for Manhattan, where Sondheim resides, so that Dracula can make her his "bride." Sondheim's boyfriend, Dr. Rosenberg, is a direct descendant of the original Dr. Van Helsing, who in this version is called Fritz rather than Abraham (his name in the novel). Once he sees the telltale marks of the vampire on his girlfriend's neck, he tries to convince the police that Dracula is loose in the city. Hilarity supposedly ensues, but *Love at First Bite* is no *Young Frankenstein*. The script by Robert Kaufman just isn't very good, going for the most obvious jokes at the expense of various racial, ethnic and sexual groups.

What's really missing, though, is the kind of respect for the source material that Brooks and Wilder demonstrated in *Young Frankenstein*. Dragoti, a journeyman director who would eventually go on to helm the hugely successful *Mrs. Doubtfire* (1993) with Robin Williams, doesn't invest any heart into *Love at First Bite*. Although Hamilton does a reasonably good Bela Lugosi impression and tries to maintain some dignity as Dracula, the story and direction work against him at every turn. When he's forced to utter such lines as, "I don't drink wine and I don't smoke shit," one loses all hope for his attempts to elevate the film to a higher level.

The rest of the cast tries valiantly too, with Johnson in particular doing a good parody of Dwight Frye as Renfield, even to a passable version of his maniacal laugh. But he isn't given all that much to do, as most of the screen time is filled with the various neuroses of Rosenberg and Sondheim (sounds like a law firm). Rosenberg is the stereotypical nutty psychiatrist, while Sondheim is such an emotional mess that it's difficult to see why Dracula would even pursue her.

"Ah, Cindy Sondheim," Dracula says to her. "You should have lived in an earlier age. Things were simpler, less complicated. Do you know how many women had nervous breakdowns in the fourteenth century? Two."

If the script had included more lines such as that one to give Dracula a bit more sensitivity, the film on the whole may have worked. But bringing Dracula into the midst of 1979 Manhattan, complete with discos, drugs, promiscuous sex and street crime, is a mistake. The movie is hopelessly dated now, unlike *Young Frankenstein*, which still seems as fresh as it did in 1974. If the filmmakers had kept *Love in First Bite* in period as a direct parody of the novel (as Brooks later did in *Dracula: Dead and Loving It*, 1995) they could have had a comedy classic on their hands. Ultimately, however, the character of Dracula is lost amidst lame jokes about psychiatry, sex and Manhattan ennui.

There are a couple of amusing gags, such as when Rosenberg pulls out a Star of David instead of a crucifix and tries to chase away an unfazed Dracula. Hamilton's best line comes early in the film, when the wolves howl outside his Transylvanian castle, making quite a din. "Children of the night ... shut up!" he says. And they do.

Attempts have been made over the years to do a sequel to *Love at First Bite*, but so far, none of them have gotten off the ground. Maybe it's just as well.

7

THE EIGHTIES
American Werewolves and Toxic Avengers

Everything goes in cycles and much about the eighties seemed like, as Yogi Berra once famously said, "*Deja vu* all over again." Like the fifties, a Republican was in the White House for the entire decade. Conservatism began to creep into both politics and culture, and the casual sex that had dominated the seventies was very much "out" due to the scare surrounding the AIDS virus.

Movies are always a reflection of their times, and they became safer and more conservative as well. And yet, comedy-horror films kept pushing the envelope. Since sex had become dangerous, it also made a good subject for comedy-horror filmmakers. And since "splatter movies" such as George A. Romero's *Dawn of the Dead* (1978) had become standard fare for those fans known as "gorehounds," comedy-horror movies had to follow suit and add even more blood and guts to the mix.

Motel Hell

British director Kevin Connor helmed a number of movies for Amicus Productions in the seventies, beginning with *From Beyond the Grave* (1973), their final—and one of their best—anthology films. The four segments were based on stories by R. Chetwynd-Hayes, who had a tendency to punctuate his horror tales with black humor. One of the stories in the film, "The Elemental," which stars Ian Carmichael and Margaret Leighton, is played for total comedy. Carmichael meets Leighton on a train. Supposedly a famous medium, she tells him quite bluntly, "There is an elemental on your shoulder." Her attempts to exorcise the entity once Carmichael gets home are very funny indeed, with one of those bizarre endings that are typical of Chetwynd-Hayes.

There was nothing in *From Beyond the Grave*, however, to prepare the viewer for Connor's 1980 American film, *Motel Hell*. A project originally slated for Tobe Hooper, director of the original *The Texas Chain Saw Massacre* (1973), it's a gory parody of the slasher films that were popular at the time.

Connor came to America after the virtual collapse of the British film industry, and of Amicus in particular. He had gained a good deal of international prominence with his Amicus-produced Edgar Rice Burroughs movies such as *The Land That Time Forgot* (1975), *At the Earth's Core* (1976) and *The People That Time Forgot* (1977), the latter featuring British blues singer Dana Gillespie in a cavegirl outfit that practically thrust her sumptuous figure into the faces of audience members. These films were all very successful, and Connor decided to strike out for Hollywood while the iron was hot, so to speak.

The Hooper project had been scheduled for Universal, but because of its bizarre and over-the-top nature, the studio dropped it and gave Hooper another horror project, *The Funhouse* (1980), to direct instead. The script for *Motel Hell*, written by Robert Jaffe, Steven-Charles Jaffe and Tim Tuchrello, ended up at United Artists.

Ultimately, Connor was hired on the strength of his Amicus horror and fantasy films to direct *Motel Hell*. The screenplay parodied elements from *Texas ChainSaw* as well as Wes Craven's *Last House on the Left* (1972) with a bit of the old legend of "Sweeney Todd" added to the brew. There's also some EC horror comics flavor to the film in its story of Farmer Vincent Smith (veteran Hollywood actor Rory Calhoun) who lives with his sister Ida (Nancy Parsons) on a farm which is also a motel. Vincent is renowned for his smoked meats, for which everybody for a hundred miles around pays him a pretty penny. It turns out that Vincent's secret is that he uses human flesh in his meats to give it that extra "spicy" flavor.

Vincent fills the isolated roads around his motel with various booby traps to snare unsuspecting travelers. These are the poor souls who end up, quite literally, as dead meat. Perhaps the nastiest scenes in the film are those involving his victims, who are placed in a "garden" where they're buried up to their necks. He then slits their vocal chords so they can't scream. Keeping them in there until they've "aged" enough to be killed, he then cuts them up into quarters and "cures" them. His sister aids him in his hideous endeavors and, if anything, seems to enjoy the ghastliness of it more than he does.

What makes this unpleasant-sounding story work is Connor's no-nonsense direction. The film is totally unpretentious, with no unnecessary flourishes. It simply is what it is: a comedy-horror film offered up complete with gore, cannibalism and no apologies.

The performances by the supporting cast are nothing special; if you look closely you'll spot John Ratzenberger a couple of years before he became "Cliff" on TV's *Cheers* as a member of an ill-fated punk rock band called "Ivan and the Terribles." But Calhoun is terrific as Vincent, a "down-to-earth" sort of fellow who is very pragmatic about his work. "Meat's meat, and a man's gotta eat," he says. "There's too many people and not enough food. Now this takes care of both problems at the same time."

Vincent's certainty about his craft, however, is challenged by his younger brother Bruce (Paul Linke), who just happens to be the town sheriff. Apparently, Bruce hasn't been a terribly bright policeman, since it's taken him years to figure out what his brother's been up to. When he discovers the secret, he's properly horrified. Vincent admits, "Sometimes I wonder about the karmic implications of these actions."

But his self-doubt ultimately extends in a rather unexpected direction. "I'm the biggest hypocrite of them all. My meats ... I used ... preservatives!" he confesses.

Released on October 18, 1980, *Motel Hell* was sold with the advertising tagline, "You might just die ... laughing!" As a parody of slasher films, it still holds up today. Although not especially successful financially at the time of its release, it's become a fondly remembered cult movie over the years and, beyond its other charms, it contains one of Calhoun's very best performances. The sight of him wearing a slaughtered pig's head over his face while wielding a chainsaw is not easily forgotten. Nor is his business motto: "It takes all kinds of critters to make Farmer Vincent's fritters."

An American Werewolf in London

I once interviewed Stephen King upon the release of a film he wrote and George Romero directed, *Creepshow* (1982). A five-story omnibus film, it has some very effective moments of comedy and horror. During the interview, King commented that he felt *An American Werewolf in London* (1981) "didn't know when to be funny and when to be horrifying." Although the film, directed by John Landis, has become a cult movie over the years, I tend to agree with that statement.

Landis, a self-professed horror fan, wrote the first draft of *An American Werewolf in London* in 1969. The title is a cross between the classic musical *An American in Paris* (1952) and Universal's *Werewolf of London* (1935), starring Henry Hull as the screen's first all-talking, all-howling werewolf.

In 1971, Landis broke into the movie business by writing and directing *Schlock*, a movie that was somewhat inspired by *King Kong* (1933). It's safe to say that *Schlock* lives up to its title. Landis himself plays the monster, a sort of apeman who ends up carrying off a woman, King Kong–style. The ape costume was designed by future Oscar winner Rick Baker. Shot in 16mm, *Schlock* is full of the sophomoric humor that would become Landis' trademark, as well as cameos by superfans such as Forrest J Ackerman (editor of *Famous Monsters of Filmland* magazine) and Donald F. Glut (future filmmaker of such direct-to-DVD fare as *Dinosaur Valley Girls*). Cameos would also become a Landis hallmark in future films.

Schlock became a minor cult film, and Landis went on to direct a segment of the omnibus comedy film *Kentucky Fried Movie* (1977) and hit it big with *National Lampoon's Animal House* (1978), virtually inventing the "slob comedy." He next did *The Blues Brothers* (1980) before deciding to go back and rework his old werewolf screenplay.

Universal seemed the obvious choice to finance the film, given their history in horror, and the budget was set at a fairly hefty ten million dollars. Landis hired his old friend Rick Baker to do the werewolf makeup effects, which were much heralded upon the release of the film in August, 1981.

Landis decided to film on location in England and Wales, and he hired first-rate cinematographer Robert Paynter to give the film an expensive look. The opening shots are of moors near Hay Bluff in Brecon Beacons National Park, a mountain on the border between Wales and England. The hamlet of Cickadarn, about ten miles west of Hay Bluff, is seen as the town of East Proctor. One of the most effective locations is Tottenham Court Road tube station, used as a scene of a werewolf attack.

As usual, Landis filled the film with cameos and in-jokes. Frank Oz appears in many Landis films, and he's actually in *American Werewolf* twice, first as Mr. Collins from the American Embassy, and later as the voice of Miss Piggy in a dream sequence. "Naughty Nina," who is seen on a television promo, is actually Nina Carter, a London "Page Three Girl" and future wife of Yes keyboard player Rick Wakeman. In the climactic Piccadilly Circus sequence, Landis himself plays the man hit by a car and thrown through a shop window.

There are also some actors in the film who would later become very well-known in England, including Julian Glover and rising actor-comedian Rik Mayall as characters in the Slaughtered Lamb pub. They appeared together again ten years later in Mayall's comedy TV series *Bottom*. One of the policemen chasing the werewolf toward the end of the film is John Altman, who would later star as "Nasty" Nick Cotton in the long-running British soap opera *EastEnders*. Michael Carter, the werewolf's victim at the tube station, would next appear as Bib Fortuna in *Return of the Jedi* (1983). And Allan Ford, who plays a taxi driver, would later play crime boss "Brick Top" in Guy Ritchie's gangster film *Snatch* (2000).

Landis has a running gag through many of his films concerning a fictitious film called *See You Next Wednesday*. In *American Werewolf*, it's a porn film playing in Piccadilly Circus. One of its stars is the very busty Linzi Drew, porn actress and sometime *Penthouse* magazine editor. As the undead Jack (Griffin Dunne) points out ironically in *American Werewolf*, "Good movie!"

Irony pretty much sums up the tone of *American Werewolf*. The film is pervaded with a juvenile, frat-boy kind of humor that ultimately works against the story. The production's financiers feared that the movie was too horrible to be a comedy and too funny to be a horror film. It may have been Landis' intention to catch the audience off guard, to lull them into a false sense of security with the jokes and then hit them hard with a shock sequence. But *American Werewolf*, much to its detriment, never achieves a consistent tone.

One of the biggest problems is the script, which lurches from one scene to the next without concern for continuity or believability. The dialogue often rings false; it's an American imagining how British people might speak. "Whereas I am a victim of your carnivorous lunar activities," the undead tube station victim says at one point. "Why don't you watch telly whilst I take a shower?" says Alex (Jenny Agutter) at another.

On the other hand, Landis seems to have a certain contempt for the British. When the American werewolf himself, David Kessler (David Naughton), tries to get arrested in Trafalgar Square so that he'll be behind bars when the full moon rises and he transforms, he shouts out to a policeman and a gathering crowd, "Queen Elizabeth is a man! Prince Charles is a

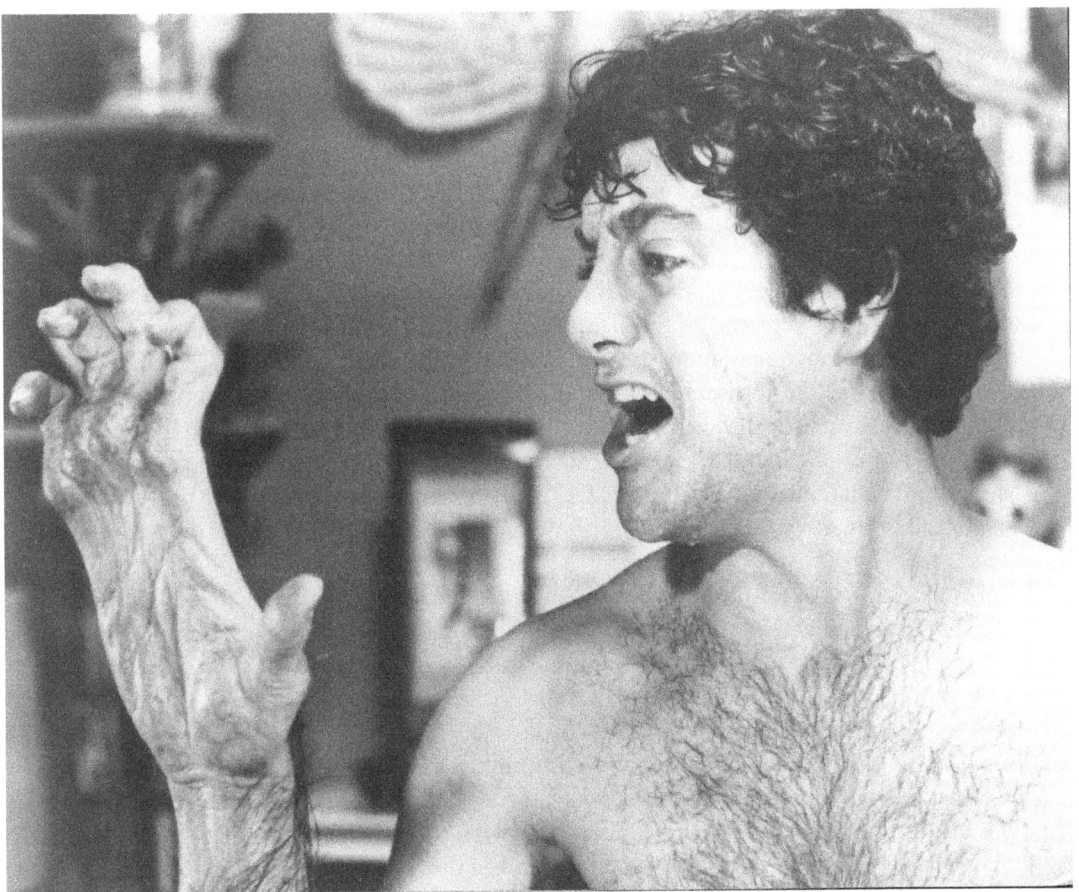

David Naughton experiences the curse of the full moon in John Landis's ***An American Werewolf in London*** (1981).

faggot! Winston Churchill was full of shit! Shakespeare's French!" Perhaps to atone for these tasteless remarks, the end credits include a congratulatory note to Prince Charles and Lady Diana Spencer for their wedding, which occurred shortly before the film was released. You don't really get the feeling that this lame attempt at a *mea culpa* is sincere; it seems to be just as ironic as the rest of the film.

Landis also takes great liberties with the werewolf myth itself. Kessler's friend Jack comes back from the dead several times, and each time he looks a little worse. Kessler refers to him as "a walking meatloaf," but for my money, he looks more like a pizza that's been in the fridge a bit too long. "On the moors," Jack tells Kessler, "we were attacked by a lycanthrope, a werewolf. I was murdered, an unnatural death, and now I walk the earth in limbo until the curse is lifted."

The twist of all of the werewolf's victims walking the earth in limbo until the beast is destroyed never appears in any of the classic films Landis claims to love so much. It's just another example of his disregard for the source material, a plot point dropped in as an excuse to show a lot of walking corpses.

And what are those storm trooper ghouls (or whatever they are) that keep popping up in Kessler's nightmares? They appear for no particular reason than to slaughter his family; later on, he talks to one of his siblings on the telephone, so obviously the dream wasn't prophetic. Nothing bad has happened to his family. Again, the nightmare sequence was just dropped in for shock effect, regardless of whether it had anything to do with the plot.

But there are things about the film that work. Rick Baker's makeup effects, particularly in the transformation scene, are extremely well executed and in fact won him an Oscar for Best Special Effects Makeup. Although Rob Bottin had pioneered similar effects in Joe Dante's *The Howling* (1981), Baker did him one better by having the transformation take place in a fully lighted room. The sequence is still powerful today.

Landis also manages one very effective, almost Val Lewton–type fright sequence, when the werewolf tracks down the man in the tube station. Very little of the werewolf is actually seen here, until the very end of the sequence when it slowly crawls into frame. This scene lingers in the memory, and almost seems to come from another film.

Naughton, as the tormented "hero" of the piece, appears to be attempting to give a thoughtful performance, but he's undercut by the script at every turn. The sophomoric lines he is forced to utter ("I didn't mean to call you a meatloaf, Jack!") do little to gain audience sympathy. The fact that we do, in fact, feel badly for him when he is killed (not with silver bullets, but ordinary ones) is more of a tribute to Naughton's talent than it is to Landis' direction.

The one sincere performance, despite the dialogue written for her, is that of Jenny Agutter. A former child actress in such films as Lionel Jeffries' *The Railway Children* (1970), she received a lot of attention for appearing nude in Nicolas Roeg's *Walkabout* (1971) at the age of sixteen. She made a big impression on American audiences in the sci-fi thriller *Logan's Run* (1976), appearing opposite Michael York.

In *American Werewolf*, Agutter's role is underwritten, but she does a great deal with it. Her relationship with Kessler is quite believable, despite its sleazy beginnings: She's a nurse who brings him home from the hospital to stay with her in her flat. But her love for him appears genuine, and it's her emotion at the end of the film that rings true. Her scenes with a difficult child in the hospital also have a very natural, authentic feel about them; one gets the sense that they were partly ad-libbed. Agutter remains an underrated actress to this day. Anyone who can take a poorly written character and make something out of it has a special kind of skill, and Agutter proves she has the right stuff in *American Werewolf*. Too bad it's in the wrong movie.

Landis' sense of irony carries over into the film's soundtrack. Although the original score was composed by the great Elmer Bernstein, Landis chose to use just about every song ever written with the word "moon" in the title to point out that, yes, we're watching a werewolf movie. Van Morrison's "Moondance," Creedence Clearwater Revival's "Bad Moon Rising" and three different versions of "Blue Moon" really hammer this point home. Okay, we get it, John. The werewolf transforms when the moon rises. Now can we get on with the movie?

This points out one of Landis' great failures as a director: He clutters his films with in-jokes, celebrity cameos and self-referential music to such an extent that the movie stops dead for the audience. Instead of just telling the story, Landis constantly feels the need to play "wink, wink" with the viewer, which is fine if the jokes are funny. But more often than not, they fall flat.

An *American Werewolf in London* certainly has its fans, and there are some highly effective moments. But to this writer, it's neither fish nor fowl, a mishmash that never quite gels. It pointed the way to more self-referential movies to follow, some good, some bad. But thanks to the director's insincerity, slapdash approach and what appears to be a thinly veiled contempt for the material, it succeeds neither as comedy nor as horror.

Eating Raoul

Eating Raoul (1982) is a "cannibal comedy," although cannibalism doesn't enter into it until the final scene. The story concerns a very conservative couple, Paul and Mary Bland (Paul Bartel and Mary Woronov), who, unfortunately for them, live in an apartment complex full of swingers. Their dream is to open a restaurant someday, but their financial situation worsens when Paul loses his job at a wine shop. Mary's pay as a nurse will have to sustain them for now, despite the fact that their rent has just been raised.

Their lives take a new direction when one of the swingers breaks into their apartment and tries to rape Mary. Paul bops him over the head with a frying pan, killing him. Going through his pockets, they discover that "swingers have a lot of money," so they take his cash and put him in the trash compactor. They decide that they can make enough money to open their restaurant if they kill enough "rich perverts."

What follows is a murder spree as Paul and Mary lure swingers to their apartment (mostly through Mary's sex appeal) and kill them with their weapon of choice, the frying pan. They continue on their merry yet murderous way until their locksmith Raoul (Robert Beltran), a part-time cat burglar, breaks into their apartment and finds the body of a Nazi fetishist in a rather provocative position. Paul confronts Raoul and they make a bargain: Raoul will keep their secret and take the corpses to a dog food company where he gets cash for them. Unbeknownst to Paul and Mary, he also steals the dead swingers' cars and sells them.

Things get even stickier when Paul is out buying groceries and a hippie (Ed Begley, Jr.) shows up as Mary's next customer. He attempts to rape her, but Raoul happens to walk in and strangles the man to death with his belt. After this charming interlude, Raoul offers Mary the dead hippie's marijuana and they begin what turns out to be an ill-fated affair.

Raoul wants Mary to run away with him and he decides to kill Paul, but Mary, who loves her husband despite everything, kills Raoul with the frying pan instead. Their real estate agent, who is helping them buy their restaurant, is scheduled to come over for dinner that night, and with very little time to prepare anything, the homicidal couple cooks Raoul and serves him to their guest, who remarks on how good the meal is. Paul thanks him and says, "It's amazing what you can do with a cheap piece of meat if you know how to treat it."

Bartel not only starred in *Eating Raoul*, he wrote and directed it as well. It was something of a labor of love; he financed the film as he went along with the help of friends and family members and shot whenever he had the money. It was released to critical acclaim and good box office, mainly playing in art houses, in the spring of 1982.

The Brooklyn-born Bartel had been knocking around the movie scene for years, mainly working as an actor in such Roger Corman–produced movies as *Death Race 2000* (1975), Joe Dante's first feature *Hollywood Boulevard* (1976) and the cult classic *Rock'n'Roll High School* (1979). He also directed a genuinely creepy and disturbing black comedy-horror film called *Private Parts* (1972) that had echoes of Alfred Hitchcock's *Psycho* (1960) as well as of Michael Powell's infamous *Peeping Tom* (also 1960). Bartel made no secret of the fact that he was gay at a time when openly gay actors were not really accepted by Hollywood studios. He found that he had many more opportunities in the wild world of independent filmmaking.

Woronov came up from the ranks of the Andy Warhol Factory. By 1982, she had already appeared in several of the Corman films with Bartel, but *Eating Raoul* was the breakthrough movie that made her a cult "star." Tall and lanky, she became an unlikely sex symbol due to her frequent nudity in the film, and became sought-after by producers because of her expert comic timing, appearing in such films as *Night of the Comet* (1984), again with her good friend Bartel.

Although no actual gore is shown in the film, the concept of *Eating Raoul* is so, well, tasteless that blood and guts would seem superfluous. It's also very funny, full of ironic, witty lines. The offhand way in which the Blands kill people is both chilling and laughable. When Paul volunteers to go get groceries, Mary calls out to him, "At the store, can you buy a new frying pan? I'm a little squeamish about using the one we use to kill people."

After killing the Nazi fetishist, Paul says to Mary, "Why don't you go to bed, honey? I'll bag the Nazi and straighten up." When Raoul incredulously asks them, "You killed two people for less than a thousand dollars?" Mary deadpans, "One of them short changed us."

The movie has some naughty fun at the expense of conservative morality. Paul and Mary are like a two-person Moral Majority, killing people who don't subscribe to their values because they're "worthless." After murdering the first victim, Paul says to Mary, "I just killed a man." She replies matter-of-factly, "He was a man. Now he's just a bag of garbage."

But Bartel also encourages us to laugh at the swingers, who come across as kinky fetishists who think of nothing but how they're going to score their next orgasm. In a sense, they're no better than the Blands; if they can't get consensual sex, they're willing to attempt rape. After dispatching one swinger, Paul attempts to assuage what little guilt Mary feels by telling her, "Well, there's one consideration. If you'd done what he asked, he would have died anyway."

In a strange sort of way, the most "moral" character in the film is Doris the Dominatrix (Susan Saiger), a single mom who seems very middle class until she dons her leather gear and humiliates her customers at their request. It's just a job to her, capitalism at its finest.

During a radio interview in 1984, Woronov told me that she didn't feel that Mary Bland was an evil character, just "criminally naive." She also mentioned that a sequel called *Bland Ambition* was in the works. It was to have co-starred Chevy Chase as a man who attempts to blackmail the Blands with his knowledge of their killing spree. Bartel was never able to get the project off the ground, and his untimely death of liver cancer in 2000 meant that we would never see Paul and Mary Bland together again. *Eating Raoul* remains one of a kind, a unique black comedy-horror film that leaves a not unpleasant taste in the mouth. As the film's end credits read, "Bon Appetit!"

House of the Long Shadows

By 1983, the British Gothic horror film was already a thing of the past. The cycle had petered out in the mid-seventies, with Hammer's final Gothic feature *To the Devil ... a Daughter* (1976) a failure at the box office. The small British companies could no longer compete with the American studios, who were beating them at their own game with such big-budget scare-fests as *The Exorcist* (1973), *The Omen* (1976) and *Carrie* (1976). So it was perhaps surprising that London Cannon Films announced in 1982 that they were going to reunite the classic horror stars for one more feature.

House of the Long Shadows, as the film eventually came to be known, was actually the seventh version of an oft-filmed play written by, of all people, George M. Cohan. The play was in turn based on Earl Derr Biggers' 1913 mystery novel *Seven Keys to Baldpate*, in which an author makes a wager that he can spend the night in an old mansion and write a 10,000-word novel that is good enough to publish.

Seven Keys to Baldpate (1917) features one of Cohan's few screen appearances. Nearly forgotten today, the silent film nevertheless gives one a sense of Cohan's stage and screen presence, as he plays the lead role of the author. It was filmed again in 1929 with Richard Dix, and several more times in the thirties and forties. But none of these adaptations were comedy-horror films. They were all rather tepid comedy-mysteries crawling with underworld hoodlums, gunshots in the dark and ... well, lots of talk, talk, talk.

This was not to be the case with the 1983 version. Everyone connected with it had a background in horror films. The writer, Michael Armstrong, had made a name for himself with the infamous European film *Mark of the Devil* (1969), the first film to be jokingly rated "V for Violence" (by its distributor, Hallmark Films) in the United States. Armstrong had also written the Tigon-AIP thriller *The Haunted House of Horror* (1970) starring Frankie Avalon.

The director, Pete Walker, was an even better-known purveyor of on-screen gore, having directed such low-budget shockers as *The Flesh and Blood Show* (1975) and *House of Whipcord* (1974). *The Confessional* (1976), one of his better films, revolved around a homicidal priest. Walker was a journeyman director whose main claim to fame was pushing the envelope when it came to gore and brutality.

While the contributions of both gentlemen to world cinema may be questionable, there was no question about the quality of the cast. *House of the Long Shadows* is historically important because it's the only film to co-star a classic quartet of horror cinema: Vincent Price, Christopher Lee, Peter Cushing and John Carradine. For that reason alone, the film is well worth watching. It was the final teaming of Lee and Cushing in a theatrical feature, although they did appear together in the television documentary *Flesh and Blood*, broadcast on the BBC in 1998, four years after Cushing's death.

Cannon Films being what they were, however—a B-movie company without anyone really creative at the helm—they also cast Desi Arnaz Jr. in the lead role of Kenneth Magee, the author. To say that the young Arnaz is out of his league is to put it mildly. Although he has moments of charm during the course of the film, he mostly comes across as a young punk who is barely believable as a best-selling author.

The horror stars, though, appear to be having a wonderful time. The screenplay allows each one of them to make a grand entrance, as one by one they enter the house on a stormy night for a rather strange family reunion. Price is the very flamboyant Lionel Grisbane; Lee is a rich businessman named Corrigan who wants to buy the house; Cushing is the fussy Sebastian Grisbane, who speaks a lot like Elmer Fudd; and Carradine is Lord Grisbane, the family patriarch.

Rounding out the cast is Walker regular Sheila Keith as dotty old Victoria, who plays the piano and sings off-key; Richard Todd as Sam Allyson, Magee's agent; and Julie Peasgood as Mary Norton, Allyson's attractive young secretary. There are also a couple of stragglers who end up stranded in the old dark house, Diana (Louise English) and her boyfriend Andrew (Richard Hunter). Once everyone is assembled, the murders begin, and we have a sort of *And Then There Were None* situation in which the characters are bumped off in various gory ways, one at a time.

This is where *House of the Long Shadows* differs from the six other versions of *Seven Keys to Baldpate*. Walker, as might be expected, doesn't hold back on the gore, and we see close-ups of hangings, stabbings, acid in the face and even an ax murder. Nothing is quite as it seems, however. There are several plot twists: One is that Corrigan is the murderer, actually a mad member of the Grisbane family himself; then it's revealed that Lionel was actually the mad one who had his brother put away in his place. Before long, however, we discover that every murder has been staged and all of the characters are actors from a local theater. In the final twist, it turns out that everything we have just witnessed is in fact Magee's novel; he has succeeded in writing his book overnight, and he collects the wager from his agent.

All of these plot twists are rather dizzying but they certainly keep one guessing. The final shot, in which Magee walks off with Mary, asking her if she believes in love at first sight, is a bit too cute, but the film on the whole works almost in spite of itself. There are some amusing, self-referential lines that give the film a post-modern appeal. When Magee asks the stationmaster (Norman Rossington) how to get to Baldpate Manor, the man says, "It is a cursed place." Magee sarcastically replies, "I'm sure it's drenched in evil." The stationmaster repeats, "A cursed place," to which Magee retorts, "Filled with things best not spoken of. Yes, I saw the movie."

Although Carradine doesn't have a great deal to do as the old patriarch, the three other horror icons relish their roles. Price spoofs his own horror image, hamming it up alarmingly as Lionel; his "murder" by ax is reminiscent of his death at the end of Michael Reeves' *Witchfinder General* (1968). Lee is obviously enjoying himself as the sophisticated Corrigan, whom Diana refers to as "a real man." He's typically aloof in a role that is quite similar to the equally untrustworthy character he played in Vernon Sewell's *Curse of the Crimson Altar* (1969).

But it's the immortal Cushing who seems to be having the most fun here. An avowed fan of Warner Bros. Looney Tunes cartoons, his Fudd-like dropping of his "R's" is something of an inside joke and is hugely enjoyable. It wasn't that often that Cushing got to do comedy, and that's unfortunate. When it's revealed at the penultimate plot twist that he's merely an actor, he notes that his ability to cry on cue has led to him being referred to as "The Big Drip."

And Price's last words to Christopher Lee in the film? It turns out that the two of them have been (in the movie, that is) bitter rivals and at odds with each other for some time. After Lee makes a crack about Price's age, Price calls him a "bitch." And that was the final word Price had for Lee in any film.

House of the Long Shadows may not be well remembered today, and in fact it was barely released in 1983. Nevertheless, it was a movie that celebrated horror film history while making a bit of history itself. The old dark house movie was already passé when the film was made, and in fact the writer and director made few movies afterward. Of the four horror icons, only Lee (at this writing) is still with us. The others have gone to that bijou in the sky, where, if there is any justice in the universe, they're still playing to capacity audiences, making them laugh and scream for eternity.

Ghostbusters

It's easy to understand why *Ghostbusters* (1984) remains the most financially successful comedy-horror film of all time. There's something in it for everyone: off-the-wall humor, romance, great special effects and a memorable musical score (by Elmer Bernstein). Fun, as they say, for the whole family.

The film was really comedy legend Dan Aykroyd's "baby." Long before he began his stint on NBC's *Saturday Night Live* in the seventies, he had nurtured a fascination for the paranormal, UFOs and cryptozoology. Originally, *Ghostbusters* was conceived in the late seventies as a project that would have starred Aykroyd and fellow *SNL* veteran John Belushi, according to Don Shay in his 1985 book *Making* Ghostbusters. The first draft of the script dealt with time, space and inter-dimensional travel in which the Ghostbusters battled bizarre entities. Aykroyd pitched the script to director-producer Ivan Reitman, who had just scored hits with two movies starring Bill Murray, *Meatballs* (1979) and *Stripes* (1981), the latter of which also featured *Second City* TV alum John Candy. Reitman liked the concept of *Ghostbusters* but felt that the screenplay was overly ambitious and next to impossible to film with the technology and budgetary constraints of the time. He asked for a rewrite, so Aykroyd got together with friend Harold Ramis (another SCTV veteran) and rewrote the script from start to finish. According to Ramis' commentary on the *Ghostbusters* DVD, the screenplay was completed by the duo in an old bomb shelter on Martha's Vineyard.

The script was written specifically with their friends in mind. There were roles included for John Belushi (Dr. Peter Venkman), Eddie Murphy (Winston Zeddemore) and John Candy (Louis Tully). But Belushi died of a drug overdose before production could begin and Murphy and Candy couldn't commit to the film due to prior engagements, so more rewrites and script polishes were in order.

The role of Louis Tully went to another SCTV performer, Rick Moranis. Originally conceived as a conservative man who always wore a suit, Moranis loosened the character up to become the kind of nerdy nebbish he was so good at playing on television.

The Zeddemore role ended up going to Ernie Hudson, who made it his own. In the draft that was written with Eddie Murphy in mind, Zeddemore had more screen time and came into the story much earlier. When the role went to Hudson, Aykroyd and Ramis turned it into an opportunity to bring the character in later, giving the first third of the film more build-up to demonstrate that the Ghostbusters needed a little more help to keep those pesky ghosts at bay.

The role written for Belushi went to Bill Murray, who had an excellent working relationship with Reitman. The whole nature of the movie changed with Murray's casting; his casual, improvisational style is one of the best-remembered things about the film. It's difficult at this point to imagine Belushi or anyone else as Dr. Peter Venkman.

Filmed partially on location in Manhattan, *Ghostbusters* benefits enormously from a lav-

Sigourney Weaver and Rick Moranis are possessed and having a wonderful time in Ivan Reitman's *Ghostbusters* (1984).

ish budget courtesy of Columbia Pictures. Some of the money went into Gozer's temple, the largest, most expensive set ever built for a movie up to that time. The sets representing the Sedgwick Hotel hallway had originally been built for the film *Rich and Famous* (1981). Location shooting took place at New York's famed Biltmore Hotel, in which the Ghostbusters appear in their "gear" for first time.

The special effects team, headed by Richard Edlund, pulled off some wonderful moments, including the Library Ghost, which was originally even scarier but was toned down in order to get a PG rating. The discarded concept was later used for a vampiric apparition in Columbia's R-rated *Fright Night* (1985), for which Edlund also did the special effects.

Slimer, the ghost who "slimes" Dr. Venkman ("I feel so funky!" exclaims the good doctor), is another great creation, a green, amorphous blob that does nothing but eat. Rumor has it that the crew referred to it as "the ghost of John Belushi" during the filming.

The Stay-Puft Marshmallow Man was in Aykroyd's original draft of the script, and thankfully made it into the final version. When the demonic entity Gozer (Slavitza Jovan) delves into the Ghostbusters' minds to uncover their worst fears, they all clear their minds and try not to think of anything, except for Dr. Raymond Stantz (Aykroyd), who instead chooses to dwell on something childlike and innocent. "I tried to think of the most harm-

Left to right: Harold Ramis, Dan Aykroyd, Bill Murray and Ernie Hudson in Ivan Reitman's megahit *Ghostbusters* (1984).

less thing," Stantz tells them. "Something I loved from my childhood. Something that could never, ever possibly destroy us. Mr. Stay-Puft!"

Needless to say, Mr. Stay Puft is transformed by Gozer's power into the most menacing apparition of all, a gigantic, Godzilla-like thing that stalks through the concrete canyons of Manhattan, destroying everything in its path. "I'm terrified beyond the capacity for rational thought," says Dr. Egon Spengler (Ramis).

Sigourney Weaver, who became an overnight star in *Alien* (1979), was cast as Dana Barrett, Venkman's classy and sophisticated love interest. She has the misfortune of being possessed by an entity called Zuul, the gatekeeper, one of Gozer's minions. Tully is possessed by Vinz Clortho, the Keymaster, another of Gozer's doglike demons.

Possessed or not, Weaver has never been more beautiful nor more appealing than she is in *Ghostbusters*. A gifted actress who excels in dramatic roles, she rarely gets a chance to let herself go in a comedy, but her scenes with Murray when she's inhabited by Zuul are tremendous fun. "Take me now, subcreature!" she commands, hyperventilating all the while.

The movie is chock full of hilarious lines, most of them uttered by Murray. There's great debate as to whether he ad-libbed his way through the film or whether he used his vast improvisational experience to merely make it seem as though everything he said was off the cuff. Whatever the case, there is no scene featuring Murray that isn't funny. One of my

Dan Aykroyd, Bill Murray and Harold Ramis sense their prey is near in Ivan Reitman's *Ghostbusters* (1984).

personal favorites is his prediction of what will happen when "a disaster of Biblical proportions" takes place in the city: "Human sacrifice, dogs and cats living together, mass hysteria!"

When Dr. Stantz notes that library books have been stacked symmetrically, "just like the Philadelphia mass turbulence of 1947," Venkman deadpans, "You're right, no human being would stack books like this."

At one point, Dana tells Venkman that he doesn't look like a scientist. "You're more like a game show host," she observes. Actually, he does come across like one particular game show host: Groucho Marx, host of the fifties television show *You Bet Your Life*. With a quip for every situation, a put-down for everyone who deserves it and an ability to rise above it all, Venkman is a lot like Groucho. In fact, the four Ghostbusters have a rapport that's very much like that of The Marx Brothers. Murray is certainly the ringleader, but they all have their moments of hilarity. Stantz is more or less the straight man, à la Zeppo. Spengler is the quiet type, rather like Harpo. And Zeddemore is a bit more of a streetwise rogue in the way that Chico was; when Ghostbusters secretary Janine (Annie Potts) asks him at his job interview, "Do you believe in UFOs, astral projections, mental telepathy, ESP, clairvoyance, spirit photography, telekinetic movement, full trance mediums, the Loch Ness Monster and the theory of Atlantis?" Zeddemore answers, "Uh, if there's a steady paycheck in it, I'll believe anything you say."

Everyone in *Ghostbusters* looks like they're having fun, from Moranis, who has a great time being possessed by Vinz Clortho, to Potts, who's very droll as Janine. Even the bit players look like they're having a ball. And that sense of fun communicates to the audience.

When *Ghostbusters* was released by Columbia Pictures on June 8, 1984, it became an immediate sensation. The film grossed $240 million in the United States alone, more than what had been predicted to be the year's biggest hit, *Indiana Jones and the Temple of Doom*. It became the biggest box office bonanza of the year and was followed by a sequel, *Ghostbusters II* (1989), and two animated television series, *The Real Ghostbusters* and *Extreme Ghostbusters*. The term "ghostbusters" has become part of the language; I once worked in a New York State licensing office in which employees assigned to find out which licensees were deceased were unofficially referred to as "ghostbusters."

Ivan Reitman has never made a film nearly as good as *Ghostbusters*, and there have been few comedies, horror or otherwise, to serve up so many scenes that tickle your funny bone. I have no idea what "Mother pus bucket!" means, but when Murray says it, it makes me laugh.

Gremlins

Comedy-horror delivered a one-two punch during the summer of 1984. The same weekend that *Ghostbusters* was released also saw the debut of Joe Dante's *Gremlins*, a movie that took comedy-horror to new heights of screams and laughter, and one of the two films (the other being Steven Spielberg's *Indiana Jones and the Temple of Doom*) released that summer that led to a new movie rating: PG-13, for films that were too dark or violent for a PG rating but not quite nasty enough for an R.

Spielberg's film was heavily criticized for a ritual sequence in which a living man's beating heart is ripped out of his chest. *Gremlins* was the recipient of similar criticism for a scene in which one of the title creatures is thrown into a microwave oven, whereupon it explodes in a welter of blood and viscera. But that's part of the brilliance of Dante's approach: Although *Gremlins* is essentially a mainstream, family-friendly film, there is a dark and subversive undercurrent that keeps the viewer off guard, wondering in which direction it will veer next. This is not to say that it has an inconsistent tone, such as John Landis' *An American Werewolf in London*; quite the contrary. Dante, like the Gremlins themselves, is having mischievously wicked but childlike fun with his audience.

Dante was born Joseph Dante, Jr. in Morristown, New Jersey, on November 18, 1946. After a brief bout with polio when he was seven years old, he decided to take up art as a profession; his parents were professional golfers, but after his health scare, he decided the athletic life was not for him.

After graduating from high school, Dante went to the Philadelphia College of Art. Always a fan of the horror and sci-fi genres, he contributed to the magazine *Famous Monsters of Filmland* while still a teenager; his piece, titled "The Fifty Worst Horror Movies Ever Made," became quite controversial among readers of the magazine.

He became a film critic for a local newspaper after he graduated from college, and eventually got into the film business when a friend convinced him to move to California and work with him for Roger Corman's New World Pictures. Dante started out as an editor for New World trailers, but Corman soon gave him the opportunity to direct his first feature film,

Hollywood Boulevard (1976), shot in ten days on a $50,000 budget, but one that nevertheless showed real promise. Two years later, Corman assigned Dante to do what started out as a rip-off of Spielberg's *Jaws* (1975), entitled *Piranha*. From a witty script by young writer John Sayles, Dante made his first attempt at combining humor with horror. *Piranha*, like *Hollywood Boulevard*, quickly became a cult favorite.

After working as second unit director on *Rock 'n' Roll High School* (1979), Dante accepted an offer from independent producer Mike Finnell to direct another John Sayles script, *The Howling*, based on a novel by Gary Brandner. Released in 1981 by Avco-Embassy, *The Howling* became Dante's first "mainstream" hit. It arrived in theaters several months before the more highly touted *An American Werewolf in London* and benefited strongly from Rob Bottin's excellent werewolf transformation effects. Sayles' script was even wittier than the one he wrote for *Piranha* and is filled with in-jokes. For example, all of the main characters are named after directors who had made werewolf films: George Waggner, Terry Fisher, Fred Francis and so on.

Dante's contributions to the success of the film include the casting of veteran genre actors such as Kevin McCarthy, Kenneth Tobey and Dick Miller; this became a Dante trademark that would continue on throughout his career. And, in a nice moment of payback, he even cast Forrest J Ackerman, editor of *Famous Monsters of Filmland*, in a memorable cameo.

Continuing his dizzying ascent up the Hollywood ladder, Dante next found himself working for Steven Spielberg on the anthology film *Twilight Zone: the Movie* (1983), directing perhaps the most imaginative and darkly comic segment, "It's a Good Life," based on the classic *Twilight Zone* episode of the same title.

Duly impressed with his work, Spielberg hired Dante to direct *Gremlins* for Warner Bros. The screenplay by Chris Columbus, a young writer who, like John Sayles, would later go on to direct his own highly successful films, was very dark comedy-horror indeed. Juxtaposed against an idyllic Christmas season setting, the story was about a young fellow who receives an unusual creature for a pet. He is admonished to make sure that water never touches it, to keep it away from sunlight and to "never feed it after midnight." Needless to say, he breaks all those rules and the creature reproduces itself at an alarming rate, spawning a horde of "gremlins" whose only purpose in life seems to be destruction.

Early drafts of the screenplay contained far more gruesome elements than producer or director wanted. The word "gremlin" came from World War II pilots who jokingly said that any mechanical failures that happened to their planes were caused by tiny, mischievous creatures. In 1943, Roald Dahl seized upon this new urban legend and came out with a book entitled *The Gremlins*.

Columbus was aware of these stories when he came to write his screenplay. He claimed that the inspiration for it occurred to him when he was trying to get some sleep in his loft apartment and heard mice skittering around in the darkness. He wrote the script as a writing sample to show to producers with the hope that they would take an interest in his work. It fell into Spielberg's hands, he felt it "was one of the most original things I've come across in many years," and Columbus never had to worry about impressing producers again.

Nevertheless, Spielberg asked for several more drafts until the screenplay achieved the right tone. In the original version, the main character's mother is killed by the gremlins and her head goes bouncing down the stairs. Dante agreed that such a scene was a bit too much, and in the final filmed version, the character lives to defeat the gremlins—including popping one into the aforementioned microwave.

The cast that Dante assembled was a wonderful mixture of old and new faces. Unknown

Never feed him after midnight: Mogwai in Joe Dante's *Gremlins* (1984).

Zach Galligan was cast as Billy, the young man who receives the pet "mogwai," or gremlin. As the object of his affections, Spielberg and Dante cast Phoebe Cates, who had just created a sensation of sorts by playing a teenage sexpot in *Fast Times at Ridgemont High* (1982). Kate, her character in *Gremlins*, was more of the "sweet and innocent" type, but Spielberg in particular was impressed by the chemistry she and Galligan demonstrated together in their auditions.

In an unusual casting move, country singer and songwriter Hoyt Axton was given the role of Billy's father, a failed inventor. Axton had previously acted in *The Black Stallion* (1979) and exhibited a natural, relaxed presence before the camera. Veteran character actor Keye Luke was cast as Mr. Wing, the elderly Chinese shopkeeper who has the mogwai in his possession. And Polly Holiday, at the time a recurring character on the TV show *Alice*, was chosen to play Mrs. Deagle, a character vaguely based on Margaret Hamilton's Wicked Witch of the West in *The Wizard of Oz* (1939).

But it was in the casting of the smaller character roles where Dante really had some fun. Once again, he cast the venerable Dick Miller, this time playing a World War II veteran who is the first to refer to the mogwai as gremlins: "They're the same gremlins that brought down our planes in the big one," he notes. Another nice touch is the casting of Jackie Joseph as his wife, reuniting them from Corman's *The Little Shop of Horrors* (1960).

Kenneth Tobey (*The Thing from Another World*, 1951) has a cameo as a gas station attendant, and Dante's other favorite, Kevin McCarthy, is in the film by proxy, in a scene from Don Siegel's *Invasion of the Body Snatchers* (1956) that a character is watching on television.

But Dante's cameo casting goes even further than in his previous films: Legendary Warner Bros. animator Chuck Jones shows up as Mr. Jones, a man in a bar who gives Billy a compliment on the cartoon he has just drawn. In fact, *Gremlins* probably owes more of its zany, anarchic humor to the legendary Warner Bros. cartoon factory than to any other source of inspiration. One particular Bugs Bunny short, *Falling Hare* (1943), directed by Robert Clampett, was an introduction for most audiences to the concept of the gremlin, with its little green guy causing all sorts of mischief for Bugs. "I like him [Bugs]; he's silly!" the gremlin says to Mr. Bunny at one point in the short.

Robby the Robot, originally from *Forbidden Planet* (1956), makes an appearance at an "inventor's convention"; veteran character actor William Schallert (Jack Arnold's *The Incredible Shrinking Man*) appears as Father Bartlett; Spielberg himself shows up in a wheelchair: and *Gremlins* music composer Jerry Goldsmith appears wearing a cowboy hat. As if they weren't enough, western star Harry Carey Jr. and veteran B-movie actor Scott Brady (*Castle of Evil*, 1964, among others) make appearances of the "blink and you'll miss them" variety.

Even if you don't get all the inside jokes, however, *Gremlins* remains a fun and exciting romp. The title creatures, mostly sophisticated puppets, frequently upstage the live performers, especially the sweet and cuddly Gizmo (voiced by Howie Mandel) and the malicious Stripe (voiced by Frank Welker). The puppets were designed and created by special effects ace Chris Walas, and, although problematic to operate, they end up being worth all the trouble.

Filmed on a studio back lot rather than on location to add to that Frank Capra–esque quality, *Gremlins* references Capra's *It's a Wonderful Life* (1946) a number of times. In fact, pop culture references, like the Gremlins themselves, are legion in the film. Everything from urban legends (such as Kate's darkly humorous but poignant story of her father, dressed as Santa Claus, getting stuck in the chimney and dying on Christmas Eve) to sly nods to Spielberg's other films such as *E.T.* (1982) and *Close Encounters of the Third Kind* (1977) are thrown into the mix, adding immeasurably to the texture and subtext of the movie.

Goldsmith's music perfectly captures the mischievousness of the title characters and Dante's headlong direction never flags. Generally well-received critically (although the filmmakers were admonished for its violence), *Gremlins* was the fourth biggest money maker of the year, coming in just behind *Beverly Hills Cop*, *Ghostbusters* and Spielberg's own *Indiana Jones and the Temple of Doom*. A sequel was definitely in order, although it wouldn't arrive until six years later. And by that time, as we shall see, it may have been a bit late.

Bloodbath at the House of Death

Vincent Price did one last British comedy-horror film in the eighties, the title of which suggested an Amicus anthology: *Bloodbath at the House of Death* (1984). Sold with the tagline, "The movie it took a lot of guts to make," the film was an outright parody of numerous other horror films. The basic plot is taken from *The Legend of Hell House* (1973), a film directed by John Hough and based on a novel by Richard Matheson.

Bloodbath opens in the year 1975 (not coincidentally, the year of the events that inspired the book and movie *The Amityville Horror*) at an old dark house called Headstone Manor, which, the sign outside tells us, is a "businessman's weekend retreat and girls' summer camp."

A group of evil cultists dressed as monks (one of whom has painted toenails) breaks into the mansion and murders eighteen people who are staying there. The ways in which they kill them are eclectic, to say the least: two are axed, two have their throats slit, four are stabbed, two are struck by lightning, one is hanged, six are frozen to death in the house's freezer, and a witness to the carnage explodes through spontaneous human combustion. The nineteenth occupant, a woman, survives to tell the tale.

Flash forward to "the present," when a team of paranormal investigators is sent to Headstone Manor, which is now known by the nearby villagers as "The House of Death." Dr. Lucas Mandeville (Kenny Everett) and Dr. Barbara Coyle (Pamela Stephenson), set up their equipment in the house; the several other scientists include a pair of gay men (Stephen Wilson and *The New Avengers*' Gareth Hunt).

Meanwhile, in the surrounding forest, the Sinister Man (Price), who is in fact a 700-year-old black magic priest, oversees a Satanic rite to rid the house of the investigators. The Sinister Man speaks to some invisible demonic entity and relays the message to his gathered flock: "He says we must gather up all the faggots and burn them." Brother Theresa, the monk with the painted toenails, protests, "I'm not sure I like the sound of this!" Another cult member reassures him, saying, "Don't worry, Brother Theresa, he means wood."

The rather cheap gay jokes would be more offensive were it not for the fact that Everett, for whom the film was written, was an outspoken homosexual at a time when very few were out of the closet, particularly in show business. Everett was a former disc jockey for a pirate radio station that was hugely popular in England. He went on to have his own television show, and *Bloodbath* was an attempt to parlay that success into movies. While the film was not well-received at the time, it's developed a small cult following since due to video releases and television showings.

There isn't a great deal of wit in the movie, although there are some moments of not-quite-inspired silliness. Perfunctorily directed by Ray Cameron, who also helmed some of Everett's TV episodes, *Bloodbath*'s jokes are of the hit-or-miss variety. There are a lot of sex jokes, including a scene in which the voluptuous Stephenson (who previously appeared in Mel Brooks' *A History of the World Part One* and was a regular on NBC's *Saturday Night Live* in the eighties) is ravished by a ghost, a sequence lifted straight out of *The Legend of Hell House*.

Price has very little to do, although it looks like he had a fun time doing it. Much of the humor in his scenes comes from his uncharacteristic (for him) use of crude language. At one point, he tells another character to "piss off," and during the Satanic ceremony, a candle burns his hand, and he shouts "Oh, shit, my hand!" In true Mel Brooks fashion, the monks, who have been repeating every word he has said, chant in unison, "Oh, shit, my hand!"

The movie falls apart in the third act, when it turns out that the strange occurrences around the house are not satanic in nature, but extraterrestrial. The monks take off in a UFO; it seems they were space aliens using the house for their Earthbound pursuits. The whole film collapses into an incoherent mess of doppelgangers, aliens, flatulence jokes and "smart-arse paranormal research crap."

Nevertheless, any movie that includes the line, "Sounds like a lot of monks exploding," can't be all bad. With some dead-on parodies of scenes from such films as *The Amityville Horror* (1979), *The Shining* (1980), any number of slasher films and an ending cribbed from *The Rocky Horror Picture Show*, *Bloodbath at the House of Death* is an amusing time-waster that displays just a tiny amount of Everett's talent. The actor died of AIDS in 1995, and remains virtually unknown in the United States.

Once Bitten

Two of the biggest cinematic trends during the eighties were teen slasher films in the "vein" of *Halloween* (1978) and *Friday the 13th* (1980) and teen sex comedies à la *Porky's* (1982) and its many variations. It seemed an obvious little notion, then, to combine the two genres, thereby creating the teen sex comedy-horror film.

Canadian-born Jim Carrey had already starred in *Copper Mountain* (1983), a comedy set at a ski resort, when he played the lead in the teen vampire comedy *Once Bitten* (1985), directed by television veteran Howard Storm. It took three writers—David Hines, Jeffrey Hause and Terence Marsh—to concoct the trifle of a story involving a high school student and part-time ice cream truck driver (Carrey) who is seduced by a sexy vampire countess (Lauren Hutton). The basic plot in which the countess must have the blood of a virgin in order to remain youthful is a variation on *Blood for Dracula* (1974).

It just so happens that Mark is still a virgin thanks to his girlfriend Robin (Karen Kopins), a sweet young thing who is not ready to go all the way. Desperate to lose the curse of virginity (a big plot point in dozens of teen sex comedies), Mark goes along with some friends to an L.A. nightclub where he is picked up by the countess. He goes back to her place, a neo–Gothic mansion overseen by her butler-chauffeur Sebastian (*Blazing Saddle*'s Cleavon Little), where she slips him a mickey and proceeds to bite the buttons off his shirt. She also nips the inside of his thigh, marking him as her victim. When he wakes up, he thinks they've had sex, and the countess implies that he is part of her now.

The countess must feed twice more before midnight on Halloween or she will transform into an old crone. After she bites Mark a second time, he begins to act very strangely; he takes to sleeping in a trunk in his room, dresses entirely in black and orders raw hamburgers for lunch. Eventually, Robin consults an eccentric dealer in occult books (Peter Elbling) and comes to realize that Mark is the victim of a female vampire. She tracks the countess to her lair and relieves Mark of his virginity before the countess can have her final bite. The countess ages before their eyes and is taken to her coffin by the ever loyal Sebastian, who promises her that she's sure to find virgin blood "in places like Kansas and Nebraska."

Once Bitten is a routine comedy-horror movie which, despite its strong sexual theme, is rated PG-13. Apparently, the producers wanted to ensure they'd get the biggest teen audience they could. There are a few amusing moments here and there, many of them provided by Mark's friends Jamie and Russ (played by Thomas Ballatore and Skip Lackey). Perpetual nerds, they desperately want sex but are usually in the wrong place at the wrong time. They're involved in an unpleasant incident in the school shower after Robin asks them to see if they can find the tell-tale vampire bite on Mark's inner thigh. In the shower, they go through a number of awkward contortions to try to locate Mark's mark, but only succeed in causing a riot among homophobic students. Later, Mark says to them, "You could have just asked," and they have a homosexual panic: "Oh, my God, we liked it! We're homos! We're rump rangers!"

Carrey has a couple of nice moments and is actually more restrained than he would become. He looks appropriately gawky and seems genuinely bemused by his vampiric condition. "I can't be a vampire. I have to go to college!" he complains at one point.

Hutton, a former model who was never a great actress, acquits herself well as the countess, whose name we never learn. She's basically a centuries-old diva used to getting her own way. When she gets rather bitchy with Sebastian, he asks her, "Did we get up on the wrong side of the coffin this morning?"

Wearing an interesting variety of costumes, Hutton does give the impression of aging decadence; by the time she made the film, her modeling days were over and she was considered somewhat "long in the tooth." How appropriate, then, for the role. She gives particular relish to such lines as, "I haven't had anything this pure since the Vienna Boys' Choir hit town." And, not incidentally, she looks great throughout the film.

Once Bitten suffers from tired, anemic writing and perfunctory direction. While there are a few bright spots, they can't save the film from sinking into mediocrity. But it did point the way to the future: Jim Carrey became a big star in movies such as *Ace Ventura, Pet Detective* (1994) and *The Mask* (also 1994). And sex-comedy-horror films with teenage protagonists are still with us, for better or worse.

Fright Night

A far more successful vampire film, Tom Holland's delightful *Fright Night* (1985) is a loving homage to both Hammer and AIP vampire classics. Holland, who had written the screenplay for *Psycho II* (1983), a sequel to Hitchcock's masterpiece, specialized in darkly humorous stories and situations. Although *Psycho II* isn't really a comedy-horror film, it certainly contains many moments of gallows humor. Holland, who also wrote the rather interesting *The Beast Within* (1982) and the violent, gripping *Class of 1984* (1982), was hired by Columbia Pictures to direct *Fright Night* from his own screenplay.

Vampire films had been languishing since 1979's *Love at First Bite*, but it's safe to say that *Fright Night* injected new blood into the genre in much the same way that Hammer had in 1958 with *Horror of Dracula*, the first Technicolor vampire film and an acknowledged classic. The fact that *Fright Night* is comedy-horror doesn't dilute its truly frightening sequences, and it paved the way for bigger-budgeted Hollywood vampire epics such as *The Lost Boys* (1987), *Bram Stoker's Dracula* (1992) and *Interview with the Vampire* (1994).

"If you love being scared, it'll be the night of your life," read the tagline for *Fright Night*. Filmed for around seven million dollars, a considerable sum for a horror film at the time, *Fright Night* benefits from some excellent casting. The young leads, William Ragsdale, Stephen Geoffreys and Amanda Bearse, all acquit themselves nicely in the film, but the real fun lies in the casting of vampire and vampire hunter.

Veteran stage, film and television actor Chris Sarandon plays vampire Jerry Dandridge, "the vampire next door." He had made a big impression in such films as *Dog Day Afternoon* (1975) and in Michael Winner's horror film *The Sentinel* (1977), and in his stage work he had shown an affinity for the classics.

Sarandon was a perfect foil for the actor who was cast as his nemesis, beloved child star turned adult actor Roddy McDowall. Born in London in 1928, McDowall had appeared in several British films at a very young age before his family moved to America because of the Blitz in 1941. There he was quickly cast in such major Hollywood productions as *How Green Was My Valley* (1941) and *Lassie Come Home* (1943). As an adult he became popular in character roles, such as his recurring appearances in the *Planet of the Apes* film series between 1968 and 1973, as well as in the 1974 television series based on the movies. No stranger to the horror genre, he had also appeared in such shockers as *It!* (1967) and *The Legend of Hell House* (1973), as well as contributing a memorable performance in the 1969 television movie *Night Gallery*, which launched Rod Serling's series of the same name.

In *Fright Night*, Holland cast McDowall as Peter Vincent (the name is an homage to both Peter Cushing and Vincent Price), a has-been TV horror host and actor who finds himself in an encounter with a real vampire. Not exactly the "fearless vampire killer" that he portrayed in his old films, Vincent nevertheless rises to the occasion and battles the vampire on his home turf, an old mansion situated next door to the home of Judy Brewster (Dorothy Fielding) and her teenage son Charley (Ragsdale).

Essentially a cross between Hitchcock's *Rear Window* (1954) and Paul Landres' clever B-movie *The Return of Dracula* (1958), *Fright Night* brings the vampire legend into 1980s suburbia. Charley Brewster is a big horror fan who idolizes Peter Vincent. One night after watching Vincent's program *Fright Night*, Charley sees new neighbors moving in next door, carrying what looks like a coffin. A few nights later, he happens to see the new neighbor undressing a beautiful hooker he has hired for the evening. But after the lights go out next door, Charley hears a scream. The next day, he sees the woman's face on a television news story; her mutilated corpse has been found.

Needless to say, no one believes Charley when he tells them that his new neighbor may be a vampire, not even his friend "Evil" Ed Thompson (Geoffreys) and girlfriend Amy Peterson (Bearse). In desperation, Charley seeks Vincent's help. At first, Vincent believes that Charley is merely an obsessed fan, but a trip to Dandridge's house convinces him otherwise. The final act of the film takes place entirely in and around the old mansion, and under Holland's spirited, confident direction, the last third of the film has the feel of a good old-fashioned Hammer horror (with a bit of AIP's 1970 *Count Yorga Vampire* thrown in) but with state-of-the-art (for 1985) special effects by Richard Edlund, who had handled the effects for *Ghostbusters* the year before.

Jan Kisser's fluid cinematography, with its muted, pastel color schemes, is reminiscent of the work of such Hammer "lighting cameramen" as Jack Asher (*The Brides of Dracula*, 1960) and Alan Hume (*The Kiss of the Vampire*, 1963). One doesn't expect an autumnal look to a film shot in Southern California, but Kisser does wonders in lighting John De Cuir Jr.'s elegant sets. Once our "heroes" enter the mansion, the film takes on the look of a period piece, which is in a sense where it was heading all along.

Holland's screenplay cleverly updates the vampire myth for a new audience. Early in the film, Vincent loses his job at the TV station due to low ratings and laments to Charley, "Apparently your generation doesn't want to see vampire killers anymore, nor vampires either. All they want to see is slashers running around in ski masks hacking up young virgins." The interesting thing about that statement is that, early in the eighties, Vincent's observations would have been correct. But in the wake of *Fright Night*, vampires were very much "in" again, and remain so to this day.

McDowall is superb as the cowardly yet likable Vincent, who helps to save the day almost in spite of himself. In another nod to Hammer, he tears the curtain from Dandridge's basement window, exposing him to sunlight just as Cushing had done to Christopher Lee in *Horror of Dracula*. Life imitates art, and the actor who has played a vampire killer in several movies becomes one in "real" life.

Astute horror fans will notice a number of in-jokes, especially in Vincent's apartment. His walls are decorated with artwork by Basil Gogos, cover artist for *Famous Monsters* magazine, and there's one particularly beautiful painting of John Carradine as Dracula, spreading his cape in Universal's *House of Dracula* (1945). The ratlike head and clawlike hands of Klaus Kinski's Dracula from Werner Herzog's *Nosferatu the Vampyre* (1979) also rest on Vincent's mantel.

But you can't have a great hero—however reluctant—without a great villain, and Sarandon's Dandridge more than fills the bill. Boyishly charming, given to wearing flamboyant scarves and sucking on blood oranges, he makes the ladies swoon (including Charley's girlfriend Amy) while at the same time appealing to Charley's nerdy friend "Evil" Ed with a speech that would be compelling to any teenage "outsider." Cornering Ed in a dark alley, Dandridge croons to him in a silken voice: "Hello, Edward. You don't have to be afraid of me. I know what it's like being different. Only they won't pick on you any more, or beat you up. I'll see to that. All you have to do is take my hand."

Later, in the old dark mansion, Vincent whips out a crucifix and shoves it toward Dandridge's face. "Back, spawn of Satan!" Vincent shouts. Dandridge just laughs at him: "Oh, really!" Unlike any Hammer vampire, Dandridge takes the cross and crushes it in his hand, tossing it onto the floor. "You have to have faith for this to work on me!" he tells Vincent. The vampire has indeed been brought up to date: In a world where religion no longer holds the influence it once did, all the old symbols and icons may not be effective. Only the devout, apparently, are safe from vampires in the eighties, and there aren't many of those left.

Edlund's effects are exciting and startling. When Dandridge turns into a bat, as any self-respecting vampire would do, it isn't just some flapping rubber toy on a string, it's a full-blooded, full-fanged flying demon. Likewise, when Ed, who is more or less the Renfield character, transforms into a wolf, it looks like the genuine article, and it's actually quite disturbing to see the beast impaled on an upturned table leg.

The most frightening effect, though, is the one that was cut from Edlund's work on *Ghostbusters*. Originally, it was supposed to have been the face of the "ghost librarian" in that film, but it was dropped because it was deemed too horrific. But a movie titled *Fright Night* was expected to go for the jugular, and Edlund finally got to use the effect when Amy is bitten by Dandridge. For a moment, she transforms into a hellish, vampiric creature that is nearly all mouth and fangs, a nightmare vision if there ever was one. It was such a shocking image that it was used in the film's poster and advertising art.

Fright Night is one of the few comedy-horror films that features genuine scares. The humor arises out of the characters and situations and isn't just dropped in for its own sake. Upon its release on August 2, 1985, the movie became a sleeper hit, grossing just under $25 million domestically, a tidy sum. It also won several awards, including three Saturn Awards from the Academy of Science Fiction, Fantasy and Horror Films, who named *Fright Night* "the best horror movie of 1985."

Spawning a highly entertaining sequel (*Fright Night II*, 1985, with Ragsdale and McDowall reprising their roles), Tom Holland's first directorial effort managed to make vampires scary again for a new generation of filmgoers. More vampire films have been made since 1985 than ever before, and our toothsome friends (and fiends) continue to delight and terrify us in the twenty-first century.

The Return of the Living Dead

The genesis of *The Return of the Living Dead* (1985) is a long and convoluted one. In a sense, it begins in 1968, when George A. Romero's *Night of the Living Dead* became an instant cult classic. Unfortunately, Romero himself saw little of the film's profits due to a bad distribution deal and the fact that the film was never properly copyrighted, which is why there are so many "unofficial" versions of the movie available on DVD today. The original title of the film was *The Night of Anubis*, but as the distributor, The Walter Reade Organization, felt that no one would know that Anubis was the Egyptian god of the dead, it was changed to the more generic *Night of the Living Dead*. Apparently, because of this eleventh hour decision, prints without copyrights on them were rushed out to theaters.

Flash forward to 1978: That year, Romero made his even more groundbreaking and influential *Dawn of the Dead*, the second in his proposed "Dead" trilogy. John Russo, one of Romero's partners on the original film, disagreed with Romero on how to continue the series and wrote a novel called *Return of the Living Dead*. He sold the film rights in 1979 to independent producer Tom Fox, who set up the production and assigned the screenplay to be written by Dan O'Bannon, who had just written the blockbuster sci-fi horror film *Alien*. Tobe Hooper was hired to direct, but dropped out of the production to work on *The Funhouse* for Universal.

At that point, the whole nature of the project changed and O'Bannon decided to rewrite it as a comedy-horror film rather than a "serious" sequel to *Night of the Living Dead*. O'Bannon was now set to direct the film himself, with Russo adapting this new version into another novel, also titled *The Return of the Living Dead*. This time, the film was made and the novel was published, in that order.

Producers Fox and Graham Henderson supposedly attempted to contact Romero several time to offer him producing credit on the film, but he never returned their phone calls. It's safe to say that there was "bad blood," so to speak, between Russo and Romero. After all, Romero was considered by most fans to be the auteur of the series, while Russo and company seemed to be blurring the line between what was the "official" series and a film that seemed to be attempting to cash in on the *Night* franchise. In fact, Richard P. Rubenstein, who had produced *Dawn of the Dead*, attempted to get an injunction to prevent the producers from using the words *Living Dead* in the title, but the arbitrators of the Motion Picture Association of America ruled in favor of Fox and Henderson.

Whatever the case, *The Return of the Living Dead* attempted to clear up any confusion by presenting itself as an out-and-out spoof. In Louisville, Kentucky, a medical supply warehouse foreman named Frank (James Karen) tells his young employee (Thom Matthews) that *Night of the Living Dead* was based on a "true story"—what really happened when a gas developed by the military (something called 2-4-5 Trioxin) was accidentally spilled in the morgue of a VA hospital in Pittsburgh. The gas caused cadavers to return to life, but the military stepped in, cleaned up the spill and destroyed the zombies. The story was somehow leaked (just like the gas) and the military allowed *Night of the Living Dead* to be made, but only if the details were changed.

This conceit allowed *Return*'s makers to have some fun with the premise and do things that Romero likely would not have done: fill the movie with "splatstick," camp up the dialogue and even throw in copious amounts of nudity. The result is a movie that was a big success for Orion Pictures, who released it on August 16, 1985.

Director O'Bannon originally planned on playing Frank himself, but when Karen came in to read for another role, O'Bannon hired him on the spot for the role. Also cast was veteran actor Clu Gulager as Burt, Frank's boss, with Don Calfa as Ernie, a mortician. According to liner notes in the collector's edition DVD, O'Bannon had no idea that Burt and Ernie were also the names of two very famous *Sesame Street* characters.

The other cast members were all young, with the standout of the "punks" being Linnea Quigley as Trash, who does her now-famous striptease in the cemetery early in the film. Her character is a pretty sick puppy. Before she gets naked, she says to another character: "Do you ever wonder about all the different ways of dying? You know, violently? And wonder, like, what would be the most horrible way to die.... For me, the worst way would be for a bunch of old men to get around me and start biting and eating me alive."

Needless to say, Trash meets a fate very much like that, as do many other characters. It transpires that the medical warehouse contains several of the Trioxin canisters, as well as one cadaver from the original event in Pittsburgh. Predictably, the canisters spring a leak, releasing the cadaver (Allan Trautman) to newfound zombie-hood and poisoning Frank and Freddy. Several body parts in the warehouse, including a "split dog," start moving about, and the two warehouse employees slowly turn into zombies themselves.

Burt and Ernie conspire to cremate the animated body parts and cadaver, but the smoke issuing up from the crematorium's chimney carries the toxic gas with it. Mixing with a cloud, it forms into rain and falls onto the very cemetery where Trash is dancing naked with her friends.

Coincidence piles upon coincidence, ensuring that *Return* can never be taken seriously. The arch dialogue and over-the-top acting drive the point home. At first, the effect is rather unsettling: Audiences aren't sure if they should laugh, scream or throw up. Eventually, the movie settles on a tone that calls for all of those reactions.

There are some very funny lines. When a zombie refuses to die, even though it's received a pickaxe to the head, Burt says to Frank, "I thought you said if we destroyed the brain, it would die!" Frank lamely replies, "Well, it worked in the movie." Freddy blurts out, "You mean the movie lied?"

The zombies are very different from those in Romero's films. Instead of shambling along like, well, zombies, they move fast, can speak and seem as intelligent as they were when they were alive. But because their bodies are rotting away, they're in constant pain, and the only way they can alleviate it is by eating the brains of human beings.

At one point, the corpse of a woman—well, really she's just half a corpse—is strapped to a table by Ernie. She wails about the "pain of being dead" and says, "I can feel myself rotting." Ernie asks her, "Eating brains ... how does that make you feel?" The half-corpse is quite adamant on this point: "It makes the pain go away!"

Again, unlike in Romero's mythos, shooting these zombies in the head has little or no effect; it seems that the only way to dispatch them is to cremate them. But then you have that smoke problem...

Although it's more successful than *An American Werewolf in London* at mixing comedy with horror, *The Return of the Living Dead* suffers from O'Bannon's undisciplined direction. While Gulager, Calfa and especially Karen are fun to watch, O'Bannon allows them to go so far over the top at times that the film loses all credibility. More amusing, in a sick sort of way, are the scenes in which the zombies attack the paramedics sent to one of the scenes of carnage; one zombie gets on the car radio, smiling, begging, "Send more paramedics!" The joke is repeated when some of the zombies attack policemen sent to the scene, and a zombie gets on the police radio, pleading, "Send more cops!"

Where the film suffers most is in the scenes involving the punks, a group of foul-mouthed delinquents just crying out—literally in Trash's case—to be slaughtered. This is where the movie becomes a loud, annoying mess. By the end of the film, when the whole concept has pretty much run its course, it seems as though the only solution is to nuke the whole city ... which is what happens. How the military plans to cover up nuking Louisville is anybody's guess, but by that time, the audience has pretty much ceased to care, as any sense of reality has been tossed out the window.

The Return of the Living Dead spawned several sequels despite its faults, none of them featuring the participation of O'Bannon or Russo. The redundantly titled *Return of the Living Dead Part II*, written and directed—poorly—by Ken Wiederhorn, was released on January 15, 1988, and was a modest box office success. Each film in the series fared worse, however.

Return of the Living Dead 3 (no roman numerals this time) was produced and directed by Brian Yuzna of the *Re-Animator* films. Although somewhat stylishly done, it's more of a teen horror film than the others and had a limited release in 1993 when it failed miserably, earning a paltry $54,000. Despite this setback, the series continued in 2005 with *Return of the Living Dead: Necropolis* (dispensing with the numbers altogether), which premiered on the SciFi Channel in edited form. Peter Coyote starred, and the less said about this one the better. As of this writing, the dead have returned one more time in *Return of the Living Dead: Rave from the Grave*, another SciFi Channel premiere that was released later on DVD in its uncut form. Let's hope this is the final nail in the coffin.

Re-Animator

A new chapter in the history of the comedy-horror film was written in late 1985, when director Stuart Gordon's version of H. P. Lovecraft's *Re-Animator* was unleashed upon the world. Bold and innovative, both in its Grand Guignol gore effects and its mordant humor, it was a film that owed as much to Hammer horror as to Lovecraft.

Lovecraft's original story "Herbert West: Reanimator" was, in a sense, one of the author's throwaways. It was originally serialized in an amateur press magazine called *Home Brew*; he wrote it on commission and was paid a whopping five dollars for each installment. In later years, he said that he felt his work had been compromised because the publisher forced him to end each installment with a cliffhanger and start the next one with a recap of the previous chapter.

"Herbert West: Reanimator" is not one of Lovecraft's better tales; it's over-the-top, clichéd and blatantly racist. It has very little of the "cosmic horror" for which the author ultimately became famous. What it does possess in abundance is a love of the Gothic horror tale; ultimately, the story is both an homage to and an affectionate parody of Mary Shelley's *Frankenstein*.

It is perhaps understandable, then, that one of Lovecraft's more gruesome, less cosmic stories was chosen for a film treatment. Up to that point, film adaptations of his work were spotty, to say the least. The best was probably the first, Roger Corman's *The Haunted Palace* (1963), which was sold as an Edgar Allan Poe movie but was in fact a fairly faithful adaptation of H.P. Lovecraft's short novel *The Case of Charles Dexter Ward*. The next Lovecraft film, *Die Monster Die!* (1965) was allegedly based on Lovecraft's *The Colour Out of Space*, but very little of the story remains in the finished film. After that came *The Dunwich Horror* (1970), a movie that has its moments but co-stars a woefully miscast Sandra Dee; Gidget didn't belong in Lovecraft's world.

It was left to Gordon to make the first truly successful Lovecraft film, one that influenced a whole sub-genre that is still prevalent today. A fan of both the reclusive Providence author and of Hammer's Frankenstein pictures starring Peter Cushing, Gordon was a well-known stage director in Chicago with his company, Organic Theater, a troupe of actors and directors dedicated to bringing original works to the stage.

In the book *Lurker in the Lobby: A Guide to the Cinema of H.P. Lovecraft* by Andrew Migliore and John Strysik, Gordon recounted how he came to make *Re-Animator*, his first feature:

> In our company we had several talented actors just starting out in their careers, and whenever a movie would come into town, they would be cast in the movie. So it occurred to me that we should do an Organic Theater movie. I was trying to come up with an idea for a

project when a friend of mine suggested that we do a horror film. He said, no matter how badly the film comes out you can always get your money back, and you can do it for under a million dollars. So I was trying to find a good topic. I was talking to someone about the fact that there were all these vampire and Frankenstein movies being made, and he asked if I had ever heard of 'Herbert West: Reanimator,' an H. P. Lovecraft story. I had never heard of it, and I thought I had read a lot of Lovecraft. So eventually I went to look for it in the Chicago Public Library.... The book was an old crumbling pulp but the stories were fantastic so we started adapting them to the movie that eventually became *Re-Animator*.

In an interview with Gordon on the 2007 Anchor Bay Collection DVD of *Re-Animator*, Gordon talked about being inspired by Hammer's Frankenstein series; clips are shown of *The Curse of Frankenstein* (1957) and *The Revenge of Frankenstein* (1958), Hammer's seminal horror films that established Cushing as an arrogant, obsessed, even psychotic Baron Frankenstein who is far worse than any monster he creates. In fact, he becomes his own creation at the end of *Revenge*.

The tone and plot structure of *Re-Animator* is very similar to that of Hammer's Frankenstein series, in particular *Revenge*, in which Frankenstein, under the name of "Dr. Stein," operates a hospital for the poor while "borrowing" numerous body parts from his patients to build his next creation. In *Re-Animator*, Herbert West (Jeffrey Combs) is kicked out of medical school in Switzerland (home country of Frankenstein, according to Shelley) for trying to bring a corpse back to life. He ends up at Miskatonic University in Massachusetts, where he enlists the aid of medical student Dan Cain (Bruce Abbott) to help him in his experiments, much as Cushing's Dr. Stein had enrolled Dr. Kleve (Francis Matthews) as his assistant in *Revenge*.

The *Re-Animator* screenplay was written by Gordon, Dennis Paoli and William J. Norris. Paoli had worked with Gordon at Organic Theater and in his interview in *Lurker in the Lobby*, pointed out: "[The humor] wasn't there in the first draft—that I can tell you. We certainly weren't making fun of these characters' desires and these characters' neuroses. We were simply expressing them."

Paoli went on to say that the humor started to come out in subsequent drafts and when the film actually went into production:

> You know, Lovecraft's not funny either, except he's so outre, so beyond, so far past where everybody else is thinking literature should go. I don't think that by adding humor we negated the spirit of Lovecraft at all. And I think it's there in all Gothics. I think when the Gothic genre takes itself so seriously, you start laughing at it as opposed to laughing with it.... In *Re-Animator* you are with Herbert West—you oddly identify with Herbert West.

Fortuitously, producer Brian Yuzna was in search of a project; he had just raised money for a film that had fallen apart. Gordon pitched *Re-Animator* to Yuzna and the rest is history. Gordon took a leave of absence from Organic Theater and went to Los Angeles to make the film, which was shot in eighteen days, shooting a full twenty-four hours on the last day.

One of Gordon's best decisions, as it turned out, was the casting of Combs as Herbert West. Combs, an actor with a very strong theater background, is perfect in the role. It's a star-making performance. His Herbert West is, like Frankenstein, an arrogant mad scientist type who has developed a formula for reanimating dead tissue. Combs has a marvelous Peter Cushing theatricality about him in the part, although he more closely resembles Ralph Bates, who played the baron in Hammer's *Horror of Frankenstein* (1970).

In an interview that I did with Combs for the magazine *Imagi-Movies* (#3, Spring 1994), his macabre sense of humor came through loud and clear. "What's your blood type, Bruce?"

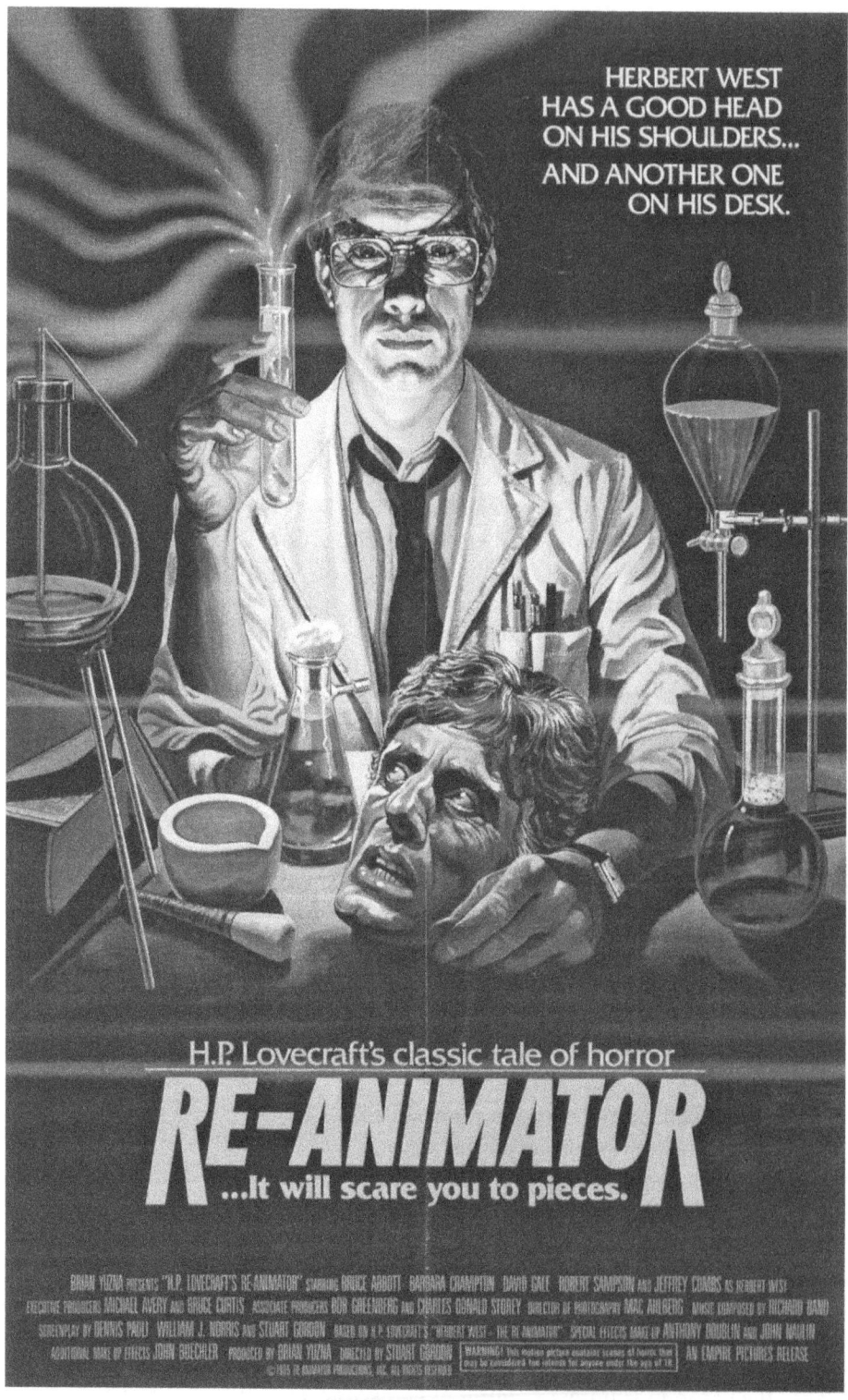

Original poster art for Stuart Gordon's ground-breaking comedy-horror film of H.P. Lovecraft's *Re-Animator* (1985).

was he first thing he said to me on the telephone. When I told him I didn't know, he said quietly, "I'm sure we can find out."

Combs was not at all familiar with Lovecraft before he walked into Gordon's office to audition for the role of West. That wasn't what he told the producers, however: "They would say, 'You know, this movie's based on H.P. Lovecraft,' and like any actor who wants a job, I said, 'Oh! Ah, sure!' I'd heard the name, but I really didn't know his writings at all. But I went out and read quite a bit of it after that."

Combs was at first taken aback by the script. He recalled, "I went through some quandaries. I wondered, 'What is this?' Actually, when I first read the script for *Re-Animator*, I thought, 'Oh, God, this is quite strong. But I'll do it, because work is work, and no one will ever see it anyway.' How wrong can you be?"

Probably the only actor working in horror films today who recalls some of the grandeur of the classic horror actors such as Karloff, Lugosi, Cushing and Lee, Combs told me that he wanted to "bring back some of that style. All of those guys in the earlier horror films were stage-based. That's where that kind of grand attitude comes from—a little larger than life. A lot of actors don't have that sort of base. They just come in and don't kick it in the rear. It's very flattering to be compared to people like Vincent Price, Peter Cushing and all those great actors."

Combs and Gordon turned out to be a match made in Heaven, according to Combs: "He understands the process. A lot of film directors don't really know how to talk to actors other than to say, 'Stand there,' or 'Can you say it louder and faster?' Stuart really knows how to get the detail. He can really base it in honest-to-goodness motivation and reality. Although it's fantastical, he likes to base it in fact. He's a great guy. We have a lot of good laughs."

And many of those good laughs are on-screen in *Re-Animator*. It's a certifiable cult classic, released to an unsuspecting world at 1985's Cannes Film Festival, becoming one of the first movies to find its true audience on video, where it was unashamedly unrated. Its status and its influence have only grown over the years, and it remains one of the few films to successfully combine scares—real scares—with real laughs.

West's first experiment, a revitalized cat, gets splattered against a wall. "Don't expect it to tango," he tells Cain. "It has a broken back."

His human experiments don't fare much better. And there is, of course, one of the most over-the-top gore scenes of all time, in which a re-animated human head (David Gale) tries to get fresh with a lovely—and very naked—coed (Barbara Crampton). That notorious scene also features one of the best lines in the film, when West admonishes the head by saying, "Who's going to believe a talking head? Get a job in a freak show!"

Re-Animator broke down the barriers between "splatter movies" and comedy-horror films. Its buckets of gore mixed with barrels of laughs, and it opened up a whole new realm where nothing was sacred and nothing was taboo. It could easily have been a disaster, but thanks to Gordon and his cast, it virtually invented a whole new sub-genre of the comedy-horror film: "splatstick." The sequels are worthy too—but more on those later.

The Toxic Avenger

A good candidate for "most tasteless film ever made" might just be *The Toxic Avenger*, produced and released by Troma Entertainment, long known for making campy B-movies. Officially released on April 11, 1986, the movie became a cult favorite at midnight screenings at the famous Bleecker Street Cinema in New York City. There's something in the film to offend everyone: graphic child murder and mutilation, the senseless shooting of a seeing-eye dog, attempted rape of a blind girl, the beating of an elderly woman, etc., etc.

The fact that none of these atrocities are meant to be taken seriously only adds to its offensiveness. The movie's genesis began back in 1975, when Troma president Lloyd Kaufman was pre-production supervisor on Sylvester Stallone's *Rocky*. At that year's Cannes Film Festival, Kaufman had read an article in "Variety" indicating that horror films were no longer popular. As sick flicks such as *Bloodsucking Freaks* (and the less said about that, the better) were Troma's stock in trade, the perverse filmmaker decided to produce a horror film in a health club, the set of the training scenes in *Rocky*. From such modest beginnings, *The Toxic Avenger* (originally titled *The Health Club Horror*) was born.

Troma's offices are located in a little hole in the wall in New York City's Hell's Kitchen. Because of their low-budget roots, the company takes special pleasure in making their films as extreme, exploitative and shoddy as possible. The *Toxic Avenger* is no exception. It's the tragi-comic story of Melvin Ferd (Mark Torgl), a ninety-eight-pound weakling and nerd who mops up the floors at Tromaville Health Club, where he is continually mocked by members. The worst offenders are Bozo (Gary Schneider), Slug (Robert Pritchard), Wanda (Jennifer Baptist) and Julie (Cindy Manion). But then again, they're not nice people. When they're not harassing Melvin, they're out on the road running down children in their souped-up muscle car and taking pictures of the carnage, to which Wanda masturbates. How's that for political incorrectness?

Things come to a head when, back at the health club, Melvin's "torturers" trick him into putting on a pink tutu and kissing a sheep. Humiliated, Melvin runs from the laughing crowd and jumps out of a window, landing in a drum of toxic waste that just happens to have been dumped outside. Hideously deformed by the poisonous garbage, he returns to town as The Toxic Avenger (Mitch Cohen), dedicated to ending evil in particularly nasty, gory and sadistic ways.

Needless to say, the whole concept is just an excuse on which to hang numerous gruesome set-pieces, including a scene in a Mexican restaurant that involves a gang of three holdup men who shoot the aforementioned dog and attempt to rape the blind girl ("I always wanted to cornhole me a blind bitch," one of them says with glee) and even point a shotgun into a baby's face. That particular scene caused the actor, Patrick Kilpatrick, who held the gun, to quit the film. He didn't like being directed to point the gun at the baby, and who can blame him?

In any case, the Toxic Avenger's treatment of the criminals is even more horrific than anything they've done. He rips off the would-be rapist's arm and beats him with it, turns another's face into a human milkshake, and commits other such atrocities. There is a rare tender moment, however, when he falls in love with the blind girl (Andree Maranda) who loves him despite his deformity.

The extreme gore effects seen in the unrated version were created by a woman, Jennifer Aspinall. Although done quickly and cheaply, her special makeup effects are as unsettling as anything done by Tom Savini; the ghastly scene in which a child's head is run over by a car was done with a dummy, a melon with a wig on it (for the head) and red food dye. Supposedly, the scene was based on an actual incident in which Kaufman was backing his car out of the garage and accidentally hit his sister. She was unharmed, but the incident haunted Kaufman. Now, thanks to *The Toxic Avenger*, it haunts all of us.

The restaurant hold-up man who has his arm ripped off was actually a one-armed actor.

Simply enough, his prosthetic arm was pulled off for the scene. And the dog that is shot was trained to glide across the floor; its "intestines" were spaghetti covered in gray paint.

But knowledge of how the tricks were done doesn't make them any less disturbing. Unlike *Flesh for Frankenstein* and *Blood for Dracula*, however, a true sense of irony is sorely missing from *The Toxic Avenger*. It's a movie that revels in its own tastelessness, that seems to say that the only way to deal with evil is to be twice as sadistic as those who perpetrate it. It's a very mean-spirited film.

Of course, to imply that the makers of *The Toxic Avenger* were interested in making a political statement is to miss the point. Kaufman and his partner Michael Herz (who receives co-directing credit) were just trying to make money by appealing to the lowest common denominator. In that respect, they succeeded. Although produced on a budget of only $475,000, *The Toxic Avenger* has made millions over the years, spawning three sequels: *The Toxic Avenger Part II* (1989), *The Toxic Avenger Part III: The Last Temptation of Toxie* (1989) and *Citizen Toxie: The Toxic Avenger IV* (2001). They're all as intentionally cheesy as they sound, albeit less gory than the original.

It's impossible to critique a film like *The Toxic Avenger* in the ordinary way. It is disgusting, sick, vile, poorly acted and sloppily produced. The fact is, that is exactly what the filmmakers intended it to be. So in that respect, it's a great success. Incredibly, it spawned not only sequels, but a short-lived children's cartoon show, *Toxic Crusaders*, and an equally short-lived Marvel Comic. Most bizarre of all, it also inspired a stage musical, *Toxic Avenger: the Musikill*, which was produced at Omaha's Blue Barn Theatre in 2004. "Toxie," now Troma's trademark character, has influenced everything they've done since, including *Class of Nuke 'Em High* (1986) and their latest "spectacle," *Poultrygeist: Night of the Chicken Dead* (2006). The name Troma has become associated with campy, intentionally atrocious filmmaking. You have to give Kaufman and Herz credit for one thing: They have set the bar low and have continued to produce films on that level of "quality" for over twenty years now.

Critters

Stephen Herek's *Critters* (1986) may be the only comedy-horror film based on a "true" event, however loosely. It's a case referred to in *The Encyclopedia of Extraterrestrial Encounters* edited by Ronald D. Story as "The Kelly-Hopkinsville (Kentucky) goblins."

The book entry, written by Coral and Jim Lorenzen, relates an incident that occurred on August 22, 1955, near Hopkinsville, Kentucky:

> The basic details include the beginning of the episode when visiting relative Bill Taylor went out to the well for a drink and came back to tell of a "spaceship" which had landed in a nearby field. Just a scant few minutes later the aroused household saw a small specter-like figure approaching the house.
>
> It appeared to be lit by an internal source, had a roundish head, huge elephantine ears, a slit-like mouth which extended from ear to ear. The eyes were huge and wide-set. Only about three or three and one-half feet in height, the creature had no visible neck, and its arms were long and ended in clawed hands. Although it stood upright, it dropped to all fours when it ran.

According to the Frank Sutton family, several of the creatures converged on the house, climbing trees, and one managed to climb onto the roof. The Lorenzens wrote, "At one point Sutton fired a shotgun through the screen door at one of the little men. Although struck and knocked over by the blast, the little fellow got up and scuttled away on his hands and feet."

The bizarre events continued for most of the night until the family piled into their car and drove into town to report the incident to the police. When Deputy Sheriff George Batts and two state policemen arrived at the house, they found no evidence of the "little men," although researchers who later interviewed the family "were inclined to believe the incident did take place."

Whatever the case, it remains one of the most famous cases in the realm of UFOs. Screenwriter Domonic Muir took the basic "facts" of the encounter and, along with director Herek, turned it into the film *Critters*. In the movie, the "little green men" became small, round creatures called Crites (or Krites) who looked a bit like bipedal porcupines and rolled like tumbleweeds when they were in a hurry.

Although the filmmakers have been criticized for trying to cash in on the success of *Gremlins*, Herek pointed out in an interview on the liner notes for the British VHS release of the film that the original draft of *Critters* was actually written by Muir months before *Gremlins* started production and that he and Muir did several rewrites to eliminate many of the coincidental similarities between the two films. The design for the gremlins themselves in Joe Dante's film is very similar to that of the so-called "Kelly-Hopkinsville creatures," whereas the Crites are just weird little fur balls.

Whatever strange synchronicities may have been going on with the two films, the plot-line of *Critters* is embellished to give it something of an "outer space western" flavor: Two bounty hunters from another planet hunt down the Crites, who have landed their spaceship near a small Kansas town.

The cast that Herek assembled is an excellent combination of seasoned veterans and talented youngsters. Dee Wallace-Stone, previously seen in Joe Dante's *The Howling* (1981) and Steven Spielberg's *E.T.* (1982), was cast as Helen Brown, a mother of two who lives in a farmhouse with her husband Jay (Billy Green Bush). The great character actor M. Emmett Walsh, who had just appeared in Joel and Ethan Coen's stunning debut film *Blood Simple* (1985), had the role of Harv, the local police chief. Stage actor Terrence Mann was given the dual role of rock singer Johnny Steele and Ug, the interstellar bounty hunter who "borrows" Steele's physical features during his stay on Earth. And a young Billy Zane ended up being eaten by Crites in a small role as the boyfriend of Helen and Jay's daughter Alice (Nadine Van Der Velde).

Critters was very well-received upon its release on April 11, 1986. New Line Cinema, a company that was still building its reputation on such horror fare as Sam Raimi's *The Evil Dead* (1982) and Wes Craven's *A Nightmare on Elm Street* (1984), had a real "sleeper" success with *Critters*. Film critics Gene Siskel and Roger Ebert, on their syndicated television program *Siskel and Ebert at the Movies*, gave the film "two thumbs up."

Much of the humor in the movie involves the bounty hunters, who steal a police car and, due to their lack of knowledge regarding earthbound vehicles, drive it backwards around town. Walsh seems to be having fun in his role of bewildered cop, but unfortunately he's sadly underused in the film. Wallace-Stone and the other members of "the Brown family" are warmly convincing; they don't seem like an eighties family at all, though. They're more like "salt of the earth" Eisenhower-era types, perhaps a sort of homage to the Sutton family in the original Kelly-Hopkinsville case.

Critters is an amiable little movie, fast-paced at a mere 86 minutes and full of loony sight gags. The Crites are even given subtitles so that we can understand their language. They don't have much to say, with the exception of one of them shouting "Fuck!" when his companion is blown apart by a shotgun.

The film was successful enough to spawn three sequels, none of them directed by Herek, who went on to helm such mainstream movies as *Bill and Ted's Excellent Adventure* (1989) and *Mr. Holland's Opus* (1995).

House

In the mid-eighties, it almost seemed at times that comedy-horror films outnumbered the "serious" kind. *House* (1986), an off-the-wall haunted house story, was conjured up by Fred Dekker (who would later direct two comedy-horror films himself) with a screenplay by Ethan Wiley. Produced by fun-loving New World Pictures (once owned by Roger Corman but by this time in other hands), *House* was directed by journeyman filmmaker Steve Miner, who had previously helmed the first two *Friday the 13th* sequels.

In the film, Roger Cobb (William Katt), a Vietnam veteran, is also a horror novelist à la Stephen King. After his son vanishes while visiting his aunt in her rambling old house, he moves into the house to write a novel based on his war experiences. Weird happenings ensue and bizarre apparitions are seen. It's haunted by, among other "things," the specter of his old war buddy Big Ben (Richard Moll), who harbors a grudge against Cobb for leaving him to die in the jungle. Meanwhile, Cobb's estranged wife (Kay Lenz) starts snooping around the place and everything comes to a head when Cobb discovers that the house itself is evil (and, in Lovecraftian fashion, is also a gateway to another dimension).

House has an ambitious concept, although the film's budget isn't quite enough to see it through. There are some imaginative touches, such as Cobb falling through a window into some eldritch dimension, complete with a flying demon that looks like one of Lovecraft's "Night Gaunts." But much of the humor is forced, for example the scene in which Cobb cuts up the body of what he thinks is his wife (actually a demon) to the tune of the Linda Ronstadt hit "You're No Good."

Where the film does work, however, is in the Vietnam subtext. Cobb is forced to literally face his demons when Big Ben shows up, even though the ghost is somewhat inept. "Damn!" the specter exclaims when he's trying to shoot his old buddy "Come back from the grave and I run out of ammunition!"

George Wendt, "Norm" of *Cheers* fame, has some funny lines as Cobb's neighbor, Harold Gorton. "Solitude's always better with somebody else around," he quips at one point. Cobb's other neighbor, Tanya (Mary Slavin) is a gorgeous Nordic blonde who's always coming on to him. "I can tell when a man wants to work," she coos. "I can also tell when a man wants to play."

Between the ghosts, his neighbors and the house itself, Cobb doesn't get much writing done; in a sense the story recalls that of *House of the Long Shadows* (1983). The film, produced by Sean S. Cunningham (who directed the original *Friday the 13th*), has its charms, including an appealing performance by Katt, who had made a huge impression on audiences ten years earlier in *Carrie*. Mac Ahlberg's cinematography is fluid and attractive and Harry Manfredini (another *Friday the 13th* veteran) contributes a pleasantly effective musical score. Released at a time when the entire genre seemed on the verge of self-parody, *House* was a modest success, earning just under twenty million dollars. As the film's budget was only around three million, it was a tidy enough profit to warrant three sequels, 1987's *House II: The Second Story*, 1989's *The Horror Show*, known in Great Britain and Australia as *House III*, and 1992's *House IV*. Unfortunately, all the sequels are negligible and contributed little to the genre.

Night of the Creeps

"What is this?" asks Detective Cameron (Tom Atkins). "A homicide, or a bad B-movie?" The answer: It's *Night of the Creeps* (1986), the story of parasitic slugs from outer space who enter human beings through their mouths and turn them into marauding zombies. Needless to say, teenagers fight against them and win the day ... or do they?

Written and directed by Fred Dekker, who was only twenty-seven years old at the time, *Night of the Creeps* is indeed a B-movie, although not a bad one. It revels in its cheesiness and its inside jokes: Six characters are named after horror directors, the celebrated "worst movie of all time," Ed Wood's *Plan 9 from Outer Space* (1959), is referenced, and the film's title itself is a take-off of George Romero's *Night of the Living Dead* (1968).

Played mostly for laughs, the film opens in 1959, the year that *Plan 9* was released. The plot, in fact, parodies Wood's cult "classic" in that an alien experiment has gone wrong and crashed to Earth, bringing about the expected zombie holocaust. After some initial carnage in which a teenager is infected by the parasites, we flash forward to 1986, where college student Chris Romero (Jason Lively) becomes infatuated with Cynthia Cronenberg (Jill Whitlow). The zombie outbreak begins when the infected body, which has been cryogenically frozen and kept in a lab since 1959, is accidentally unfrozen by Romero and his friend James Carpenter Hooper (Steve Marshall) during a hazing initiation. The body returns to life and escapes from the lab, going on a rampage that leads to the infection of most of the nearby town.

The zombies' heads have a tendency to split open and release the slug-like parasites, which is what happens to one of them outside Cynthia's sorority house. Our heroes impress her by recognizing the problem (parasitic alien invasion) and dealing with it (burning the zombies to a crisp). The climax seems to indicate that the menace is destroyed, but a coda shows Chris and Cynthia standing in front of the sorority house, watching it burn with the zombies and parasites inside. A zombified dog, however, has been overlooked, and it wanders into the scene. Cynthia bends down to pet the creature when it opens its mouth and a parasite jumps out of its mouth.

This was not the ending that Dekker intended. The final scene that he originally shot started in the same way, with the sorority house burning. Police cars are all over the place, and we see Detective Cameron, who is now a zombie, shambling down the street towards a cemetery. He falls to the ground and the parasites crawl out of him and go into the cemetery. The UFO that we saw in the film's opening scene shows up and the aliens try to retrieve their failed experiment.

The original ending wasn't used because the studio, Tri-Star Pictures, didn't like what Dekker showed them. The special effects were unfinished and the studio execs had a hard time picturing what the final version would look like, so they demanded a new ending with the clichéd cheap shock.

The funniest scene involves a busload of undead football players that head for the sorority house on the night of the formal dance. Detective Cameron, who has been guarding the girls at the sorority, looks out the window and sees the approaching horde. "I've got good news and bad news," he says. "The good news is, your dates are here." "What's the bad news?" asks one of the sorority sisters. "They're dead," Cameron replies.

Atkins is very good as the gruff detective, who always answers his phone with the sarcastic phrase, "Thrill me!" A veteran of such John Carpenter movies as *Halloween* (1978) and *The Fog* (1980), Atkins is by far the most watchable actor in the movie. The teenagers are okay, but they're upstaged by the over-the-top gore effects at every turn. *Night of the Creeps* is by no means a classic, but it's a movie with a strong cult following made by a writer-director who is a true fan of the genre, and as such, it seldom fails to elicit a smile or two.

The Monster Squad

Fred Dekker's next comedy-horror film is even better remembered by those who grew up in the eighties. *The Monster Squad* (1987) was co-written by Dekker and Shane Black, who also wrote 1987's *Lethal Weapon*. Most of *The Monster Squad*, however, reflects Dekker's love of the old Universal monster movies. In fact, the film is basically a cross between the *Our Gang* comedies and *Abbott and Costello Meet Frankenstein*. As in the A&C movie, Dracula (played here by Duncan Regehr) is the head villain, supervising Frankenstein's Monster (Tom Noonan), the Wolf Man (Carl Thibault), the Mummy (Michael Reid MacKay) and even the Creature from the Black Lagoon (Tom Woodruff Jr.). Jack Gwillim, a veteran of such big-budget movies as *Thunderball* (1965) and *Clash of the Titans* (1981), plays Dr. Van Helsing in the prologue, one of the best parts of the movie.

The plot has something to do with an amulet that maintains the balance between good and evil; once every hundred years or so, the artifact becomes vulnerable to destruction by the forces of darkness. Count Dracula, who has recently been revived, tries to reach the amulet ahead of our heroes, the Monster Squad, a ragtag band of kids who have a treehouse where they tell each other scary tales of the classic monsters.

The treehouse is one of Dekker's nods to the *Our Gang* comedies of the thirties. Others include a "No Girls" sign on the treehouse door and a dog named Pete (an homage to the *Our Gang* dog Petey).

The classic Universal monsters provided the other inspiration, but as the film was distributed by Tri-Star Pictures and not Universal, the filmmakers were not allowed to use the trademarked Universal monster makeups. Nevertheless, the monsters are all very recognizable variations.

There's a certain childlike charm to Dekker's film; those of us who grew up on the classic monsters will certainly relate to the wide-eyed wonder experienced by the Monster Squad (Andre Gower, Michael Faustino, Jason Hervey, Robby Kiger, Ryan Lambert and five-year-old Ashley Bank) when they meet Frankenstein's Monster in the flesh. The Monster turns out to be a sweet soul who immediately bonds with the five-year-old girl, in a tip of the hat to the scene with the little girl in James Whale's 1931 *Frankenstein*.

Not so Dracula, the incarnation of evil, who commands the other monsters to do his bidding. But the members of the Monster Squad know how to dispatch such creatures, even though one of them is shocked to discover that "The Wolfman has nards!" After all, even werewolves were not allowed to walk around naked in the forties movies these kids love.

The youngsters get some help from their local "scary German guy" (Leonardo Cimino) to translate Van Helsing's diary, which has somehow turned up in their neighborhood. The plot, shall we say, stretches credulity, but its charm is in the telling.

There are times when Dekker goes too far; the relationship between the little girl and the Monster travels uncomfortably into *E.T.* territory and borders on the maudlin. But the important thing to remember is that *The Monster Squad* is aimed at kids, and as a family-themed comedy-horror film, it does what it's supposed to do for its intended audience.

Thanks to Bradford May's excellent cinematography, the movie (budgeted at around twelve million dollars) looks bigger than it is. The visual effects, supervised by *Fright Night*'s Richard Edlund, are first-rate, as is Bruce Broughton's musical score.

Although the humor tends to rely a bit too much on flatulence jokes and swear words (guaranteed to elicit laughs from twelve-year-olds everywhere), the movie's overall sweetness and obvious love of its source material tend to compensate for the cheap jokes. There are some genuinely funny lines, such as when a little boy complains, "Creature stole my Twinkie!" At one point, another character bemoans, "Where am I gonna find silver bullets? K-Mart?"

Tri-Star Pictures released *The Monster Squad* on August 14, 1987. It wasn't especially well-received by critics or audiences at the time, but like *Night of the Creeps*, it has developed a cult following over the years. After decades of legal wrangling over who owned the rights, it was finally released to DVD by Lionsgate on July 24, 2007, in a special two-disc twentieth anniversary edition, much to the delight of its fans. *The Monster Squad* has its flaws, but it makes you wish that Dekker had made more films in the intervening years. Perhaps a *Monster Squad II*, in which our now grown-up heroes return to battle evil, is not out of the question?

Evil Dead 2: Dead by Dawn

Sam Raimi's low-budget horror film *The Evil Dead* (1981) had a hard time finding a distributor. Its graphic violence and excessive gore combined with a relentless pace made it a tough sell; ultimately it was picked up by New Line Cinema and, after being championed by author Stephen King, it became a cult movie.

The story contains elements of the works of H.P. Lovecraft, as well as strong echoes of another independent horror film, *Equinox* (1970). Five young people go to an old and isolated cabin in the woods for an vacation. There they find an audiotape made by a researcher who recites a spell to conjure up ancient forest demons. By merely playing the tape, the group inadvertently calls up the demons, who attempt to possess all of them.

Although there are strong elements of black humor in Raimi's film, it can hardly be called a comedy-horror film. In fact, it was advertised as "the ultimate experience in grueling terror." But the film's success ultimately led to a sequel that remains one of the greatest comedy-horror films of all time.

After *The Evil Dead*, Raimi decided to do something different, resulting in a comedy-thriller called *Crimewave*. It was not well received by press or public. Irvin Shapiro, a publicist who had been highly efficient at promoting *The Evil Dead*, suggested a sequel. Raimi had actually thrown around some ideas during *Evil Dead*'s production in which the hero, Ash (Bruce Campbell), went through a time portal and ended up in the Middle Ages. Raimi and his partner, producer Robert Tapert, decided that now was a good time to go along with Shapiro's suggestion. They met with legendary film producer Dino De Laurentiis, who at that time owned DEG Studios, located in North Carolina.

Initially, De Laurentiis offered Raimi the chance to direct a film version of Stephen King's novel *Thinner*, but Raimi declined. King heard that Raimi was attempting to finance a sequel to *The Evil Dead*, which he had so favorably reviewed at the Cannes Film Festival. King intervened and personally asked De Laurentiis, who was then producing several films based on King novels, to fund the sequel.

Raimi and Tapert asked for $4 million for the production, a far cry from the $325,000 they had received to make their first film. But the sequel was to be on a much larger scale. De Laurentiis would only agree to $3.75 million, so they decided to scale the sequel down to take place in and around the cabin, and would save the medieval scene for the very end. Ultimately, they brought the film in for $3.6 million, earning some "brownie points" from De Laurentiis for coming in under budget.

To help him complete the script, Raimi contacted his old friend from his home state of Michigan, Scott Spiegel, who had worked with him on several of his Super-8 "backyard productions" when they were kids. It was primarily Spiegel who brought humorous elements to the sequel, as many of the films he and Raimi had collaborated on in their teenage years had been comedies, and he felt comfortable with that genre.

And so 1987's *Evil Dead 2* (also known as *Evil Dead 2: Dead by Dawn*) became perhaps the first horror movie to be inspired as much by the Three Stooges as by H.P. Lovecraft. When Ash (Campbell again) is forced to battle his own disembodied hand, eventually imprisoning it under a bucket on top of which he places the book *A Farewell to Arms* by Ernest Hemingway, we know we've entered the realm of "splatstick". The scene was actually almost a shot-for-shot remake of *Attack of the Helping Hand*, a short film that Spiegel had made as a teenager (inspired by a commercial for Hamburger Helper).

Bruce Campbell goes a little wacky in Sam Raimi's *Evil Dead 2: Dead by Dawn* (1987).

Raimi's younger brother Ted plays a demon-possessed woman named Henrietta. For the role, he was required to wear a latex costume that covered his entire body. In the North Carolina heat, the younger Raimi often found the costume unbearable, and it ultimately became filled with his own sweat.

Evil Dead 2 was written with an R rating in mind, but that isn't what it received. When it was released on March 13, 1987, not by DEG but by an affiliate called Rosebud Releasing, it went out to theaters unrated.

It may be hard for horror fans to believe now, but when *Evil Dead 2* was originally released, it was not a success. I interviewed Raimi for *Metroland* magazine shortly after the film's opening weekend; he thanked me for the positive review I had written and encouraged me to "spread the word." When I asked him how *Evil Dead 2* was doing at the box office, he replied, "Not so good, unfortunately. They had to sell it to Rosebud, at least for domestic [distribution], because Rosebud is not affiliated with the MPAA. So they sold the title to them for domestic; Rosebud is actually a real company that does very little business. I know that they are closely affiliated with DEG."

Raimi went on to verify that they had indeed shot the film for an R rating, but that "DEG said it wasn't an R. Rather than cut it, they said to just release it as it is to another company."

The ever-affable Raimi continued, "If I had known it would be unrated, I think I would have hit a little harder with it. There wasn't initially a lot of pressure, but they did ask us to deliver an R-rated picture; that was one of the conditions of the funding. That was really what we tried to do, and I guess we failed. I guess I don't know how to make an R-rated picture!"

I asked Raimi why scenes from the first film were recreated in the opening of the sequel, and he answered:

The first movie was shot in 16mm and looked grainy. And I didn't want to step on any toes; so many people were involved in the distribution of that picture, I wasn't sure if we could get the rights or not. It could have been a legal problem and it could have looked crummy, so we just decided to bypass it and retell it to a new audience. So few people have seen *Evil Dead* we decided to retell it using the exact same cabin and the exact same actors we'd be seeing later in the film. It turned out to be the simplest way and, I think, the most effective for the audience.

Raimi also revealed that he filmed most of the "shaky cam" shots in *Evil Dead 2* himself. "This was a very pleasant picture to make. The money made it a lot easier. I didn't have to go into debt to pay our office bills, we could pay all the people their salaries, we didn't have to keep running and stopping the production, and we could shoot in 35mm. I had more room to be creative, basically."

At the time of the interview, Raimi used an expression to describe the film that has since become a cliché: "a roller coaster ride." It's one of the few times that phrase has been accurate: *Evil Dead 2* is indeed a ninety-minute roller coaster ride that reaches the heights of comedy one moment and horror the next.

After all the abuse that Campbell suffers in the film, I had to ask Raimi if the actor was a masochist. He laughed:

No, he's just a good sport. He really endured a lot; we broke plates over his head—actually, he broke plates over his own head, even more horrible—so he couldn't blame anyone else for that. We dumped a few thousand gallons of blood on the poor guy and strapped him upside down, flew him on wires, slammed him into walls, broke beams over his head ... everything from having him fall down the steps to being batted around by zombies; he really goes through a lot. He does all his own stunts too.

Campbell certainly made an impression in the original *Evil Dead*, but it was the sequel that transformed him into a comedy-horror movie icon. When I asked Raimi if he specifically instructed the actor to go way over the top, he said, "Yeah, I guess I did. He trusted me, and maybe I led him down the wrong path, but we felt it was that type of picture where we didn't want to hurt the audience, we wanted to make them laugh and have a good time. So we decided to make it a little more extreme than we usually do."

Raimi expressed misgivings about this approach at the time: "I don't know if this will work with a mass audience. Maybe next time."

It's safe to say that Raimi had probably never dreamed in 1987 that he would someday be directing movies on the level of *Spider-Man* (2002) and its sequels, but the sense of fun he had making movies was very obvious. He took particularly devilish glee in personally drenching the actors in "blood and green bile," and noted that they were all very good about it.

"Sarah Berry, who plays Annie," he told me, "is a New York actress, and she had no problem with the gore except for one scene. The scene is the one in which her boyfriend is now possessed by the spirit of evil and he's being cut up by Bruce Campbell. She's supposed to be screaming, and while she screams, green bile—one of my favorite substances—spurts into frame and hits her on the cheek. Well, I had the squeegee, and I told them to roll camera, and I shoot the bile and I miss and I hit her right in the eye. I guess it got beneath her contact lens and, oh, man, she was a little upset at me."

Raimi was also very proud of what he called "the flyball eyeball" scene, in which actress Kassie Wesley screams at the same time that a popped-out eyeball flies into her mouth. "I had a scene in the script," Raimi continued, "where she's running in the woods later and she coughs it back up. But in the film as it is, I guess she just swallows that thing. We were also going to have a point of view shot of it going down into her stomach, but we never shot it."

The ending of *Evil Dead 2* really wasn't a set-up for a sequel, Raimi said. "I just wanted to create an ending that was very different from the other one," he noted. "I thought it would be the most different and unusual ending that I could put on the picture. I just didn't want to end it the way all horror movies end. And I thought it completed the cycle of the film, that Ash is bound up with the Book of the Dead for all eternity, trapped forever to battle this evil. I thought that was kind of a frightening idea. That's really why we ended it there."

Of course, the series didn't end there, as we shall see later on. When *Evil Dead 2* was released to home video in the fall of 1987, it really took off and became the cult film we know and love today. This is the movie in which Campbell becomes King of (Horror) Comedy, uttering such immortal lines as "You're goin' down. Chainsaw," and, best of all, when he puts the chainsaw at the end of his arm in place of his missing hand and proclaims, "Groovy!" "Movie magic at its most outlandish"; that pretty much sums up *Evil Dead 2*.

The Three Stooges influence is everywhere, but perhaps most noticeably behind the scenes: The re-animated, possessed "zombies" are always referred to by Raimi and his crew as "Fake Shemps" after Shemp Howard. Raimi may be a bigshot director, but he still hasn't forgotten his roots; somewhere in his psyche, that teenage boy who used to shoot comedy films in his backyard still lurks. And for the sake of movie audiences anywhere, let's hope he lurks there for decades to come.

Beetlejuice

One of the more bizarre comedy-horror films to be released by a major studio, Tim Burton's *Beetlejuice* (1988) was an unexpected sleeper hit. The young filmmaker had already proven his directing chops as far as the studios were concerned with another offbeat success, *Pee-wee's Big Adventure* (1985), a film made on a budget of seven million dollars that grossed more than forty million. Even before he had made his first feature, however, Burton had forced Hollywood executives to sit up and take notice.

Timothy William Burton was born in Burbank, California, on August 25, 1958. A highly imaginative child, he once staged an ax murder with his brother to scare the neighbors; the result was that they called the police. Burton liked to escape the mundane reality of his home and school life by watching low-budget horror films on television; one of his idols was Vincent Price. He was also a huge fan of Ray Harryhausen's special effects work.

These influences led him to a career in films. Upon graduation from high school, he received a Disney scholarship to attend the California Institute of the Arts in Valencia. There, he studied for three years as an animator, getting his first film job at the age of twenty on Ralph Bakshi's animated version of *The Lord of the Rings* (1979). Shortly afterward, he was hired by the Walt Disney Studios as an apprentice animator; it was during this period that he wrote and directed his first short film, *Vincent* (1982), a stop-motion animation piece about a young boy who believes himself to be Vincent Price. It was an instant cult favorite with horror fans.

He followed this up with a live-action short called *Frankenweenie*, which co-starred Daniel Stern, Shelley Duvall and Barret Oliver. Filmed in black and white, it was inspired by the look of James Whale's 1931 *Frankenstein*, but its story of a boy who re-animates his dead dog did not sit well with Disney executives, despite the fact that it did very well at film festivals. The "suits" at Disney, concerned that it was too scary for their family market, quietly shelved the film, which didn't receive a video release until 1992, when Burton had become famous for his two *Batman* films.

Frankenweenie, however, led directly to Burton directing his first feature. Actor Paul Reubens, who played Pee-wee Herman on Saturday morning television at the time, saw *Frankenweenie* and chose Burton to direct *Pee-wee's Big Adventure*, the series' first theatrical spin-off. Burton set another path for himself on the film when he chose Danny Elfman, from the oddball rock group Oingo Boingo, to compose the music. Since then, they've collaborated on all but two of Burton's directorial efforts.

Beetlejuice turned out to be a natural choice for Burton to direct; although he didn't write it, nearly all of his trademark touches are there. The screenplay by Michael McDowell and Warren Skaaren (from a story by McDowell and Larry Wilson) concerns a young couple (Alec Baldwin and Geena Davis) who die in an auto accident and become ghosts. They haunt their rambling old house in New England, only to be put off by its new owners (Jeffrey Jones and Catherine O'Hara), who move in with their teenage daughter (Winona Ryder).

To force out the yuppie couple, the ghosts hires a "bio-exorcist" called Betelgeuse (named after a red star in the constellation of Orion and pronounced "Beetlejuice"), who tries all sorts of outlandish pranks to scare the new owners away. Meanwhile, the daughter, an early example of a Goth girl, bonds with the ghosts while drifting apart emotionally from her own parents. It's an outlandish premise by any standards, but because of the bright script and Burton's assured direction, it all works.

Burton got the job as director of *Beetlejuice* partly because of the success of *Pee-wee's Big Adventure*, but also because he had become bogged down working with writer Sam Hamm on developing a script for *Batman*. The superhero adventure was languishing in Development Hell, with Warner Bros. waffling on whether or not they would greenlight it.

During the period between his first two features, Burton had worked in television, directing, among other things, episodes of the revived *Alfred Hitchcock Presents*. One of these episodes, "The Jar," was written by Michael McDowell. During pre-production work on *Batman*, producer David Geffen gave a copy of McDowell's script for *Beetlejuice* to Burton. The young director was taken by the originality and imagination of the story and brought on Larry Wilson to help McDowell with rewrites. Ultimately, the finished screenplay was attributed to McDowell and Warren Skaaren.

Originally, Burton had been interested in casting song-and-dance legend Sammy Davis Jr. as Beetlejuice; it was Geffen who suggested Michael Keaton for the part. After meeting with Keaton, Burton was convinced that he was perfect for the role. Burton cast young actress Winona Ryder after seeing her in David Seltzer's appealing romantic teenage drama *Lucas* (1986).

Geena Davis had just received considerable acclaim for her co-starring role in *The Fly* (1986), David Cronenberg's visceral remake of the 1958 classic. But *Beetlejuice* was not her first foray into comedy-horror. She had previously played a very fetching faux vampire in Rudy De Luca's wildly unfunny *Transylvania 6-5000* (1985).

Alec Baldwin had just appeared in Stanley Kubrick's *Full Metal Jacket* (1987), while character actor Jeffrey Jones had previously made a big impression as the long-suffering high school principal in the John Hughes teen comedy *Ferris Bueller's Day Off* (1986). Catherine O'Hara was a veteran of the long-running comedy series *Second City TV*. The oddball casting that Burton eventually became known for was on full display in *Beetlejuice*, with television talk show host Dick Cavett and singer Robert Goulet cast in small but pivotal roles. Veteran actress Sylvia Sidney also has a memorable turn as an "afterlife case worker."

The film's thirteen million dollar budget was only allotted one million for special effects.

Michael Keaton in the title role of Tim Burton's *Beetlejuice* (1988).

Burton, no stranger to low budgets, got the most for the money when he created (or supervised) the film's stop-motion animation, makeup effects, puppetry and blue screen work. Production designer Bo Welch (who would later work with Burton on *Edward Scissorhands*, 1990, and *Batman Returns*, 1991) contributed a delightfully off-kilter, Edward Gorey–like look to the film.

According to Mark Salisbury's book *Tim Burton: Burton on Burton*, (Faber and Faber, 2006), Warner Bros. didn't like the film's title and pushed to call it *House Ghosts*. Burton, as a joke, said he thought a good title would be *Scared Sheetless* and was properly appalled that the studio actually put that title under consideration. Burton won out in the end and *Beetlejuice* was released on April Fool's Day of 1988. It brought in over eight million dollars in its first weekend. The movie became the tenth biggest box office hit of the year in the U.S. and critics were generally kind to it as well. Vincent Canby, under the headline "*Beetlejuice* Is Pap for the Eyes," called it "a farce for our time" in his March 30 *New York Times* review.

Interestingly enough, Canby expressed a wish in his review that Keaton had more screen time in the movie. Indeed, the title character doesn't show up until around fifty minutes into the picture, but he quickly makes up for lost time with his zany sight gags and bizarre bits of business. "I'm the ghost with the most, babe," he announces to Davis' character; he also comes out with some wacky and off-handed non sequiturs such as, "I have a photo shoot with *GQ* in about an hour and a half. They've been trying to get me for weeks. Some underwear thing or something."

Some of Burton's visuals are wonderful, especially considering the low special effects budget. The explorer with the shrunken head was such a great effect it was included in the film's trailer, and the animated sandworm is memorable too. In fact, the look of some of the creatures almost seems to be a warm-up for the various monsters in Burton's much-beloved *The Nightmare Before Christmas* (1993).

Burton's expertise with effects paid off in a big way when *Beetlejuice* won the Oscar for Best Makeup Effects. Instead of creating a sequel, Burton chose to be executive producer of a Saturday morning cartoon spin-off called *Beetlejuice*. It ran on ABC from September 9, 1989, to December 6, 1991. A theatrical sequel tentatively titled *Beetlejuice Goes Hawaiian* has been bandied about for years, but maybe it's just as well it hasn't been made. *Beetlejuice*, after all, is a true original and remains to date Burton's only real comedy-horror film. *Mars Attacks!* (1986) was comedy-science-fiction, not horror, while his stylish version of *Sleepy Hollow* (1999) surprisingly removed most of the humor of Washington Irving's tale and substituted gore and violence. Although a visually stunning homage to Hammer and AIP, *Sleepy Hollow* could have benefited from more of the ghoulish humor that distinguished *Beetlejuice*.

Killer Klowns from Outer Space

Any movie with a title like *Killer Klowns from Outer Space* lets you know from the outset that it is, shall we say, tongue in cheek, if not completely deranged. It was directed by Stephen Chiodo and written by his brothers Charles and Edward Chiodo, all of whom had worked on the special effects of *Critters*.

Killer Klowns is virtually an uncredited remake of Edward L. Cahn's 1957 teenage monster movie for AIP, *Invasion of the Saucer Men*. Both films feature teenagers who discover an alien invasion in a wooded area used as a lovers' lane; both films feature local police officers who think the kids are just pulling pranks; and both films feature really weird-looking alien creatures. *Saucer Men* has "Martians" with bug eyes and heads the size of beach balls. But *Killer Klowns* tops it in the strangeness department with its army of, well, clowns. Add to that the idea that they land in the woods not in a flying saucer but in a circus tent, shoot people with "popcorn guns" and cocoon their victims in cotton candy, and you have a recipe for a movie that's an instant cult classic, which it became upon its May 27, 1988, video release.

The acting is mostly dreadful, with the exceptions of veteran performers John Vernon as Sergeant Mooney and Royal Dano as a hapless farmer who becomes the first victim of the Klowns. The film is hampered by an obviously low budget, but the designs of the Klowns are so imaginative and individual set-pieces are so clever that *Killer Klowns* is an enjoyable romp almost in spite of itself.

"Nobody stores cotton candy like this," notes Debbie (Suzanne Snyder) as she and her boyfriend Mike (Grant Cramer) investigate what's inside the sinister circus tent that has mysteriously appeared in the woods. The Klowns wreak murderous mischief upon the nearby town, laughing all the way. Their weapons are unique: a balloon animal that turns into a bloodhound, ray guns that look like toys and—best of all—a shadow puppet of a Tyrannosaurus Rex that devours unsuspecting people waiting at a bus stop.

One of the title characters designed by the Chiodo Brothers for Stephen Chiodo's *Killer Klowns from Outer Space* (1988).

There's also the obligatory gratuitous shower scene featuring the leading lady, although there's no nudity (the film is rated PG-13); instead, popcorn fired from the Klowns' guns turns into weird snakelike creatures with clown faces, which Debbie dispatches with the help of the shower head and some hairspray.

Sergeant Mooney, who's been acting like your basic small-town fascist cop through the whole film, is ultimately strangled by one of the Klowns and turned, post-mortem, into a ventriloquist's puppet, complete with face paint. Although it's a colorfully grotesque scene, it's a pity the character is killed off, as he had some of the best lines in the film. When his office phones are ringing off the hook with reports of strange happenings, his exasperated takes on such lines as "You say your wife was carried off in a balloon?" are hard to forget.

Once you get past the basic premise, the story is simple and uncomplicated, leading to a predictably happy ending in which the Klowns are vanquished, including their leader, a giant "King Klown" played by Charles Chiodo. The film is bracketed by a title song at the beginning and end credits performed by a cult punk band, The Dickies.

Killer Klowns from Outer Space really does live up to its title. Its tagline, "In space no one can eat ice cream," is a take-off on "In space no one can hear you scream" from Ridley Scott's *Alien*. With a surreal atmosphere that sometimes suggests the mood of Ray Bradbury's *Something Wicked This Way Comes*, plus some genuine laugh-out-loud sequences (try to keep a straight face when one of the smaller clowns literally knocks a biker's block off), *Killer Klowns from Outer Space* has a kind of low-budget charm that is rarely seen in these days of overblown special effects extravaganzas. It's a movie that knows what it wants to do—make the audience laugh and scream, often at the same time—and then it goes and does it. In a way, it's surprising that a sequel was never made, but the fact that it stands alone makes it even more special.

Waxwork

There are a number of dedications in the end credits of *Waxwork* (1988): to Romero, Argento, etc., etc. But the first and foremost dedication is to Hammer, and part of the fun of watching the movie is catching all of the Hammer references. It's no coincidence that the writer-director, Anthony Hickox, is British, but even more interesting is that he's the son of Douglas Hickox, who directed the brilliant *Theater of Blood* (1973) with Vincent Price.

Like father, like son: Anthony does an admirable job with *Waxwork*, his first feature. Only twenty-three at the time of its production, he shows his love for the genre by giving us what is, in essence, an anthology film à la Amicus Productions. The conceit is a clever one: A wax museum owner (David Warner) lures people into his exhibits, which consist of representations of werewolves, vampires, zombies and mummies. The victims enter into the world of the exhibits themselves, and the unlucky ones must stay forever as part of the waxwork.

This gives Hickox an opportunity to showcase a number of monsters in the various vignettes presented. John Rhys-Davies (*Raiders of the Lost Ark*, 1981) becomes a very effective werewolf; Miles O'Keefe, who played Tarzan in the execreble *Tarzan the Ape Man* (1981) to Bo Derek's Jane, here plays a Count Dracula who talks rather like Clint Eastwood; there's an excellent Hammer-styled mummy sequence, complete with an actor who's a dead ringer for Andre Morell in Hammer's *The Mummy's Shroud* (1967); and finally, there's the requisite George A. Romero–type zombie sequence filmed in black and white.

Despite some indifferent acting (although Warner as the villain and Patrick Macnee as the Van Helsing type seem to enjoy chewing the scenery), *Waxwork* is a lot of fun, both in concept and execution. Gerry Lively's cinematography, with its accent on strong lighting and color effects, smacks of the best in classic British horror film imagery, despite the fact that the movie was made in Los Angeles. Some of the camera set-ups are nearly exact duplicates of those in the films they parody, particularly in the mummy segment.

Zach Galligan (*Gremlins*, 1984) is okay in the lead role of Mark, a rich high schooler who discovers that his destiny is to end evil in the world; Sarah Brightman (the name was based on the English pop singer, perhaps?) as played by Deborah Foreman (*Valley Girl*, 1983) belies her wholesome image by becoming fascinated by the works of the Marquis De Sade; and China (Michelle Johnson, *Blame It on Rio*, 1983) is a curvy, conceited twit who ends up being victimized by Dracula in a scene that pours on so much blood that much of it was cut by the MPAA.

Foreman is the most interesting of the young performers; the lustful look on her face when she's being whipped by De Sade (J. Kenneth Campbell) while the English prince (Hickox himself in a cameo) looks on is downright disturbing. Her girl-next-door looks only add to the depravity of the scene; she's Gidget gone masochistic.

Waxwork goes a bit too far out of control toward the end: A wheelchair-bound Macnee leads the forces of good in a charge against the forces of evil inside the waxwork. For a moment, it starts to look like the finale of *Casino Royale* (1967) in its chaotic battle scenes, including a shot of a midget being fed to a gigantic man-eating plant that screams, "Feed me!" à la *The Little Shop of Horrors* (1960). Then again, this is Hickox's first film and one can forgive a certain lack of discipline in such a young director when, for the most part, *Waxwork* holds up as a comedy-horror romp with enough going on in it for two or three movies. Sure enough, there was a sequel, but more on that later.

Elvira, Mistress of the Dark

In addition to being a passable comedy-horror film, *Elvira, Mistress of the Dark* (1988) is probably the most extravagant breast fetish movie since the days of soft-core pioneer Russ

Meyer's films. Some critics have counted no less than fifty-six breast jokes in the film, fifty-seven if you count the movie's tagline, "Here comes the best DOUBLE FEATURE ever made!"

Lest you think that the leading actress is being exploited, however, it's important to know that the character of Elvira was created by Cassandra Peterson, the actress who plays her, and she's only too happy to exploit what God (or plastic surgery) has given her.

A somewhat unsuccessful actress, singer and dancer who had bounced around between the U.S. and Europe in the 1970s, Peterson eventually settled in Los Angeles, where, in 1981, a casting call went out for a "horror hostess" for a late-night movie series at KHJ-TV. Peterson won the role, auditioning against two hundred other actresses. She was given carte blanche to create the character's image, and she and her best friend Robert Redding came up with the Gothic punk vampire look that the character has to this day. Originally, she was going to call herself Vampira, after Maila Nurmi's similar horror hostess character of the fifties, but shortly before the initial taping, the producers received a "cease-and-desist" letter from Nurmi, who was still living in Los Angeles. Peterson changed the name of the character to Elvira, and a star was born.

Elvira's Movie Macabre became a huge hit and was quickly syndicated around the country. Elvira's low-cut black costume sported more cleavage than had ever been seen on local television up to that time, and her sexy but slightly air-headed Valley Girl persona (with just a hint of Mae West) brought

Elvira (Cassandra Peterson) is about to be burned at the stake in James Signorelli's *Elvira, Mistress of the Dark* (1988).

viewers back again and again, even when the movies she was hosting weren't very good. In fact, the whole basis of her act—along with rather naughty double entendres—was to lampoon the movies themselves.

Her show became such a success that movies were in the offing, and New World Pictures was there to produce one. John Paragon, who produced the TV show, was hired to co-write *Elvira, Mistress of the Dark* with Sam Egan. James Signorelli, a veteran director-producer of NBC's *Saturday Night Live*, was assigned to direct, although it's pretty obvious that Peterson directed herself. Her TV character is virtually unchanged in the film: Still showing as much cleavage as a PG-13 rating will allow, still self-deprecating, still making corny jokes.

The plot, such as it is, is really just an excuse for the jokes: Art imitates life when Elvira, the hostess of a horror movie program, inherits her aunt's spooky old mansion in Falwell, a sort of misplaced "Bible Belt" town in New England. She discovers that her aunt was a well-known witch, and a warlock (W. Morgan Sheppard) is trying to uncover her black magic secrets, putting him in direct conflict with Elvira. Meanwhile, the townspeople—except for the hip young folks, of course—find Elvira to be rather inappropriate in her manner of dress, her manner of speech, and her manners in general.

This small-minded attitude is perhaps best expressed by Chastity Pariah (Edie McClurg), who attempts to come to Elvira's "defense" in front of the townspeople: "Please, I don't think we need to resort to name-calling. I think what Calvin is trying to say is that Elvira is a person of easy virtue, a purveyor of pulchritude, a one-woman Sodom and Gomorrah, if you will. A slimy, slithering succubus, a concubine, a streetwalker, a tramp, a slut, a cheap whore."

Of course the town's name, Falwell, is based on Jerry Falwell, the televangelist who supposedly represented the Moral Majority, a right-wing Christian movement that was becoming more and more visible in eighties America. In its own little way, *Elvira, Mistress of the Dark* takes aim at religious hypocrisy, and while the jokes are never on the level of Oscar Wilde's, they do make their points.

After serving the townspeople a "pot luck" dinner spiked with aphrodisiacs ("Believe me, when they open that pot, they'll need all the luck they can get," says the Mistress of the Dark), Elvira is accused of being a witch and is about to be burned at the stake. Before the match is struck, she pleads to a friend: "And if they ever ask about me, tell them I was more than just a great set of boobs. I was also an incredible set of legs ... and tell them ... tell them that I never turned down a friend. I never turned down a stranger, for that matter. And tell them ... tell them that when all is said and done, I only ask that people remember me by two simple words ... any two, as long as they're simple."

In a scene that carries breast worship to a nearly unparalleled height in world cinema, Elvira escapes her bonds by using her breasts as weapons. Breathing heavily, she breaks the chains and all ends happily when she recreates a scene from *Flashdance* (1983) by swinging the tassels on her breasts while black paint is dumped upon her.

As previously noted, there isn't much of a plot here, but Peterson is so amiable and unflappable, with an almost Groucho Marx–type delivery of one-liners, that she's impossible to dislike. The movie may be indifferent, but Elvira lives on—and keeps on stretching the fabric of her tacky black dress.

Brain Damage

Writer-director Frank Henenlotter found his own "sick" comedy-horror film, the low-budget and nasty *Basket Case* (1982), a tough act to follow. It took six years for him to mount another production, but for his fans, it turned out to be well worth the wait. *Brain Damage* (1988) is a more polished piece of work than *Basket Case* and there's more going on in the film than blood and gore, although there is plenty of that. The subtext has to do with drug addiction, and it definitely has a point of view: Addiction is a very, very bad thing.

In *Brain Damage*, Rick Herbst plays Brian, a young man who lives in an apartment complex with his brother (Gordon MacDonald). Brian is involved in a romantic relationship with Barbara (Jennifer Lowry), but all of his human relationships go to hell when a slug-like parasite called Aylmer (voiced by John Zacherle, aka famed TV horror host Zacherley) crawls into the back of his head. Aylmer, who has already possessed two other people in the apartment complex, secretes a blue fluid into Brian's brain that is highly addictive. And all Aylmer wants in return is to feast on human brains.

Brain Damage is really one of the better film metaphors for drug addiction. Brian's inner torment is well conveyed by Herbst, who later went on to become a soap opera star on such venerable series as *The Bold and the Beautiful* and *General Hospital* under the name of Rick

Hearst. Essentially a quiet, peaceful young man, Brian is compelled by the drug—and by Aylmer's insistent whisperings in his inner ear—to find victims for the gruesome little parasite.

In some respects, *Brain Damage* is Henenlotter's homage to David Cronenberg's *They Came from Within* (aka *Shivers*, 1976): Both films feature parasitic slugs that crawl within people and make them do evil things. In Cronenberg's film, they become sex addicts, but Henenlotter's drug allegory could not be more blatant.

Aylmer (not "Elmer," as some viewers have thought) is a peculiar name. It's explained by a character in the film as having some mystical meaning, but any genre fan must wonder if it's really a sort of tribute to the great British character actor Felix Aylmer, who played Merlin in *Knights of the Round Table* (1954) and who had his back broken by Christopher Lee's Kharis in Hammer's *The Mummy* (1959). Whatever the origin of the name, it's a memorable character, a combination hand puppet and vocal performance punctuated, at the strangest moments, by Zacherle's trademark laugh. It even breaks into song occasionally and provides most of the film's best moments of dark comedy.

Brain Damage didn't create the kind of cult that *Basket Case* had, but in many ways it's the superior film. More intelligently written and better acted (especially by Herbst), it's a comedy-horror film with a social conscience. Henenlotter seems to know a lot about drug addiction, and the constant cravings of Brian for the mysterious blue fluid get under your skin. Just like Aylmer.

Alert viewers will notice that the man seen on the subway holding a wicker basket towards the end of the film is Kevin Van Hentenryck, the star of *Basket Case*. Henenlotter's next film would in fact be the unimaginatively titled *Basket Case 2*.

The Lair of the White Worm

Comedy-horror films can be derived from the most unlikely sources. It is perhaps not surprising that Ken Russell's *The Lair of the White Worm* (1988) is based on the last novel that Bram Stoker wrote in 1911, a year before his death. What is surprising is that the film draws more heavily on an old English folk legend than it does on Stoker's book.

Russell's *Lair* is based quite explicitly on the story of the Lambton Worm, a legend from the north east of England that goes back at least as far as the time of the Crusades. It's very famous in its home country, having been passed down through the centuries by oral tradition, songs, and even children's pantomimes.

The story concerns one John Lambton, heir to the Lambton estate in County Durham, who battles with a gigantic "worm" or "dragon" that has been terrorizing the local populace. Lambton eventually vanquishes the worm near the River Wear with the help of a witch who tells him where to find it and how to destroy it. According to the witch's instructions, he covers his armor in spikes; then, when he battles the worm, it coils around him in an attempt to suffocate him, but is cut to pieces by the spikes.

There are many such folk tales in the British Isles, but the story of the Lambton Worm has been linked to everything from Stoker's novel to the Loch Ness Monster. Russell's film version delves into the legend more deeply than Stoker ever did, and makes more explicit the conflict between paganism and Christianity that is implied in the legend.

In the film, John Lambton's descendant becomes Lord James D'ampton (Hugh Grant), a modern-day nobleman whose ancestor supposedly had slain a gigantic white worm by chopping off its head. When an archaeological dig near his property turns up something like

Lady Sylvia Marsh (Amanda Donohoe) makes like a snake in Ken Russell's *The Lair of the White Worm* (1988).

the skull of a dinosaur, a connection is made to the old legend. Could it have been based on a real incident?

The plot thickens when Lady Sylvia Marsh (Amanda Donohue), a reclusive and wealthy neighbor of the D'Amptons, hears of the discovery. Lady Sylvia is in fact an immortal priestess of the snake (or worm) god Dionin and her home, Temple House, was built on the site of an ancient pagan temple that was the lair of the snake-worshipping cult.

As if that weren't strange enough, it's further discovered that Eve Trent (Catherine Oxenberg), who lives at Mercy House where the skull was discovered, is a reincarnation of one of the nuns who had built a convent in the Middle Ages on the site of what is now her home. The nuns were forever at odds with the snake cult, and now Lady Sylvia sees an opportunity for an ironic revenge: She finds out that Eve is still a virgin and would make the ideal sacrifice to Dionin, the worm that still dwells in the old well on her estate.

Ken Russell was the famous middle-aged "bad boy" of British cinema, having established himself with such over-the-top and controversial films as *Women in Love* (1969), with its homo-erotic nude wrestling scene between Oliver Reed and Alan Bates; *The Music Lovers* (1970), with Richard Chamberlain as the tortured Russian composer Tchaikovsky; and perhaps most shocking of all, *The Devils* (1971), in which hysterical, sex-starved nuns are responsible for having a priest whom they all lusted after (Reed again) burned at the stake for spurning their advances.

Because of his flamboyant, operatic style, Russell turned out to be the perfect choice to film (in 1975) The Who's famous rock opera *Tommy*, which became a huge mainstream hit. His career waxed and waned over the next decade, during which he made some American films, including the highly successful *Altered States* (1980) and the wildly unsuccessful *Crimes of Passion* (1984) with Kathleen Turner and Anthony Perkins.

Unhappy with the reception to the latter film, Russell returned to England and did several movies for Vestron Pictures, a video distributor that was branching out into theatrical features. The first was *Gothic* (1986), his typically larger-than-life look at Lord Byron (Gabriel Byrne), Mary Shelley (Natasha Richardson) and their infamous weekend in Switzerland that inspired Shelley to write *Frankenstein*.

The next film in the Vestron deal was *Salome's Last Dance* (1988), which reunited him with his *Women in Love* star, Glenda Jackson. But Russell really hit his stride with the next Vestron movie, *The Lair of the White Worm*. Here was an opportunity to let his feverish imagination run rampant on his favorite subjects: sex, religion and death.

You know you're watching a Ken Russell film when a character named Eve starts having hallucinations about a snake wrapped around a crucified Christ, nuns being raped by Roman soldiers and vampiric demons with snakelike fangs. Russell has never been known to be subtle, and the imagery in *Lair* is as lush, sexual and violent as in any of his films.

But there's more to Russell's films than meets the eye, particularly the ones he has written as well as directed, as is the case with *Lair*. There's a great deal of subtext in all his films, but the pagan/Christian dichotomy of *Lair* seems to have inspired him to do some of his most startling work since *The Devils*. To some extent, it's a parody of Hammer vampire films, since everyone who is bitten by Lady Sylvia becomes a fanged, vampiric snake demon with poisonous venom.

In its quieter moments, the movie also features some witty references to other films, such as the wonderful scene in which Lady Sylvia explains her fascination with snakes to Lord D'Ampton, then decides to burn her "Snakes and Ladders" board game in the fireplace, while uttering the line, "Rosebud," from *Citizen Kane* (1941).

Donohoe is a delight throughout, wearing a variety of slinky, sensuous costumes that make her appear serpentine. The scene in which she reclines on the branches of a tree and seductively tempts Eve is blatant enough in its symbolism; you'd have to be a dolt to miss the Biblical reference. But it's filmed and performed so stylishly, one forgives its obvious metaphor.

Most of the cast members seem to be having a good time, including a very young Hugh Grant, who makes a stalwart hero; Sammi Davis as Eve's appealing sister, Mary; Peter Capaldi as the befuddled archaeologist; and Stratford Johns as a very weird butler. Oxenberg is the weak link, rather stiff in her performance and obviously unwilling to do the nudity that's required in a Russell film. Her sacrifice to the worm at the film's climax is nonetheless memorable, in part because of the virginal white underwear she's wearing.

But it's Donohoe who's the star here. She had made a big splash two years before by co-starring with Oliver Reed in Nicolas Roeg's *Castaway*, in which both performers had extensive nudity. In 1991, she became famous for performing the first lesbian kiss on American television in the series *LA Law*, when her character C.J. Lamb kissed Abbie Perkins (Michelle Greene). Openly bisexual, Donohoe has been linked romantically to both Sandra Bernhard and Jim Carrey.

Her performance in *Lair* may be Donohoe's finest on-screen moment. An actress of considerable presence, she has a flair for this kind of outrageous material, and obviously works well with Russell. She worked for him again the following year, in his adaptation of D.H. Lawrence's *The Rainbow*, but her Lady Sylvia Marsh is a truly iconic character; it is to her as Dracula is to Christopher Lee.

Who could forget the following dialogue exchange: When she picks up a Boy Scout named Kevin and takes him back to her place for a "bite," he asks her: "Do you have any children?" Smiling a thin-lipped smile, she replies, "Only when there are no men around."

8

THE NINETIES
Screams and Cemetery Men

By 1990, the age of irony was in full force. It was an age in which nothing was off limits for the public to know, whether it was every intimate detail of what the president did with an intern in the Oval Office or who fathered whose child on *The Jerry Springer Show*. It seemed as though class had gone out of culture, that good taste was a thing of the past. Some pundits even referred to the U.S. as "White Trash Nation," referring to this new culture—or lack of it.

On the other side of the coin, the so-called Religious Right was at the vanguard of the Culture Wars, bemoaning the fact that America had gone astray and had traveled too far from religion. Their answer—as it had been in the fifties with comic books and rock 'n' roll music—was to suppress or ban whatever they didn't like, such as the phenomenally popular *Harry Potter* books, which (to the religious fundamentalists, at least) promoted witchcraft.

Years of *Saturday Night Live*–style frat boy humor in which there were no sacred cows led to such cable TV cult series as *Mystery Science Theatre 3000*, on which old horror and sci-fi B movies were shown and became the butt of sophomoric jokes. There were very few "serious" horrors being made at the time for theatrical release; even those characters who were mainstays of the slasher film, Freddy and Jason, had degenerated into self-parody.

Frankenhooker

It was a good time for writer-director Frank Henenlotter to get back into action. Beloved by fans for both *Basket Case* (1982) and *Brain Damage* (1988), he chose for his next project none other than a unique "re-imagining" of Mary Shelley's *Frankenstein*, called *Frankenhooker*.

Needless to say, Henenlotter's vision of the story is unlike anyone else's, although there are echoes of the Warhol-Morrissey version. But *Frankenhooker* takes place completely in the present, in *The Toxic Avenger*'s home turf of New Jersey.

Co-written by onetime *Fangoria* magazine editor Robert Martin, *Frankenhooker* tells the tragi-comic tale of Jeffrey Franken (James Lorinz), a medical school dropout and would-be mad doctor whose beautiful fiancée Elizabeth Shelley (Patty Mullen) is horribly killed at a garden party when a huge, industrial-strength lawnmower goes out of control and cuts her to pieces. As a television newscaster puts it: "In a blaze of blood, bones and body parts, the vivacious young woman was instantly reduced to a tossed human salad—a salad that police are still trying to gather up. A salad that was once named ... Elizabeth."

Unbeknownst to the police, Franken has already gathered up the "salad" and is attempting to put his beloved fiancée back together again in a laboratory he has built in his garage, which looks much bigger on the inside than it does on the outside. Part of his mad scheme involves creating an explosive form of crack cocaine, which he gives to some New York City prostitutes. When they blow up after using it, he gathers up their body parts and takes them back to his mad lab.

He rejects certain parts for not measuring up to his standards of perfection: for example, mismatched breasts which he refers to as "Mutt and Jeff" and then tosses into the trash. And he's horrified to find a beautiful leg with a bunion-infested foot on the end of it. He files down the bunions and that seems to satisfy him.

When he brings his creation to life, she escapes out into the night, carrying her purse. Although she has Elizabeth's head, she is apparently possessed by the souls of all the hookers that went into making her new body. With a nervous twitch, scars and stitches all over her face and body, she nevertheless asks every "john" she sees: "Wanna date? Got any money?"

One of the new Elizabeth's many problems is that anyone she kisses blows up, thanks to the explosive crack that is still in her system. In an ending that resembles that of *Re-Animator* (1985), the body parts that Franken threw away band together and wreak their vengeance upon him. He finally ends up with his head stitched onto a woman's body. Franken's last line in the film is, "Where's my johnson?"

Subtle parody is not Henenlotter's forte. He was weaned on the exploitation films of New York City's grindhouses, and *Frankenhooker* may be his ultimate tribute to those sleazy films of his youth. Filmed in surreal, day-glo colors, the movie oozes outrageous humor from every frame. Lorinz's off-hand delivery of such lines as, "Medical schools upset me, Mother. I'm antisocial. I'm becoming dangerously amoral," add tremendously to the ironic fun. A former movie theater usher, Lorinz makes the most of his first starring role; his New Jersey accent and sense of innocence, especially in regard to the prostitutes he meets on the city streets, make him almost endearing in the role.

Of course, the character name "Elizabeth Shelley" is an inside joke: Elizabeth was the first name of Victor Frankenstein's bride in Shelley's novel. Mullen was a former Penthouse Pet who had also appeared in a low-budget New York–produced horror film titled *Doom Asylum* (1987). She is very funny indeed in *Frankenhooker*, completely deadpan as she wanders the streets in her purple outfit with matching purse, and is quite nonplussed when she inadvertently causes people to explode.

As with all of Henenlotter's work, *Frankenhooker* is about as far out of the mainstream as feature films get. It's an instant cult movie, and if there were still a midnight movie circuit, it would no doubt still be playing in those very grindhouses (if they still exist) where Henenlotter spent his misspent youth. Instead, the film lives on DVD; when it was released to that format in 2006, a quote attributed to Bill Murray was displayed prominently on the box cover: "If you see one movie this year, it should be *Frankenhooker*."

Gremlins 2: The New Batch

Joe Dante had resisted making a sequel to *Gremlins* since its huge financial success in 1984. He felt that the film had a proper ending and there was no need for a sequel; in addition, the making of *Gremlins* had been long and arduous and he had no great desire to repeat the experience. The studio, aching for another cash cow, developed *Gremlins 2* without Dante, moving forward with a variety of writers and directors, none of whom were getting anywhere.

Eventually, after such concepts as having the gremlins go into outer space, or (even more fantastic perhaps) to Las Vegas, Warner Bros. finally came back to Dante with an offer he couldn't refuse: Not only would he be given three times the budget of the original film, he would have complete creative control over the sequel. Dante agreed to these terms.

Gremlins 2 would be set in one office building in New York City, giving the little creatures a new location to terrorize. Screenwriter Charles S. Haas came up with the idea of keeping the action within one building after Warner Bros. balked at the concept of the gremlins at large in Manhattan. Perhaps they felt it would look too much like *The Muppets Take Manhattan* (1984); in any case, Haas created a character named Daniel Clamp, who was basically a cross between media mogul Ted Turner and real estate maven Donald Trump, and made him the owner of the building.

Since the studio had given Dante his head, the director decided to push the envelope with the sequel—not in the direction of violence, but rather toward anarchic humor. In the DVD commentary for *Gremlins 2: The New Batch* (the film's final title), Dante noted that his intention with the sequel was "to make one of the most unconventional studio pictures ever." He conceived *Gremlins 2* not just as a sequel, but as a parody of sequels in general. He also wanted it to be his ultimate tribute to the Warner Bros. cartoons that he loved so much. As a result, one gremlin is called Daffy and two others are referred to as Lenny and George; anyone who has spent any time at all watching Looney Tunes or Merrie Melodies will recognize those references. Daffy, of course, for Daffy Duck, and Lenny and George for the characters from John Steinbeck's *Of Mice and Men* that are frequently satirized in Warner Bros. cartoons. A scene from Robert Clampett's classic Bugs Bunny short *Falling Hare* (1943), which introduced the concept of the gremlin to the screen, is included in *Gremlins 2*. In fact, the pop culture references in the sequel fly so fast and so furiously that it's difficult to keep up with them.

Zach Galligan, Phoebe Cates, Dick Miller, Jackie Joseph and Keye Luke all returned from the original *Gremlins*, with Miller and Joseph's roles agreeably expanded upon from the first film. Hoyt Axton was originally set to appear in a cameo toward the end of the film, but the scene was not shot due to the movie's length.

New cast members included Robert Picardo, who had appeared in Dante's *The Howling* (1981), Robert Prosky as Grandpa Fred, a takeoff on Al Lewis's character from the TV series *The Munsters*, and John Glover as Clamp. Cast as the evil Dr. Catheter was none other than Christopher Lee, who has two assistants called Martin and Lewis. In a nod to his Count Dracula roles for Hammer, Lee has a scene with a bat, which he injects with something called "genetic sun block." He points out to his assistant: "Sometimes they feed on blood."

Chris Walas had done the gremlin effects for the first film; for the sequel, Dante hired the equally talented Rick Baker to handle those chores. Originally, Baker turned the project down, but Dante convinced him that he could make a wider variety of gremlins than the first film had, thereby making the project his own rather than just following in Walas' footsteps.

One of the conceits of the sequel is that, when the gremlins run loose in the building, they break into Dr. Catheter's laboratory and take some of the drugs that they find there. Thus, one gremlin merges with a bat, another with a spider, and so on. There's even a "Vegetable Gremlin." One of the film's funniest bits occurs in this scene: a gremlin picks up a beaker which has a label that reads: "Acid. Do not throw into face." Needless to say, the nasty little creature throws the acid into the face of a fellow gremlin, who immediately puts on a *Phantom of the Opera* mask from the Andrew Lloyd Webber musical that was then playing on Broadway.

This kind of "cartoony" violence, slapstick as opposed to "splatstick," is what distinguishes *Gremlins 2* from its predecessor. Dante even hired famous Warner Bros. cartoon animator Chuck Jones to do some animation featuring Bugs Bunny, Daffy Duck and Porky Pig. Jones came out of retirement to do it, placing the animation over the beginning and end titles of the film.

One of the movie's myriad of in-jokes occurs when film critic Leonard Maltin, who had disliked the 1984 original because of its violence, is killed by the gremlins. It's another very funny pop culture moment.

Other cameo players include Dante himself as the director of Grandpa Fred's TV show, Belinda Belaski from Dante's *The Howling* as a woman in a movie theater, Paul Bartel from *Eating Raoul* (1982) as the theater manager, Kenneth Tobey (one of Dante's favorites) as the projectionist, professional wrestler Hulk Hogan as himself, the film's screenwriter Charles S. Haas as one of Dr. Catheter's assistants, John Astin (TV's Gomez Addams) as a janitor, *Rowan and Martin's Laugh-In* veteran Henry Gibson as an employee of Cramp's, and pro football stars Dick Butkus and Bubba Smith as men attacked by the gremlins in a restaurant.

Critical reaction to *Gremlins 2: The New Batch* was mixed, just as it had been with the original film. This time, it wasn't the violence that was criticized, but the anarchic tone. Although many reviewers appreciated the movie's wit, some complained that the story degenerated quickly into what was merely a series of gags.

More to the point, however, *Gremlins 2* was not a financial success. Made for roughly fifty million dollars, it only grossed forty-one million in the U.S. Perhaps there had been too long a gap between the first and second films.

Nevertheless, *Gremlins 2* is underrated. In some respects it surpasses the first film, at least in sheer lunacy. Its tone is perfectly exemplified by a movie theater scene in which the gremlins break the film, then make shadow puppets on the screen. This breaking of "the fourth wall" is reminiscent not only of a similar scene in William Castle's *The Tingler* (1959), but of many scenes in Chuck Jones' classic cartoons.

One final bit of irony: The original *Gremlins* had been heavily criticized for being too violent for its PG rating and was one of the films that led to the creation of the PG-13 rating. Its less violent sequel was immediately slapped with a PG-13. As Christopher Lee once observed, "That's show business!"

Tremors

One of the big theatrical sleepers of 1990, Ron Underwood's *Tremors* came out of nowhere and delighted audiences everywhere. Released by Universal early in the year to excellent reviews and good box office, *Tremors* is a light-hearted version of classic monster movies from the fifties such as Gordon Douglas' *Them!* (1954) and Jack Arnold's *Tarantula* (1955). It shares its desert setting with both of those films and its story structure is much the same. But the infusion of "good old boy" humor and first-rate special effects give it a "nineties feel" and a charm all its own.

A very small town (only fourteen residents) called Perfection, Nevada, has a worm problem. A very big worm problem involving some very big, burrowing underground worms that suddenly start appearing and laying waste to the town.

As was the case with most fifties monster movies, *Tremors* unfolds like a mystery. Two out-of-work handymen, Val (Kevin Bacon) and Earl (Fred Ward), meet up with Rhonda

(Finn Carter), a college student who is majoring in geology; she's doing some seismographic work near the town and is coming up with some strange, anomalous readings.

Much more troubling to Val and Earl, however, is the discovery of the body of Edgar Deems (Sunshine Parker), the town drunk: Apparently he had climbed to the top of an electrical tower, where his body now hangs, and has died of dehydration. What, the two men wonder, would have made him stay up there for days until he died?

It turns out that they don't have to wait long for the answer. The immense burrowing worms finally make their first appearance by breaking through the sandy soil underneath their horses, throwing Val and Earl to the ground. The rest of the film is one action scene after another, with Val, Earl and the other town residents attempting to survive and to save what's left of Perfection.

One of the aspects of *Tremors* that makes it so enjoyable is the casting of its oddball characters. Bacon and Ward play off each other like a well-honed comedy team; Carter is a perky, cute but resourceful scientist; and Burt Gummer (TV actor Michael Gross) and his wife Heather (country singer Reba McEntire) are survivalists who have an arsenal in their home with which they hope to battle the creatures.

Eventually, the worms are dubbed "graboids" by Walter Chang (Victor Wong), a restaurant owner who, moments later, is indeed grabbed by one and horribly killed. The same scene features some exposition which in the fifties versions would have involved some sort of "scientific" explanation for what the creatures were and why they were there. But the clever screenplay by Brent Maddock and S. S. Wilson, from a story co-written by Underwood, subverts such audience expectations. Half-jokingly, Val offers, "They're mutations caused by radiation. No, wait, the government made 'em. Big surprise for the Russians."

The best Rhonda can come up with is, "Well, there's nothing like them in the fossil record. Okay, they predate the fossil record. That would make them a couple of billion years old, and we've never seen one until now. Yeah, right."

And that's as far as *Tremors* goes in explaining what the graboids are and why they've suddenly popped up. Like the mountains in the background (the film was shot in and around Lone Pine, California), they're just "there." And now everyone in town has to deal with them.

The fact that our ragtag band of heroes does deal with them—and how they do it—turns *Tremors* into a "feel good" monster movie. For all the film's action, there's very little gore. The movie could easily have passed the censors back in the fifties, except for the salty dialogue. The resourcefulness of the characters is admirable, especially in a genre often derided for having smart people do stupid things. The only truly "brainy" character is Rhonda, but the others, common folks all, rise to the occasion and ultimately destroy the threat.

Tremors is often compared to Steven Spielberg's *Jaws* (1975): The desert sand is a stand-in for water and the graboids are stand-ins for the shark. (One of the working titles for *Tremors* was *Land Sharks*.) The fact is, though, that Spielberg's film also owed a great deal of its story sense to fifties monster films such as *Creature from the Black Lagoon* (1954) and *The Monster That Challenged the World* (1957). So who was imitating whom?

Each of the characters in *Tremors* ends up being indispensable in one way or another. Rhonda has the scientific smarts and comes up with the idea of "pole vaulting" from one rock to another to escape the graboids that lie in wait under the sand; Burt and Heather have the weapons and other hardware to help defeat the monsters; and Val and Earl have the "street smarts." It is Val who ultimately saves the day, "stampeding" the last graboid by letting it chase him to the edge of a cliff, blowing it up with a bomb and letting it plummet to its death.

Part-western, part-comedy, part-monster movie, *Tremors* is a delight from start to finish.

It was successful enough to spawn three direct-to-video sequels and even a short-lived Sci-Fi Channel television series, but none of those offshoots came close to recreating the sheer fun of the original. *Tremors* is truly one of a kind.

Bride of Re-Animator

Stuart Gordon paved the way for direct-to-video horror hits with *Re-Animator*, which had only a few theatrical playdates before finding its audience on video. The inevitable sequel, *Bride of Re-Animator*, would bypass theaters altogether and go straight to video for its American release on February 22, 1991.

Although it's a clever (and extremely gory) parody of James Whale's *Bride of Frankenstein* (1935), *Bride of Re-Animator* goes even farther toward emulating the Hammer Frankenstein films than the first film did. This time, it's directed by Brian Yuzna, who produced the original, from a screenplay he co-wrote with Rick Fry and Woody Keith.

Most of the lead actors from the first film were brought back, with the exception of Barbara Crampton, meaning that the end of the original, in which Dan Cain (Bruce Abbott) used the re-animating agent to bring back his girlfriend Megan, had to be ignored. The story picks up eight months after the events of the first movie, and we find West (Jeffrey Combs) and Cain working as medics in a sort of MASH unit in a Peruvian civil war. There is no shortage of body parts to experiment with, but eventually the war becomes too, shall we say, distracting, and they're forced to return to Arkham, Massachusetts, and good old Miskatonic University Hospital, where Cain goes back to work as a doctor.

West discovers that the heart of Cain's dead girlfriend is being stored in the hospital morgue. West tells Cain that he will create him a new Megan if he helps him. Meanwhile, a mortician appropriately named Dr. Graves (Mel Stewart) comes across a vial of the re-animating fluid in the lab and restores the severed head of Dr. Carl Hill (David Gale), which just happens to be lying around with all the other evidence from the "Miskatonic Massacre" that ended the first film. Dr. Graves re-animates Dr. Hill's head, which, incredibly enough, forces Dr. Graves to graft bat wings onto his neck so that he can fly about as a sentient human head with the wings of a night creature.

As if that isn't weird enough, the Hill head also uses his mental powers to re-animate all of the original zombies so that he can avenge himself on West. At the same time, Cain's most beautiful patient, Gloria (Kathleen Kinmont), dies from injuries sustained in a car crash, thereby unwittingly supplying the head for West's creation. When the "bride" is brought to life, she is, to say the least, a patch job. Cain rejects her and sides with Francesca (Fabiana Udenio), the woman he's been dating, causing the distraught "bride" to rip Megan's heart from her body, at which point she falls to bits all over the floor of the lab.

Dr. Hill leads an assault of zombies against West and Cain and traps them in a graveyard crypt. The crypt collapses under the attack and West is buried inside with the zombies, while Cain and Francesca escape.

As can be gleaned from this brief synopsis, there's a lot going on in *Bride of Re-Animator*, although it doesn't all make a great deal of sense. For one thing, West had apparently been horribly killed by one of his own creations in *Re-Animator*, but he's back here with no explanation at all. Megan is conspicuous by her absence, and her heart is really no replacement for her—as Cain ultimately finds out. There's also a subplot involving Police Lt. Leslie Chapham (Claude Earl Jones), who is convinced that West and Cain were behind the "Miskatonic Massacre" but can't prove it. Dr. Hill turns him into a zombie as well.

Original poster art for Brian Yuzna's homage to James Whale and Hammer, *Bride of Re-Animator* (1990).

Bride of Re-Animator is not up to the quality of the original, but it has a lot going for it. Combs, for example, seems to be channeling Peter Cushing's Baron Frankenstein even more than he was before. A blatant misogynist (as Cushing's baron was), he admonishes Cain to "Think with the big head, not the little head," when he becomes obviously infatuated with Francesca. Again like the Hammer Frankenstein, he uses and manipulates all the people around him, insisting that Cain help him create a "new Megan," while he's really just indulging his own passion for playing around with dead tissue.

It wouldn't be too much of a stretch to see something of Udo Kier's Baron from *Flesh for Frankenstein* (1973) in West's character as well; instead of having normal sexual relations, he'd rather fool around with various body parts. But mostly he's the Cushing model, arrogant, cold (when his creation tears Megan's heart from her own chest, he merely notes, "Tissue rejection") and impervious to the charms of beautiful women. He's totally obsessed and single-minded in his purpose, so dedicated to restoring life to corpses that he barely notices their spastic movements and unseemly appearance. He's done what he set out to do, and that's that.

The ending is like a Hammer Frankenstein too: The good-guy assistant (Cain here, but usually named Hans in the Hammer films) escapes with the girl, while West/Frankenstein is left buried alive in the rubble of the crypt/castle.

The big difference between *Re-Animator* and *Bride* is in the direction. It's a pity that Gordon didn't return for the sequel; although Yuzna is a highly competent director, his style and handling of actors are no match for Gordon's. What he does well, though, is to achieve a certain level of Lovecraftian weirdness. The bat-winged head of Dr. Hill is truly bizarre, like something out of the Providence author's nightmares, as are the other freakish, stitched-together zombies.

As a sequel, *Bride of Re-Animator* is highly respectable—if that's not too lofty a word for a film that trades in dismemberment and gore. It lacks the wit and originality of the first movie but goes even farther into the gruesome concept of re-animation. It's carried almost entirely by Combs' performance, and one gets the distinct impression by film's end that there will be more chapters in the tale to come. Which, of course, there were.

Buffy the Vampire Slayer

To the casual observer, it may seem obvious that the movie *Buffy the Vampire Slayer* (1992) is the "origin story" of the character in the identically titled (and wildly successful) television series that ran on American TV from 1997 through 2003. But according to Joss Whedon, the writer behind both the film and series, it is no such thing.

At the time of the film's production, Whedon was mainly known as a writer for the TV show *Roseanne*. Although he commanded a certain respect within the industry for being a proficient writer, he didn't have much clout at the time that his screenplay for *Buffy* was produced. Consequently, his script underwent several revisions by the producers, who didn't see eye to eye with Whedon.

Originally, *Buffy the Vampire Slayer* was conceived as something called "Rhonda the Immortal Waitress." Whedon's idea was to create a female character who seemed fairly nondescript or "unimportant" and endow her with superpowers. The concept eventually morphed into a screenplay about Buffy Summers, a high school cheerleader who has been chosen by fate to be the latest in a long line of vampire slayers.

In the film, Buffy is played by the lovely blonde actress Kristy Swanson, who had already made her mark in such genre productions as Wes Craven's *Deadly Friend* (1986) and the adaptation of V. C. Andrews' best-selling novel *Flowers in the Attic* (1987). In contrast to Sarah Michelle Gellar's multi-layered interpretation of Buffy in the TV series, Swanson plays the character as a vapid, air-headed Valley Girl.

Her co-star, Donald Sutherland, was no stranger to the horror genre or to vampire movies. He had, in fact, driven a stake into his vampiric wife in *Dr. Terror's House of Horrors* (1965) and had given a fine performance in the 1978 remake of *Invasion of the Body Snatchers* (1956). In *Buffy*, he essays the role of the Slayer's mentor, Merrick Jamison-Smythe, who informs her of her legacy and helps her develop her vampire-fighting skills.

Rutger Hauer, who plays Lothos, a local vampire "king," was at the time best-known to American audiences as the "replicant" in Ridley Scott's *Blade Runner* (1982). The Dutch-born actor frequently worked with European directors like Paul Verhoeven and had given robust, larger-than-life performances in such films as Verhoeven's *Flesh and Blood* (1985).

Paul Reubens, who was cast as Lothos' assistant Amilyn, was known to American television audiences as Pee-wee Herman, star of the Saturday morning children's show *Pee-wee's Playhouse*. The show was cancelled and the star was fired in 1991 after he was arrested for masturbating publicly in an adult movie theater. His role in *Buffy* was Reubens' first acting job since his arrest.

Buffy also has the distinction of featuring the first film performance of Hilary Swank, who later won the Oscar for *Boys Don't Cry* (1999) and *Million Dollar Baby* (2004). In *Buffy*, she plays the small but pivotal role of Kimberly Hannah, a rich, snooty high school student.

Ben Affleck has a "blink and you'll miss it" cameo as "Basketball Player Number Ten." The former child actor would later share an Oscar with best friend Matt Damon for their *Good Will Hunting* (1997) screenplay. Other well-known actors in the film include Candy Clark (*American Graffiti*, 1973) as Buffy's self-centered mother, and David Arquette, who would later star in Wes Craven's *Scream* trilogy, as Buffy's classmate Benny Jacks.

Despite all this talent, however, *Buffy the Vampire Slayer* is an indifferent film. The central conceit of "Rhonda the Immortal Waitress" is there: Buffy is destined to fight and destroy vampires. But the tone of the movie is markedly different from that of the television series, which was both darker and more complex.

It's easy to see that the screenplay went through numerous rewrites, because the finished film has little of Whedon's trademark wit. It's been pared down to the basics and much has obviously been cut, as its running time is a mere eighty-six minutes. Reportedly, Whedon was so frustrated with the way his vision was being treated through the various rewrites that he left the set during production and never returned.

The blame for this mishandling must fall on both producer (Howard Rosenman) and director (Fran Rubel Kuzui). It was Kuzui who had discovered Whedon's screenplay and gathered the financing to get it produced, but the finished film demonstrates not only her lack of understanding of what Whedon was attempting to achieve, but her ignorance of and apparent contempt for the whole vampire genre.

Again unlike the television series, the vampires in the movie lack any sense of style or menace, there is no real depth to any of the characters and the action scenes are not especially well-handled. Kuzui eventually became one of the executive producers of the series, but as a director, she came up with a film that is flat and uninvolving, which utterly fails to do anything notable with a wonderful premise. Even the presence of two fine actors such as Sutherland and Hauer are not enough to raise *Buffy* out of the doldrums.

It was up to Whedon himself to turn the concept into the pop culture phenomenon it

Poster for Fran Rubel Kuzui's feature film *Buffy the Vampire Slayer* (1992).

became. At this point, Whedon pretty much disowns the original film explaining that, because of its commercial and artistic mishandling, it is not part of the "canon" of his "Buffyverse." Indeed, the opening episodes of the series reference what was supposed to have been the ending of the movie: Buffy burns down the school to get rid of the vampires, a darker ending that was completely changed by the time the various rewrites had all but destroyed Whedon's carefully wrought story.

But Whedon had his revenge: *Buffy* the television series has made him a very rich man and he is much in demand in Hollywood. It just goes to show that the old saying is true: If you want to do something right, do it yourself.

Waxwork II: Lost in Time

Writer-director Anthony Hickox was back in 1992 for a sequel to his 1988 horror anthology *Waxwork*, appropriately titled *Waxwork II: Lost in Time*. Rather inappropriately, however, there's no waxwork involved in the sequel: The film opens with the last few minutes of *Waxwork*, although Deborah Foreman has been replaced in the role of Sarah Brightman by Monika Schnarre. The reason for this has more to do with Hollywood romance than with any artistic decision: After the original film, Hickox and Foreman were an item for a few years, but by the time the sequel rolled around, they had parted ways. And so the pivotal role of Sarah went to another actress, which tends to play hell with the continuity, since Zack Galligan returns as Mark and there's even a cameo by Patrick Macnee, despite the fact that his character died in the first one.

Aside from continuity, however, *Waxwork II* has a lot going for it. The central conceit has been changed; as the waxwork has burned down, Mark and Sarah discover a compass-like device that once belonged to the Macnee character. With this device, they can travel through time (which Macnee refers to as "God's Nintendo game") to fight the evil forces that they had tried to conquer in the first film. And there's a personal side to their quest: Sarah has been blamed for the murder of her abusive father, and the only way they can prove her innocence is by bringing back the re-animated severed hand that actually committed the killing.

The fun is, once again, in the variety of stories, most of them parodies of other films, that are offered up on the menu. The time dimension through which Mark and Sarah travel is a mythical one consisting of legends that have been turned into realities by the forces of evil.

One of the stories concerns Baron von Frankenstein, played with relish (and a little blood-red ketchup) by British actor Martin Kemp. As those pesky villagers with their torches attack the castle, Mark and Sarah escape into another time. And so it goes through the rest of the film; just as they're in a cliffhanger situation, they escape into another one, going from the frying pan into the fire.

The most amusing story is probably the one based on the Robert Wise version of *The Haunting* (1963). Its cast is wonderful: Bruce Campbell plays the Richard Johnson character from the original, except that in this case, he ends up with a vulture feeding on his split-open chest while someone literally throws salt into the wound. It's just another case of Campbell being used as a punching bag for some "splatstick" fun, but it works. And the fact that the entire sequence has been filmed (as was the original *Haunting*) in black and white keeps the scene from being overwhelmed with the red stuff. Marina Sirtis (of *Star Trek: The Next Generation*) plays the Claire Bloom character, a lesbian who has the hots for Elenore (Sophie

Ward), the Julie Harris character. And Jim Metzler fills in nicely for Russ Tamblyn, semi–Beatle haircut and all. It's a delightful parody of *The Haunting*, lovingly imitated down to the last detail, even recreating some of the original film's camera angles.

A take-off on *Alien* (1979) works less well, but there's a great deal of fun to be had in the final (and longest) tale, a parody of the Roger Corman Poe films. David Carradine has a nice cameo as "The Beggar," explaining to Mark and Sarah that they are now in Medieval England, and that an evil sorcerer named Scarabus (the name of Boris Karloff's character in Corman's *The Raven*, 1963) is trying to usurp the throne of King Arthur (John Ireland) for his own nefarious purposes. His castle is located in "Bedloe's Swamp," and sharp-witted audiences will recall that Bedloe was the name of Peter Lorre's character in *The Raven*.

When they reach the castle, the story pretty much becomes Corman's *The Masque of the Red Death* (1964), with Scarabus (Alexander Godunov), one of those bored aristocratic types, using black magic on his subjects to amuse himself. One scene, in which a woman who looks exactly as Hazel Court did in *Masque* before Scarabus transforms her into a hideous demon, could easily have been directed by Corman himself. Again, Hickox's love for genre films shines through as he uses the same camera set-ups that Corman used.

More *Raven* parallels are drawn when Sir Wilfred (the Macnee character) shows up in the guise of, well, a raven, just as Lorre had done in Corman's film. All of these in-jokes are wonderful fun for the fans, but unlike what John Landis does—stopping the film for an in-joke that mainstream audiences may not get—Hickox never lets the jokes get in the way of the action. The movie keeps on roaring along at full speed.

As with the first film, the ending gets a bit out of control as it zips through one time and then another, but it is fun to see even Nosferatu get in on the act. But the rap song at the end, is, let's face it, out of place and out of ... time.

For the most part, however, *Waxwork II: Lost in Time* is a gift to the fans and a valentine to the films which its creator loved so much. It reminds us once again that what makes a comedy-horror film work is the care with which it is made, and that the best, most timeless parody grows from affection for the source material.

Army of Darkness

Sam Raimi's long-awaited sequel to *Evil Dead 2* had a troubled history. Raimi entered the "big time" with his production of *Darkman* (1990) for Universal. Plans to make a third *Evil Dead* film actually began during the production of the second one: Originally, *Evil Dead 2* had been intended to take the character of Ash (Bruce Campbell) back to 1300, but the budget given to Raimi by Dino De Laurentiis wouldn't allow for it, so the 1300 sequence was relegated to the film's final few minutes.

A draft of the screenplay for what would eventually come to be known as *Army of Darkness* was written by Raimi in 1988. *Evil Dead 2* had been a mild financial success for De Laurentiis, and, after *Darkman* had earned a profit for Universal, Raimi found himself suddenly hot. Universal offered to contribute half the budget for *Army of Darkness*, with De Laurentiis putting up the other half. The total budget was just under $12 million, a far cry from the first *Evil Dead*, which cost a mere $350,000.

To polish up the script, Raimi brought in his brother Ivan, who had also worked on the script for *Darkman*. More humor was added to the mix and *Army of Darkness* went into production in California's Bronson Canyon, home to many a B-movie shoot, and Vasquez Rocks Natural Area Park. There was also a good deal of studio work at the Introvision Inernational stage in Hollywood, which used a type of front projection process. When the movie ran into problems, Raimi, Campbell and co-producer Rob Tapert were forced to put up $1 million of their own money to film a new opening and ending.

As Campbell wrote in his autobiography, *If Chins Could Kill: Confessions of a B Movie Actor*, the whole idea of "going Hollywood" with an *Evil Dead* film was new to him, Raimi and Tapert: "With a shooting schedule of 111 days, the new film, *Army of Darkness*, far outreached any challenge the three of us had faced so far.... After years of making it up as I went along, I had to learn new skills. Since the film took place mainly in the 1300s, the main mode of transportation was by horse. I couldn't ride to save my life, so lessons were arranged.

"The character Ash, now elevated to full-blown hero, also had to know his way around medieval combat. This required fighting lessons, which included hand-to-hand techniques as well as staffs and swords. The main reason for this was because Sam wanted the climactic sword fight to play out as elegantly as in a Fred Astaire movie and he wanted it all in one crane shot."

A large castle set was built on location on the outskirts of the Mojave Desert, and cast and crew suffered through extreme ranges of temperature: very hot during the day, and, typically for a desert location, very cold at night.

Raimi had no complaint with De Laurentiis and company: They had given him free rein during the shoot. But once filming had been completed, Universal took over post-production chores, and that was where things got complicated.

The studio's first objection was to the film's ending. An unnamed medieval character (possibly Merlin, as the king's name in the movie is Arthur) gives Ash a potion and tells him that if he drinks three drops of it, he will awaken in his own time. Ash goes into a cave where his Oldsmobile (which has transported through time with him) awaits. While sitting in the car, he takes the potion, but he's distracted by the sound of a boulder falling and takes one drop too many. He awakes, with a long, flowing beard, in some post-apocalyptic time and shouts, "Oh, God! I've slept too long."

Universal found the ending too downbeat and it didn't test well with audiences. Raimi, Campbell and Tapert were asked to shoot a new ending, as well as a new beginning to help explain the plot to those who hadn't seen the first two films. Things were further complicated when Universal refused to give them the money to do so. At that point, the three co-producers had to put in money from their own salaries to finish the picture.

Raimi cut the film twice before Universal was happy with it, but then ran into more trouble: The violence and gore were deemed too much by the MPAA ratings board, who were threatening to impose an NC-17 rating upon it. This would have been the kiss of death at the box office, and Universal would have no part of it. Eventually, the movie was pared down to an R rating and clocked in at a brisk 81 minutes.

But there was one more unexpected hurdle to overcome: Universal was itching to acquire the rights to the Hannibal Lecter character so that they could film a sequel to Jonathan Demme's Oscar-winning thriller *The Silence of the Lambs* (1991). De Laurentiis had so far refused to grant them the rights, so because of all the legal wrangling, the release of *Army of Darkness* was delayed from its original summer 1992 date. Eventually, the legal matters were ironed out and Universal did indeed receive the rights to do a film featuring Hannibal Lecter. *Army of Darkness* was finally released to theaters in February 1993.

Despite all the studio interference, *Army of Darkness* is one of Raimi's best and most entertaining films. It's completely dominated by Campbell's performance; he chews the scenery with relish throughout. Whether he's trying to remember the magic words, "Klaatu

Barada Nikto" (a tribute to the famous line uttered by Michael Rennie and Patricia Neal in Robert Wise's *The Day the Earth Stood Still*, 1951) or doing his version of the Three Stooges routines, he seems to be having a wonderful time. And so does the audience.

Campbell's one-liners have become legend, but they're always worth repeating. When he encounters the medieval villagers, it's a scene like something out of Mark Twain's *A Connecticut Yankee in King Arthur's Court*. Ever ready with his shotgun, he quips, "Okay, you primitive screwheads, listen up! You see this? This is my boom stick!'

Later in the same scene, he further admonishes the crowd: "I swear, the next one of you primates even touches me, I'll...." When Duke Henry the Red (Richard Grove) introduces himself ("I am Henry the Red, Duke of Shale, Lord of the Northlands and leader of its people"), Ash responds with, "Well, hello, Mr. Fancy Pants! Well, I've got news for you, pal. You ain't leadin' but two things, Jack and shit. And Jack just left town."

His exchanges with Sheila (Embeth Davidz), a medieval "babe," are just as memorable. In a moment of passion, he commands her, "Give me some sugar, baby," in a delivery somehow reminiscent of Elvis Presley's. Later, feeling ignored, Sheila asks him, "But what of all those sweet words you spoke in private?" His deadpan response: "Oh, that's just what we call pillow talk, baby, that's all."

The third time is the charm, and by the time he stars in *Army of Darkness*, Bruce Campbell's Ash has become an iconic character, just as Sean Connery's James Bond had in the third film in that series, *Goldfinger* (1964). Full of bluster and bravado, but constantly screwing up, Ash is impossible not to like. In the first film, he was a serious character dealing with serious issues, i.e., having to decapitate his girlfriend when she comes back from the dead. In *Evil Dead 2*, his uttering of a single line ("Groovy!") helped to push the character over the line into parody, and in *Army of Darkness*, he relishes the idea of being a hero, even if it's to a bunch of medieval cretins.

The new ending may not have been Raimi's choice, but it's more fun than the original one and adds even more to Ash's character. Having told his entire story to a fellow clerk at S-Mart ("Shop Smart! Shop S-Mart!"), he is suddenly attacked by a possessed "she-bitch" from the past. "Lady, I'm gonna have to ask you to leave the store," he deadpans. "Who the hell are you?" she shouts. He replies, "Name's Ash. Housewares," then blows her away with his ubiquitous shotgun.

With wonderful special effects by the KNB EFX Group that pay homage to everything from *The Manster* (1962) to the Ray Harryhausen classic *Jason and the Argonauts* (1963), *Army of Darkness* is consistently fun and the pace never flags. A good score by Raimi regular Joseph De Luca is enhanced by a terrific main theme by Danny Elfman. With Campbell's performance towering over all, *Army of Darkness* may not be the goriest of the *Evil Dead* trilogy, but it certainly is the funniest.

Campbell, with his usual self-effacing humor and absolute refusal to take himself seriously, has the last word on the film in his book: "The only saving grace of shooting a new beginning and ending was that Bridget Fonda was involved. She had been a fan of the series and asked for a small role. What were we gonna say, 'No'?"

Cemetery Man

One of the most extraordinary comedy-horror films of all time, Michele Soavi's *Cemetery Man* (aka *Dellamorte Dellamore*, 1994) has an unusual back story. It's based in part on an Italian comic book series called "Dylan Dog," about a paranormal investigator who encounters all types of monsters, both human and otherwise. The physical appearance of the character is modeled after openly gay British actor Rupert Everett. Dylan Dog is quite heterosexual and in fact pursues a variety of women throughout the series. But the film that Soavi eventually came to direct was based not on the comic, but on a novel written by the creator of "Dylan Dog," Tiziano Sclavi. The novel *Dellamorte Dell'amore* (English translation: "Of Love, Of Death") concerned one Francesco Dellamorte, a cemetery caretaker whose real job is making sure that the dead don't return to life ... and if they do, to kill them again.

This simple but effective premise was turned into a screenplay by Giovanni Romoli, who had written the story for Dario Argento's *Trauma* in 1993. He had also written the screenplay for Soavi's previous horror film *The Devil's Daughter* (aka *La Setta*, 1991). Romoli took the character of Dellamorte and gave him the appearance of Dylan Dog, which meant that the only actor who could play the role would be Everett.

Everett had never heard of Dylan Dog or Francesco Dellamorte, but apparently Soavi appealed to the actor's vanity and convinced him to play the role. Soavi, a protégé of Argento's, was already an accomplished director in Italy when he decided to do *Dellamorte Dellamore*.

Born in Milan in 1957, Soavi began his film career as an assistant to hack director Aristide Massacessi (aka Joe D'Amato), who made both porn films and horror films. But a match was made in Heaven when Soavi teamed up with Argento, who was one of his idols, as assistant director on such films as *Tenebrae* (1982) and *Phenomena* (1984). Having cut his teeth on horror, he graduated to directing his own films, the first one being *Stage Fright* (aka *Deliria*, 1987), a giallo thriller obviously styled on Argento's films. He found his own voice on his next directorial effort, *The Church* (aka *La Chiesa*, 1989), which featured some inspired Gothic imagery and eerie supernatural atmosphere.

After the international success of *La Setta*, Soavi decided to make a film that was uniquely his own. His film of *Dellamorte Dellamore* is rich in imagery, subtext and romance. It combines such disparate elements as political satire, film noir, zombie film clichés, sex and "splatstick" humor in a delirious and heady brew. It shouldn't work, but with Soavi's self-assured style and Everett's commanding performance, it's one of the best horror films—comedy or otherwise—of the nineties.

With a Raymond Chandler–esque voice-over narration provided by Everett helping to draw us into Dellamorte's unique world, we discover that he lives in a little house in a cemetery in the small town of Buffalora, Italy, with his corpulent mute assistant Gnaghi (Fancois Hadji-Lazaro, who looks like Curly Howard of the Three Stooges). Together, they destroy the dead, who have a pesky habit of returning from their graves after being buried for seven days. The reason for this is never explained, although it seems to have something to do with the mandragora roots that grow throughout the cemetery. The time-honored George A. Romero method of shooting the zombies—whom Dellamorte calls "returners"—in the head is the method most often used, although our heroes are not above splitting the undead's heads with shovels.

One day while viewing a funeral, Dellamorte becomes infatuated with the dead man's widow, a stunningly beautiful woman (Anna Falchi). Dellamorte doesn't get out much; his only friend (aside from Gnaghi, whom he treats more like a pet) is Franco (Anton Alexander), but when they actually get together, he doesn't know what to say to him. And worse, Dellamorte's only hobby is reading outdated phone directories (he calls them "classics") and attempting to assemble some sort of three-dimensional puzzle that's shaped like a human skull.

He becomes obsessed with the widow, who is known only as "She." They make love on her husband's grave, despite the fact that Dellamorte is supposedly impotent. Apparently, her late husband isn't happy about that, as he crawls up from his grave and bites the woman, who apparently dies from loss of blood and shock. After dispatching the husband, Dellamorte shoots her in the head, believing that she will become a returner.

From that point on, Dellamorte seems to drift more and more deeply into a fantasy world. He keeps encountering women who, to him at least, look exactly like his lost love. The second half of the film is a fever dream of graphic violence, re-animated heads, near-castrations and a final attempt to escape the town to find "the rest of the world."

The Australian title of the film is *Of Love and Death*, and that certainly sums it up. Dellamorte (who eventually discovers that his real name is Dellamore) is haunted by two images: one of his beloved "She" and the other of the specter of Death. He eventually loses all sanity and comes to believe that the only way to keep the dead from returning is to shoot innocent people while they're still alive. But he is such a non-entity to people in the town that he literally can't get himself arrested, as the police believe that someone else has been doing the killings. Frustrated, he gets into his car with Gnaghi and they head for the town limits. When they reach the edge of town, though, they find the edge of a deep precipice—the end of the world. They cannot escape their destinies.

Much of Everett's narration is wonderful. "Death, death, the whore," he says with exasperation. "You and I are both the same. We kill out of indifference, out of love sometimes, but never out of hate. Now I don't know who's dead or alive. I'm sick of killing. So I'm leaving the game, brother."

In another scene he muses, "The living dead and the dying living are all the same. Cut from the same cloth. But disposing of dead people is a public service, whereas you're in all sorts of trouble if you kill someone while they're still alive."

Meanwhile, the town's mayor (Stefano Masciarelli) is so absorbed in his re-election campaign that he's completely oblivious to the nightly horrors going on in his town. "By keeping things the same, we can change more effectively," he intones without a hint of irony.

And when Dellamorte and Gnaghi finally escape the claustrophobic clutches of Buffalora, they find that there's nowhere to go. "I knew it!" shouts Dellamorte. "The rest of the world doesn't exist!" Comedy doesn't get any darker than this.

When originally released theatrically, *Dellamorte Dellamore* was well-received in its native Italy, but was a flop internationally. American critics either didn't understand the film (now retitled *Cemetery Man*) or refused to try because it was "just" a horror film. Stephen Holden's review in the April 26, 1996, *New York Times* was typical: "Obviously *Cemetery Man* is not a conventional horror movie. But what is it? For all the repulsive goings-on, the movie is oddly unscary, and after a certain number of zombies have rattled around the old graveyard, it all begins to seem terribly repetitive."

Somewhat more charitably, Bob Stephens wrote in *The San Francisco Examiner* of May 10, 1996: "Moviegoers should not go to see *Cemetery Man* for Soavi's misguided, contradictory humor but for the occasional seriousness and power of his images."

But *Cemetery Man*, as with many comedy-horror films that were slightly ahead of their time, had the last laugh. Zombie movie fans couldn't wait to get their hands on the video (both bootleg and legal) and Oscar-winning director Martin Scorsese called it one of "the best films of the 1990s" in the *New York Times* website filmography of Michele Soavi. Anchor Bay released the unrated version on DVD in 2006 under the title *Cemetery Man*, complete with a featurette about the making of the film. Under any title, Soavi's zombie-splatstick-satire-romance is now considered one of the best Italian horror movies ever made.

Dracula: Dead and Loving It

Young Frankenstein was a tough act to follow, but Mel Brooks gave it the old school try more than two decades later with *Dracula: Dead and Loving It* (1995). It was the third high-profile vampire movie from Columbia Pictures in ten years, the other two being *Fright Night* (1985) and *Bram Stoker's Dracula* (1992). The film was the second in a two-picture deal with Brooksfilms, Castle Rock Entertainment and France's Gaumont Film Company (the first was *Robin Hood: Men in Tights*, 1993).

Dracula: Dead and Loving It may not be *Young Frankenstein*, but it was produced with just as much love of the genre. In fact, it was really made for the fans; mainstream audiences probably didn't get all the inside jokes. Essentially, the screenplay by Brooks, Rudy De Luca and Steve Haberman is a comedy remake of the original Tod Browning *Dracula* (1931) with Bela Lugosi. It even includes parody versions of much of the dialogue from that film and most of the situations. Unlike *Young Frankenstein*, however, it's filmed in color, which gives it the rich look of Hammer's early Dracula films.

As with the Browning version, it is Renfield, not Jonathan Harker, who makes the trek to Castle Dracula in Transylvania. Brooks cast character actor Peter MacNicol as Renfield, and he does a spot-on impersonation of Dwight Frye from the Lugosi film, complete with maniacal laugh once Dracula makes him his slave.

Leslie Nielsen, snow-white hair and all, does a passable Lugosi impression as the count. First appearing with the weirdly piled-up hairdo that Gary Oldman sported in Francis Ford Coppola's version, he utters many of the same lines that Lugosi did when approaching Frye on the castle steps. But the resemblance ends when Nielsen's Dracula says, "Children of the night ... what a mess they make!" and slips on some bat guano, tumbling headlong down the stairs. After this ignominious entrance, he plays the courteous host and we even have the scene from the novel in which two vampire brides (there were three in the novel) ravish Renfield on an antique bed in the castle. He tells the count about it, but Dracula reassures him: "Renfield, you were having a nightmare." Renfield finds that hard to accept: "A nightmare? But it seemed so real, so vivid. Two voluptuous women grinding, heaving. I don't know how to describe it." Deadpan, Dracula asks him, "Have you ever been to Paris?"

When Dracula arrives in London, the story remains quite faithful to both the novel and the major "serious" film versions. The scene of Dracula climbing down the wall of a house to vampirize Lucy (Lysette Anthony) is based on a similar scene in John Badham's *Dracula* (1979), starring Frank Langella in the title role. When Lucy later becomes a vampire and Harker (Steven Weber) encounters her near her tomb, the lighting, set design and makeup are almost identical to a similar scene in Terence Fisher's *Horror of Dracula* (1958), the first in the Hammer series. But in this case, when she walks up to Harker and attempts to seduce him into the world of vampirism, he backs off, saying, "But Lucy! I'm British!" Lucy squeezes her considerable cleavage together: "So are these!" she announces, in an obvious tip of the hat to the kind of heavy-breathing vampire women that Hammer was known for.

The staking of Lucy is right out of Hammer too, with an additional touch lifted from Jesus Franco's cheap and tawdry *Count Dracula* (1970) starring Christopher Lee: as in that film, when Harker takes the hammer and drives the stake into the vampire's heart, untold gallons of blood gush up and hit him in the face. Supposedly, Brooks didn't tell Weber that

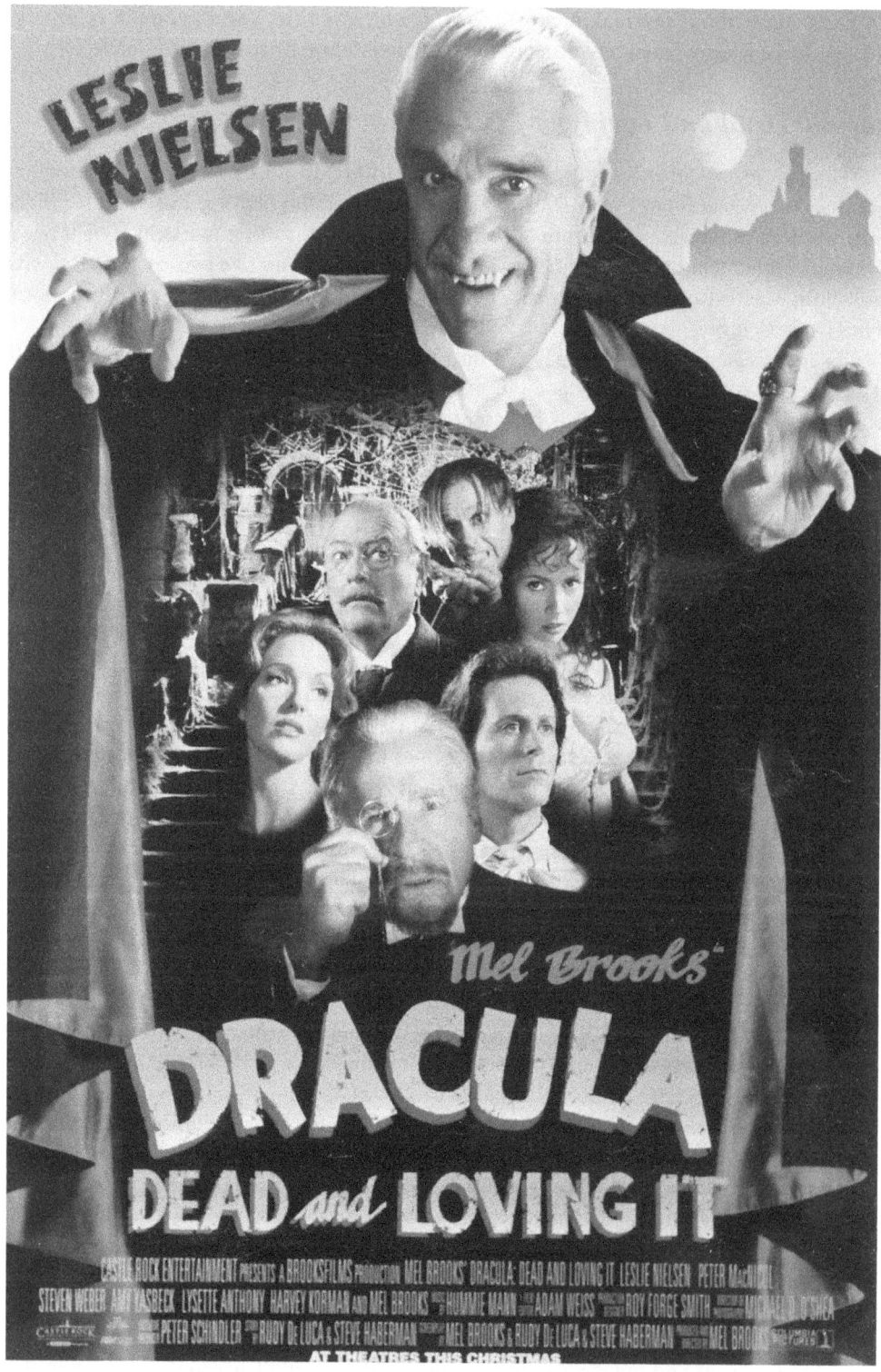

The original poster for Mel Brooks's underrated Bram Stoker parody *Dracula: Dead and Loving It* (1995).

so much blood would spray onto him, thereby ensuring a "natural" reaction. Whatever the case, Weber certainly looks surprised when he ends up with the sticky red stuff all over his face and shirt.

"Oh my God!" Harker shouts. "There's so much blood!"

Brooks, as Van Helsing, admonishes him: "She just ate! Hit her again!"

"Oh, no, I can't," says Harker. "How much blood can she have left?" Van Helsing shrugs. With considerable misgivings, Harker pounds the stake in again and is sprayed with even more blood. "She's almost dead!" Van Helsing exclaims. Harker, fed up, announces, "She's dead enough!"

There are some wonderfully silly, typically Brooksian touches. Brooks gets a lot of mileage out of Renfield's propensity to eat flies and other insects (a pretty funny idea to begin with, when you think of it), much to the consternation of Dr. Seward (Harvey Korman, apparently channeling Nigel Bruce), whose answer to everything regarding his patients is, "Give him an enema!"

About midway through the film, there's a marvelous sequence in which we see Dracula walking about in the sunlight, when he is offered a glass of wine by some picnickers. "I never drink ... wine," he says in classic Lugosi fashion. But then he lightens up and says, "Oh, what the hell!" and takes the glass. Renfield appears to let him know that he shouldn't be walking around in daylight, and when the count looks down he sees his body starting to burn. Suddenly, he wakes up in his coffin. "I was having a daymare!" he says to himself, and goes back to sleep.

The entire cast seems to be having a wonderful time, with MacNicol a standout, chewing all the scenery (and the insects) in sight. Nielsen, who found a second career for himself after appearing in the parody film *Airplane!* (1980), is in fine form as Dracula, alternating from dignity to sheer buffoonery in the blink of an eye.

As Mina, Amy Yasbeck, who also co-starred in *Robin Hood: Men in Tights* as Maid Marian, uses the same over-the-top English accent here. She looks great in period costumes and does the required Brooksian pratfalls with panache. Weber's Harker is both stalwart and silly, excelling in such moments as when Van Helsing says of Lucy, "She is Nosferatu," to which Harker inquires, "She's Italian?"

Anthony, the only member of the cast who is actually British, makes an excellent Lucy, deliberately undressing in front of her window to entice Dracula; later, as the vampire, she's a dead ringer (no pun intended) for Valerie Gaunt's vampire woman in *Horror of Dracula*. And Brooks as Van Helsing is, well, just what you would expect. After all that blood squirts all over Lucy's tomb when she is staked, he shakes his head and says, "We should have put newspapers down."

All of the technical credits are first-rate and completely in tune with the subject matter; it's as if Brooks instructed everyone involved to study the classic vampire films, which he may very well have done. Hummie Mann's music is strongly reminiscent of Wojciech Kilar's sumptuous orchestrations for *Bram Stoker's Dracula* and Michael D. O'Shea's fluid cinematography perfectly captures the feeling of Jack Asher's lighting camerawork from the early Hammer horrors. Roy Forge Smith's production design is likewise styled after Bernard Robinson's art direction for *Horror of Dracula* and other Hammer "vampers."

Not especially well-received at the time of its release, *Dracula: Dead and Loving It* suffered by comparison to *Young Frankenstein* as far as most critics and audiences were concerned. But it has a charm all its own and makes other vampire parodies such as *Love at First Bite* (1979) look even tackier than they were. In fact, it ranks with Polanski's *The Fearless*

Vampire Killers as one of the greatest vampire comedies ever made. Once again, Brooks' love for the material shows through; *Dracula: Dead and Loving It* is a valentine to the genre, not a stake through its heart.

Vampire in Brooklyn

After the loving parody that was the Mel Brooks version, it is depressing to contemplate what horror maven Wes Craven did to Bram Stoker's concept with *Vampire in Brooklyn* (1995), starring Eddie Murphy. It's a low point in the careers of both men (although some may say that the film that gained Craven his notoriety, *The Last House on the Left*, 1972, is a low point in film history in general). *Vampire in Brooklyn* is an ill-conceived, high-profile mess that effectively ended Murphy's long contract with Paramount Pictures. The fact that it was co-written by Murphy (with Vernon Lynch and Charles Q. Murphy) and produced by his own production company hammers home the point that, director Craven aside, Murphy has only himself to blame for the failure of the movie.

Despite all the talent involved, *Vampire in Brooklyn* has virtually nothing to recommend it. There's a good supporting cast, including Angela Bassett and Joanna Cassidy, but Murphy's tendency to hog the whole show (he plays three characters in the film) bogs the whole enterprise down in foul-mouthed, poorly written comedy routines that just don't work.

The plot essentially follows the blueprint of John Badham's film of *Dracula* that starred Frank Langella. A ship full of corpses crashes into a Brooklyn dock; some time later, Maximillian (Murphy), a suave man with a Caribbean accent, infects Julius (Kadeem Hardison), a petty crook, with his tainted blood, turning him into his Renfield-like slave. In a long bit of exposition, Maximillian explains that he has come to Brooklyn to search for a "dhampir," the daughter of a vampire from his native island, so that he can live through the next full moon.

The fact that this exposition is all nonsense from a "movie vampire" point of view is among the least of the film's problems. The "dhampir" turns out to be a police detective named Rita (Bassett), whom Maximillian seduces, eventually putting the bite on her, turning her into a vampire, but with one caveat: Provided that he is killed before she bites someone else, she can revert to being human. Again, more nonsensical vampire "lore" made up specifically for this film.

The movie ends, predictably enough, with Rita staking Maximillian. In a "disintegration" scene lame enough to have been helmed by Ed Wood, he dissolves into the usual pile of dust. An equally impotent epilogue has Julius finding Maximillian's ring and placing it on his finger, which transforms him into a supposedly debonair and sexy vampire.

From virtually any standpoint, quickie director Fred Olen Ray's ultra-cheap *Beverly Hills Vamp* (1988, with its title inspired by Murphy's hugely successful *Beverly Hills Cop*, 1984) is a far better comedy-horror movie, filled with knowing nods to the Hammer and Universal films. *Vampire in Brooklyn* isn't really a direct parody of anything, and has the same sort of schizoid, inconsistent tone that "distinguishes" John Landis' *An American Werewolf in London* (1981).

Vampire in Brooklyn succeeds neither as comedy, romance nor horror. Murphy fails to register as a vampire; if he is trying to pay homage to William Marshall in *Blacula* (1972), he completely misses the mark. His other two roles consist of wearing over-the-top makeup and uttering long strings of profanities.

Craven's direction matches Murphy's wooden acting note for note. Although Craven is capable of some interesting work (notably *A Nightmare on Elm Street*, 1984), he seems to be at sea when it comes to vampires. Even beyond his lack of affinity for the genre, however, the film is simply directed sloppily, with poor continuity, barely workmanlike camera set-ups and tepid performances, even from the usually reliable Cassidy (*Blade Runner*, 1982). Although *The Last House on the Left* is repellent in its violence, it can be argued that it was a kind of auteur work for Craven; he's referred to it, among other things, as a parable for the Vietnam experience. *Vampire in Brooklyn*, on the other hand, looks as though it required no thought whatsoever. Craven's direction of the film is strictly of the "I'll just collect my paycheck" variety.

Murphy didn't return to the Paramount lot for eleven years, as his once dynamic career went into a downward slide after audiences stayed away in droves from *Vampire in Brooklyn*. In 2006, he finally got back into his stride when he was Oscar-nominated for his performance in Paramount's *Dreamgirls*, but it had been a long road back.

The Frighteners

For New Zealand filmmaker Peter Jackson, one thing led to another. Literally. His rise from amateur filmmaker to low-budget "splatstick" auteur to mainstream, Oscar-winning director of the massively budgeted, uber-successful *Lord of the Rings* trilogy has been nothing less than meteoric. And few filmmakers of his caliber have been such unabashed fans of the genre.

Born on Halloween in 1961, Jackson became an amateur filmmaker at a very young age. His first "professional" feature, *Bad Taste* (1987), is an exercise in, well, bad taste. Originally, it was one of Jackson's many amateur weekend projects. He was working regular jobs to fund his films when he came up with the idea of a comedy-horror film about aliens who invade Earth to turn it into part of an intergalactic fast-food franchise, with humans as the main course. The movie was shot on weekends over the course of four years, between 1983 and 1987. It had originally been planned as a ten-minute short, but eventually expanded into a full-length feature.

Using friends, family and local people as actors, Jackson was otherwise a one-man show on *Bad Taste*: he wrote, produced, directed and photographed it, and he even played one of the main characters. Thanks to some connections to the professional film industry, he got it into the Cannes Film Festival, where it received considerable acclaim. Critics and audiences responded to its bizarre, off-the-wall humor and over-the-top gore effects. It was quickly picked up by a distributor and became a world-wide cult hit.

Jackson quit his job at a local photographer's shop and went into filmmaking full-time. His next film, *Meet the Feebles* (1989), was an even weirder project, a musical comedy (starring puppets) that was filled with gross-out humor. Although not a comedy-horror film, it was made in recognizably the same style as *Bad Taste* and solidified Jackson's reputation as a low-budget cult director.

His next feature was a "splatstick" comedy called *Braindead* (1992), which was released in the U.S. as *Dead Alive*. It was a comedy-horror-zombie film, or "Zom-Com," with a budget of around three million dollars, quite a step up for the young filmmaker. It begins on Skull Island, a name that Jackson took from his favorite film, the original *King Kong* (1933), which inspired him to become a filmmaker when he first saw it at the age of nine. From there, the story moves to a house in New Zealand that is filled with zombies.

Although the first half of *Braindead* is fairly low-key, the second half becomes wilder and wilder; the film set a record for the most fake blood ever used in a movie (a record that it still supposedly holds), with no less than 300 liters of the sticky red stuff used in the final scene. Again, the movie was a success internationally. Jackson was suddenly the new king of comedy-horror films.

His next film, *Heavenly Creatures* (1994), couldn't have been more different. Based on a true event that happened in New Zealand in the fifties, the film portrayed the story of two teenage girls (Melanie Lynskey and a very young Kate Winslet) who commit a murder together; worse, the murder is that of the mother of one of the girls. Sensitively directed, with an accent not on gore but on the inner workings of twisted minds, the film received great critical acclaim and led to Jackson's first Oscar nomination, for the screenplay he co-wrote with Fran Walsh.

Hollywood came calling, and Jackson was quick to answer. Director Robert Zemeckis, who had helmed all three *Back to the Future* films starring Michael J. Fox, "presented" Jackson's next feature, *The Frighteners* (1996), with Fox again in the lead role. This time, the American actor played Frank Bannister, a "psychic private detective" who encounters a homicidal spirit that has killed at least twenty-eight people.

Although the story, again co-written by Jackson and Walsh, takes place in America, he filmed it in his beloved New Zealand. The cast supplied to him by Zemeckis was an excellent one. It was the first time Jackson was able to use name actors: Winslet had been an unknown when he discovered her for *Heavenly Creatures*. John Astin, Gomez from TV's *The Addams Family*, was cast as "The Judge," one of several ghost accomplices that Bannister uses to dupe unsuspecting clients. Jeffrey Combs, now known the world over for his Lovecraftian roles, assumed the role of eccentric FBI agent Milton Dammers. Dee Wallace-Stone of Joe Dante's *The Howling* (1981) and Steven Spielberg's *E.T.* (1982) played the pivotal role of Patricia Bradley; Jake Busey was Johnny Charles Bartlett, the serial killer she loved. And W. Lee Ermey spoofed his drill sergeant role in Stanley Kubrick's *Full Metal Jacket* (1987) as Sergeant Hiles, the "commander" of a graveyard full of ghosts.

The film's digital effects and computer animation were quite groundbreaking for the time, and led directly to New Line Cinema's decision to let Jackson's effects company, Weta, handle all the effects for the *Lord of the Rings* films. Particularly impressive is the sight of a Grim Reaper–like figure (actually the spirit of Bartlett, the serial killer) that swoops down from the skies and kills its victims by reaching into their chests and causing their hearts to stop. It's as frightening an apparition as you'd ever want to see in a "serious" horror movie, and Jackson's vacillations between comedy and dark terror in *The Frighteners* are genuinely unsettling.

In fact, the tone of the film was so disturbing to the MPAA ratings board that they slapped the film with an R rating. Ironically, Jackson had not drenched the film in gore as he had with *Bad Taste* and *Braindead*, and in fact had shot the film with a PG-13 rating in mind. But the MPAA would not be moved from their decision, and the film went out with an R rating, which Jackson felt hurt its box office. He had hoped that the movie would find the same kind of audience that had made *Ghostbusters* (1984) and *Beetlejuice* (1987) into big hits.

The box office take for *The Frighteners* was disappointing, despite the presence of Fox and the other name actors. Released in July of 1996, it couldn't compete with more family-friendly Hollywood blockbusters such as *Independence Day*, the sci-fi spectacle that made Will Smith a movie star. Once again, home video came to the rescue and now *The Frighteners* is regarded as another cult film for the director, albeit with a larger budget than usual.

The Frighteners is a rollicking comedy-horror film, brimming with energy and style.

Busey is a terrifying villain and Fox a likable yet reluctant hero. All of the actors have their moments, but Combs is a standout as the obsessive-compulsive, paranoid special agent Dammers. "My body is a road map of pain," he says to Lucy Lynskey (Trini Alvarez). Mumbling to himself and overacting wildly, Combs creates a character that is at once funny and unsettling. He can't stand people getting too close to him ("You are violating my territorial bubble!") and becomes physically ill when women yell at him. With a bizarre haircut and body language that suggests autism, Combs creates another memorable character to add to his ever-growing list of comedy-horror credits.

Astin, whose son Sean appears in all three *Lord of the Rings* movies, has some good moments as well; in makeup that suggests his jawbone is gradually coming loose from his skull ("When a man's jawbone drops off, it's time to reassess the situation"), Astin seems to be having more fun than he's had since his Gomez Addams days. Perhaps surprisingly, he's in the film's most tasteless scene, a brawl in a museum that ends with him having sex with a mummy. "I like it when they lie still like that," he says to no one in particular. Still, one supposes that it can't really qualify as necrophilia, since he's just as dead as the mummy.

Despite these occasional lapses into "bad taste," Jackson's directorial hand is assured in *The Frighteners*. Unlike the awkward shift in tone that pervades John Landis' *An American Werewolf in London*, Jackson's inventive, headlong style carries the film to lofty heights of humor and horror. To him, they're two sides of the same coin. Why can't an audience laugh and scream at the same time?

Jackson has now made his own version of *King Kong*, with a whopping price tag somewhere in the area of $200 million. But splatstick fans hope that maybe someday, he'll return to the genre that endeared him to them. He's one of the few New Zealand directors to continue to make films in his home country. But then, as they say, blood is thicker than water.

Scream

After the unholy mess that was *Vampire in Brooklyn*, director Wes Craven virtually reinvented himself—and, to a certain extent, the slasher genre—with *Scream* (1996), a movie that successfully combined scares with satire. The slasher film in general had become moribund by 1996, with perhaps one too many Freddy and Jason films; the sub-genre of the horror film that Craven had helped to popularize had reached a point of self-parody. Why not make a film, therefore, that was an intentional parody of the genre?

As slasher films have always been primarily a teen commodity, *Scream* was written by Kevin Williamson (the TV series *Dawson's Creek*) with a teenage cast in mind. Craven, with Williamson's assistance, assembled a dream cast of young stars: Neve Campbell, Drew Barrymore, Rose McGowan, Skeet Ulrich and future married couple David Arquette and Courteney Cox.

Scream is perhaps the ultimate post-modern slasher film: Williamson, who has claimed that his favorite movie of all time is John Carpenter's *Halloween* (1978), fills his screenplay with ironically self-aware characters who are huge slasher movie fans. Craven takes the premise and runs with it, creating a film that is so aware of itself that it becomes unsettling. It's like watching a movie that stars members of the audience with whom you're watching it.

Randy Meeks (Jamie Kennedy) recites the "rules" of a typical slasher film once it becomes apparent that there is, indeed, a film-obsessed slasher on the loose: "You may not survive the movie if you have sex. You may not survive the movie if you drink or do drugs. You may not survive the movie if you say, 'I'll be right back.'"

The killer, who starts off the movie with the ringing of a phone that is answered by a doomed Drew Barrymore, provides one more rule of his own: "You may not survive the movie if you ask, 'Who's there?'"

All of the characters are familiar with these genre clichés, and respond to them accordingly when they actually occur. On top of the irony inherent in the script, Craven drenches the film with visual cues that recall other movies, including his own. A scene with Skeet Ulrich climbing through a window references a scene involving Johnny Depp's character in *A Nightmare on Elm Street* (1984) doing exactly the same thing. Ulrich even looks like Depp.

True to Williamson's contention that *Halloween* is his favorite film, the spirit of Carpenter's classic looms large over *Scream*. There's a party scene in which several of the main characters are watching *Halloween* on television, and at one point someone even says, "Go down the street to the Mackenzies' house," a line directly lifted from Carpenter's film.

Scream is almost a primer for slasher films, milking as much dark humor out of the situations as possible. The acting is mostly indifferent, and while the characters are all allegedly smart and self-assured, many of them end up dead anyway. The women are supposedly highly intelligent, empowered types, but sport more cleavage than has been in evidence since Hammer's heyday. It's what's known as having your cake and eating it too.

Janet Maslin, writing in the *New York Times* of December 20, 1996, noted, "Craven wants things both ways, capitalizing on lurid material while undermining it with mocking humor ... an exploitative mix." Whatever the case, *Scream* was hugely successful at the box office, ultimately bringing in over $173 million worldwide.

Scream 2

A sequel, of course, was immediately planned, and *Scream 2* arrived in 1997 as, appropriately, a parody of slasher sequels. The entire creative team was back, including most of the cast. A new addition was Sarah Michelle Gellar, soon to be known as Buffy the Vampire Slayer to television audiences all over the world. The plot this time involves Gale Weathers (Cox again) who has written a book called *Stab*. It's subsequently been turned into a film, and after the movie's release, copycat murders begin to take place.

Once again, Randy (Jamie Kennedy), one of the survivors from the first movie, is the ultimate film geek. He lays down the rules for slasher sequels to the other characters: "The body count is always bigger. The death scenes are always much more elaborate, with more blood and gore. If you want your films to become a successful franchise, never, ever, under any circumstances, assume the killer is dead." That last rule only appeared in the film's trailer; in the actual movie, Randy is interrupted by another character, and never finishes his sentence.

Interestingly enough, although the body count is indeed bigger in *Scream 2*, there is actually less blood and gore than in the original. The film on the whole is just as clever as the first one, and as it's a parody of sequels, its self-awareness becomes, well, even more aware. Williamson's screenplay is, again, constructed as much like a mystery as a slasher film and keeps you guessing as to the killer's identity up until the end. Cotton (Liev Schrieber) has the last line in the film: "It would make one hell of a movie."

Bride of Chucky

"Chucky gets lucky" was the tagline for *Bride of Chucky* (1998), the third in the series of *Child's Play* movies that began courtesy of screenwriter Don Mancini and director Tom Hol-

Jennifer Tilly tries to become a living doll for her lover in Ronny Yu's *Bride of Chucky* (1998).

land (*Fright Night*, 1985) ten years earlier. The difference between *Bride* and the first three films (rather unimaginatively titled *Child's Play*, *Child's Play 2* and *Child's Play 3*) is that, while the concept of a murderous, foul-mouthed child's doll is inherently amusing, the fourth film in the series is out-and-out comedy-horror.

Again written by Mancini, *Bride of Chucky* is directed with maximum energy by Ronny

Yu, leaving no darkly comic stone unturned. After being chopped to pieces in the previous entry, Chucky (again voiced by Brad Dourif) is brought back to life by his human girlfriend Tiffany (Jennifer Tilly), whom he had been involved with ten years before when he had been murderer Charles Lee Ray. His soul, transferred into the doll through voodoo, is still manipulative where the naïve, blowsy and voluptuous Tiffany is concerned.

The title of the film is an obvious nod to James Whale's *Bride of Frankenstein* (1935), which is directly referenced in a scene when Tiffany is taking a bath while watching the film on TV. It is at this point that Chucky pushes her TV set into the bathtub, electrocuting her, after which he uses voodoo to transfer her soul into a little bride doll. Now she's just the right size (and species?) for him.

There are numerous subplots in *Bride of Chucky*, but the best scenes are the comedic ones. Dourif's delivery as Chucky's "voice" is iconic; he's a doll with a very bad attitude and a raunchy vocabulary. When Tiffany confronts him about the fact that he had left a ring for her before his soul was transferred into the Chucky doll, he tells her that he had stolen it so that he could sell it for a large sum of money. "So you weren't going to ask me to marry you?" she asks him. "What, are you fucking nuts?" he says (cue diabolical laughter).

What makes *Bride of Chucky* really fun is that Tilly is every bit as good as Dourif, matching him stroke for stroke with her amazingly annoying voice and spot-on comic timing. Yes, she is upstaged by her cleavage in nearly every scene (at least until she's transformed into the doll), but she's a genuinely gifted comedic actress.

Like most comedy-horror films, *Bride of Chucky* wasn't especially well-received by mainstream critics. Lawrence Van Gelder, writing in the October 17, 1998, *New York Times*, opined: "A handful of jokes about Martha Stewart, a dig at Barbie and an excursion into the sex life of toys cannot rescue the comic Grand Guignol that is *Bride of Chucky* from the graveyard of horror sequels that lose the heartbeat of inspiration long before they die of box office anemia." Critics rarely understand comedy-horror movies, and once again, they were missing the point.

Despite its gore, *Bride of Chucky* is a comedy-horror movie with a romantic heart. A pulsating, blood-dripping heart to be sure, but you do end up rooting for this oddest of odd couples.

The fifth (and so far final) film in the series is, predictably enough, *Seed of Chucky* (2004), in which our protagonists, both now dolls, are revived by their own son (Billy Boyd). Dourif and Tilly are back, with Tilly in especially good form. The film, directed by series screenwriter Don Mancini, isn't quite as clever as *Bride*. Shot on the cheap in Romania, it nevertheless professes to be a spoof of Hollywood itself, with the usual in-jokes and some surprise cameos, including one by John Waters.

It's apparent, though, that the *Chucky* franchise has gone about as far as it can. Perhaps the next step could be a TV sitcom starring Dourif, Tilly and Boyd as a dysfunctional doll family. *Here's Chucky*, perhaps?

9

Comedy-Horror in the New Millennium

"The Age of Irony comes to an end," wrote Roger Rosenblatt in *Time* magazine immediately after the horrific events of September 11, 2001. "In the age of irony," he continued, "even the most serious things were not taken seriously. Movies featuring characters who 'see dead people' or TV hosts who talk to the 'other side' suggested that death was not to be seen as real ... that is unlikely to happen again."

It has become a cliché to say that 9/11 changed everything, but it's true. We think of life before that dreadful day and life afterwards, and never the twain shall meet. Before 9/11, our society was open and welcoming. Now, as it was in the McCarthy era of the early fifties, we are closed and suspicious.

It's safe to say that many pundits felt in the wake of 9/11 that no one would want to see horror movies any more, and that comedy-horror, which is essentially poking fun at death, would never rise from the grave. The fact that they were utterly wrong should not come as a surprise; as we have seen before, people flock to entertainment full of shock and terror and black humor when real life is at its worst, whether it's the Great Depression, World War II or the War on Terror.

Halloween of 2001 may have been low-key, but it was still celebrated. There was even a horror movie released the previous weekend called *Thirteen Ghosts*, a remake of the 1960 William Castle movie. It isn't anywhere near as good as the original, but it did rather well at the box office and proved that horror was still very much a viable commodity in the film business.

The Age of Irony returned, with a vengeance, in no time at all. Although Wes Craven's *Scream* franchise was coming to an end, there was another, even more popular series of films waiting in the wings to take its place.

Scream 3

Scream 2 had been very successful and it was clear that a third film was in order. But by the time *Scream 3* appeared in February 2000, the tide had turned. Slasher fans were tired of the self-referential tone of the series, which purists among their number felt demeaned the genre. Movies such as *The Blair Witch Project* and *The Sixth Sense* (both 1999) were more serious and less gruesome, made with a more psychological approach. *Scream 3* was the only film in the trilogy that made less than $100 million.

Kevin Williamson was missing as screenwriter this time, having been replaced by Ehren Kruger, who used the characters that Williamson had created. Neve Campbell was again the main character, and most of the other cast members returned as well.

Scream 3 (or, as it was rather pretentiously known in theatres, *Scr3am*) is an indifferent affair compared to the first two. Perhaps because it's the only one of the trilogy not written by Williamson, who was busy producing the short-lived TV series *Wasteland*, both dialogue and story are showing their seams. Kruger (*Arlington Road*) penned the script from notes left to him by Williamson, and most of his dialogue consists of endless variations on the F-word. It all becomes quite a bore after awhile.

Even Wes Craven's heart doesn't seem to have been in it. By this time, the whole self-aware, self-referential approach has started to seem tired. The plot revolves around the making of *Stab 3*, so you have the movie-within-a-movie gimmick; in addition, cast members Parker Posey and Matt Keeslar are playing characters based on those played in *Scream 3* by Courteney Cox Arquette and her then-new husband, David Arquette. But the characters played by Posey and Keeslar are also partly based on real-life performers Angelina Jolie and Tom Cruise. It all becomes rather confusing, and, ultimately, it's one joke too many.

With *Scream 3*, the franchise becomes a parody of a parody of a parody, effectively rendering it meaningless. There are the usual celebrity cameos, including an amusing turn by Carrie Fisher, who pokes fun at her Princess Leia character from *Star Wars*. Pop culture references this time are aimed squarely at Brad Pitt and Jerry Seinfeld, among others, and once again the slasher film "rules" are updated, this time by Jamie Kennedy in a video viewed by the main characters: He points out that, in the third movie, "all bets are off."

Perhaps the scariest thing about *Scream 3* is just how emaciated, even skeletal, some of the lead actresses appear to be. The unfortunate tendency that Hollywood actresses have to starve themselves has seldom been more in evidence. Cox Arquette looks as though she had spent the past several years in a concentration camp, and her appearance is not helped by an unflattering hairdo; her performance is fine as far as it goes, but it's hard to shake the feeling while watching her that she's in desperate need of, at least, a sandwich. Posey and Emily Mortimer look equally anorexic. Only Jenny McCarthy, as the short-lived Sarah Darling, and the everpresent Neve Campbell as Sidney Prescott look reasonably healthy, but both are betrayed by the ridiculous dialogue they're forced to spout. One wonders how screenwriter Kruger would have fared if he'd been forced to write a script without expletives. It probably would have been about three pages long.

Predictably, *Scream 3* was the least successful of the three films at the box office and effectively ended (at least at this writing) the franchise. But was it possible to parody a series that was already a parody of itself? The answer was yes, and it was provided by the same studio, Dimension Films.

Scary Movie

The *Scary Movie* franchise is, like each of its individual films, a hit-and-miss affair. The original *Scary Movie* (2000) spoofed slasher films, such as *Scream*, which was a spoof to begin with, and *I Know What You Did Last Summer* (1997). But the parody didn't stop there; no quarter was given to such blockbusters as *The Blair Witch Project* (1999), *The Sixth Sense* (1999), *The Usual Suspects* (1995) and *The Matrix* (1999). The film was directed by Keenen Ivory Wayans, who had previously scored a big hit on the Fox TV Network with his sketch comedy show *In Living Color*. He had also directed a very funny parody of blaxpoitation movies called *I'm Gonna Git You Sucka* (1989), among other features.

Scary Movie, however, suffers from a plethora of writers: Wayans' brothers Shawn and Marlon, Buddy Johnson, Phil Beauman, Jason Friedberg and Aaron Seltzer. Too many cooks spoiled the broth, and, although the movie was an immediate hit, it pales in comparison to many of the films it parodies, as well as to genuinely great spoofs such as Mel Brooks' *Young Frankenstein* (1974) and Roman Polanski's *The Fearless Vampire Killers* (1967). The reason is painfully obvious when you watch the film. Instead of bringing out the humor in the concept with affection, as Brooks and Polanski do, Wayans merely reveals his contempt for the entire horror genre, as well as for big-budget movies that are more successful than his own.

In various media interviews, the Wayans brothers said as much, noting that characters in horror films are always stupid, so they just made them a little stupider in their version. Indeed, the character of Cindy Campbell (Anna Faris) is based on Sidney Prescott from the *Scream* trilogy; her first name is a play on Sidney and her last name is taken from Neve Campbell, who played the *Scream* character. Cindy and her friend Brenda Meeks (Regina Hall) are the only two characters who appear in the entire *Scary Movie* series.

Faris is the real discovery of *Scary Movie*, the one performer who tries valiantly to hold everything together, a nearly impossible task in a film that's really just one raunchy sketch after another. And therein lies one of the major problems with the original: It revels in its R rating like a giggly kid revels in poo-poo jokes. *New York Times* reviewer A. O. Scott opined (July 7, 2000):

> If you're amused by jokes involving male genitals, female pubic hair, flatulence and dismemberment, it should be a big hit. If you're not, and you haven't seen the half-dozen or so blockbusters it alludes to ... then by all means miss it.... Mr. Wayans faces a new challenge: How do you make fun of something [*Scream*] that's already a parody of itself?... The plot, as you would expect, is a slapdash piece of scaffolding on which to hang bits of humor that are annoying less for their vulgarity than for their tiredness. Couch-bound pot smokers, prison sex, mannish female gym teachers ... hasn't it all been done to death?

Perhaps the scariest thing about *Scary Movie* was that a lot of parents took their children to see it; one can only pray that some of the more disgusting jokes went over the kids' heads, but as the humor is applied with a sledgehammer, that may be too much to hope for.

Despite the hard R rating (or because of it), *Scary Movie* was a huge success, eventually earning nearly $300 million worldwide. The inevitable sequel followed a year later, and it was even more revolting than the first; it made less than half the money that the first one did. The producers decided that there was still life in the concept, but that making the series more family-friendly might be a wise financial move.

The first three films were distributed by Dimension Films through Miramax Films, Bob Weinstein and Harvey Weinstein's company. Later, the Weinsteins formed The Weinstein Company, which produced the fourth edition. Their decision to go for a PG-13 rating on the third film did indeed prove to be a smart move; the Wayans were out (except for the characters that they had created) and David Zucker, one-third of the directing team behind *Airplane!* (1980), was in. The series improved considerably under his direction.

Scary Movie 3 (2003) is an altogether more agreeable enterprise than the first two, in part because it doesn't rely so much on gross-out humor, in part because Zucker, a true film buff, doesn't display disgust or contempt for the source material as the Wayans brothers had done. The film on the whole is more slickly produced, faster paced and, well, funnier.

Among the many films spoofed in *Scary Movie 3* are M. Night Shyamalan's *Signs* (2002), as crop circles feature heavily in the plot. It also owes a heavy debt to Gore Verbinski's *The Ring* (2002), which is a remake of Hideo Nakata's *Ringu* (1998). A weird videotape is being passed around and after you've watched it, you supposedly have only seven days to live. Cindy (Faris) is given just such a message. In a convoluted but amusing plot twist, the farmers who have found crop circles in their fields discover that aliens are landing on Earth to destroy the killer who murders those who have watched the mysterious tape. Got it?

The movie starts out well, with blonde sexpots Pamela Anderson and Jenny McCarthy the first victims of the mystery videotape. Charlie Sheen is one of the farmers who find the crop circles. He asks his brother George (Simon Rex), "What do you think it means?" The camera pulls back to show us that the "circle" is actually arrow-shaped, and that it's pointing toward the farm with a sign on it that reads, "Attack here!"

Obviously, the humor is not on the level of, say, Oscar Wilde, but for those who love the other films that Zucker directed, such as *The Naked Gun: From the Files of Police Squad!* (1988), there is almost as much to laugh at here. Zucker teamed up with his frequent co-writer, Pat Proft, along with Craig Mazin, and the jokes—both physical and verbal—fly fast and furiously. And sure enough, there's Leslie Nielsen (Lt. Frank Drebin from *The Naked Gun*), one of the funniest people on the planet, as the president of the United States.

Ruthless fun is had at the expense of "King of Pop" Michael Jackson (Edward Moss), who is portrayed as a child molester whose nose comes off during a fight. Jackson supposedly talked about filing a lawsuit against the producers, but nothing ever came of it. Parody, after all, is protected by the First Amendment.

But Jackson was only one of many pop culture references in *Scary Movie 3*. Also skewered are rap singers, the *Jeopardy!* TV show, *American Idol* (with judge Simon Cowell himself in a cameo), and movies ranging from *Air Force One* (1997) to *Pootie Tang* (2001). There are effective cameos from Denise Richards, Queen Latifah, and Ja Rule, among others.

To be sure, many of the jokes are tasteless, such as the running gag involving the child Cody (Drew Mikuska) constantly being horribly injured. But Zucker keeps the proceedings moving at such a fast clip we don't have time to object to anything, and he somehow succeeds in keeping the jokes from seeming at all mean-spirited. Faris does her usual excellent job of both throwing herself full force into the action and blithely getting on with things, no matter what bizarre situation is thrust at her.

Needless to say, Nielsen's President Baxter Harris is a total dimwit, and at the end of the film beats the tar out of people he believes to be aliens. Of course, he's wrong.

Scary Movie 4, again directed by Zucker, benefits from a screenplay co-written by his old *Airplane!* collaborator Jim Abrahams, along with Pat Proft and Craig Mazin. Following the formula of the other films in parodying the latest genre releases, this one pokes fun at Steven Spielberg's version of *War of the Worlds* (2005) and Takashi Shimuzu's *The Grudge* (2004). There are also spoofs of James Wan's *Saw* (2004), M. Night Shyamalan's *The Village* (2004) and Iain Softley's *The Skeleton Key* (2004). And there are numerous references to non-genre films such as Clint Eastwood's *Million Dollar Baby* (2004) and Ang Lee's *Brokeback Mountain* (2005), among many others.

Once again, Anna Faris steals the show as Cindy Campbell, this time pretty much playing Sarah Michelle Gellar's role in *The Grudge*. And Leslie Nielsen returns as President Harris, especially effective in a scene inspired by Michael Moore's *Fahrenheit 9/11* (2004), in which he is sitting in an elementary school listening to a book being read, when his aide (Alonzo Bodden) enters the room to tell him about an alien invasion. The president wants to stay and hear the rest of the story.

Many of the jokes in *Scary Movie 4* are similarly right on the money, and as for those that aren't ... well, another good one comes along in a second to pick up the slack. The film proper ends when James Earl Jones, delivering Morgan Freeman's lines from *War of the Worlds*, is suddenly hit by a bus. There follows a coda in which *Mad TV* alumnus Debra Wilson does a spot-on impersonation of Oprah Winfrey interviewing Tom Cruise during the infamous "couch jumping" episode, which, needless to say, gets completely out of control before the screen goes black. Memorable cameos are once again provided, this time by Michael Madsen, Carmen Electra, Dr. Phil McGraw, Shaquille O'Neal, Cloris Leachman and Charlie Sheen.

The great thing about Zucker's *Scary Movie* films is that they look as though they were as much fun to make as they are to watch. *Scary Movie 4* was the first in the series to be shot in high-definition video, with no perceptible difference in visual quality from the usual 35mm film. The special effects, mostly parodying those in *War of the Worlds*, are almost as good as those in Spielberg's film.

So far, *4* is the final *Scary Movie*. A mixed bag as a franchise, the first two are needlessly raunchy and mean-spirited while the last two are as much fun as those in Zucker's *Naked Gun* series. But is this really the end of the series? Perhaps one should read the *Scary Movie* "rules" that Brenda (Regina Hall) holds up in the movie's poster:

> I. Let the scary movies be seen, we will mock them.
> II. Let the weepy dramas be seen, we will give them something to cry about.
> III. Let the romantic comedies beware, for we are coming.

Bubba Ho-Tep

Don Coscarelli's *Bubba Ho-Tep* (2002) certainly has one of the weirdest concepts of any comedy-horror movie: Elvis Presley (Bruce Campbell) is still alive circa 2002 and living in a nursing home; so is a man who claims to be John F. Kennedy (Ossie Davis). A mummy from ancient Egypt somehow ends up in their East Texas town and feeds upon the souls of the nursing home residents late at night. Elvis and JFK team up to battle the mummy and save the souls of their fellow residents, as well as their own.

Bubba Ho-Tep is based upon a novella of the same title by horror author Joe R. Lansdale. It originally appeared in *The King Is Dead: Tales of Elvis Post-Mortem*, edited by Paul M. Sammon and published by Delta in 1994. A more unlikely idea for a film would be hard to find: The whole story takes place in a nursing home, the heroes are in their eighties and Elvis has a cancerous growth on his penis. There goes the most coveted demographic in Hollywood: what eighteen- to twenty-four-year-old audiences would be interested in such a film?

As it turned out, quite a few. At the time of the movie's production, Coscarelli already had a long track record in the genre. Born in Libya in 1954, Coscarelli was raised in Southern California and, like so many genre filmmakers, made short films with his friends while still in high school. At nineteen, the release of his first feature film, a drama called *Jim, the World's Greatest* (1976), made him the youngest director ever to have a feature film distributed by a major studio (Universal).

It was Coscarelli's sophomore effort, *Phantasm* (1979), that put him on the genre map. A bizarre horror tale about a boy who is pursued by strange supernatural creatures, *Phantasm* was a big hit commercially and garnered good reviews for its surreal, dreamlike quality. It also spawned three sequels.

Coscarelli has had an erratic career since then, only occasionally coming out with more fantastic-themed pictures such as *The Beastmaster* (1982) or the odd thriller such as *Survival Quest* (1989). At the time he made *Bubba Ho-Tep*, Coscarelli hadn't directed a film since *Phantasm IV: Oblivion* (1998).

Whatever the reason for Coscarelli's relatively low output of movies, *Bubba Ho-Tep* was worth the wait, and then some. Undoubtedly Coscarelli's most polished work to date, it's that rare comedy-horror film that not only effectively combines shrieks and laughs, it has an emotional impact as well. And it even has something to say about aging in our society, and of how the elderly are often made to feel both worthless and helpless.

The conceit of having Elvis alive in contemporary times is just the beginning; in many ways, he wishes he wasn't. Elvis narrates the film and his monologues are quite revealing. "Where did my youth go?" he laments. "Why didn't fame hold off old age and death?"

As the story develops, we are told that Elvis grew tired of the responsibilities of his fame in the 1970s and switched places with an Elvis impersonator named Sebastian Haff (also Campbell). It was Haff who died in 1977, while Elvis himself continued to live the quiet life as an Elvis impersonator.

Interestingly, there's a certain ambiguity as to whether or not Campbell's Elvis really is "The King" or Sebastian Haff deluding himself. Coscarelli's screenplay, which deservedly won the prestigious Bram Stoker Award, leans in the direction of convincing us that we're watching a movie about Elvis in his golden years, but the only "proof" we're given is that the lead character claims to be Elvis; a flashback tells us that all of his documentation was lost in, of all things, a barbecue explosion, so we're left with only his word that he is, indeed, Elvis Aron Presley.

There's considerably more doubt about the Davis character being JFK; for one thing, he's the wrong race. "No offense, Jack," Elvis says to him, "but President Kennedy was a white man." Jack has an answer for that: "They dyed me this color! That's how clever they were!"

This type of apparent paranoid delusion seems to pervade the nursing home; another character thinks he's The Lone Ranger. Ultimately, though, it doesn't really matter whether the two lead characters are who they claim to be. What counts is the fact that they are two elderly men who aren't taken seriously by society any more. "Get old," Elvis muses to himself, "you can't even cuss someone and have it bother them. Everything you do is either worthless or sadly amusing."

But the appearance of the mysterious mummy—which wears boots and a cowboy hat—gives the two men a new purpose. The mummy, which was stolen during a museum tour of the country, ends up in the river when the bus driven by the thieves careens off a bridge during a violent thunderstorm. Somehow, the mummy revives and sucks the souls of the nursing home residents, which give it more strength.

Elvis and Jack get together to destroy the mummy. "In the movies," Elvis tells us in voice-over, "I always played the heroic types. But when the stage lights went out, it was time for drugs and stupidity and the coveting of women. Time to be a little of what I always fantasized of bein' ... a hero."

As they move in slow motion down the corridors of the rest home (a parody of every western showdown you've ever seen), Elvis using his walker and Jack in his wheelchair, the excellent, spaghetti western–styled music by Brian Tyler swells to a crescendo. "Ask not what your rest home can do for you," proclaims Elvis. "Ask what you can do for your rest home." To which, of course, Jack retorts, "Hey, you're copying my best lines!"

Sadly, although they do eventually vanquish the mummy, both Elvis and Jack are mortally wounded during the battle. Elvis, lying near the river where the mummy is now merely ashes, looks up at the night sky. Just before he dies, he sees the stars move into a sort of constellation made up of Egyptian hieroglyphics. It translates into, "All is well." In typical Elvis fashion, the King says, "Thank you ... thank you very much," and then expires.

Bubba Ho-Tep features Campbell's finest performance. His Elvis is a tragic figure, an old man who can't quite figure out how he got that way. His internal musings frequently border on existentialism: "In the end," he asks himself, "does anything really matter?" And on another occasion, when he looks at himself in a mirror: "How could I have gone from the king of rock 'n' roll to this? An old guy in a restroom in East Texas with a growth on his pecker."

And when he lies dying at the end of the film, the effect is strangely moving. It may be in part because we're watching one pop culture icon—Campbell—playing another—Elvis. Whatever the case, it's one of the few moments in the history of comedy-horror films that brings tears to the eyes—not from laughter, but from the sheer emotion of the acting and the beauty of the way the scene is filmed.

Throughout the course of the film, it's amusing to hear such a distinguished actor as Davis spouting the outrageous lines he's given. We are sad, too, when his character dies. But it's Campbell's towering performance that drives *Bubba Ho-Tep*.

When it was originally released to theaters, only 32 prints of *Bubba Ho-Tep* were struck. Those prints were sent on the art house and film festival circuits, to great audience and critical response. It was an official selection at the Toronto International Film Festival and became an instant cult film. When the DVD release rolled around, it was a hit on that format as well.

The end credits feature a tantalizing hint of things to come: *Bubba Nosferatu: Curse of the She-Vampires* is announced as "coming soon." This was originally intended as a joke, but the response to the title was so great that Coscarelli did have plans for a time to produce this alleged "prequel." But apparently, the project died aborning. *Bubba Ho-Tep* would be a tough act to follow, in any case. Even if Coscarelli never makes another film, *Bubba Ho-Tep* will go down in history as a wonderfully witty, bizarre, emotional and unforgettable piece of pop iconography.

Beyond Re-Animator

The third film in the *Re-Animator* series, Brian Yuzna's *Beyond Re-Animator* is virtually an uncredited remake of Hammer's final Frankenstein film, Terence Fisher's *Frankenstein and the Monster from Hell* (1974). In the Hammer film, Peter Cushing's Baron Frankenstein is now ensconced in an insane asylum, where he can continue his experiments without being noticed. A young doctor (Shane Briant) is sent to the asylum as an inmate because of his Frankenstein-like experiments with the dead. Needless to say, he now teams up with the baron, and they stitch another ill-fated creature (David Prowse) together. This time, the object is to mate the creation with a human, and the baron chooses Sarah (Madeline Smith), a mute asylum inmate. At the film's gory climax (at least in the original British version), the creature is literally torn to pieces by the inmates.

In *Beyond Re-Animator* (2003), we learn that Dr. Herbert West (Jeffrey Combs again) has been serving time at Miskatonic Prison for the past fourteen years, due to his participation in the Miskatonic Massacre. Again, continuity has gone astray; at the end of the previous outing, *Bride of Re-Animator*, West had been buried under the rubble of a collapsing tomb. The lack of continuity from film to film, however, is yet another mirror of Hammer's Frankenstein series: In *Frankenstein and the Monster from Hell*, Cushing's baron has been in the asylum for an undisclosed number of years; in the previous entry, *Frankenstein Must be Destroyed* (1969), he had apparently been killed by his own creation (Freddie Jones), who had died in a fire with him.

So the assumption is, as with Cushing's Frankenstein, that Comb's West is somehow eternal. Again, following the plot line of *Monster from Hell*, a young doctor (Jason Barry) comes to work at the prison. It transpires that he has been fascinated by West's work since he was a child, when his sister was murdered by one of West's creations. West gets the doctor to aid him in acquiring the ingredients he needs to complete his experiments, and, like Cushing and Briant in the Hammer film, they're off and running.

The prison warden (Simon Andreu) discovers what West and the young doctor are up to, and he is ultimately killed and then re-animated by West. He becomes another freakish creation, having been injected with the "nano-plasmic energy" of a rat. The result is a rat-like warden who scuttles around through the halls of the prison looking for victims.

All movies set in prisons have to feature at least one riot, and *Beyond Re-Animator* is no exception. The last third of the film descends into total chaos, featuring such atrocities as multiple hangings, eviscerations, castration by fellatio and even a re-animated penis that fights with a rat under the end credits.

Beyond Re-Animator fails to live up to the previous two films in the series for a number of reasons. It would have been a real treat to have seen Stuart Gordon return as director, but, for whatever reason, Yuzna directed again, as he had done with *Bride of Re-Animator*. His direction of *Beyond* is competent but uninspired.

The biggest problem with *Beyond*, however, lies with the international nature of its production. In the year 2000, Yuzna had set up a new production company in Barcelona, Spain, where films could be produced more cheaply than in the U.S. With Spanish producer Julio Fernandez, he formed Fantastic Factory as a sub-division of the Barcelona film company Filmax. The intention was to produce modestly budgeted genre films shot in English for the international market. English-speaking and Spanish actors would be used, with an accent on developing local (Spanish) talent.

The nature of this set-up meant that most of the cast and crew of *Beyond Re-Animator* were required to be Spanish. For a film set in New England, this presented a bit of a problem. Combs is the only American in the cast; Barry is Irish, and his accent keeps popping up at inopportune moments. The rest of the cast is Spanish and their voices are obviously dubbed. They are apparently speaking English to begin with, but their accents required that their lines had to be re-voiced by other actors. This does not make for a happy creative compromise. The film has more of a Euro-horror feel to it than that of a Re-Animator movie.

As a result, there is little tension in the film and not much comedy either. Gone are West's witticisms (the screenplay was written by Jose Manuel Gomez, with Xavier Berrando listed as "Script Collaborator," probably meaning that he translated it into English). The dialogue is flat, with West reduced to mouthing such lines as "Religion has nothing to do with this," when Howard Phillips (Barry) cries, "God damn you!"

Nevertheless, Combs is the saving grace of *Beyond Re-Animator*. He's still very much the Cushing Frankenstein in modern dress, still the misogynist, still the obsessed seeker of death's mysteries. The problem is, he has no one to play off of; Barry is a poor replacement for Bruce Abbott, leading lady Elsa Pataky is no Barbara Crampton and Andreu, a veteran of such Spanish horror films as Vicente Aranda's *The Blood-Spattered Bride* (1972), is impressive physically, but the role as written is the clichéd sadistic warden stereotype—and the post-dubbing works against his performance.

As with *Frankenstein and the Monster from Hell*, there is a certain feeling of finality, even of sadness, to the story. Both films are shot in unusually muted colors. Both have claustrophobic settings. And both Frankenstein and West have tried repeatedly to play God, to master the secrets of life and death, but each time they have been foiled. Their creations keep going mad, are destroyed in conflagrations or are torn asunder. Yet after every failure, they press on, eternally optimistic that if they have one more chance they can succeed. Indeed, both films end much the same way: "Best thing that could have happened to him," says Cushing's baron after his latest creation has been torn to bits. He's already thinking about the next experiment.

Similarly, Combs' West is allowed to live at the end of *Beyond Re-Animator*, the first time he has done so in the series. We see him walking away from the prison, and from the intensity in his eyes, we know that he's already planning on doing some more re-animating. But the joy has gone out of his face. He's just going through the motions now, waiting for the series itself to be re-animated—by Stuart Gordon, perhaps?

Shaun of the Dead

The year 2004 turned out to be a big one for zombies. Early that spring, a remake of George A. Romero's 1979 neo-classic *Dawn of the Dead* was released by Universal to considerable success. Meanwhile, in the U.K., Edgar Wright's *Shaun of the Dead* was, well, knockin' 'em dead, although it didn't arrive in the U.S. until September. By that time, zombie fans in this country were ready for a spoof; what they got was the first "rom-zom-com," or "romantic zombie comedy."

The British horror movie scene had been moribund for many years before it was revitalized by Danny Boyle's *28 Days Later* (2002), a low-budget post-apocalyptic zombie tale shot on digital video. *Shaun of the Dead*, which was originally called *Tea-Time of the Dead*, was shot in the same format, mostly at the venerable Ealing Studios, where such black comedy classics as *Kind Hearts and Coronets* (1949) and *The Ladykillers* (1955) had been filmed.

Shaun of the Dead was the brainchild of Simon Pegg and Wright, who had collaborated on the British television sitcom *Spaced* between 1999 and 2001. In fact, the entire concept of *Shaun* came from an episode of that series, in which Tim (Pegg) hallucinates that he's battling zombies. Series director Wright and Pegg got such a kick out of the premise that they decided to do their own zombie film, based on a mutual love for the Romero zombie movie series.

Many performers from *Spaced* acted in *Shaun*, including Pegg, who was cast in the title role. Jessica Stevenson, Nick Frost and Peter Serafinowicz from *Spaced* all signed onto the "rom-zom-com" along with a slew of other British comic actors, including Dylan Moran and Lucy Davis. Working Title Films and StudioCanal pooled their resources to produce the film, and zombie extras were recruited from a *Spaced* fan website.

Spaced had been notable for its fast cutting, high-energy visual style and pop culture references, and *Shaun of the Dead* followed suit. The plot follows that of your average Romero zombie romp: Several characters are trapped in an enclosed setting, fighting off the undead hordes that are trying to break in and devour them. As it's a British film, however, it's set in a pub—that bastion of British social life—rather than in a shopping mall.

The story revolves around Shaun (Pegg), a slacker who is trying to reconcile with his ex-girlfriend Liz (Kate Ashfield) and sort out some issues with his mother (Penelope Wilton) and stepfather (Bill Nighy). Most of his life is spent in the local pub, The Winchester. His routine is suddenly unhinged when the dead start returning, for no discernible reason, to make meat pies of the living. This startling development doesn't make his domestic problems go away, it just exacerbates them.

The fact that Shaun makes it clear at one point that he doesn't know what the word "exacerbate" means proves that he isn't the sharpest tool in the shed, but he has a good heart. And he would rather keep it in his chest than let one of the zombies eat it, so he devises some very novel ways of dispatching the living dead, such as throwing old vinyl record albums, Frisbee-style, into their skulls and whacking them with cricket bats. Once everyone is holed up in the pub, things start to get really nasty and some of the characters find themselves being literally torn apart or turned into zombies. When Shaun's beloved mum is bitten, she says to him with typical British understatement, "It's been a funny sort of day, hasn't it?"

Shaun of the Dead actually has some very poignant, even compelling moments, such as when Shaun's friends try to convince him that his mother must be destroyed before she comes back to devour them. It's a frightening idea, straight out of Romero, but it hits home even harder because much-loved family members—a proper English mum and her devoted son—are thrust into this horrific situation. The fact that the film works both as a comedy and as a horror film is a tribute to Wright and Pegg (who co-wrote the script) and to all of the highly effective cast.

The dialogue is so rapid-fire (especially if you're not used to thick British accents) that *Shaun* may require a couple of viewings before you catch all the jokes, but the movie bears multiple visits anyway. The pop culture jokes fly fast and furiously, touching on everything from Batman to rock music to, of course, Romero zombie films. We realize at one point that the only reason Shaun's mother is named Barbara is so that a character can say to her, "They're coming to get you, Barbara," à la the original *Night of the Living Dead*.

Shaun of the Dead is a brash, wild, outrageously entertaining roller coaster of a movie that succeeds on just about every level. The zombie makeups and gore effects are as good as any that Tom Savini pulled off in Romero's films, and the production values are solid for the relatively little money spent (about four million pounds). Pegg is ultimately endearing in the title role, a lovable loser who becomes a kind of hero, eventually winning back his girlfriend.

A commercial and critical success on both sides of "the pond," the film impressed Romero so much that he had Pegg and Wright play cameo roles in the fourth in his *Dead* series, *Land of the Dead* (2005). Sharp-eyed viewers will spot the two Brits as zombies in the Universal release.

And so it was that two British sitcom veterans helped to keep the living dead genre "alive." And make us laugh very, very hard in the process.

Dead and Breakfast

Matthew Leutwyler's *Dead and Breakfast* (2004) might just as easily have been called "Head and Breakfast," as there are probably more decapitated heads per square feet in this film than in any other movie ever made. At least thirty-four gallons of blood were used during the course of production, with nearly five gallons of the stuff used just in one scene in which the character played by Erik Palladino is beheaded.

Dead and Breakfast references many other genre films, including the other contender for most blood used in a movie, Peter Jackson's *Braindead* (1992). There are also nods to Sam Raimi's *Evil Dead* (1981) and Sergio Leone's *The Good, the Bad and the Ugly* (1967). Unfortunately, none of these in-jokes is especially amusing. Leutwyler throws in everything but the proverbial kitchen sink, but ultimately demonstrates that more is less.

The plot is pretty basic: Six young people stop to spend a night in the small town of Lovelock, somewhere in the American southwest. The inn is owned by Robert Wise (David

Carradine) playing a character named after the famed director of *The Haunting*, 1963). Interestingly, one of the travelers is played by Carradine's niece, Ever Carradine. Even stranger, she bears a striking resemblance to Uma Thurman, the elder Carradine's co-star in Quentin Tarantino's *Kill Bill* (2003) and *Kill Bill Volume 2* (2004). But aside from this unique bit of casting, there isn't much interesting about *Dead and Breakfast*. Most of the characters are either annoying or stupid, they're all incredibly foul-mouthed and the film quickly degenerates into a routine, albeit extremely gory, series of zombie attacks.

Even worse, the film trades on the most blatant redneck stereotypes and makes the assumption that its audience is in total agreement that people who live in the country are ignorant, cow-chip-throwing cretins. There's even an ersatz country singer-rapper (Zach Selwyn) who pops up throughout the film to act as a kind of Greek chorus; alas, he isn't very funny either.

In short, *Dead and Breakfast* lacks a likable lead character à la Bruce Campbell in *Evil Dead 2* and is entirely devoid of the kind of wit that made *Shaun of the Dead* so enjoyable. Instead, Leutwyler throws buckets of blood at us in lieu of any discernible story and expects us to laugh uproariously when one of the zombies uses a character's cut-off head as a hand puppet. Like Queen Victoria, we are not amused.

Leutwyler doesn't understand the genre well enough to effectively satirize it. Every bit of so-called humor is delivered, quite literally, like a bludgeon to the head. It's the splatstick equivalent of a Martin and Lewis movie, with too much mugging and too many pointless musical interludes.

The tagline for *Dead and Breakfast*, which is also a line of dialogue from the film, read: "Like a bad horror movie, only worse."

For once, there was truth in advertising.

Black Sheep

One of the more successful comedy-horror films of recent years, Jonathan King's *Black Sheep* (2007) is a throwback in style and substance to Peter Jackson's early films such as *Bad Taste* (1987) and *Braindead* (aka *Dead Alive*, 1992). As with Jackson's low-budget features, the gore flows freely, but there's wit and intelligence at work in both script and direction. It's far more slick-looking than Jackson's early work, due in part to—ironically enough—the special effects, courtesy of Jackson's own company, Weta Workshop.

"Get ready for the violence of the lambs," read one tagline. "There are forty million sheep in New Zealand ... and they're pissed off!" read another. Elegantly produced on beautiful New Zealand locations, *Black Sheep* may (or may not) have been inspired by an old *Monty Python's Flying Circus* routine about "killer sheep." These particular sheep, however, are victims of genetic experiments performed on them by the usual "mad scientists," and what makes matters even worse is that, if a human is bitten by a mutated sheep, they transform, vampire-like, into sheep monsters themselves.

The idea of sheep morphed into blood-thirsty mutants is almost as funny as the unintentionally hilarious *Night of the Lepus* (1972), in which flop-eared bunnies grow to phenomenal size and mass together to destroy the planet. But King's film is meant to be funny, albeit in very gruesome and irreverent ways. And along the way, it satirizes both scientists without ethics and radical environmentalists, a tricky balancing act.

The acting is uniformly good, with Nathan Meister as Henry, the lead character, a standout. His main foil is his older brother Angus (Peter Feeney), who is hell-bent on genetically creating "the perfect sheep." Angus becomes so infatuated with the idea, in fact, that ... well,

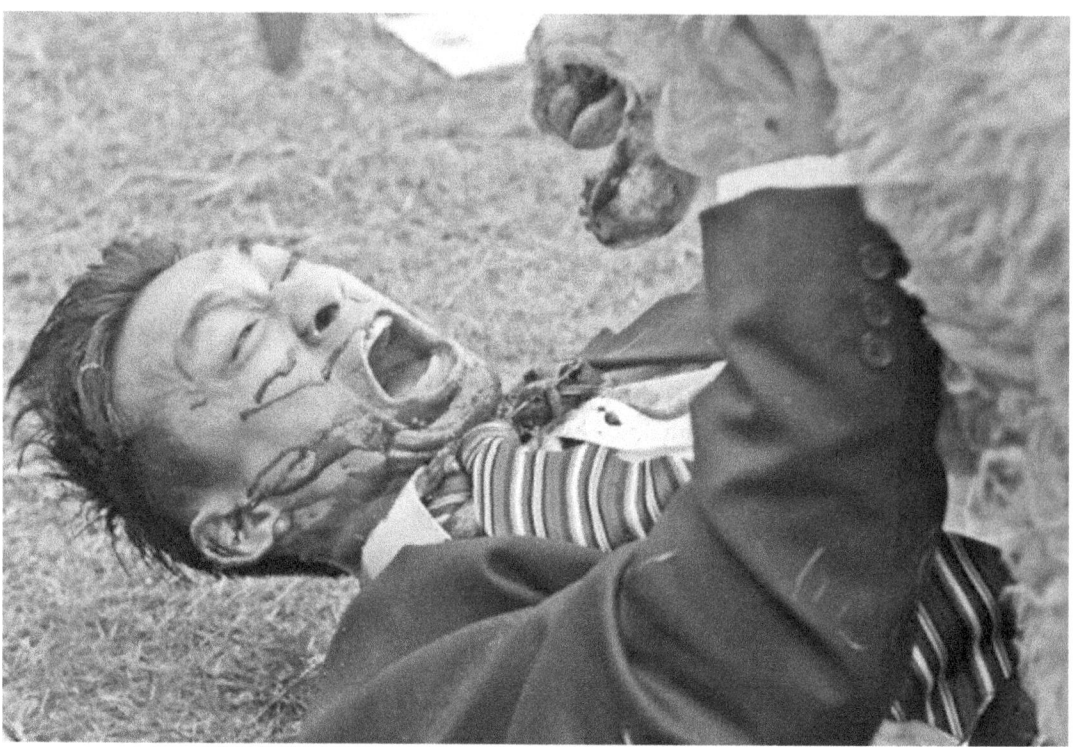

It's the violence of the lambs in Jonathan King's New Zealand feature *Black Sheep* (2007).

let's put it this way: There's a scene where he's sitting on the floor in his study, smoking a cigarette, not wearing any pants, his prize sheep at his side. "What are you doing in here?" Henry asks him. "You wouldn't understand," his brother replies.

Pretty much any sight gag involving sheep is bound to be funny. There's a riotous scene in which a killer sheep sits calmly in the front seat of a truck, not quite knowing how to drive it as it careens off a cliff. There are some very funny lines as well, especially after Henry hooks up with an environmental activist named Experience (Danielle Mason). She wraps herself around such overstuffed dialogue as, "I thought you of all people would appreciate efforts to deconstruct the colonialist paternalistic agrarian hierarchy that disenfranchises the Tangata Whenua and erodes the natural resources of Aotearoa."

While he is being attacked by a murderous sheep, Henry goes into panic mode. "What is wrong with you?" Experience asks him. "Ovinophobia, my therapist calls it." She asks him, "Well, what's that?" Deadpan, he replies, "Just the completely unfounded and irrational fear that one day this is going to happen!"

Released directly to DVD in the U.S., *Black Sheep* won several prizes in Europe, including the Golden Raven at the Brussels International Festival of Fantasy Films. Its tour-de-force style put King on the map as a director to watch. The film's lush orchestral music score by Victoria Kelly gives it a touch of class that Jackson's early films never had.

The Lost Skeleton of Cadavra

Larry Blamire's *The Lost Skeleton of Cadavra* (2004) is more of a science-fiction parody than a comedy-horror film, but it paves the way toward a new sensibility in movie spoofs.

Original poster art for Larry Blamire's "post-post-modern" spoof *The Lost Skeleton of Cadavra* (2001).

Independently produced on a minuscule budget (under $100,000) and shot on video, it was converted to black and white film for its ultimate release on DVD. Blamire, a self-professed admirer of classic Roger Corman B-movies of the fifties (he lists Corman's *Attack of the Crab Monsters*, 1957, as one of his favorite films), went so far as to ask his cast, game actors all, to give intentionally wooden performances and speak some of the silliest dialogue ever written. He even filmed it in Bronson Canyon, a favorite location for B-moviemakers throughout the years, including *Crab Monsters*, among many others.

In *The Lost Skeleton of Cadavra*, the famous Bronson Cave is home to the titular skeleton, a rather petulant demon voiced by Blamire himself. His oft-repeated phrase "I sleep now!" is meant to dismiss those to whom he doesn't feel like talking. The film, which took five days to write and ten days to shoot, is a funny valentine to all the movies of the fifties spoofed on *Mystery Science Theatre 3000*. But Blamire's movie is far more clever than that overrated TV series could ever hope to be.

Most of the film concerns space aliens who somehow get mixed up with the so-called Lost Skeleton; one of the worst-looking monsters since Gene Corman's *Night of the Blood Beast* (1958) is also on the loose in the canyon. The intentionally stilted dialogue causes chuckles, sometimes outright belly laughs. Ranger Brad (Dan Conroy) tells scientist Dr. Paul Armstrong (Blamire) and his wife Betty (Fay Masterson), "We take our horrible mutilations seriously in these parts." There are bizarre non sequiturs, such as when Betty proclaims, "I must make a skeleton meatier using a crowbar covered in lettuce." And the Skeleton himself (itself?) moves on wires, or is simply pushed by the other actors to give the appearance of movement.

There are visual cues in the film that hark back to *Cat Women of the Moon* (1953), *Plan 9 from Outer Space* (1959) and any fifties sci-fi movie filmed in Bronson Canyon you'd care to name. Blamire truly captured the look and feel of these movies, and he's done it with a real love and appreciation for the genre. One suspects that his best work is yet to come, and indeed, his followup film is more a parody of sci-fi horror films of the sixties, and it's quite brilliant in its lunacy.

Trail of the Screaming Forehead

In 2008, Blamire and his cast of zanies from *The Lost Skeleton of Cadavra* returned to the screen with a new and even more deranged film. *Trail of the Screaming Forehead*, like *Lost Skeleton*, owes its inspiration to B horror and science fiction movies from the fifties. But this time it's in blazing color, the kind of rich Eastman Color look that the late fifties and early sixties genre films were known for. And it's filmed in "Craniascope, the new miracle of the screen," which means absolutely nothing but sounds great.

Blamire, who wrote, produced and directed the film, brought some big names into the mix this time. *Trail of the Screaming Forehead* is "presented" by fantasy film icon and special effects genius Ray Harryhausen (who also animates the "crawling foreheads") and there are several acting cameos from thespians beloved by fans of the genre. Dick Miller (Corman's *A Bucket of Blood* et al.) shows up as Eddie the bartender; James Karen (*Return of the Living Dead*, *Poltergeist*) puts in a very funny appearance as Reverend Beaks; veteran TV character actress Betty Garrett appears as Mrs. Cuttle, who notes when she's taken over by aliens that a carrot "smells like burning toothpaste"; and Kevin McCarthy (Don Siegel's *Invasion of the Body Snatchers*, 1956) pops in as "The Latecomer," who doesn't show up until the end credits are over.

Brian Howe, hilarious in *Lost Skeleton*, is equally laugh-out-loud funny here as Big Dan Frater, a salty sea-dog. New additions to the Blamire stock company include Alison Martin as Millie Healey, a librarian, who gets to utter such lines as, "This is really fun! I hope we don't get killed," and Trish Geiger as Mary Latham, whose husband Dr. Philip Latham (Andrew Parks) has been injected with Foreheadazine, which causes him to grow a head the size of a pumpkin.

The visual effects are handled by Stephen Chiodo (*Killer Klowns from Outer Space*, 1987) and the theme song, written by Blamire, is warbled by The Manhattan Transfer. There are also two *a capella* versions of "Love Ballad of the Screaming Forehead" done to perfection by Blamire's wife, Jennifer Blaire, who steals every scene she's in. Blamire gives her some of the worst (or perhaps one should say best) jokes in the film. As the hard-drinking, hard-living bar chanteuse Droxy, Blaire outdoes her performance as Animala in *Lost Skeleton*. When Dr. Sheila Bexter (Fay Masterson) asks Nick Vassidine (Blamire), "You Nick?" Droxy chimes in, "Only when he shaves," and then laughs hysterically at her own lame joke. Later, she drunkenly quips, "Foreheads are better than none!"

The plot mixes up elements of *Invasion of the Body Snatchers* and *Fiend Without a Face* (1958), with a little bit of *Critters* (1986) thrown in for good measure. Dr. Bexter is trying to prove her theory that the seat of intelligence (or, as she calls it, "thinking-up-stuff ability") is in the forehead, not the brain. Using her feminine wiles, she convinces Dr. Latham to take injections of Foreheadazine, the cranium-enlarging drug she's developed.

By some strange coincidence, an invasion of the little town of Longhead Bay, in which Bexter and Latham live, is taking place at the same moment; foreheads from outer space are landing at an alarming rate and attaching themselves to town residents, taking over their "thinking-up-stuff ability." Meanwhile, a pair of seamen vaguely patterned after the Skipper and Gilligan from TV's *Gilligan's Island* have arrived in town and are staying at a local bed and breakfast. Frater's sidekick, Dutch "The Swede" Annacrombie, is played by Dan Conroy, "Ranger Brad" from *Lost Skeleton*.

Ultimately, the two sailors come closer than anyone else to being the "heroes" of the piece, aided by Millie, who notes that an inordinate number of her library patrons are checking out books on "foreheadology." The three of them ring bells at the townspeople who have been "taken over," having discovered through their library research that people with large foreheads can't stand the sound of any sort of bell.

As was the case with *Lost Skeleton*, a mere synopsis of *Screaming Forehead* can't begin to describe its, shall we say, unique quality. And the humor is, again, of the "you either get it or you don't" variety. But if you do, there are many treasures to be found in Kevin F. Jones' marvelous "retro" color photography; the excellent music by Chris Aisncough and Blamire; and the slap-happy yet completely deadpan performances of the game cast, right down to the smallest bit players.

After its world premiere at the Seattle Film Festival in 2007, Ken Eisner (*Variety*) wrote: "The not-quite-right names, nonsensical plot turns and belabored pseudo-scientific gibberish are all nicely tuned, capturing the know-nothing ethos of Eisenhower-era filmmakers angling to cash in on events (and better movies) they only vaguely understood. Dick Tracy colors, wonderfully clunky staging, and lush musical interludes ... add to the sense of a forgotten comic book sprung to life."

Blamire may be at the forefront (or the forehead) of a new sensibility in filmmaking, just as Roger Corman was in 1960 when he said, "Nobody was making films like these." Call it post-postmodern. Blamire's next feature is a sequel to *Lost Skeleton*, called *The Lost Skeleton Returns Again*, and then an old dark house thriller called *A Dark and Stormy Night*. Say, isn't that where we came in?

Afterword

It's clear that comedy-horror films are here to stay because they appeal to two of the most basic human emotions: fear and amusement. Authors like Robert Bloch understood this; so does Stephen King, who even included a clown as a symbol of terror in his novel *It*.

And, as we have seen, this marriage of genres is extremely resilient. It has survived wars, depressions and terrorist attacks. In fact, that which does not kill it only makes it stronger.

The most basic fear we have is the fear of death. What happens at the moment of death? Where do we go, if anywhere, after we die? Does human consciousness survive?

We only have one weapon with which to fight off the inevitability of death: humor. It works in the trenches, it works for prisoners of war, it works for doctors who hold people's lives in their hands every day. If we can laugh in the face of death, we can pretend to be invincible. Humor won't save us from the Grim Reaper, but at least we can laugh in his face before he takes us away to what we fervently hope will be the Elysian Fields.

No matter how bad times may get, we'll always have comedy-horror films to comfort us with the knowledge that they could be worse. Zombies could be at the door, and they could be our loved ones. We could be transformed into werewolves or vampires or we could be re-animated after death by mad scientists.

But we can fight back. We can laugh at our fears, no matter what they may be, and vanquish them. Even when confronted by the Army of Darkness, we can throw down a banana peel and make the undead hordes fall flat on their faces.

We all need to whistle past the cemetery. And ultimately, we all need to laugh, from cradle to grave.

APPENDIX A
A Chronological Checklist of Films

This list includes nearly 100 more titles than are given extensive coverage in the text. Where possible, specific U.S. release dates are included.

The Ghost Breaker
Directed by Cecil B. DeMille, Oscar Apfel. Produced by Cecil B. DeMille, Jesse L. Lasky. Written by Cecil B. DeMille, Oscar Apfel, Paul Dickey, Charles W. Goddard, James Montgomery. Starring H. B. Warner. Release: December 7, 1914. 60 minutes (USA)

One Exciting Night
Directed, Produced and Written by D. W. Griffith. Starring Carol Dempster, Henry Hull, Morgan Wallace, Porter Strong. Cinematography: Hendrik Sartov. Distributed by United Artists. Release: October 1922. 128 minutes (USA)

The Ghost Breaker
Directed by Alfred Green. Produced by Jesse L. Lasky. Written by Walter de Leon. Starring Wallace Reid, Lila Lee, Walter Hiers, Arthur Carewe, J. Farrell MacDonald, Snitz Edwards. Cinematography: William Marshall. Distributed by Famous Players–Lasky. Release: 1922. 57 minutes (USA)

The Headless Horseman
Directed by Edward D. Venturini. Produced by Carl Stearns Clancy. Written by Washington Irving (story), Carl Stearns Clancy (adaptation). Starring Will Rogers, Lois Meredith, Ben Hendricks, Jr., Charles Graham, Mary Fox, Bernard A. Reinold, Downing Clarke, Jerry Devine, James Sheridan, Kary MacCausland, Nancy Chase. Cinematography: Ned Van Buren. Distributed by W. W. Hodkinson. Release: November 5, 1922. 68 minutes (USA)

Puritan Passions
Directed and Written by Frank Tuttle. Starring Maude Hill, Glenn Hunter, Osgood Perkins, Thomas Chalmers, Mary Astor. Cinematography: Fred Waller. Distributed by W. W. Hodkinson. Release: September 9, 1923. 70 minutes (USA)

The Monster
Directed by Roland West. Produced by W.L. Heywood. Written by Crane Wilbur (play), Roland West, Willard Mack, Albert Kenyon. Starring Lon Chaney, Johnny Arthur, Gertrude Olmstead. Distributed by MGM. Release: March 16, 1925. 86 minutes (USA)

The Bat
Directed and Produced by Roland West. Written by Avery Hopwood, Mary Roberts Rinehart (play), Roland West, Julien Josephson. Starring Tullio Carminati, Charles Herzinger, Jewel Carmen, Louise Fazenda, Emily Fitzroy, Arthur Houseman, Robert McKim. Cinematography: Arthur Edeson. Distributed by MGM. Release: 1926. 86 minutes (USA)

The Cat and the Canary
Directed by Paul Leni. Produced by Paul Kohner. Written by John Willard (play), Walter Anthony (titles), Alfred A. Cohn, Robert F. Hill (adaptation). Starring Laura La Plante, Creighton Hale, Forrest Stanley. Cinematography: Gilbert Warrenton. Editing by Martin G. Cohn. Distributed by Universal Pictures. Release: September 9, 1927. 82 minutes (USA)

The Gorilla
Directed and Produced by Alfred Santell. Written by: Ralph Spence (play and adaptation). Starring Charlie Murray, Fred Kelsey, Alice Day, Tully

Marshall, Walter Pidgeon. Cinematography: Arthur Edeson. Distributed by First National Pictures. Release: November 13, 1927. 80 minutes (USA)

The Gorilla

Directed by Bryan Foy. Written by Ralph Spence (play), B. Harrison Orkow, Herman Ruby (adaptation). Starring Joe Frisco, Harry Gribbon, Lila Lee, Walter Pidgeon, Purnell Pratt. Cinematography: Sid Hickox. Editing by George Amy. Distributed by First National Pictures. Release: November 2, 1930. 65 minutes (USA)

The Cat Creeps

Directed by Rupert Julian. Produced by Carl Laemmle, Jr. Written by John Willard (play), William Hurlbut, Gladys Lehman. Starring Helen Twelvetrees, Raymond Hackett, Neil Hamilton. Music by Heinz Roemheld. Cinematography: Hal Mohr. Editing by Maurice Pivar. Distributed by Universal Pictures. Release: November 10, 1930. 71 minutes (USA)

The Bat Whispers

Directed by Roland West. Produced by Joseph M. Schenck. Written by Avery Hopwood, Mary Roberts Rinehart (play), Roland West (screenplay). Starring Chester Morris, Chance Ward, Una Merkel, Richard Tucker, Maude Eburne. Cinematography: Ray June (35mm version), Robert H. Planck (70mm version). Editing by Hal C. Kern, James Smith. Distributed by United Artists. Release: November 13, 1930. 83 minutes (USA)

The Monster Walks

Directed by Frank Strayer. Produced by Cliff P. Broughton. Written by Robert Ellis. Starring Rex Lease, Vera Reynolds, Sheldon Lewis, Mischa Auer, Martha Mattox, Sidney Bracey, Willie Best. Cinematography: Jules Cronjager. Editing by Byron Robinson. Distributed by Mayfair Pictures Corporation. Release: February 10, 1932. 63 minutes (USA)

The Old Dark House

Directed by James Whale. Produced by Carl Laemmle, Jr. Starring Boris Karloff, Melvyn Douglas, Charles Laughton, Gloria Stuart, Lillian Bond. Music by Bernhard Kaun. Cinematography: Arthur Edeson. Editing by Andrew Cohen. Distributed by Universal Pictures. Release: October 20, 1932. 71 minutes (USA)

Night of Terror

Directed by Benjamin Stoloff. Written by Beatrice Van, William Jacobs, Lester Nielson. Starring Bela Lugosi, George Meeker, Tully Marshall, Bryant Washburn, Edwin Maxwell. Cinematography: Joseph A. Valentine. Editing by Arthur Hilton. Distributed by Columbia Pictures. Release: April 24, 1933. 65 minutes (USA)

The Ghost Walks

Directed by Frank Strayer. Produced by Maury M. Cohen. Written by Charles S. Belden. Starring John Miljan, June Collyer, Richard Carle, Spencer Charters, Johnny Arthur. Cinematography: M. A. Anderson. Editing by Ronald D. Reed. Distributed by Chesterfield Motion Pictures Corporation. Release: December 1, 1934. 69 minutes (USA)

A Face in the Fog

Directed by Robert Hill. Produced by Sam Katzman. Written by Al Martin. Starring June Collyer, Lloyd Hughes, Lawrence Gray, Jack Mulhall, Al St. John. Cinematography: Bill Hyer. Editing by Earl Turner. Distributed by Victory Pictures Corporation. Release: February 1, 1936. 66 minutes (USA)

Mummy's Boys

Directed by Fred Guiol. Produced by Samuel J. Briskin. Written by Jack Townley, Philip G. Epstein, Charles Roberts. Starring Bert Wheeler, Robert Woolsey, Barbara Pepper, Moroni Olsen. Cinematography: Jack Mackenzie. Editing by John Lockert. Distributed by RKO Pictures. Release: October 2, 1936. 68 minutes (USA)

Super-Sleuth

Directed by Benjamin Stoloff. Produced by Edward Small. Written by Harry Segall (play), Gertrude Purcell, Ernest Pagano (screenplay). Starring Jack Oakie, Ann Sothern, Edgar Kennedy, Eduardo Ciannelli, Willie Best, Paul Guilfoyle. Cinematography: Joseph H. August. Editing by William Hamilton. Distributed by RKO Pictures. Release: July 16, 1937. 75 minutes (USA)

Sh! The Octopus

Directed by William C. McGann. Produced by Bryan Foy, Hal B. Wallis, Jack L. Warner. Written by Ralph Spence, Ralph Murphy, Donald Gallaher (play), George Bricker (screenplay). Starring Hugh Herbert, Allen Jenkins, Marcia Ralston, John Eldredge, George Rosener, Brandon Tynan, Eric Stanley, Margaret Irving, Elspeth Dudgeon. Cinematography: Arthur Todd. Editing by Clarence Kolster. Distributed by First National Pictures. Release: December 14, 1937. 54 minutes (USA)

The Cat and the Canary

Directed by Elliott Nugent. Produced by Arthur Hornblow, Jr. Written by John Willard (play), Walter de Leon, Lynn Starling. Starring Bob Hope, Paulette Goddard, John Beal, Douglass Montgomery, Gale Sondergaard. Music by Ernst Toch. Cinematography: Charles B. Lang. Editing by Archie Marshek. Distributed by Paramount Pictures. Release: November 10, 1939. 72 minutes (USA)

The Ghost Breakers

Directed by George Marshall. Produced by Arthur Hornblow, Jr. Written by Walter de Leon. Starring Bob Hope, Paulette Goddard, Richard Carlson, Paul Lukas, Willie Best, Anthony Quinn, Paul Fix. Music by Ernst Toch. Cinematography: Charles B. Lang. Editing by Ellsworth Hoagland. Distributed by Paramount Pictures. Release: June 21, 1940. 83 minutes (USA)

King of the Zombies

Directed by Jean Yarbrough. Produced by Lindsley Parsons. Written by Edmond Kelso. Starring Dick Purcell, Joan Woodbury, Mantan Moreland. Music by Edward J. Kay. Cinematography: Mack Stengler. Editing by Richard C. Currier. Distributed by Monogram Pictures Corporation. Release: May 14, 1941. 67 minutes (USA)

Hold That Ghost

Directed by Arthur Lubin. Produced by Burt Kelly, Glenn Tryon. Written by Robert Lees, Fred Rinaldo, John Grant. Starring Bud Abbott, Lou Costello, Richard Carlson, The Andrews Sisters, Shemp Howard, Joan Davis, Evelyn Ankers. Music by H.J. Salter. Editing by Philip Cahn. Distributed by Universal Pictures. Release: August 6, 1941. 85 minutes (USA)

The Smiling Ghost

Directed by Lewis Seiler. Produced by Bryan Foy. Written by Kenneth Gamet, Stuart Palmer. Starring Wayne Morris, Brenda Marshall, Alexis Smith, Lee Patrick, Alan Hale, David Bruce, Willie Best. Cinematography: Arthur Todd. Editing by Jack Killifer. Distributed by Warner Bros. Release: September 6, 1941. 77 minutes (USA)

Spooks Run Wild

Directed by Phil Rosen. Produced by Sam Katzman. Written by Carl Foreman, Charles R. Marion. Starring Bela Lugosi, Leo Gorcey, Huntz Hall. Music by Johnny Lange, Lew Porter. Cinematography: Marcel Le Picard. Editing by Robert Golden. Distributed by Monogram Pictures Corporation. Release: October 24, 1941. 65 mins. (USA)

Ghosts on the Loose

Directed by William Beaudine. Produced by Jack Dietz, Sam Katzman, Barney A. Sarecky. Written by Kenneth Higgins. Starring Leo Gorcey, Huntz Hall, Bobby Jordan, Bela Lugosi, Ava Gardner. Cinematography: Mack Stengler. Editing by Carl Pierson. Distributed by Monogram Pictures Corporation. Release: July 30, 1943. 67 minutes (USA)

Ghost Catchers

Directed by Edward F. Cline. Produced and Written by Edmund L. Hartmann. Starring Ole Olsen, Chic Johnson, Gloria Jean, Martha O'Driscoll, Leo Carrillo, Lon Chaney, Jr., Walter Catlett, Jack Norton. Cinematography: Charles Van Enger. Editing by Arthur Hilton. Distributed by Universal Pictures. Release: June 16, 1944. 68 minutes (USA)

The Canterville Ghost

Directed by Jules Dassin, Norman Z. McLeod (uncredited). Produced by Arthur Field. Written by Oscar Wilde (story), Edwin Blum (screenplay). Starring Charles Laughton, Robert Young, Margaret O'Brien. Cinematography: Robert Planck, William H. Daniels. Editing by Chester W. Schaeffer. Distributed by MGM. Release: July 1944. 95 minutes (USA)

Crazy Knights

Directed by William Beaudine. Produced by Jack Dietz, Sam Katzman, Barney A. Sarecky. Starring Billy Gilbert, Maxie Rosenbloom, Shemp Howard, Jayne Hazard, Minerva Urecal, Tim Ryan, Art Miles. Cinematography: Marcel Le Picard. Editing by Richard C. Currier. Distributed by Monogram Pictures Corporation. Release: December 8, 1944. 63 minutes (USA)

Zombies on Broadway

Directed by Gordon Douglas. Produced by Benjamin Stoloff. Written by Robert Faber, Charles Newman (story), Robert Kent, Lawrence Kimble (screenplay). Starring Bela Lugosi, Alan Carney, Wally Brown, Anne Jeffreys, Sheldon Leonard. Music by Roy Webb. Cinematography: Jack Mackenzie. Editing by Philip Martin. Distributed by RKO Radio Pictures. Release: May 1, 1945. 68 minutes (USA)

The Cat Creeps

Directed by Erle C. Kenton. Produced by Howard Welsch. Written by Gerald Geraghty (story), Edward Dein (screenplay). Starring Fred Brady, Lois Collier, Paul Kelly, Douglass Dumbrille, Noah Beery, Jr., Rose Hobart. Cinematography: George Robinson. Editing by Russell Schoengarth. Distributed by Universal Pictures. Release: May 17, 1946. 58 minutes (USA)

Dead of Night

Comedy Sequence: "Golfing Story." Directed by Alberto Cavalcanti, Charles Crichton, Basil Dearden, Robert Hamer. Produced by Michael Balcon. Written by John Baines, Angus MacPhail. Starring Michael Redgrave, Mervyn Johns, Frederick Valk, Roland Culver, Googie Withers, Sally Ann Howes. Music by Georges Auric. Cinematography: Jack Parker, Stanley Pavey, Douglas Slocombe. Editing by Charles Hasse. Distributed by Universal Pictures. Release: June 28, 1946. 102 minutes (UK)

Spook Busters

Directed by William Beaudine. Produced by Jan Grippo. Written by Tim Ryan, Edmond Seward. Starring Leo Gorcey, Huntz Hall, Douglass Dumbrille, Bobby Jordan, Gabriel Dell. Cinematography: Harry Neumann. Editing by William Austin. Distributed by Monogram Pictures Corporation. Release: August 24, 1946. 68 minutes (USA)

Genius at Work

Directed by Leslie Goodwins. Produced by Herman Schlom. Written by Robert E. Kent, Monte Brice. Starring Wally Brown, Alan Carney, Anne Jeffreys, Lionel Atwill, Bela Lugosi. Cinematography: Robert de Grasse. Editing by Marvin Coil. Distributed by RKO Pictures. Release: October 20, 1946. 61 minutes (USA)

Abbott and Costello Meet Frankenstein

Directed by Charles Barton. Produced by Robert Arthur. Written by Robert Lees, Frederic I. Rinaldo, John Grant. Starring Bud Abbott, Lou Costello, Lon Chaney, Jr., Bela Lugosi, Glenn Strange. Music by Frank Skinner. Editing by Frank Gross. Distributed by Universal Pictures. Release: June 15, 1948. 83 minutes (USA)

Abbott and Costello Meet the Killer, Boris Karloff

Directed by Charles Barton. Produced by Robert Arthur. Written by John Grant, Hugh Wedlock, Jr., Howard Snyder. Starring Bud Abbott, Lou Costello, Boris Karloff, Lenore Aubert. Music by Milton Schwarzwald. Editing by Edward Curtiss. Distributed by Universal Pictures. Release: August 22, 1949. 82 minutes (USA)

The Adventures of Ichabod and Mr. Toad

Directed by Jack Kinney, Clyde Geronimi, James Algar. Produced by Walt Disney. Written by Homer Brightman, Winston Hibler, Erdman Penner, Harry Reeves, Joe Rinaldi, Ted Sears. Starring Bing Crosby, Eric Blore, Basil Rathbone, Pat O'Malley, Colin Campbell, John McLeish, Campbell Grant, Claud Allister, Leslie Denison, Edmond Stevens, Oliver Wallace, The Rhythmaires. Music by Oliver Wallace. Distributed by RKO Radio Pictures. Release: October 5, 1949. 68 minutes (USA)

Someone at the Door

Directed by Francis Searle. Produced by Anthony Hinds. Written by A.R. Rawlinson. Starring Yvonne Owen, Michael Medwin, Hugh Latimer, Danny Green, Garry Marsh. Cinematography: Walter Harvey. Editing by John Ferris, Ray Pitt (both uncredited). Distributed by Exclusive Films. Release: 1950. 65 minutes (UK)

Abbott and Costello Meet the Invisible Man

Directed by Charles Lamont. Produced by Howard Christie. Written by Frederic I. Rinaldo, John Grant, Robert Lees, Hugh Wedlock Jr, Howard Snyder. Starring Bud Abbott, Lou Costello, Nancy Guild, Arthur Franz. Music by Erich Zeisl. Cinematography:George Robinson. Editing by Virgil Vogel. Distributed by Universal Pictures. Release: March 19, 1951. 82 minutes (USA)

Bela Lugosi Meets a Brooklyn Gorilla

Directed by William Beaudine. Produced by Maurice Duke. Written by Tim Ryan. Starring Bela Lugosi, Duke Mitchell, Sammy Petrillo. Music by Richard Hazard. Cinematography: Charles Van Enger. Editing by Philip Cahn. Distributed by Realart Pictures Inc. Release: September 4, 1952. 74 minutes (USA)

Mother Riley Meets the Vampire (aka *My Son the Vampire*)

Directed and Produced by John Gilling. Written by Val Valentine. Starring Arthur Lucan, Bela Lugosi, Dora Bryan, Hattie Jacques, Dandy Nicholls, Richard Wattis, Charles Lloyd-Pack, Graham Moffatt. Cinematography: Dudley Lovell. Editing by Len Trumm. Distributed by Blue Chip Productions, Inc. Release: (released in UK in 1952, released in the U.S. in 1963 under the title *My Son the Vampire*)

Scared Stiff

Directed by George Marshall. Produced by Hal B. Wallis. Written by Herbert Baker, Walter DeLeon, Norman Lear. Starring Dean Martin, Jerry Lewis, Lizabeth Scott, Carmen Miranda. Music by Leith Stevens. Distributed by Paramount Pictures. Release: April 27, 1953. 108 minutes (USA)

Abbott and Costello Meet Dr. Jekyll and Mr. Hyde

Directed by Charles Lamont. Produced by Howard Christie. Written by Howard Dimsdale, Sid Fields, Grant Garett, John Grant, Lee Loeb. Starring Bud Abbott, Lou Costello, Boris Karloff. Cinematography: George Robinson. Editing by Russell Schoengarth. Distributed by Universal Pictures. Release: August 10, 1953. 76 minutes (USA)

The Bowery Boys Meet the Monsters

Directed by Edward Bernds. Produced by Ben Schwalb. Written by Edward Bernds, Elwood Ullman. Starring Leo Gorcey, Huntz Hall, Lloyd Corrigan, Ellen Corby, John Dehner, Laura Mason. Cinematography: Harry Neumann. Editing by William Austin. Distributed by Allied Artists Pictures. Release: June 6, 1954. 65 minutes (USA)

Abbott and Costello Meet the Mummy

Directed by Charles Lamont. Produced by Howard Christie. Written by John Grant. Starring Bud Abbott, Lou Costello, Marie Windsor, Michael Ansara. Editing by Russell Schoengarth. Distributed by Universal Pictures. Release: May 23, 1955. 79 minutes (USA)

The Phantom of the Red House

Directed by Miguel M. Delgado. Produced by Pedro Galindo, Jr. Written by Maria Cristina Lesser (story), Ramon Perez P. (adaptation), Miguel M. Delgado (screenplay),. Starring Alma Rosa Aguirre, Raul Martinez, Antonio Espino. Cinematography: Jose de la Vega. Editing by Jorge Bustos. Distributed by Trans-International Films. Release: (released in Mexico in 1956, in USA in 1964). 91 minutes (Mexico)

Castle of the Monsters

Directed by Julián Soler. Produced by Heberto Dávila Guajardo, Jesús Sotomayor Martínez. Written by Fernando Galiana, Carlos Orellana, Julián Soler. Starring Antonio Espino, Evangelina Elizondo, Carlos Orellana. Music by Gustavo César Carrión. Cinematography: Víctor Herrera. Editing by Sigfrido García, Carlos Savage. Distributed by Columbia Pictures. Release: October 16, 1958. 90 minutes (Mexico)

House on Haunted Hill

Directed by William Castle. Produced by William Castle, Robb White. Written by Robb White. Starring Vincent Price, Carolyn Craig, Elisha Cook Jr., Carol Ohmart, Alan Marshal, Julie Mitchum. Music by Richard Kayne, Richard Loring, Von Dexter. Cinematography: Carl E. Guthrie. Editing by Roy V. Livingston. Distributed by Allied Artists. Release: 17 February 1959. 75 minutes (USA)

Uncle Was a Vampire (aka Hard Times for Vampires)

Directed by Steno (Stefano Vanzina). Produced by Mario Cecchi Gori. Written by Edoardo Anton, Dino Verde, Alessandro Continenza. Starring Chrstopher Lee, Renato Rascel, Sylvia Koscina. Cinematography: Marco Scarpelli. Editing by Eraldo Da Roma. Distributed by Embassy Pictures. Release: (released in Italy in 1959, USA in 1964). 85 minutes (Italy)

The Bat

Directed by Crane Wilbur. Produced by C.J. Tevlin. Written by Avery Hopwood, Mary Roberts Rinehart (play), Crane Wilbur. Starring Vincent Price, Agnes Moorehead, Gavin Gordon, John Sutton, Lenita Lane, Elaine Edwards, Darla Hood, John Bryant, Harvey Stephens. Music by Louis Forbes. Cinematography: Joseph F. Biroc. Editing by William Austin. Distributed by Allied Artists. Release: August 9, 1959. 80 minutes (USA)

A Bucket of Blood

Directed and Produced by Roger Corman. Written by Charles B. Griffith. Starring Dick Miller, Barbara Morris, Antony Carbone. Music by Fred Katz. Cinematography: Jacques R. Marquette. Editing by Anthony Carras. Distributed by American International Pictures. Release: October 21, 1959. 66 minutes (USA)

The Headless Ghost

Directed by Peter Graham Scott. Produced by Herman Cohen. Written by Herman Cohen, Kenneth Langtry. Starring Richard Lyon, Lilian Sottane, David Rose, Jack Allen, CLive Revill, Alexander Archdale, John Stacy, Carl Bernard. Cinematography: John Wiles. Editing by Bernard Gribble. Distributed by American International Pictures. Release: 1959. (UK)

The Little Shop of Horrors

Directed and Produced by Roger Corman. Written by Charles B. Griffith. Starring Jonathan Haze, Jackie Joseph, Mel Welles, Dick Miller. Music by Fred Katz, Ronald Stein. Cinematography: Archie R. Dalzell, Vilis Lapenieks. Editing by Marshall Neilan Jr. Distributed by The Filmgroup Inc. Release: September 14, 1960. 70 minutes (USA)

Creature from the Haunted Sea

Directed by Roger Corman. Produced by Roger Corman, Charles Hannawalt. Written by Charles B.

Griffith. Starring Antony Carbone, Betsy Jones-Moreland, Edward Wain [Robert Towne]. Music by Fred Katz. Cinematography: Jacques R. Marquette. Editing by Angela Scellars. Distributed by The Filmgroup Inc. Release: June, 1961. 63 minutes (USA)

Bring Me the Vampire

Directed by Alfredo E. Crevenna. Produced by Mario Carcia Camberos. Written by Mario Garcia Camberos, Alfredo Ruanova. Starring Fernando Soto, Joaquin Garcia Vargas, Alfonso "Pompin" Iglesias, Jose Jasso, Roberto Cobo. Cinematography: Fernando Alvarez Garces. Distributed by Trans-International Films. Release: 1961 in Mexico, 1964 in USA. 100 minutes (Mexico/Venezuela)

Frankenstein, the Vampire and Company

Directed by Benito Alazraki. Produced by Guillermo Calderon. Written by Alfredo Salazar. Starring Manuel Loco Valdes, Jose Jasso, Joaquin Garcia Vargas. Cinematography: Enrique Wallace. Editing by Jose Bustos. Distributed by Trans-International Films. Release: 1961 in Mexico, 1968 in USA. 80 minutes (Mexico)

Tales of Terror

Comedy Sequence: "The Black Cat." Directed by Roger Corman. Produced by James H. Nicholson, Samuel Z. Arkoff, Roger Corman. Written by Richard Matheson. Starring Vincent Price, Peter Lorre, Basil Rathbone. Music by Les Baxter. Cinematography: Floyd Crosby. Editing by Anthony Carras. Distributed by American International Pictures. Release: July 4, 1962. 89 minutes (USA)

What a Carve Up! (aka No Place Like Homicide)

Directed by Pat Jackson. Produced by Monty Berman, Robert S. Baker. Written by Ray Cooney, Tony Hilton. Starring Kenneth Connor, Sidney James, Shirley Eaton, Donald Pleasence, Esma Cannon, Dennis Price, Michael Gough, Michael Gwynn, Valerie Taylor, George Woodbridge. Cinematography: Monty Berman. Editing by Gordon Pilkington. Distributed by Embassy Pictures Corporation. Release: September 12, 1962. 88 minutes (UK)

The Raven

Directed and Produced by Roger Corman. Written by Edgar Allan Poe (poem), Richard Matheson. Starring Vincent Price, Peter Lorre, Boris Karloff, Jack Nicholson, Hazel Court. Music by Les Baxter. Cinematography: Floyd Crosby. Editing by Ronald Sinclair. Distributed by American International Pictures. Release: January 25, 1963. 86 minutes (USA)

The Old Dark House

Directed by William Castle. Produced by William Castle, Anthony Hinds. Starring Tom Poston, Robert Morley, Janette Scott, Fenella Fielding, Mervyn Johns. Music by Benjamin Frankel. Cinematography: Arthur Grant. Editing by James Needs. Distributed by Columbia Pictures. Release: October 31, 1963. 86 minutes (USA)

The Comedy of Terrors

Directed by Jacques Tourneur. Produced by Anthony Carras. Written by Richard Matheson. Starring Vincent Price, Peter Lorre, Boris Karloff, Basil Rathbone, Joyce Jameson, Joe E. Brown. Music by Les Baxter. Cinematography: Floyd Crosby. Editing by Anthony Carras. Distributed by American International Pictures. Release: January 22, 1964. 88 minutes (USA)

The Horror of It All

Directed by Terence Fisher. Produced by Robert L. Lippert. Written by Ray Russell. Starring Pat Boone, Erica Rogers, Dennis Price, Andree Melly, Valentine Dyall, Jack Bligh, Archie Duncan, Erik Chitty. Cinematography: Arthur Lavis. Editing by Robert Winter. Distributed by Twentieth Century-Fox Film Corporation. Release: 1963. 75 minutes (UK)

Dr. Terror's House of Horrors

Comedy Sequence: "Voodoo." Directed by Freddie Francis. Produced by Max J. Rosenberg, Milton Subotsky. Written by Milton Subotsky. Starring Peter Cushing, Christopher Lee, Max Adrian, Ann Bell, Peter Madden, Donald Sutherland. Music by Elisabeth Lutyens. Cinematography: Alan Hume. Editing by Thelma Connell. Release: February 23, 1965. 98 minutes (UK)

The Ghost and Mr. Chicken

Directed by Alan Rafkin. Produced by Edward J. Montagne Jr. Written by Jim Fritzell, Everett Greenbaum. Starring Don Knotts, Joan Staley, Liam Redmond, Dick Sargent, Skip Homeier. Music by Vic Mizzy. Cinematography: William Margulies. Editing by Sam E. Waxman. Distributed by Universal Pictures. Release: January 20, 1966. 90 minutes

Munster, Go Home!

Directed by Earl Bellamy. Produced by Joe Connelly, Bob Mosher. Written by Joe Connelly, Bob Mosher, George Tibbles. Starring Fred Gwynne, Yvonne DeCarlo, Al Lewis, Butch Patrick, Debbie

Watson, Robert Pine, Terry-Thomas, Hermione Gingold, Jeanne Arnold, John Carradine. Distributed by Universal Pictures. Release: June 15, 1966. 97 minutes (USA)

The Wrong Box

Directed by Bryan Forbes. Produced by Bryan Forbes, Jack Rix, Larry Gelbart, Burt Shevelove. Written by Larry Gelbart, Burt Shevelove. Starring John Mills, Ralph Richardson, Michael Caine, Nanette Newman, Peter Cook, Dudley Moore. Music by John Barry. Cinematography: Gerry Turpin. Editing by Alan Osbiston. Distributed by Columbia Pictures. Release: May 27, 1966. 107 minutes (UK)

The Undertaker and His Pals

Directed and Written by T.L.P. Swicegood. Produced by David C. Graham, Alex Grattan. Starring Ray Dennis, Warrene Ott, Rad Fulton, Robert Lowery. Cinematography: Andrew Janczak. Editing by Thomas Luther. Distributed by Howco International Pictures. Release: 1966. 63 minutes (USA)

It!

Directed by Herbert J. Leder. Produced by Robert Goldstein. Written by Herbert J. Leder. Starring Roddy McDowall, Jill Haworth, Paul Maxwell, Alan Sellers. Music by Carlo Martelli. Distributed by Warner Bros./Seven Arts. Release: November 15, 1967. 97 minutes (UK)

The Fearless Vampire Killers

Directed by Roman Polanski. Produced by Gene Gutowski. Written by Roman Polanski, Gérard Brach. Starring Jack MacGowran, Roman Polanski, Sharon Tate, Ferdy Mayne. Music by Krzysztof Komeda. Cinematography: Douglas Slocombe. Editing by Alastair McIntyre. Distributed by MGM. Release: November 13, 1967. 91 minutes; (Director's Cut is 107 minutes). (UK/US)

Spider Baby

Directed by Jack Hill. Produced by Paul Monka, Gil Lasky. Written by Jack Hill. Starring Lon Chaney, Jr., Sid Haig, Jill Banner, Beverly Washburn. Music by Ronald Stein. Cinematography: Alfred Taylor. Editing by Jack Hill. Distributed by American General Pictures. Release: January 18, 1968. 86 minutes (US)

The Maltese Bippy

Directed by Norman Panama. Produced by Robert Enders, Everett Freeman. Written by Everett Freeman, Ray Singer. Starring Dan Rowan, Dick Martin, Carol Lynley, Julie Newmar. Cinematographer William H. Daniels. Editing by Homer Powell, Ronald Sinclair. Distributed by MGM. Release: 1969. 88 minutes (USA)

Girly (aka Mumsy, Nanny, Sonny and Girly)

Directed by Freddie Francis. Produced by Ronald J. Kahn. Written by Brian Comport. Starring Michael Bryant, Ursula Howells, Pat Heywood, Vanessa Howard, Howard Trevor, Robert Swann, Imogen Hassall, Michael Ripper, Hugh Armstrong. Cinematography: David Muir. Editing by Tristam Cones. Distributed by Cinerama Releasing Corporation. Release: February 12, 1970. 101 minutes (UK)

The House That Dripped Blood

Comedy Sequence: "The Cloak." Directed by Peter Duffell. Produced by Milton Subotsky, Max J. Rosenberg. Written by Robert Bloch, Russ Jones. Starring Christopher Lee, Peter Cushing, Nyree Dawn Porter, Denholm Elliott, Jon Pertwee. Music by Michael Dress. Cinematography: Ray Parslow. Editing by Peter Tanner. Distributed by Amicus Productions. Release: March 1971. 102 minutes (UK)

The Horror of Frankenstein

Directed and Produced by Jimmy Sangster. Written by Jimmy Sangster, Jeremy Burnham (screenplay). Starring Ralph Bates, Kate O'Mara. Veronica Carlson, David Prowse. Music by Malcolm Williamson. Cinematography: Moray Grant. Editing by Chris Barnes. Distributed by Continental. Release: November 8, 1970. 95 minutes (UK)

The Vampire Happening

Directed by Freddie Francis. Produced by Pier A. Caminnecci. Written by August Rieger, Karl Heinz Hummel (from "Clarimonde" by Theophile Gautier). Starring Pia Degermark, Thomas Hunter, Ingrid van Bergen, Ferdy Mayne, Lyvia Bauer, Joachim Kemmer, Daria Damer, Yvor Murillo. Cinematography: Gerard Vandenberg. Editing by Alfred Srp. Distributed by Aquila Film Enterprises. Release: June 4, 1971. 102 minutes (West Germany)

The Abominable Dr. Phibes

Directed by Robert Fuest. Executive Producers: Samuel Z. Arkoff, James H. Nicholson. Produced by Ronald S. Dunas, Louis M. Heyward. Written by James Whiton, William Goldstein. Starring Vincent Price, Joseph Cotten, Terry-Thomas, Virginia North. Music by Basil Kirchin. Cinematography: Norman Warwick. Editing by Tristam Cones. Distributed by American International Pictures. Release: May 18, 1971. 94 minutes (USA)

Psychomania

Directed by Don Sharp. Produced by Andrew Donally. Written by Arnaud d'Usseau, Julian Zimet. Starring Nicky Henson, Mary Larkin, Ann Michelle, Roy Holder. Music by John Cameron. Cinematography: Ted Moore. Editing by Richard Best. Distributed by Scotia International. Release: January 1974. 95 minutes (UK)

The Horrors of Burke and Hare (aka Burke and Hare)

Directed by Vernon Sewell. Produced by Guido Coen. Written by Ernie Bradford. Starring Harry Andrews, Darren Nesbitt, Glynn Edwards, Dee Shenderey, Yootha Joyce, Francoise Pascal, Alan Tucker, Paul Greaves, Yutte Stensgaard, Joan Carol. Cinematography: Desmond Dickinson. Editing by John Colville. Distributed by New World Pictures. Release: 1972. 91 minutes (UK)

Dr. Phibes Rises Again

Directed by Robert Fuest. Produced by Samuel Z. Arkoff, Richard F. Dalton, Louis M. Heyward. Written by Robert Blees, Robert Fuest. Starring Vincent Price, Robert Quarry, Valli Kemp, Fiona Lewis. Music by John Gale. Cinematography: Alex Thomson. Editing by Tristam V. Cones. Distributed by American International Pictures. Release: 1972. 88 minutes (USA)

Private Parts

Directed by Paul Bartel. Produced by Gene Corman. Written by Philip Kearney, Les Rendelstein. Starring Ayn Ruymen, Lucille Benson, John Ventantonio. Music by Hugo Friedhofer. Cinematography: Andrew Davis. Editing by Martin Tubor. 87 minutes. Release: September 1972. Distributed by MGM. (USA)

The Folks at Red Wolf Inn (aka Terror House)

Directed by Bud Townsend. Produced by Michael Macready. Written by Allen J. Actor. Starring Linda Gillin, John Neilson, Mary Jackson, Arthur Space. Cinematography: John McNichol. Editing by Al Maguire. Distributed by Intercontinental Releasing Corporation. Release: 1972. 90 minutes (USA)

Children Shouldn't Play With Dead Things

Directed by Bob Clark. Produced by Bob Clark, Gary Gochl, Peter James. Written by Bob Clark, Alan Ormsby. Starring Alan Ormsby, Jeffrey Gillen, Paul Cronin, Roy Engleman, Bob Filep, Bruce Solomon, Alecs Baird, Seth Sklarey. Distributed by Geneni Film Distributors. Release: 1972. 87 minutes (USA)

Please Don't Eat My Mother

Directed by Carl Monson. Produced by Carl Monson, Harry N. Hovak. Written by Eric Norden. Starring Buck Kartalian, Lyn Lundgren, Art Hedberg, Rene Bond. Cinematography: Jack Beckett. Editing by Paul Heslin. Distributed by Boxoffice International Pictures. Release: March 5, 1973. 98 minutes (USA)

Theater of Blood

Directed by Douglas Hickox. Produced by Gustave Berne, Sam Jaffe, John Kohn, Stanley Mann. Written by Anthony Greville-Bell (screenplay), Stanley Mann, John Kohn (idea). Starring Vincent Price, Diana Rigg, Ian Hendry. Music by Michael J. Lewis. Cinematography: Wolfgang Suschitzky. Editing by Malcolm Cooke. Distributed by United Artists. Release: April 5, 1973. 104 minutes (UK)

Cannibal Girls

Directed by Ivan Reitman. Produced by Daniel Goldberg, Ivan Reitman. Written by Daniel Goldber, Ivan Reitman (story), Robert Sandler (screenplay). Starring Eugene Levy, Andrea Martin, Ronald Ulrich, Randall Carpenter, Bonnie Neilson, Mira Pawluk. Music by Doug Riley. Cinematography: Robert Saad. Editing by Daniel Goldberg. Distributed by American International Pictures, Cinépix Film Properties Inc. Release: June 8, 1973. 84 minutes (Canada)

The Werewolf of Washington

Directed by Nina Schulman. Written by Milton Moses Ginsberg. Starring Dean Stockwell, Biff McGuire, Clifton James, Beeson Carroll, Jane House, Michael Dunn. Distributed by Diplomat Pictures. Release: 1973. 90 minutes (USA)

Dr. Death: Seeker of Souls

Directed and Produced by Eddie Saeta. Written by Sal Ponti. Starring John Considine, Barry Coe, Cheryl Miller, Stewart Moss, Leon Askin, Jo Morrow, Florence Marly, Sivi Aberg, Jim Boles, Athena Lorde, Moe Howard. Cinematography: Ken Wakeford, Emil Oster. Editing by Anthony DiMarco. Distributed by Cinerama Releasing Corporation. Release: 1973. 89 minutes (USA)

From Beyond the Grave

Comedy Sequence: "The Elemental." Directed by Kevin Connor. Produced by Max J. Rosenberg, Milton Subotsky. Written by R. Chetwynd-Hayes (stories), Robin Clarke, Raymond Christodoulou. Starring Peter Cushing, David Warner, Rosaline Ayres, Ian Bannen, Donald Pleasance, Diana Dors, Angela Pleasance, Margaret Leighton, Ian Carmichael, Nyree Dawn Porter, Ian Ogilvy, Lesley-Anne Down, Jack Watson. Cinematography: Alan Hume. Editing by John Ireland. Distributed by Howard Mahler Films/Teitel Amusement. Release: 1973 in UK, 1975 in USA. 98 minutes (UK)

Horror Hospital

Directed by Antony Balch. Produced by Richard Gordon. Written by Antony Balch, Alan Watson. Starring Robin Askwith, Michael Gough. Release: 1973 in UK, April 1975 in USA. 85 minutes (UK)

The House in Nightmare Park (aka *Night of the Laughing Dead*)

Directed by Peter Sykes. Produced by Clive Exton, Terry Nation. Written by Clive Exton. Starring Frankie Howerd, Ray Milland, Hugh Burden, Kenneth Griffith, John Bennett, Rosalie Crutchley. Cinematography: Ian Wilson. Editing by Bill Blunden, Harry Robertson. Distributed by Constellation Films, Inc. Release: 1973 in UK, 1977 in USA. 95 minutes

The Vault of Horror

Comedy Sequences: "The Neat Job, Bargain in Death." Directed by Roy Ward Baker. Produced by Milton Subotsky, Max J. Rosenberg. Written by Milton Subotsky. Starring Daniel Massey, Anna Massey, Michael Pratt, Terry-Thomas, Glynis Johns, John Forbes-Robertson, Curt Jurgens, Dawn Addams, Jasmina Hilton, Michael Craig, Edward Judd, Arthur Mullard, Tom Baker, Denholm Elliott, Terence Alexander, John Witty. Distributed by Cinerama Releasing Corporation. Release: 1973. 83 minutes (UK)

Psychomania

Directed by Don Sharp. Produced by Andrew Donally. Written by Arnaud d'Usseau, Julian Zimet. Starring Nicky Henson, Mary Larkin, Ann Michelle, Roy Holder. Music by John Cameron. Cinematography: Ted Moore. Editing by Richard Best. Distributed by Scotia International. Release: January 1974. 95 minutes (UK)

The Cars That Ate Paris

Directed and Written by Peter Weir. Produced by Hal McElroy, Jim McElroy. Starring John Meillon, Terry Camilleri. Distributed by New Line Cinema. Release: 1974. 91 minutes (Australia)

Flesh for Frankenstein (aka *Andy Warhol's Frankenstein*)

Directed by Paul Morrissey. Produced by Andrew Braunsberg, Andy Warhol, Lou Peraino, Carlo Ponti, Jean-Pierre Rassam. Written by Paul Morrissey, Tonino Guerra. Starring Monique van Vooren, Udo Kier. Distributed by Bryanston Distributing Company. Release: March 17, 1974. 95 minutes (Italy-France)

Homebodies

Directed by Larry Yust. Produced by Marshall Backlar. Written by Larry Yust, Howard Kaminsky, Bennett Sims. Starring Peter Brocco, Frances Fuller, William Hansen. Cinematography: Isidore Mankofsky. Editing by Peter Parasheles. Distributed by Avco Embassy Pictures. Release: September 1974. 96 minutes (USA)

Shanks

Directed by William Castle. Produced by Steven North. Written by Ranald Graham. Starring Marcel Marceau, Tsilla Chelton, Phillippe Clay. Cinematography: Joseph Biroc. Editing by David Berlatsky. Distributed by Paramount Pictures. Release: October 9, 1974. 93 minutes (USA)

Phantom of the Paradise

Directed and Written by Brian De Palma. Produced by Edward R. Pressman. Starring Paul Williams, William Finley, Jessica Harper. Music by Paul Williams. Editing by Paul Hirsch. Distributed by 20th Century-Fox. Release: October 31, 1974. 92 minutes (USA)

Blood for Dracula (aka *Andy Warhol's Dracula*)

Directed and Written by Paul Morrissey. Produced by Andrew Braunsberg, Andy Warhol. Starring Joe Dallesandro, Udo Kier. Distributed by Bryanston Distributing Company. Release: November 27, 1974. 103 minutes (Italy-France)

Young Frankenstein

Directed by Mel Brooks. Produced by Michael Gruskoff. Written by Mel Brooks, Gene Wilder. Starring Gene Wilder, Peter Boyle, Teri Garr, Marty Feldman, Cloris Leachman, Madeline Kahn, Kenneth Mars, Gene Hackman. Music by John Morris. Cinematography: Gerald Hirschfeld. Distributed by 20th Century-Fox. Release: December 15, 1974. 106 minutes (USA)

Vampira (aka *Old Dracula*)

Directed by Clive Donner. Produced by Jack Wiener. Written by Jeremy Lloyd. Starring David

Niven, Teresa Graves. Music by David Whitaker. Cinematography: Anthony B. Richmond. Editing by Bill Butler. Distributed by American International Pictures. Release: 1974 in UK, 1975 in USA. 88 minutes (UK)

Tender Dracula

Directed by Pierre Grunstein. Starring Peter Cushing, Nathalie Courval, Miou-Miou, Benard Menez. Distributed by Scotia American. Release: January 1975. 98 minutes (France)

The Rocky Horror Picture Show

Directed by Jim Sharman. Produced by Michael White. Written by Richard O'Brien, Jim Sharman. Starring Tim Curry, Susan Sarandon, Barry Bostwick, Richard O'Brien, Patricia Quinn, Nell Campbell, Meat Loaf. Music by Richard O'Brien. Cinematography: Peter Suschitzky. Editing by Graeme Clifford. Distributed by 20th Century-Fox. Release: September 26, 1975. 98 minutes (USA)

The Love Butcher

Directed by Mikel Angel, Don Jones. Produced by Gar Williams, Micky Belski. Written by Don Jones, James Evergreen. Starring Erik Stern, Kay Neer, Jeremiah Beecher. Cinematography: Don Jones, Austin McKinney. Editing by Robert Freeman. Distributed by International Film Distributors. Release: December 1, 1975. 83 minutes (USA)

Blood Sucking Freaks (aka The Incredible Torture Show)

Directed and Produced by Joel M. Reed. Written by Joel M. Reed. Starring Seamus O'Brien, Viju Krem, Niles McMaster, Dan Fauci, Alphonso DeNoble, Ernie Pysher. Music by Michael Sahl. Cinematography: Ron Dorfman. Editing by Joel R. Herson, Victor Kanefsky. Distributed by Troma Entertainment. Release: 1976. 91 minutes (USA)

Murder by Death

Directed by Robert Moore. Produced by Ray Stark. Written by Neil Simon. Starring Eileen Brennan, Truman Capote, James Coco, Peter Falk, Alec Guinness, Elsa Lanchester, David Niven, Peter Sellers, Maggie Smith, Nancy Walker, Estelle Winwood. Music by Dave Grusin. Cinematography: David M. Walsh. Editing by Margaret Booth, John F. Burnett. Distributed by Columbia Pictures. Release: June 23, 1976. 94 minutes (USA)

Dracula and Son

Directed by Edouard Molinaro. Produced by Alain Poiré. Written by: Claude Klotz (novel), Alain Godard (screenplay). Starring Christopher Lee, Bernard Menez. Music by Vladimir Cosma. Cinematography: Alain Levent. Editing by Monique Isnardon, Robert Isnardon. Distributed by Quartet Films. Release: 1976 in France, 1979 in USA. 96 minutes (France)

Satan's Cheerleaders

Directed by Greydon Clark. Produced by Alvin L. Fast. Written by Greydon Clark, Alvin L. Fast. Starring John Ireland, Yvonne de Carlo, Jack Kruschen, John Carradine. Cinematography: Dean Cundey. Editing by G.D. Clymer. Distributed by World Amusements. Release: June 1977. 92 minutes (USA)

The Cat and the Canary

Directed by Radley Metzger. Produced by Richard Gordon. Written by John Willard (play), Radley Metzger (screenplay). Starring Honor Blackman, Carol Lynley, Michael Callan, Edward Fox, Peter McEnery, Wendy Hiller, Olivia Hussey, Daniel Massey, Wilfrid Hyde-White. Cinematography: Alex Thomson. Editing by Roger Harrison. Distributed by Columbia Pictures. 98 minutes (UK)

Piranha

Directed by Joe Dante. Produced by Jon Davison, Chako van Leeuwen. Written by John Sayles. Starring Bradford Dillman, Heather Menzies, Kevin McCarthy, Keenan Wynn, Dick Miller. Music by Pino Donaggio. Cinematography: Jamie Anderson. Editing by Joe Dante, Mark Goldblatt. Distributed by New World Pictures. Release: August 3, 1978. 94 minutes (USA)

The Hound of the Baskervilles

Directed by Paul Morrissey. Produced by John Goldstone. Written by Arthur Conan Doyle (novel), Peter Cook, Dudley Moore, Paul Morrissey (screenplay). Starring Peter Cook, Dudley Moore, Dana Gillespie, Denholm Elliott, Terry-Thomas, Kenneth Williams. Music by Dudley Moore. Cinematography: Dick Bush, John Wilcox. Editing by Glenn Hyde, Richard Marden. Distributed by Atlantic Releasing Corporation. Release: October 1978. 85 minutes (UK)

Love at First Bite

Directed by Stan Dragoti. Produced by Joel Freeman. Written by Robert Kaufman. Starring George Hamilton, Susan Saint James, Richard Benjamin, Arte Johnson, Dick Shawn. Music by Charles Bernstein. Cinematography: Edward Rosson. Editing by Mort Fallick, Allan Jacobs. Distributed by American International Pictures. Release: April 13, 1979. 94 minutes (USA)

Dracula Blows His Cool

Directed and Written by Carl Schenkel. Produced by Martin Friedman. Starring Gianni Garko, Betty Verges, Giacomo Rizzo, Linda Grondier. Cinematography: Heinz Hoelscher. Editing by Jutta Herring. Distributed by Martin Films. Release: 1979 in West Germany, October 1983 in USA. 97 minutes (West Germany)

Motel Hell

Directed by Kevin Connor. Produced by Robert Jaffe, Steven-Charles Jaffe. Written by Robert Jaffe, Steven-Charles Jaffe, Tim Tuchrello (uncredited). Starring Rory Calhoun, Paul Linke, Nancy Parsons, Nina Axelrod, Wolfman Jack. Music by Lance Rubin. Cinematography: Thomas Del Ruth. Editing by Bernard Gribble. Distributed by United Artists. Release: October 18, 1980. 102 minutes (USA)

The Monster Club

Directed by Roy Ward Baker. Produced by Milton Subotsky. Written by Edward Abraham, Valerie Abraham. Starring Vincent Price, Donald Pleasence, John Carradine, Stuart Whitman. Music by Douglas Gamley. Cinematography: Peter Jessop. Editing by Peter Tanner. Release: 1980. 97 minutes (UK)

Mama Dracula

Directed and Produced by Boris Szulzinger. Written by Tony Hendra (dialogue), Pierre Sterckx, Boris Szulzinger, Marc-Henri Wainberg. Starring Louise Fletcher, Maria Schneider, Marc-Henri Wainberg. Cinematographer Rufus Bohez, Willy Kurant. Editing by Claude Cohen. Distributed by Trans World Entertainment. Release: 1980. 90 minutes (France)

Student Bodies

Directed by Mickey Rose, Michael Ritchie (uncredited). Produced by Allen Smithee [Michael Ritchie]. Written by Mickey Rose. Starring Kristen Riter, Matthew Goldsby, Cullen Chambers. Cinematography: Robert Ebinger. Editing by Kathryn Ruth Hope. Distributed by Paramount Pictures. Release: August 7, 1981. 86 minutes (USA)

An American Werewolf in London

Directed and Written by John Landis. Produced by George Folsey Jr. Starring David Naughton, Griffin Dunne, Jenny Agutter. Music by Elmer Bernstein. Cinematography: Robert Payner. Editing by Malcolm Campbell. Distributed by Universal Pictures. PolyGram Filmed Entertainment. Release: August 21, 1981. 97 minutes (USA)

Saturday the 14th

Directed by Howard R. Cohen. Produced by Julie Corman. Written by Howard R. Cohen, Jeff Begun. Starring Richard Benjamin, Paula Prentiss, Severn Darden, Jeffrey Tambor, Kari Michaelsen. Music by Parmer Fuller. Cinematography: Daniel Lacambre. Editing by Kent Beyda, Joanne D'Antonio. Release: October 30, 1981. 75 minutes (USA)

Full Moon High

Directed, Produced and Written by Larry Cohen. Starring Adam Arkin, Ed McMahon, Roz Kelly. Music by Gary William Friedman. Cinematography: Daniel Pearl. Editing by Armond Lebowitz. Release: 1981. 93 minutes (USA)

Creepshow

Directed by George A. Romero. Produced by Salah M. Hassenein, Richard P. Rubinstein. Short Stories & Screenplay: Stephen King. Starring Hal Holbrook, Adrienne Barbeau, Leslie Nielsen, Ted Danson, E. G. Marshall, Stephen King, Viveca Lindfors, Fritz Weaver, Carrie Nye, Ed Harris, Jon Lormer, Tom Atkins, Don Keefer, Robert Harper. Music by John Harrison. Cinematography: Michael Gornick. Editing by Pasquale Buba, Paul Hirsch, George A. Romero, Michael Spolan. Distributed by Warner Bros. Release: August 20, 1982 (limited release). November 12, 1982 (wide release). 120 minutes

Basket Case

Directed and Written by Frank Henenlotter. Produced by Edgar Levins. Starring Kevin Van Hentenryck, Terri Susan Smith, Beverly Bonner. Music by Gus Russo. Distributed by Analysis Film Releasing Corporation. Release: August 31, 1983. 91 minutes (USA)

House of the Long Shadows

Directed by Pete Walker. Produced by Jenny Craven, Yoram Globus, Menahem Golan. Written by Earl Derr Biggers (novel *Seven Keys to Baldpate*), Michael Armstrong (screenplay). Starring Vincent Price, Christopher Lee, Peter Cushing, John Carradine, Desi Arnaz, Jr. Music by Richard Harvey. Cinematography: Norman G. Langley. Editing by Robert C. Dearberg. Distributed by Cannon Film Distributors. Release: 1983. 100 minutes (UK)

Bloodbath at the House of Death

Directed by Ray Cameron. Produced by Laurence Myers, John Downes, Ray Cameron. Written by Ray Cameron, Barry Cryer. Starring Kenny Everett, Pamela Stephenson, Vincent Price, Gareth Hunt. Music by Mark London, Mike Moran. Cinematography: Dusty Miller, Brian West. Editing by Brian Tagg. Distributed by Media Home Entertainment. Release: 1984. 88 minutes (UK)

Gremlins

Directed by Joe Dante. Produced by Michael Finnell. Written by Chris Columbus. Starring Zach Galligan, Phoebe Cates, Hoyt Axton, Frances Lee McCain, Dick Miller, Polly Holliday, Judge Reinhold, Keye Luke, Corey Feldman, John Louie. Music by Jerry Goldsmith. Cinematography: John Hora. Editing by Tina Hirsch. Distributed by Warner Bros. Release: June 8, 1984. 106 minutes (USA)

The Toxic Avenger

Directed by Lloyd Kaufman, Michael Herz. Produced by Michael Herz, Lloyd Kaufman, Stuart Strutin. Written by Lloyd Kaufman, Joe Ritter. Starring Mitch Cohen, Mark Torgl, Andree Maranda, Pat Ryan Jr. Cinematography: Lloyd Kaufman, James London. Editing by Richard W. Haines. Distributed by Troma Entertainment. Release: 1984. 87 minutes (R-rated cut), 82 minutes (unrated cut). (USA)

Ghoulies

Directed by Luca Bercovici. Produced by Jefery Levy. Written by Luca Bercovici, Jefery Levy. Starring Peter Liapis, Lisa Pelikan, Michael des Barres, Jack Nance, Peter Risch, Tamara des Treaux, Scott Thomson. Cinematography: Mac Ahlberg. Editing by Ted Nicolaou. Distributed by Empire Pictures. Release: March 2, 1985. 81 minutes (USA)

Fright Night

Directed and Written by Tom Holland. Produced by Herb Jaffe. Starring Chris Sarandon, William Ragsdale, Roddy McDowall, Amanda Bearse, Stephen Geoffreys. Music by Brad Fiedel. Cinematography: Jan Kiesser. Editing by Kent Beyda. Distributed by Columbia Pictures. Release: August 2, 1985. 106 minutes (USA)

The Return of the Living Dead

Directed by Dan O'Bannon. Produced by Tom Fox, Graham Henderson. Written by Rudy Ricci, John A. Russo, Russell Streiner (story), Dan O'Bannon (screenplay). Starring Clu Gulager, James Karen, Don Calfa, Thom Mathews, Beverly Randolph, Linnea Quigley. Music by Matt Clifford, Francis Haines. Cinematography: Jules Brenner. Editing by Robert Gordon. Distributed by Orion Pictures Corporation. Release: August 16, 1985. 91 minutes (USA)

Mr. Vampire

Directed by Ricky Lau. Produced by Sammo Hung Kam-Bo, Mun-kai Ko. Written by Ricky Lau, Chuek-Hon Szeto, Barry Wong, Ying Wong. Starring Ching-Ying Lam, Siu-hou Chin, Ricky Hui, Moon Lee. Music by Melody Bank. Cinematography: Peter Ngor. Editing by Peter Cheung. Distributed by 20th Century-Fox. Release: 1985. 96 minutes (Hong Kong)

Polish Vampire in Burbank

Directed, Produced, Edited and Written by Mark Pirro. Starring Mark Pirro, Lori Sutton, Bobbi Dorsch, Hugh O. Fields. Cinematographer Craig Bassuk. Distributed by Simitar Video. Release: 1985. 84 minutes (USA)

Re-Animator

Directed by Stuart Gordon. Produced by Michael Avery, Bruce William Curtis. Written by H. P. Lovecraft (story), Dennis Paoli, William Norris, Stuart Gordon (screenplay). Starring Jeffrey Combs, Bruce Abbott. Music by Richard Band. Cinematography: Mac Ahlberg. Editing by Lee Percy. Distributed by Empire Pictures. Release: October 18, 1985. 86 minutes (USA)

Transylvania 6–5000

Directed and Written by Rudy De Luca. Produced by Mace Neufeld, Thomas H. Brodek. Starring Jeff Goldblum, Ed Begley, Jr., Joseph Bologna, Carol Kane, Jeffrey Jones, John Byner, Geena Davis, Michael Richards, Donald Gibb, Norman Fell, Teresa Ganzel, Rudy De Luca. Music by Lee Holdridge. Cinematography: Tomislav Pinter. Editing by Harry Keller. Distributed by New World Pictures. Release: November 8, 1985. 93 minutes (USA)

Once Bitten

Directed by Howard Storm. Produced by Frank Hildebrand, Dimitri Villard, Robert Wald. Written by David Hines, Jeffrey Hause, Terence Marsh. Starring Lauren Hutton, Jim Carrey, Cleavon Little, Karen Kopins. Music by John Du Prez. Distributed by The Samuel Goldwyn Company. Release: November 15, 1985. 94 minutes (USA)

House

Directed by Steve Miner. Produced by Sean S. Cunningham. Written by Fred Dekker (story), Ethan Wiley (screenplay). Starring William Katt, George Wendt, Richard Moll, Kay Lenz, Mary Stavin, Michael Ensign, Susan French. Music by Harry Manfredini. Cinematography: Mac Ahlberg. Editing by Michael N. Knue. Distributed by New World Pictures. Release: February 28, 1986. 93 minutes (USA)

Critters

Directed by Stephen Herek. Produced by Robert Shaye. Written by Stephen Herek, Don Keith Opper. Starring Scott Grimes, Dee Wallace-Stone, M. Emmet Walsh, Don Keith Opper, Billy Green Bush, Terrence Mann, Ethan Phillips, Billy Zane. Music by David Newman. Cinematography: Tim Surhstedt. Editing by Larry Bock. Distributed by New Line Cinema. Release: April 11, 1986. 82 minutes (USA)

Vamp

Directed by Richard Wenk. Written by Richard Wenk, Donald P. Borchers. Starring Grace Jones, Gedde Watanabe, Chris Makepeace, Robert Rusler, Dedee Pfeiffer, Sandy Baron. Distributed by New World Pictures. Release: July 18, 1986. 93 minutes (USA)

Haunted Honeymoon

Directed by Gene Wilder. Produced by Susan Ruskin. Written by Gene Wilder, Terence Marsh. Starring Gene Wilder, Gilda Radner, Dom DeLuise, Jonathan Pryce. Music by John Morris. Editing by Christopher Greenbury. Distributed by Orion Pictures. Release: July 25, 1986. 82 minutes (USA)

Night of the Creeps

Directed by Fred Dekker. Produced by Charles Gordon. Written by Fred Dekker. Starring Jason Lively, Steve Marshall, Jill Whitlow, Tom Atkins. Music by Barry De Vorzon, Stan Ridgway. Cinematography: Robert C. New. Editing by Michael N. Knue. Distributed by TriStar Pictures. Release: August 22, 1986. 88 minutes (USA)

Class of Nuke 'Em High

Directed by Richard W. Haines, Michael Herz, Lloyd Kaufman. Produced by Michael Herz, Lloyd Kaufman, James Treadwell. Written by Lloyd Kaufman, Richard W. Haines, Mark Rudnitsky, Stuart Strutin. Starring Janelle Brady, Gil Brenton, Robert Prichard, Pat Ryan. Music by Ethan Hurt, Michael Latlanzi. Cinematography: Michael Mayers. Editing by Richard W. Haines. Distributed by Troma Entertainment. Release: December 12, 1986. 85 minutes (USA)

Little Shop of Horrors

Directed by Frank Oz. Produced by David Geffen. Written by Howard Ashman. Starring Rick Moranis, Ellen Greene, Vincent Gardenia, Steve Martin, Levi Stubbs. Music by Miles Goodman, Alan Menken, Howard Ashman. Cinematography: Robert Paynter. Editing by John Jympson. Distributed by Warner Bros. Release: December 19, 1986. 94 minutes (USA)

Bad Taste

Directed and Produced by Peter Jackson. Written by Ken Hammon, Tony Hiles, Peter Jackson. Starring Terry Potter, Pete O'Herne, Peter Jackson, Mike Minett, Craig Smith. Music by Michelle Scullion. Editing by Jamie Selkirk, Peter Jackson. Distributed by New Zealand Film Commission. Release: 1987. 91 minutes (New Zealand)

Evil Dead 2: Dead by Dawn

Directed by Sam Raimi. Produced by Robert Tapert, Alex De Benedetti, Irvin Shapiro, Bruce Campbell. Written by Sam Raimi, Scott Spiegel. Starring Bruce Campbell, Sarah Berry. Music by Joseph LoDuca. Distributed by Rosebud Pictures. Release: March 13, 1987. 85 minutes (USA)

I Was a Teenage Zombie

Directed by John Elias Michalakis. Produced by Richard Hirsh, John Elias Michalakis. Written by James Aviles Martin, George Seminara. Starring Michael Rubin, Steve McCoy, George Seminara, Robert C. Sabin, Peter Bush, Allen Lewis Rickman, Kevin Nagle, Cassie Madden. Music by Jonathan Roberts, Craig Seeman. Cinematography: Peter Lewnes. Editing by John Elias Michalakis. Distributed by Horizon Films. Charter Entertainment. Release: July, 1987. 90 minutes (USA)

The Monster Squad

Directed by Fred Dekker. Produced by Jonathan A. Zimbert. Written by Shane Black & Fred Dekker. Starring Brent Chalem, Leonardo Cimino, Michael Faustino, Lisa Fuller, Andre Gower, Jack Gwillam, Jason Hervey, Robby Kiger, Ryan Lambert, Stephen Macht, Tom Noonan, Duncan Regehr. Music by Bruce Broughton. Cinematography: Bradford May. Editing by James Mitchell. Distributed by TriStar Pictures. Release: August 14, 1987. 82 minutes (USA)

House II: The Second Story

Directed and Written by Ethan Wiley. Produced by Sean S. Cunningham. Starring Arye Gross, Jonathan Stark, Royal Dano, Bill Maher, John Ratzenberger, Lar Park Lincoln, Amy Yasbeck, Gregory Walcott, Darren Galerkin. Music by Harry Manfredini. Cinematography: Mac Ahlberg. Editing by Martin Nicholson. Distributed by New World Pictures. Release: August 28, 1987. 88 minutes (USA)

Ghoulies II

Directed and Produced by Albert Band. Written by Luca Bercovovici (characters), Charlie Dolan (story), Dennis Paoli (screenplay). Starring Damon Martin, Royal Dano, Phil Fondacaro, J. Downing.

Cinematography: Sergio Salvati. Editing by Barry Zetlin. Distributed by Empire Pictures. Release: September 18, 1987. 89 minutes (USA)

Surf Nazis Must Die

Directed by Peter George. Produced by Robert Tinnell. Written by Jon Ayre. Starring Gail Neely, Barry Brenner, Robert Harden. Music by Jon McCallum. Cinematography: Rolf Kestermann. Editing by Craig Colton. Distributed by Troma Entertainment. Release: 1987. 83 minutes (USA)

Nightmare Sisters

Directed by David DeCoteau. Produced by John Schouweiler. Written by Kenneth J. Hall. Starring Linnea Quigley, Brinke Stevens, Michelle Bauer. Cinematographer Voya Mikulic. Editing by Tony Malanowski. Distributed by Trans World Entertainment. Release: 1987. 83 minutes (USA)

Return of the Living Dead Part II

Directed and Written by Ken Wiederhorn. Produced by Eugene C. Cashman, Tom Fox, William S. Gilmore. Starring Michael Kenworthy, Marsha Dietlein, Thor Van Lingen, Dana Ashbrook, Thom Mathews, James Karen, Suzanne Snyder. Music by J. Peter Robinson. Cinematography: Robert Elswit. Editing by Charles Bornstein. Distributed by Lorimar Pictures. Release: January 8, 1988. 89 minutes (USA)

Sorority Babes in the Slimeball Bowl-O-Rama

Directed by David DeCoteau. Produced by John Schouweiler. Written by Sergei Hasenecz. Starring Linnea Quigley, Michelle Bauer, Andras Jones, Hal Havins, Robin Rochelle. Music by Guy Moon. Cinematography: Stephen A. Blake, Scott Ressler. Editing by Thomas Meshelski, Barry Zetlin. Distributed by Tempe Video. Release: January 29, 1988. 80 minutes (USA)

Beetlejuice

Directed by Tim Burton. Produced by Larry Wilson, David Geffen. Written by Michael McDowell, Larry Wilson, Warren Skaaren, Tim Burton. Starring Michael Keaton, Alec Baldwin, Geena Davis, Winona Ryder, Catherine O'Hara, Jeffrey Jones, Glenn Shadix. Music by Danny Elfman. Cinematography: Thomas E. Ackerman. Editing by Jane Kurson. Distributed by Warner Bros., Geffen Pictures. Release: March 30, 1988. 92 minutes (USA)

Hollywood Chainsaw Hookers

Directed and Produced by Fred Olen Ray. Written by T.L. Lankford, Gunnar Hansen. Starring Gunnar Hansen, Linnea Quigley, Jay Richardson, Michelle Bauer. Cinematography: Scott Ressler. Editing by William Shaffer. Distributed by Camp Motion Pictures. Release: March, 1988. 75 minutes (USA)

Curse of the Queerwolf

Directed, Edited and Written by Mark Pirro. Produced by Sergrio Bandera, Mark Pirro. Starring Michael Palazzolo, Kent Butler, Taylor Whitney, Cynthia Brownell. Distributed by Raedon Video. Release: 1988. 90 minutes (USA)

Killer Klowns from Outer Space

Directed by Stephen Chiodo. Produced and Written by Charles Chiodo, Edward Chiodo, Stephen Chiodo. Starring Grant Cramer, Suzanne Snyder, John Allen Nelson, John Vernon, Michael Siegel, Peter Licassi, Royal Dano. Music by John Massari. Cinematography: Alfred Taylor. Editing by Christopher Roth. Distributed by Trans World Entertainment. Release: May 27, 1988. 88 minutes (USA)

Waxwork

Directed and Written by Anthony Hickox. Produced by Staffan Ahrenberg. Starring Zach Galligan, Deborah Foreman, Michelle Johnson. Music by Roger Bellon. Cinematography: Gerry Lively. Editing by Christopher Cibelli. Distributed by Vestron Pictures. Release: June 17, 1988. 95 minutes (R-rated), 100 minutes (unrated). (USA)

The Lair of the White Worm

Directed by Ken Russell. Produced by Dan Ireland, William J. Quigley, Ken Russell. Written by Bram Stoker (novel), Ken Russell (screenplay). Starring Hugh Grant, Catherine Oxenberg, Amanda Donohoe. Music by Stanislas Syrewicz. Distributed by Vestron Pictures Ltd. Release: September 14, 1988. 93 minutes (UK)

Elvira, Mistress of the Dark

Directed by James Signorelli. Produced by Eric Gardner, Mark Pierson. Written by Cassandra Peterson, John Paragon, Sam Egan. Starring Cassandra Peterson, William Morgan Sheppard, Daniel Greene, Susan Kellermann, Jeff Conaway, Edie McClurg, Tress MacNeille, Pat Crawford Brown. Music by James B. Campbell. Cinematography: Hanania Bier. Editing by Battle Davis. Distributed by New World Pictures. Release: September 30, 1988. 96 minutes (USA)

High Spirits

Directed and Written by Neil Jordan. Produced by David Saunders, Stephen Woolley. Starring Peter

O'Toole, Steve Guttenberg, Beverly D'Angelo, Daryl Hannah, Liam Neeson, Jennifer Tilly, John Nee. Music by George Fenton. Cinematography: Alex Thomson. Editing by Michael Bradsell. Distributed by TriStar Pictures. Release: November 18, 1988. 99 minutes (UK-USA)

Critters 2: The Main Course

Directed by Mick Garris. Produced by Robert Shaye. Written by David Twohy, Mick Garris. Starring Terrence Mann, Don Keith Opper, Scott Grimes. Music by Nicholas Pike. Cinematography: Russell Carpenter. Editing by Charles Bornstein. Distributed by New Line Cinema. Release: 1988. 93 minutes (USA)

Cannibal Women in the Avocado Jungle of Death

Directed and Written by J.F. Lawton. Starring Shannon Tweed, Bill Maher, Karen Mistal, Adrienne Barbeau. Music by Carl Dante. Cinematography: Robert Knouse. Editing by Gary W. Goldstein. Release: 1989. 90 minutes (USA)

Beverly Hills Vamp

Directed and Produced by Fred Olen Ray. Written by Ernest D. Farino. Starring Britt Ekland, Eddie Deezen, Tim Conway, Jr., Tom Shell, Michelle Bauer, Robert Quarry, Dawn Wildsmith. Cinematographer Stephen Ashley Blake. Editing by Christopher Roth. Distributed by Vidmark Entertainment. Release: 1989. 88 minutes (USA)

The Toxic Avenger Part II

Directed by Lloyd Kaufman, Michael Herz. Produced by Michael Herz, Lloyd Kaufman, Jeffrey W. Sass. Written by Lloyd Kaufman, Gay Partington Terry. Starring Ron Fazio, John Altamura, Phoebe Legere. Music by Barrie Guard. Cinematography: James London. Editing by Michael Schweitzer. Distributed by Troma Entertainment. Release: February 24, 1989. 96 minutes (USA)

Fright Night Part 2

Directed, Produced and Written by Tom Holland (characters), Tom Metcalfe, Miguel Tejada-Flores, Tommy Lee Wallace (screenplay). Starring Roddy McDowall, William Ragsdale, Traci Lind, Julie Carmen, Jon Gries, Russell Clark. Cinematography: Mark Irwin. Editing by Jay Lash Cassidy. Distributed by International Video Entertainment. Release: May 19, 1989. 104 minutes (USA)

The Toxic Avenger Part III: The Last Temptation of Toxie

Directed by Lloyd Kaufman, Michael Herz. Produced by Lloyd Kaufman, Michael Herz. Written by Lloyd Kaufman, Michael Herz. Starring Ron Fazio, John Altamura, Phoebe Legere, Lisa Gaye. Cinematography: James London. Editing by Michael Schweitzer. Distributed by Troma Entertainment. Release: November 24, 1989. 79 minutes (R-rated cut), 102 minutes (Director's Cut). (USA)

Out of the Dark

Directed by Michael Schroeder. Written by J. Greg De Felice, Zane W. Levitt. Starring Karen Witter, Karen Black, Bud Cort, Geoffrey Lewis, Tracey Walter, Divine Cameron Dye. Release: 1989. 89 minutes (USA)

Tremors

Directed by Ron Underwood. Produced by Gale Anne Hurd, Brent Maddock, S.S. Wilson. Written by Brent Maddock, S.S. Wilson, Ron Underwood (story) Brent Maddock, S.S. Wilson (screenplay). Starring Kevin Bacon, Fred Ward, Finn Carter, Michael Gross, Reba McEntire, Victor Wong. Music by Ernest Troost. Cinematography: Alexander Gruszynski. Editing by O. Nicholas Brown. Distributed by Universal Pictures. Release: January 19, 1990. 96 minutes (USA)

Frankenhooker

Directed by Frank Henenlotter. Produced by James Glickenhaus. Written by Robert ("Bob") Martin, Frank Henenlotter. Starring Patty Mullen, Louise Lasser, James Lorinz. Music by Joe Renzetti. Distributed by Levins-Henenlotter. Release: June 1, 1990. 85 minutes (USA)

Gremlins 2: The New Batch

Directed by Joe Dante. Produced by Michael Finnell, Rick Baker. Written by Charles S. Haas. Starring Zach Galligan, Phoebe Cates, John Glover, Robert Prosky, Robert Picardo, Christopher Lee, Haviland Morris, Dick Miller, Jackie Joseph, Gedde Watanabe, Keye Luke, Eric Shawn. Music by Jerry Goldsmith. Cinematography: John Hora. Editing by Kent Beyda. Distributed by Warner Bros. Release: June 15, 1990. 106 minutes (USA)

Arachnophobia

Directed by Frank Marshall. Produced by Don Jakoby, Richard Vane, Steven Spielberg. Written by Don Jakoby, Al Williams (story), Don Jakoby, Wesley Strick (screenplay). Starring Jeff Daniels, John Goodman, Harley Jane Kozak. Music by Trevor Jones. Cinematography: Mikael Salomon. Editing by Michael Kahn. Distributed by Buena Vista Pictures. Release: July 18, 1990. 105 minutes (USA)

Chopper Chicks in Zombietown

Directed and Written by Dan Hoskins. Produced by James Hardy. Starring Jamie Rose, Catherine Carlen, Lycia Naff, Vicki Frederick, Kristina Loggia, Gretchen Palmer, Nina Sonja Peterson, Whitney Reis, Billy Bob Thornton, Martha Quinn, David Knell, Don Calfa. Music by Daniel May. Cinematography: Tom Fraser. Editing by W.O. Garrett. Release: 1991. 86 minutes (USA)

Bride of Re-Animator

Directed by Brian Yuzna. Produced by Hidetaka Konno, Keith Walley, Paul White, Brian Yuzna, Michael Muscal. Written by H. P. Lovecraft (characters), Rick Fry, Woody Keith, Brian Yuzna (screenplay). Starring Bruce Abbott, Fabiana Udenio, Kathleen Kinmont, Jeffrey Combs. Distributed by Wild Street Pictures. Release: February 22, 1991. 96 minutes (USA)

Ghoulies III: Ghoulies Go to College

Directed by John Carl Buechler. Written by Luca Bercovici and Jefery Levy (characters), Brent Olson (screenplay). Starring Thom Adcox-Hernandez, Andrew Barach, Kathy Benson, Hope Marie Carlton. Cinematography: Ronn Schmidt. Editing by Adam Bernardi. Distributed by Live Home Video. Release: 1991. 94 minutes (USA)

The Addams Family

Directed by Barry Sonnenfeld. Produced by Scott Rudin. Written by Charles Addams (characters), Caroline Thompson, Larry Wilson (screenplay). Starring Anjelica Huston, Raul Julia, Christopher Lloyd, Elizabeth Wilson, Christina Ricci, Judith Malina, Carel Struycken, Jimmy Workman. Music by Marc Shaiman. Cinematography: Owen Roizman. Editing by Dede Allen, Jim Miller. Distributed by Paramount Pictures. Release: November 22, 1991. 99 minutes (USA)

Critters 3

Directed by Kristine Peterson. Produced by Rupert Harvey. Written by David J. Schow. Starring Don Keith Opper, John Calvin, Nina Axelrod, Leonardo DiCaprio. Distributed by New Line Cinema. Release: 1991. 86 minutes (USA)

Critters 4

Directed and Produced by Rupert Harvey. Written by David J. Schow, Brad Dourif. Starring Don Keith Opper, Terrence Mann, Angela Bassett, Brad Dourif. Music by Peter Manning Robinson. Cinematography: Thomas L. Callaway. Editing by Terry Stokes. Distributed by New Line Cinema. Release: 1991. 100 minutes (USA)

Buffy the Vampire Slayer

Directed by Fran Rubel Kuzui. Produced by Howard Rosenman. Written by Joss Whedon. Starring Kristy Swanson, Donald Sutherland, Paul Reubens, Rutger Hauer, Luke Perry. Music by Carter Burwell. Cinematography: James Hayman. Editing by Jill Savitt. Distributed by 20th Century-Fox. Release: July 31, 1992. 86 minutes (USA)

Death Becomes Her

Directed and Produced by Robert Zemeckis. Written by Martin Donovan, David Koepp. Starring Meryl Streep, Bruce Willis, Goldie Hawn. Release: July 31, 1992. Distributed by Universal Pictures. 104 minutes (USA)

Braindead

Directed by Peter Jackson. Produced by Jim Booth. Written by Stephen Sinclair (story), Stephen Sinclair, Fran Walsh, Peter Jackson (screenplay). Starring Timothy Balme, Diana Peñalver, Elizabeth Moody, Ian Watkin. Music by Peter Dasent. Cinematography: Murray Milne. Editing by Jamie Selkirk. Distributed by Trimark Pictures. Release: February 12, 1993. 104 minutes (New Zealand)

Army of Darkness

Directed by Sam Raimi. Produced by Dino De Laurentiis, Robert Tapert, Bruce Campbell. Written by Sam Raimi, Ivan Raimi. Starring Bruce Campbell, Embeth Davidtz, Bridget Fonda, Marcus Gilbert. Music by Joe LoDuca, Danny Elfman ("March of the Dead"). Editing by Bob Murawski. Distributed by Universal Pictures. Release: February 19, 1993. 83 minutes (USA)

My Boyfriend's Back

Directed by Bob Balaban. Produced by Sean S. Cunningham. Written by Dean Lorey. Starring Andrew Lowery, Traci Lin, Danny Zorn, Edward Herrmann, Philip Seymour Hoffman, Renée Zellweger, Matthew McConaughey, Matthew Fox. Music by Harry Manfredini. Cinematography: Mac Ahlberg. Editing by Michael Jablow. Distributed by Touchstone Pictures. Release: August 6, 1993. 85 minutes (USA)

Return of the Living Dead 3

Directed by Brian Yuzna. Produced by Lawrence Steven Meyers, Brian Yuzna, Gary Schmoeller, John Penney. Written by John Penney. Starring Melinda Clarke, J. Trevor Edmond, Kent McCord, Basil Wallace. Music by Barry Goldberg. Cinematography: Gerry Lively. Editing by Christopher Roth. Distributed by Trimark Pictures. Release: October 29, 1993. 97 minutes (USA)

Addams Family Values

Directed by Barry Sonnenfeld. Produced by Scott Rudin. Written by Charles Addams (characters), Paul Rudnick (screenplay). Starring Anjelica Huston, Raul Julia, Christopher Lloyd, Peter MacNicol, Joan Cusack, Christina Ricci, Carol Kane, Jimmy Workman, Kaitlyn Hooper, Kristen Hooper, Carel Struycken. Music by Marc Shaiman, Ralph Sall. Cinematography: Donald Peterman. Editing by Jim Miller, Arthur Schmidt. Distributed by Paramount Pictures. Release: November 19, 1993. 94 minutes (USA)

Cemetery Man

Directed by Michele Soavi. Written by Tiziano Sclavi (novel), Gianni Romoli (screenplay). Starring Rupert Everett, François Hadji-Lazaro, Anna Falchi. Music by Manuel De Sica, Riccardo Biseo. Cinematography: Mauro Marchetti. Distributed by October Films. Release: 1994. 105 minutes (Italy)

Ghoulies IV

Directed by Jim Wynorski. Produced by Gary Schmoeller. Written by Luca Bercovici, Jefery Levy (characters), Mark Sevi (screenplay). Starring Pete Liapis, Barbara Alyn Woods, Stacie Randell, Raquel Krelle, Bobby Di Cicco. Cinematography: J.E. Bash. Editing by Richard Gentner. Distributed by Columbia TriStar Home Video. Release: 1994. 84 minutes (USA)

The Day of the Beast

Directed by Álex de la Iglesia. Produced by Andrés Vicente Gómez. Written by Jorge Guerricaechevarría, Álex de la Iglesia. Starring Álex Angulo, Armando De Razza, Santiago Segura, Maria Grazia Cucinotta. Music by Battista Lena. Cinematography: Flavio Martínez Labiano. Editing by Teresa Font. Distributed by Cana+ Espana. Release: October 20, 1995. 103 minutes (Spain-Italy)

Vampire in Brooklyn

Directed by Wes Craven. Produced by Marianne Maddalena, Stuart M. Besser, Eddie Murphy. Written by Eddie Murphy, Vernon Lynch, Charles Q. Murphy. Starring Eddie Murphy, Angela Bassett. Music by J. Peter Robinson. Distributed by Paramount Pictures. Release: October 27, 1995. 100 minutes (USA)

Dracula: Dead and Loving It

Directed by Mel Brooks. Written by Bram Stoker (novel), Rudy De Luca, Mel Brooks, Steve Haberman (screenplay). Starring Leslie Nielsen, Peter MacNicol, Steven Weber, Amy Yasbeck, Mel Brooks, Lysette Anthony, Harvey Korman, Ezio Greggio. Music by Hummie Mann. Distributed by Columbia Pictures. Release: December 22, 1995. 88 minutes (USA)

Tremors 2: Aftershocks

Directed by S.S. Wilson. Produced by Christopher DeFaria, Nancy Roberts. Written by Brent Maddock, S.S. Wilson, Ron Underwood (characters), Brent Maddock, S.S. Wilson (screenplay). Starring Fred Ward, Christopher Gartin, Helen Shaver, Michael Gross, Marcelo Tubert, Marco Hernandez, José Ramón Rosario, Thomas Rosales Jr. Music by Jay Ferguson. Cinematography: Virgil L. Harper. Editing by Bob Ducsay. Distributed by Universal Pictures. Release: April 9, 1996. 96 minutes (USA)

Cannibal! The Musical

Directed by Trey Parker. Produced by Trey Parker, Matt Stone, Jason McHugh. Written by Trey Parker, Matt Stone (uncredited). Starring Trey Parker (credited as Juan Schwartz), Matt Stone, Dian Bachar, Jason McHugh, John Hegel, Toddy Walters, Stan Brakhage. Distributed by Troma Entertainment. Release: 1996. 95 minutes (USA)

Killer Condom

Directed by Martin Walz. Produced by Erwin C. Dietrich, Ralph S. Dietrich, Harald Reichebner. Written by Ralf König, Martin Walz. Starring Udo Samel, Peter Lohmeyer, Marc Richter, Leonard Lansink, Iris Berben. Music by Emil Viklicky. Cinematography: Alexander Honisch. Editing by Simone Klier. Distributed by Troma Entertainment. Release: 1996. 107 minutes (Germany)

The Frighteners

Directed by Peter Jackson. Produced by Robert Zemeckis. Written by Fran Walsh, Peter Jackson. Starring Michael J. Fox, Trini Alvarado, John Astin, Jeffrey Combs, Dee Wallace-Stone, Jake Busey, Chi McBride. Music by Danny Elfman. Cinematography: John Blick, Alun Bollinger. Editing by Jamie Selkirk. Distributed by Universal Pictures. Release: July 19, 1996. 110 minutes (Theatrical), 122 minutes (Director's Cut). (New Zealand-USA)

Scream

Directed by Wes Craven. Produced by Cathy Konrad, Cary Woods. Written by Kevin Williamson. Starring David Arquette, Neve Campbell, Courteney Cox, Matthew Lillard, Rose McGowan, Skeet Ulrich, Jamie Kennedy, W. Earl Brown, Joseph Whipp, Liev Schreiber, Drew Barrymore. Cinematographer Mark Irwin. Editing by Patrick Lussier. Distributed by Dimension Films. Release: December 20, 1996. 111 minutes (USA)

Evil Ed

Directed by Anders Jacobsson. Written by Anders Jacobsson, Göran Lundström, Christer Ohlsson. Starring Johan Rudebeck, Per Löfberg, Olof Rhodin, Cecilia Ljung, Gert Fylking. Distributed by Unipix Entertainment. Release: 1997. 93 minutes (Sweden)

Scream 2

Directed by Wes Craven. Produced by Cathy Konrad, Wes Craven, Marianne Maddalena. Written by Kevin Williamson. Starring David Arquette, Neve Campbell, Courteney Cox, Sarah Michelle Gellar, Jamie Kennedy, Laurie Metcalf, Jerry O'Connell, Jada Pinkett Smith, Liev Schreiber, Omar Epps. Cinematographer Peter Deming. Editing by Patrick Lussier. Distributed by Dimension Films. Release: December 12, 1997. 120 minutes (USA)

Bride of Chucky

Directed by Ronny Yu. Produced by David Kirschner, Grace Gilroy, Don Mancini. Written by Don Mancini. Starring Jennifer Tilly, Brad Dourif, Katherine Heigl. Music by Graeme Revell. Cinematography: Peter Pau. Editing by Randy Bricker, David Wu. Distributed by Universal Pictures. Release: October 16, 1998. 89 minutes (USA)

Idle Hands

Directed by Rodman Flender. Produced by Jeffrey Sudzin, Andrew Licht. Written by Terri Hughes, Ron Milbauer. Starring Devon Sawa, Jessica Alba, Seth Green, Elden Henson, Vivica A. Fox. Distributed by Columbia Pictures. Release: April 30, 1999. 92 minutes (USA)

Psycho Beach Party

Directed by Robert Lee King. Produced by Virginia Biddlem, Jon Gerrans, Marcus Hu, Victor Syrmis. Written by Charles Busch. Starring Lauren Ambrose, Thomas Gibson, Nicholas Brendon, Matt Keeslar. Music by Ben Vaughn. Distributed by Strand. Release: January 23, 2000 (Sundance Film Festival). 95 minutes (USA)

Scream 3

Directed by Wes Craven. Produced by Cathy Konrad, Wes Craven, Marianne Maddalena. Written by Ehren Kruger. Starring Neve Campbell, Courteney Cox Arquette, David Arquette, Jamie Kennedy, Patrick Dempsey, Jenny McCarthy, Liev Schreiber, Parker Posey, Matt Keeslar, Deon Richmond, Kelly Rutherford. Cinematography: Peter Deming. Editing by Patrick Lussier. Distributed by Warner Bros. Release: February 4, 2000. 117 minutes (USA)

Scary Movie

Directed by Keenen Ivory Wayans. Produced by Eric L. Gold, Lee R. Mayes, Shawn Wayans, Marlon Wayans, Phil Beauman, Jason Friedberg, Aaron Seltzer. Written by Shawn Wayans, Marlon Wayans, Buddy Johnson, Phil Beauman, Jason Friedberg, Aaron Seltzer. Starring Anna Faris, Jon Abrahams, Dave Sheridan, Marlon Wayans, Shawn Wayans, Regina Hall, Cheri Oteri, Shannon Elizabeth, Lochlyn Munro, Kurt Fuller, James Van Der Beek, Carmen Electra. Cinematography: Francis Kenny. Editing by Mark Helfrich. Distributed by Dimension Films. Release: July 7, 2000. 88 minutes (USA)

Scary Movie 2

Directed by Keenen Ivory Wayans. Produced by Eric L. Gold, Peter Schwerin, Bob Weinstein, Harvey Weinstein, Brad Weston, Sue Jett, Barry Rosenbush. Written by Shawn Wayans, Marlon Wayans, Alyson Fouse, Greg Grabianski, Dave Polsky, Michael Anthony Snowden, Craig Wayans. Starring Anna Faris, Christopher Masterson, Regina Hall, Shawn Wayans, Marlon Wayans, David Cross, Chris Elliott, Kathleen Robertson, Tori Spelling. Music by Ceiri Torjussen, Rossano Galante, Tom Hiel, Mark McGrath, Marco Beltrami, George S. Clinton, John Debney, Danny Lux. Cinematography: Steven Bernstein. Editing by Thomas J. Nordberg, Richard Pearson, Peter Teschner. Distributed by Dimension Films. Release: July 6, 2001. 83 minutes (USA)

Citizen Toxie: The Toxic Avenger IV

Directed and Produced by Lloyd Kaufman, Michael Herz. Written by Lloyd Kaufman, Michael Herz, Patrick Cassidy. Starring David Mattey, Clyde Lewis, Heidi Sjursen, Paul Kyrmse, Joe Fleishaker, Debbie Rochon, Ron Jeremy, Corey Feldman. Music by Wes Nagy. Cinematography: Brendan Flynt. Editing by Gabriel Friedman. Distributed by Troma Entertainment. Release: November 2, 2001. 108 minutes (R-rated cut), 99 minutes (Director's Cut). (USA)

Bio Zombie

Directed by Wilson Yip. Produced by Joe Ma. Written by Matt Chow, Siu Man Sing, Wilson Yip. Starring Jordan Chan, Sam Lee, Angela Tong Ying-Ying, Yiu-Cheung Lai, Emotion Cheung. Music by Peter Kam. Cinematography: Kwok-Man Keung. Editing by Ka-Fai Cheung. Distributed by Media Blasters (U.S. DVD). Release: April 24, 2001 (U.S. DVD). 94 minutes (Hong Kong)

Tremors 3: Back to Perfection

Directed by Brent Maddock. Produced by S.S. Wilson, Nancy Roberts. Written by S.S. Wilson, Brent Maddock, Nancy Roberts (story), John Whelpley (screenplay). Starring Michael Gross, Shawn Christian, Susan Chuang, Charlotte Stewart, Ariana Richards, Tony Genaro, Barry Livingston, John Pappas, Robert Jayne, Billy Rieck. Music by Kevin Kiner. Cinematography: Virgil L. Harper. Distributed by Universal Pictures. Release: October 2, 2001. 104 minutes (USA)

Jesus Christ Vampire Hunter

Directed by Lee Demarbre. Written by Ian Driscoll. Starring Phil Caracas, Murielle Varhelyi, Jeff Moffet, Sean Secor, Ian Driscoll. Music by Graham Collins. Editing by Lee Demarbre. Distributed by Odessa Filmworks, Inc. Release: January 15, 2002. 85 minutes (Canada)

The Happiness of the Katakuras

Directed by Takashi Miike. Produced by Hirotsugu Yoshida. Written by Kikumi Yamagishi. Starring Kenji Sawada, Keiko Matsuzaka, Shinji Takeda, Naomi Nishida, Kiyoshiro Imawano, Tetsuro Tamba. Distributed by Vitagraph Films LLC (USA). Release: February 23, 2002 (Japan). 113 minutes (Japan)

Bubba Ho-Tep

Directed by Don Coscarelli. Produced by Don Coscarelli, Jason R. Savage, Ronnie Truss, Mark Wooding. Starring Bruce Campbell, Ossie Davis, Ella Joyce, Bob Ivy, Heidi Marnhout. Music by Brian Tyler. Cinematography: Adam Janeiro. Editing by Scott J. Gill, Donald Milne. Distributed by MGM. Release: June 9, 2002. 92 minutes (USA)

Eight-Legged Freaks

Directed by Ellory Elkayem. Produced by Bruce Berman, Dean Devlin. Written by Jesse Alexander, Ellory Elkayem. Starring David Arquette, Kari Wuhrer, Scarlett Johansson, Doug E. Doug. Music by John Ottman. Distributed by Warner Bros. Release: July 17, 2002. 99 minutes (USA)

Terror Toons

Directed and Produced by Joe Castro. Written by Rudy Balli (story), Joe Castro, Steven J. Escobar, Rudy Balli (screenplay). Starring Beverly Lynne, Janet Romano (credited as Lizzy Borden), Kerry Liu. Music by J.M. Logan. Cinematography: Isaac Garza. Editing by Steven J. Escobar. Distributed by Brain Damage Films. 75 minutes. Release: August 13, 2002. (USA)

Elvira's Haunted Hills

Directed by Sam Irvin. Produced by Mark Pierson. Written by Cassandra Peterson, John Paragon. Starring Cassandra Peterson, Richard O'Brien, Mary Scheer, Scott Atkinson, Heather Hopper. Music by Eric Allaman. Cinematography: Viorel Sergovici. Editing by Stephen R. Myers. Distributed by Elvira Movie Company/Media Pro Pictures. Release: October 31, 2002. 90 minutes (USA)

Beyond Re-Animator

Directed by Brian Yuzna. Produced by Brian Yuzna, Julio Fernández, Carlos Fernández. Written by H. P. Lovecraft (characters), Miguel Tejada-Flores (story), José Manuel Gómez (screenplay). Starring Jeffrey Combs, Tommy Dean Musset, Jason Barry, Bárbara Elorrieta, Elsa Pataky, Santiago Segura, Simón Andreu. Music by Xavier Capellas. Cinematography: Andreu Rebés. Editing by Bernat Vilaplana. Distributed by Lionsgate Films. Release: April 4, 2003. 95 minutes (USA)

Battlefield Baseball

Directed by Yudai Yamaguchi. Produced by Ryuhei Kitamura. Written by Gatarô Man. Starring Tak Sakaguchi, Atsushi Ito, Hideo Sakaki. Editing by Shuichi Kakesu. Distributed by Subversive Cinema (USA). Release: July 19, 2003. 87 minutes (Japan)

Buppah Rahtree

Directed by Yuthlert Sippapak. Produced by Amorn Chanapai, Yuthlert Sippapak. Written by Yuthlert Sippapak. Starring Laila Boonyasak, Krit Sripoomseth. Music by Gancore Club. Cinematography: Prapapope Duangpikool. Editing by Tawat Siripong. Distributed by Nakomthai Picture Co. Ltd. Release: November 14, 2003. 109 minutes (Thailand)

The Haunted Mansion

Directed by Rob Minkoff. Produced by Andrew Gunn, Don Hahn. Written by David Berenbaum. Starring Eddie Murphy, Jennifer Tilly, Terence Stamp, Marsha Thomason, Nathaniel Parker. Music by Mark Mancina. Cinematography: Remi Adefarasin. Distributed by Walt Disney Pictures. Release: November 26, 2003. 99 minutes (USA)

Hey, Stop Stabbing Me!

Directed by Worm Miller. Produced and Written by Patrick Casey, Worm Miller. Starring Patrick Casey, Andy "Hippa" Kriss, Maria A. Morales, N. David Prestwood, Jack Shreck, Sean Hall, Worm Miller. Music by Sean Hall, Jack Shreck. Distributed by Sub Rosa. Release: 2003. 90 minutes (USA)

Scary Movie 3

Directed by David Zucker. Produced by Robert K. Weiss, David Zucker. Written by Shawn Wayans, Marlon Wayans, Buddy Johnson, Phil Beauman, Jason Friedberg, Aaron Seltzer (characters), Craig Mazin, Pat Proft (screenplay). Starring Anna Faris, Charlie Sheen, Simon Rex, Leslie Nielsen, Regina Hall. Music by James Venable. Cinematographer Mark Irwin. Editing by Malcolm Campbell, Jon Poll. Distributed by Dimension Films. Release: October 24, 2003. 84 minutes (USA)

Tremors 4: The Legend Begins

Directed by S.S. Wilson. Produced by Nancy Roberts. Written by S.S. Wilson, Brent Maddock, Ron Underwood (characters), Brent Maddock, S.S. Wilson, Nancy Roberts (story), Scott Buck (screenplay). Starring Michael Gross, Sara Botsford, Billy Drago, Brent Roam, August Schellenberg, J.E. Freeman, Lo Ming, Lydia Look, Sam Ly, Neil Kopit, Sean Moran, Mathew Seth Wilson, John Dixon, Dan Lemieux, Don Ruffin, Lou Carlucci. Music by Jay Ferguson. Cinematography: Virgil L. Harper. Editing by Harry B. Miller III. Distributed by Universal Pictures. Release: January 2, 2004 (USA). 101 minutes (USA)

Club Dread

Directed by Jay Chandrasekhar. Produced by Richard Perello. Written by Broken Lizard. Starring Bill Paxton, Kevin Heffernan, Brittany Daniel, Steve Lemme, Jordan Ladd, Jay Chandrasekhar, Paul Soter, Erik Stolhanske, Greg Cipes, M.C. Gainey. Music by Nathan Barr. Cinematography: Lawrence Sher. Editing by Ryan Folsey. Distributed by Fox Searchlight. Release: February 27, 2004. 103 minutes (extended cut: 118 minutes). (USA)

The Lost Skeleton of Cadavra

Directed and Written by Larry Blamire. Produced by F. Miguel Valenti. Starring Fay Masterson, Andrew Parks, Susan McConnell, Brian Howe, Jennifer Blaire, Larry Blamire, Dan Conroy, Robert Devau, Darren Reed. Music by Valentino Productions. Cinematography: Kevin F. Jones. Editing by Bill Bryn Russell. Distributed by Tri-Star Pictures. Release: March 12, 2004 (USA) (limited). 89 minutes (USA)

Dead and Breakfast

Directed by Matthew Leutwyler. Produced by Miranda Bailey, Wang Ching. Written by Matthew Leutwyler, Jun Tan, Billy Burke (story), Matthew Leutwyler (screenplay). Starring Ever Carradine, Brent David Fraser, Portia de Rossi, David Carradine, Bianca Lawson, Jeremy Sisto, Jeffrey Dean Morgan. Music by Zach Selwyn, Brian Vander Ark. Cinematography: David Scardina. Editing by Peter Devaney Flanagan. Distributed by Anchor Bay Entertainment. Release: March 2004 (SXSW Film Festival), August 19, 2005 (limited). 88 minutes (USA)

Choking Hazard

Directed by Marek Dobe. Produced by Marek Dobe, Narek Oganesjan, Vladka Poláčková. Written by Stepan Kopriva, Martin Pomothy. Music by Frantisek Fuka, Daniel Krob. Starring Jan Dolansky, Jaroslav Dusek, Eva Nadazdyova, Anna Fialkova. Cinematography: Martin Preiss, Radovan Subin. Editing by Michal Hyka. Distributed by Bontonfilm, Fangoria International. Release: April 2, 2004. 81 minutes (Czech Republic)

To Catch a Virgin Ghost

Directed by Shin Jeong-won. Produced by Jonathan Kim. Written by Lee Chang-si, Hwang In-ho. Starring Im Chang-jeong, Kwon Oh-joong, Lim Eun-kyeong. Distributed by ShowBox. Release: August 13, 2004 (South Korea). 109 mins. (South Korea). (South Korea)

Shaun of the Dead

Directed by Edgar Wright. Produced by Nira Park. Written by Simon Pegg, Edgar Wright. Starring Simon Pegg, Kate Ashfield, Nick Frost, Lucy Davis, Dylan Moran. Distributed by Rogue Pictures. Release: September 24, 2004. 95 minutes (UK)

Zombie Honeymoon

Directed and Written by David Gebroe. Produced by David Gebroe, Christina Reilly. Starring Tracy Coogan, Graham Sibley, Tonya Cornelisse, David M. Wallace. Music by Michael Tremante. Cinematography: Ken Seng. Editing by Gordon Grinberg. Distributed by Hooligan Pictures. Release: October 4, 2004. 83 minutes (USA)

Seed of Chucky

Directed by Don Mancini. Produced by David Kirschner, Corey Sienega. Written by Don Mancini. Starring Jennifer Tilly, Hannah Spearritt, John Waters, Billy Boyd, Keith-Lee Castle, Brad Dourif. Music by Pino Donaggio. Distributed by Rogue Pictures. Release: October 31, 2004. 93 minutes (USA)

Sars Wars

Directed by Taweewat Wantha. Produced by Akaradech Maneeploypech, Pracha Maleenont, Brian L. Marcar, Adirek Wattaleela. Written by Sommai Lertulan, Kuanchun Phemyad, Taweewat Wantha, Adirek Wattaleela. Starring Suthep Pongam, Supakorn Kitsuwon, Phintusuda Tunphairao, Lene Christensen, Somlek Sakdikul. Cinematography: Art Srithongkul. Editing by Doctor Head. Distributed by Chalermthai Studio. Release: December 16, 2004. 95 minutes (Thailand)

Pervert!

Directed and Produced by Jonathan Yudis. Written by Mike Davis. Starring Mary Carey, Sean Andrews, Darrell Sandeen. Music by Elliott Goldkind, Matt Piedmont. Cinematography: Guy Livneh. Editing by Michael T. Fitzgerald Jr. Distributed by TLA Releasing. Release: February 12, 2005. 81 minutes (USA)

Buppah Rahtree Phase II: Rahtree Returns

Directed and Written by Yuthlert Sippapak. Produced by Amorn Chanapai, Yuthlert Sippapak. Starring Laila Boonyasak, Krit Sripoomseth. Music by Gancore Club. Cinematography: Somkid Phukphong. Editing by Tawat Siripong. Distributed by Sahamongkol Film International. Release: March 24, 2005. 106 minutes (Thailand)

Boy Eats Girl

Directed by Stephen Bradley. Produced by Ed Guiney, Andrew Lowe. Written by Derek Landy. Starring Samantha Mumba, David Leon, Laurence Kinlan. Music by Hugh Drumm. Cinematography: Balazs Bolygo. Editing by Dermot Diskin. Distributed by Odyssey Distributors Ltd. Release: April 6, 2005. 77 minutes (Ireland)

Corpse Bride

Directed by Tim Burton, Mike Johnson. Produced by Tim Burton, Allison Abbate. Written by John August, Caroline Thompson, Tim Burton. Starring Johnny Depp, Helena Bonham Carter, Emily Watson, Tracey Ullman. Music by Danny Elfman. Cinematography: Pete Kozachik. Editing by Jonathan Lucas, Chris Lebenzon. Distributed by Warner Bros. Family Entertainment. Release: September 23, 2005. 78 minutes (USA)

Return of the Living Dead: Necropolis

Directed by Ellory Elkayem. Produced by Anatoly Fradis, Steve Scarduzio. Written by William Butler, Aaron Strongoni. Starring Peter Coyote, Aimee Lynn Chadwick. Music by Robert Duncan. Cinematography: Gabriel Kosuth. Editing by James Coblentz. Distributed by Denholm Trading Inc. Release: October 15, 2005 (TV, edited), April 18, 2006 (DVD, R-rated). 88 minutes (USA)

Night of the Living Dorks

Directed and Written by Mathias Dinter. Produced by Mischa Hofmann, Philip Voges. Starring Tino Mewes, Manuel Cortez, Thomas Schmieder, Hendrik Borgmann, Nadine Germann. Cinematographer Stephan Schuh. Editing by Connie Strecker. Distributed by Anchor Bay Entertainment. Release: 2004 in Germany, 2006 in USA. 89 minutes (Germany)

Return of the Living Dead: Rave to the Grave

Directed by Ellory Elkayem. Produced by Anatoly Fradis, Steve Scarduzio. Written by William Butler, Aaron Strongoni. Starring Peter Coyote, Aimee-Lynn Chadwick. Music by Robert Duncan, Ralph Rieckermann, Aimee-Lynn Chadwick. Distributed by Denholm Trading Inc. Release: October 15, 2005 (TV, edited). March 20, 2007 (DVD, R-rated). 86 minutes (R-rated version). (USA)

Slither

Directed by James Gunn. Produced by Paul Brooks, Eric Newman. Written by James Gunn. Starring Nathan Fillion, Elizabeth Banks, Michael Rooker, Gregg Henry, Tania Saulnier, Brenda James, Don Thompson, Jenna Fischer. Music by Tyler Bates. Distributed by Universal Pictures. Release: March 31, 2006. 95 minutes (USA)

Scary Movie 4

Directed by David Zucker. Produced by Robert K. Weiss. Written by Jim Abrahams, Pat Proft, Craig Mazin. Starring Anna Faris, Regina Hall, Craig Bierko. Cinematographer Thomas E. Ackerman. Editing by Craig Herring, Tom Lewis. Distributed by Dimension Films, The Weinstein Company. Release: April 14, 2006. 83 minutes (USA)

Severance

Directed by Christopher Smith. Produced by Jason Newmark. Written by James Moran, Christopher Smith. Starring Toby Stephens, Danny Dyer, Laura Harris. Music by Christian Henson. Cinematography: Ed Wild. Editing by Stuart Gazzard. Distributed by Pathé. Release: August 25, 2006. 91 minutes (UK-Germany)

Feast

Directed by John Gulager. Produced by Michael Leahy, Joel Soisson, Marc Joubert, Larry Tanz, Benjamin Ormand, Andrew Jameson, Alix Taylor, Alex Keledjian. Written by Marcus Dunstan, Patrick Melton. Starring Krista Allen, Balthazar Getty, Navi Rawat, Eric Dane, Clu Gulager, Jenny Wade. Cinematography: Thomas L. Callaway. Editing by Kirk M. Morri. Distributed by Dimension Films. Release: September 22, 2006. 95 minutes (USA)

Evil Bong

Directed by Charles Band. Produced by Andrea Austin, Andrew Austin. Written by August White. Starring David Weidoff, John Patrick Jordan. Music by District 78. Editing by Danny Draven. Release: October 31, 2006. 86 minutes (USA)

Fido

Directed by Andrew Currie. Produced by Trent Carlson, Patrick Cassavetti, Blake Corbet, Kevin Eastwood, Daniel Iron, Michael Shepard, Mary Anne Waterhouse, Ki Wight. Written by Robert Chomiak, Andrew Currie, Dennis Heaton. Starring Carrie-Anne Moss, Billy Connolly, Dylan Baker, K'Sun Ray, Henry Czerny, Tim Blake Nelson. Distributed by Lionsgate Films. Release: March 16, 2007. 91 minutes (Canada)

Terror Toons 2: The Sick and Silly Show

Directed and Written by Joe Castro. Produced by Steven J. Escobar. Starring Shane Ballard, Emma Bing, Bart Burson, David Alan Graf, Brinke Stevens. Music by Jason Frederick. Cinematography: Nick Saglimbeni. Editing by Steven J. Escobar. Distributed by Jesco Film Entertainment. Release: March 27, 2007. 80 minutes (USA)

Black Sheep

Directed and Written by Jonathan King. Produced by Phillipa Campbell. Starring Matthew Chamberlain, Tammy Davis, Oliver Driver, Peter Feeney. Music by Victoria Kelly. Cinematography: Richard Bluck. Editing by Chris Plummer. Distributed by The Weinstein Company. Release: March 29, 2007. 87 minutes (New Zealand)

Netherbeast Incorporated

Directed by Dean Ronalds. Produced by Brian Ronalds, Dean Ronalds, Chris Lamont, F. Miguel Valenti. Written by Bruce Dellis. Starring Darrell Hammond, Judd Nelson, Dave Foley, Steve Burns, Amy Davidson, Jason Mewes, Robert Wagner. Music by Tim Clark. Cinematography: Stefan Von Bjorn. Editing by Dean Ronalds. Release: March 30, 2007. 90 minutes (USA)

Ghost Station

Directed by Yuthlert Sippapak. Starring Kerttisak Udomnak, Nakorn Silachai. Distributed by Sahamongkol Film International. Release: April 5, 2007. 90 minutes (Thailand)

Teeth

Directed and Written by Mitchell Lichtenstein. Produced by Richard E. Chapla Jr., Mitchell Lichtenstein, Joyce M. Pierpoline. Starring Jess Weixler, Hale Appleman, John Hensley. Music by Robert Miller. Cinematography: Wolfgang Held. Editing by Joe Landauer. Distributed by Roadside Attractions. Release: January 1, 2008. 88 minutes (USA)

Trail of the Screaming Forehead

Directed and Written by Larry Blamire. Starring Daniel Roebuck, Susan McConnell, Fay Masterson, Andrew Parks, H.M. Wynant, Brian Howe, Dan Conroy, Alison Martin. Cinematographer Kevin F. Jones. Editing by Bill Bryn Russell. Release: 2008(?). 84 minutes (USA)

APPENDIX B
Selected Short Subjects

These are a few of the author's favorite short comedy-horror films, both live action and animated. (A)= Animated. (LA)= Live Action.

Shivering Spooks (LA)
Directed by Robert F. McGowan. Produced by Hal Roach. Written by Hal Roach (story), H.M. Walker (titles). Starring Harry Bowen, Joe Cobb, Jackie Condon, Johnny Downs. Distributed by Pathé Exchange. Release: August 8, 1926. 20 minutes. (USA)

Spook Spoofing (LA)
Director by Robert F. McGowan. Produced by Hal Roach Starring Farina Hoskins, Joe Cobb, Jackie Condon, Jay R. Smith, Bobby "Wheezer" Hutchins. Distributed by Pathé Exchange. Release: 1928. 30 minutes. (USA)

Haunted House (A)
Directed and Produced by Walt Disney. Voices by Walt Disney. Distributed by RKO Radio Pictures. Release: August 1, 1929. 7 minutes. (USA)

The Skeleton Dance (A)
Directed and Produced by Walt Disney. Music by Carl W. Stalling. Distributed by RKO Radio Pictures. Release: August 22, 1929 (USA). 6 minutes. (USA)

The Mad Doctor (A)
Directed by David Hand. Produced by Walt Disney. Voices by Pinto Colvig, Walt Disney. Distributed by RKO Radio Pictures. Release: January 20, 1933. 7 minutes. (USA)

Betty Boop's Hallowe'en Party (A)
Directed by Dave Fleischer. Produced by Max Fleischer. Voices by Mae Questel. Animation by Willard Bowsky, Myron Waldman. Distributed by Paramount Pictures. Release: November 3, 1933. 7 minutes. (USA)

Oliver the Eighth (LA)
Directed by Lloyd French. Produced by Hal Roach. Starring Stan Laurel, Oliver Hardy. Cinematography: Art Lloyd. Editing by Bert Jordan. Distributed by MGM. Release: January 13, 1934. 27 minutes. (USA)

Shiver Me Timbers! (A)
Directed by Dave Fleischer. Voices by William Costello, Mae Questel. Distributed by Paramount Pictures. Release: July 27, 1934. 7 minutes. (USA)

The Cobweb Hotel (A)
Directed by Dave Fleischer. Written by Bill Turner. Voices by Jack Mercer. Distributed by Paramount Pictures. Release: May 15, 1936. 8 minutes. (USA)

Skeleton Frolic (A)
Directed by Ub Iwerks. Distributed by Columbia Pictures. Release: January 29, 1937. 7 minutes. (USA)

Popeye the Sailor Meets Ali Baba's Forty Thieves (A)
Directed by Dave Fleischer. Produced by Max Fleischer. Voices by Jack Mercer, Mae Questel, Gus Wickie. Music by Sammy Timberg, Sammy Lerner, Tot Seymour, Vee Lawnhurst. Animation by Willard Bowsky, George Germanetti, Orestes Calpini. Distributed by Paramount Pictures. Release: November 26, 1937. 16 minutes. (USA)

Lonesome Ghosts (A)
Directed by Burt Gillett. Produced by Walt Disney. Voices by Clarence Nash, Walt Disney, Pinto Colvig. Distributed by RKO Radio Pictures. Release: December 24, 1937. 9 minutes. (USA)

We Want Our Mummy (LA)
Directed by Del Lord. Produced by Jules White. Written by Searle Kramer, Elwood Ullman. Starring Curly Howard, Larry Fine, Moe Howard, Dick Curtis, Bud Jamison, James C. Morton, Eddie Laughton, Theodore Lorch, Robert Williams. Distributed by Columbia Pictures. Release: February 24, 1939. 16 minutes. (USA)

Ghosks Is the Bunk (A)
Directed by Dave Fleischer. Produced by Max Fleischer. Voices by Jack Mercer, Pinto Colvig, Margie Hines. Distributed by Paramount Pictures. Release: June 14, 1939. 6 minutes. (USA)

Jeepers Creepers (A)
Directed by Robert Clampett. Produced by Leon Schlesinger. Story by Ernest Gee. Voices by Mel Blanc, Pinto Colvig (uncredited). Music by Carl W. Stalling. Animation by Vive Risto. Distributed by Warner Bros. Pictures. Release: September 23, 1939. 8 minutes. (USA)

The Hare-Brained Hypnotist (A)
Directed by I. Freleng. Produced by Leon Schlesinger. Story by Michael Maltese. Voices by Mel Blanc, Arthur Q. Bryan (uncredited). Music by Carl Stalling. Distributed by Warner Bros. Pictures. Release: October 31, 1942. (USA)

Frankenstein's Cat (A)
Directed by Mannie Davis. Produced by Paul Terry. Distributed by 20th Century-Fox. Release: November 27, 1942. 7 minutes. (USA)

Spook Louder (LA)
Directed by Del Lord. Produced by Del Lord, Hugh McCollum. Written by Clyde Bruckman. Starring Moe Howard, Larry Fine, Curly Howard, Stanley Blystone, Lew Kelly, Symona Boniface, Theodore Lorch, Stanley Brown, Charles Middleton, Shirley Patterson. Cinematography: John Stumar. Editing by Paul Borofsky. Distributed by Columbia Pictures. Release: April 2, 1943. 16 minutes. (USA)

Falling Hare (A)
Directed by Robert Clampett. Produced by Leon Schlesinger. Story by Warren Foster. Voices by Mel Blanc. Music by Carl W. Stalling. Animation by Robert McKimson, Rod Scribner, Bill Melendez, Virgil Ross. Distributed by Warner Bros. Pictures. Release: October 30, 1943. 7 minutes. (USA)

Donald Duck and the Gorilla (A)
Directed by Jack King. Produced by Walt Disney. Voices by Clarence Nash. Distributed by RKO Radio Pictures. Release: March 31, 1944. 7 minutes. (USA)

Idle Roomers (LA)
Directed by Del Lord. Produced by Hugh McCollum. Written by Del Lord, Elwood Ullman. Starring Moe Howard, Larry Fine, Curly Howard, Christine McIntyre, Vernon Dent, Duke York, Eddie Laughton. Cinematography: Glen Gano. Editing by Henry Batista. Distributed by Columbia Pictures. Release: July 15, 1944. 16 minutes. (USA)

Three Pests in a Mess (LA)
Directed by Del Lord. Produced by Hugh McCollum. Written by Del Lord. Starring Moe Howard, Larry Fine, Curly Howard, Christine McIntyre, Brian O'Hara, Vernon Dent, Snub Pollard, Victor Travers, Heinie Conklin. Cinematography: Benjamin H. Kline. Editing by Henry Batista. Distributed by Columbia Pictures. Release: January 19, 1945. 17 minutes. (USA)

If a Body Meets a Body (LA)
Directed and Produced by Jules White. Written by Elwood Ullman. Starring Moe Howard, Larry Fine, Curly Howard, Theodore Lorch, Fred Kelsey, Joe Palma, Al Thompson, Victor Travers, Dorothy Vernon. Cinematography: Benjamin H. Kline. Editing by Charles Hochberg. Distributed by Columbia Pictures. Release: August 30, 1945. 18 minutes. (USA)

Casper the Friendly Ghost (A)
Directed by Izzy Sparber. Produced by Sam Buchwald. Written by Joseph Oriolo, Seymour Reit (book), Bill Turner, Otto Messmer (story adaptation). Voices by Frank Gallop. Distributed by Paramount Pictures. Release: November 16, 1945. 9 minutes. (USA)

Hair-Raising Hare (A)
Directed by Charles M. Jones. Produced by Eddie Selzer. Story by Tedd Pierce. Voices by Mel Blanc. Music by Carl W. Stalling. Animation by Ben Washam, Ken Harris, Basil Davidovich, Lloyd Vaughan. Distributed by Warner Bros. Pictures. Release: May 25, 1946 7 minutes. (USA)

The Great Piggy Bank Robbery (A)

Directed by Robert Clampett. Produced by Edward Selzer (uncredited). Written by Warren Foster. Voices by Mel Blanc. Distributed by Warner Bros. Pictures. Release: July 20, 1946. 8 minutes. (USA)

There's Good Boos Tonight (A)

Directed by Izzy Sparber. Writen by Larry Riley, Bill Turner. Voices by Frank Gallop. Distributed by Paramount Pictures. Release: April 23, 1948. 7 minutes. (USA)

Scaredy Cat (A)

Directed by Charles M. Jones. Produced by Eddie Selzer. Story by Michael Maltese. Voices by Mel Blanc. Music by Carl Stalling. Animation by Lloyd Vaughan, Ken Harris, Phil Monroe, Ben Washam. Distributed by Warner Bros. Pictures. Release: December 18, 1948. 7 minutes. (USA)

Dopey Dicks (LA)

Directed and Written by Edward Bernds. Produced by Hugh McCollum. Starring Moe Howard, Larry Fine, Shemp Howard, Christine McIntyre, Philip Van Zandt, Stanley Price. Cinematography: Rex Wimpy. Editing by Edwin H. Bryant. Distributed by Columbia Pictures. Release: March 2, 1950. 15 minutes. (USA)

Water, Water Every Hare (A)

Directed by Charles M. Jones. Produced by Eddie Selzer. Story by Michael Maltese. Voices by Mel Blanc, John T. Smith (uncredited). Music by Carl Stalling. Animation by Ben Washam, Ken Harris, Phil Monroe, Lloyd Vaughan. Distributed by Warner Bros. Pictures. Release: April 19, 1952. 7 minutes. (USA)

Trick or Treat (A)

Directed by Jack Hannah. Produced by Walt Disney. Written by Ralph Wright. Voices by June Foray, Clarence Nash. Distributed by RKO Radio Pictures. Release: October 10, 1952. 8 minutes. (USA)

Spooks! (LA)

Directed and Produced by Jules White. Written by Felix Adler. Starring Moe Howard, Larry Fine, Shemp Howard, Philip Van Zandt, Tom Kennedy, Norma Randall, Frank Mitchell. Distributed by Columbia Pictures. Release: July 15, 1953. 15 minutes. (USA)

Dr. Jerkyl's Hide (A)

Directed by Friz Freleng. Produced by Edward Selzer. Written by Warren Foster. Voices by Mel Blanc, Stan Freberg. Distributed by Warner Bros. Pictures. Release: May 8, 1954. 7 minutes. (USA)

Claws for Alarm (A)

Directed by Charles M. Jones. Produced by Eddie Seltzer. Story by Michael Maltese. Voices by Mel Blanc. Music by Carl Stalling. Distributed by Warner Bros. Pictures. Release: May 22, 1954. 7 minutes. (USA)

Satan's Waitin' (A)

Directed by Friz Freleng. Written by Warren Foster. Voices by Mel Blanc. Distributed by Warner Bros. Release: August 7, 1954. (USA)

Fright to the Finish (A)

Directed by Seymour Kneitel. Written by Jack Mercer. Voices by Jackson Beck, Jack Mercer, Mae Questel. Distributed by Paramount Pictures. Release: August 27, 1954

Jumpin' Jupiter (A)

Directed by Chuck Jones. Written by Michael Maltese. Voices by Mel Blanc. Distributed by Warner Bros. Release: August 6, 1955. 7 minutes. (USA)

The Flying Sorceress (A)

Directed and Produced by William Hanna, Joseph Barbera. Voices by June Foray (uncredited). Music by Scott Bradley. Animation by Ed Barge, Irven Spence, Lewis Marshall, Kenneth Muse. Distributed by MGM. Release: January 27, 1956. 7 minutes. (USA)

Broom-Stick Bunny (A)

Directed by Chuck Jones. Produced by Eddie Selzer. Story by Tedd Pierce. Voices by Mel Blanc, June Foray (uncredited). Music by Milt Franklyn. Animation by Richard Thompson, Ken Harris, Ben Washam, Abe Levitow. Distributed by Warner Bros. Pictures. Release: February 25, 1956. 7 minutes. (USA)

Bewitched Bunny (A)

Directed by Chuck Jones. Written by Michael Maltese. Voices by Mel Blanc, Bea Benaderet. Distributed by Warner Bros. Pictures. Release: July 24, 1956. (USA)

A Witch's Tangled Hare (A)

Directed by Abe Levitow. Written by Michael Maltese. Voices by Mel Blanc, June Foray. Distributed by Warner Bros. Pictures. Release: October 31, 1959. 6 minutes. (USA)

Hyde and Go Tweet (A)

Directed by Friz Freleng. Produced by David H. DePatie. Voices by Mel Blanc. Music by Milt Franklyn. Animation by Arthur Davis, Gerry Chiniquy, Virgil Ross. Distributed by Warner Bros. Pictures. Release: May 14, 1960. 7 minutes. (USA)

The Abominable Snow Rabbit (A)

Directed by Chuck Jones, Maurice Noble. Produced by John Burton. Story by Tedd Pierce. Voices by Mel Blanc. Music by Milt Franklyn. Animation by Philip DeGuard, Ken Harris, Tom Ray, Bob Bransford, Richard Thompson. Distributed by Warner Bros. Pictures. Release: May 20, 1961. 8 minutes. (USA)

Transylvania 6–5000 (A)

Directed by Chuck Jones, Maurice Noble. Written by John W. Dunn. Voices by Mel Blanc, Ben Frommer, Julie Bennett. Music by Bill Lava. Distributed by Warner Bros. Pictures. Release: November 30, 1963. 7 minutes. (USA)

Haunted Mouse (A)

Directed by Chuck Jones, Maurice Noble. Produced by Chuck Jones. Story by Jim Pabian, Chuck Jones. Voices by Mel Blanc. Music by Eugene Poddany. Animation by Ben Washam, Ken Harris, Don Towsley, Tom Ray, Dick Thompson. Distributed by MGM. Release: 1965. 7 minutes. (USA)

Vincent (A)

Directed and Written by Tim Burton. Produced by Rick Heinrichs. Narrated by Vincent Price. Music by Ken Hilton. Cinematography: Victor Abdalov. Distributed by Touchstone Home Video. Release: October 1, 1982. 6 minutes. (USA)

Frankenweenie (LA)

Directed by Tim Burton. Produced by Julie Hickson. Written by Tim Burton, Leonard Ripps. Starring Shelley Duvall, Daniel Stern, Barret Oliver. Music by Michael Convertino. David Newman. Cinematography: Thomas E. Ackerman. Editing by Ernest Milano. Distributed by Buena Vista Pictures. Release: December 14, 1984. 29 minutes. (USA)

Night of the Living Duck (A)

Directed by Greg Ford, Terry Lennon. Produced by Kathleen Helppie. Story by Greg Ford. Voices by Mel Blanc, Mel Tormé. Animation by Brenda Banks. Distributed by Warner Bros. Pictures. Release: September 23, 1988. 6 minutes. (USA)

Invasion of the Bunny Snatchers (A)

Directed and Written by Greg Ford, Terry Lennon. Voices by Jeff Bergman, Noel Blanc. Distributed by Warner Bros. Pictures. Release: 1992. 12 minutes. (USA)

Read Me a Story (LA)

Directed by Bret Mix, Craig Mullins. Written by Craig Mullins. Starring Rebekah Morrison, Gage Alexander Mullins, Conan Rapson. Distributed by Unfilmable Films. Release: 2005. 8 minutes. (USA)

BIBLIOGRAPHY

Books

Aykroyd, Dan, Harold Ramis, Don Shay, et al. *Making* Ghostbusters. New York: Zoetrope, 1985.
Butler, Ivan. *The Cinema of Roman Polanski*. New York: A. S. Barnes, 1970.
Calhoun, John. *The Penguin Encyclopedia of Horror and the Supernatural*, edited by Jack Sullivan. New York: Viking, 1986.
Campbell, Bruce. *If Chins Could Kill: Confessions of a B Movie Actor*. New York: Thomas Dunne Books/St. Martin's Press, 2001.
Corman, Roger (with Jim Jerome). *How I Made a Hundred Movies in Hollywood and Never Lost a Dime*. New York: Random House, 1990.
Hamilton, John. *Beasts in the Cellar: The Exploitation Film Career of Tony Tenser*. Goldalming, Surrey: FAB Press, 2005.
Hardy, Phil. *The Encyclopedia of Horror Films*. New York: Harper and Row, 1986.
Miglore, Andrew, and John Strysik. *The Lurker in the Lobby: A Guide to the Cinema of H. P. Lovecraft*. Portland, San Francisco: Night Shade Books, 2006.
Nollen, Scott Allen. *Boris Karloff: A Gentleman's Life*. Baltimore: Midnight Marquee Press, 1999.
Polanski, Roman. *Roman by Polanski*. New York: Morrow, 1984.
Price, Victoria. *Vincent Price: A Daughter's Biography*. New York: St. Martin's Press, 1999.
Rayns, Tony. *The Time Out Film Guide*. London: Penguin Books, 1991.
Rigby, Jonathan. *English Gothic: A Century of Horror Cinema*. London: Reynolds and Hearn, 2000.
Salisbury, Mark. *Tim Burton: Burton on Burton*. London: Faber and Faber, 2006.
Sangster, Jimmy. *Do You Want It Good or Tuesday? From Hammer Films to Hollywood! A Life in the Movies*. Baltimore: Midnight Marquee Press, 1997.
Story, Ronald D. *The Encyclopedia of Extraterrestrial Encounters*. New York: New American Library, 2001.

Newspapers and Periodicals

The New York Times (in chronological order)—
    August 24, 1920 (*The Bat*, Alexander Woollcott)
    February 8, 1922 (*The Cat and the Canary*, Alexander Woollcott)
    September 18, 1927 ("Mr. Leni's Clever Film," Mordaunt Hall)
    November 17, 1927 ("Park Zoo Monkeys See a Gorilla Movie," no byline)
    January 16, 1931 (*The Bat Whispers*, Mordaunt Hall)
    February 14, 1931 ("Projection Jottings," no byline)
    October 28, 1932 (*The Old Dark House*, Mordaunt Hall)
    November 29, 1938 ("Paramount Plans to Remake *The Cat and the Canary*," no byline)
    March 2, 1939 ("Delay *in The Dictator* Seen...," no byline)
    May 28, 1939 (*The Gorilla*, Thomas M. Pryor)
    November, 1939 (*The Cat and the Canary*, Frank S. Nugent)
    July 4, 1940 (*The Ghost Breakers*, Bosley Crowther)
    September 24, 1944 (*Arsenic and Old Lace*, P. P. K.)
    May 2, 1945 (*Zombies on Broadway*, Andy Webster)

March 14, 1948 ("Hollywood Digest," no byline)
July 29, 1948 ("That One Laugh," Bosley Crowther)
March 20, 1951 (*Abbott and Costello Meet the Invisible Man*, Thomas M. Pryor)
November 14, 1967 ("Polanski Disavows Vampire Film Cuts," no byline)
March 30, 1988 ("*Beetlejuice* Is Pap for the Eyes," Vincent Canby)
April 26, 1996 (*Cemetery Man*, Stephen Holden)
December 20, 1996 (*Scream*, Janet Maslin)
October 17, 1998 (*Bride of Chucky*, Lawrence Van Gelder)
July 7, 2000 (*Scary Movie*, A. O. Scott)

The San Francisco Examiner—
May 10, 1996 ("Cemetery Man," Bob Stephens)

Time magazine—
February 1, 1963 ("Ugly Contest," no byline).
September 14, 2001 ("The Age of Irony Comes to an End," Roger Rosenblatt)

Interviews by the Author

Bates, Ralph. Interview on WQBK-AM, Albany, NY, July 7, 1984. Published in *Little Shoppe of Horrors* April 9, 1986.

Combs, Jeffrey. Interview on WABK-AM, Albany, NY, June 10, 1991. Portions appeared in *Imagi-Movies* vol. 1, no. 3, spring, 1994.

Court, Hazel. Interviewed on WQBK-AM, Albany, NY, August 12, 1990. Published in *Little Shoppe of Horrors* October 16, 2004.

Munro, Caroline. Interviewed on WQBK-AM, Albany, NY, June 16, 1984.

Raimi, Sam. Published in *Metroland Magazine*, March 16, 1987.

DVD Commentaries and Liner Notes

Blood for Dracula, essay by Maurice Yacowar (Criterion)
The Carry On Collection, liner notes by Steven Paul Davies (Anchor Bay)
Critters, DVD liner notes, quotes by Stehen Herek (New Line)
Flesh for Frankenstein, essay by Maurice Yacowar (Criterion)
Gremlins 2, DVD commentary by Joe Dante (Warner Bros.)
The Old Dark House, commentary tracks by Gloria Stuart and James Curtis; interview with Curtis Harrington (Kino Video)
Re-Animator, DVD interview with Stuart Gordon (Anchor Bay)

INDEX

Abbott, Bruce 143, 172, 173, 174, 200
Abbott, Bud 35, 36
Abbott and Costello 31, 46–59, 79
Abbott and Costello Meet Dr. Jekyll and Mr. Hyde 55–57
Abbott and Costello Meet Frankenstein 35, 47–52, 86, 151
Abbott and Costello Meet the Invisible Man 52, 54, 55
Abbott and Costello Meet the Killer, Boris Karloff 52-53
Abbott and Costello Meet the Killers 52
Abbott and Costello Meet the Monsters 49
Abbott and Costello Meet the Mummy 57–59
The Abominable Dr. Phibes 94–96
Abrahams, Jim 196
Ace Ventura, Pet Detective 137
Ackerman, Forrest J 1, 120, 132
Adair, Jean 39, 41
Adams, Don 107
Adams, Jonathan 109, 110
Addams, Charles 67
The Addams Family 67, 169, 188
Adrian, Max 78
Adventures of a Rookie 46
Affleck, Ben 175
Agutter, Jenny 121, 122
Ahlber, Mac 149
Air Force One 196
Airplane! 185, 195, 196
Aisncough, Chris 207
Aldrich, Robert 107
Alexander, Anton 181
Alexander, John 41
Alfred Hitchcock Presents 156
Alibi 15
Alice 133
Alien 128, 140, 178
All Movie Guide 29
Altered States 165
Altman, John 120
Alvarez, Trini 189
Amarcord 102
American Graffiti 175
American Idol 196

An American in Paris 120
American-International Pictures 60–62, 64, 65, 66, 67, 69, 70, 71, 72, 73, 74, 75, 94, 95, 96, 116, 125
An American Werewolf in London 119–123, 141, 186, 189
Amicus Productions 75, 76, 77, 78, 118, 119
The Amityville Horror 134, 135
Anchor Bay 143, 182
And Then There Were None 112
Anderson, Eddie "Rochester" 28
Anderson, Pamela 196
Andreu, Simon 200
Andrews, Harry 98, 99
Andrews, V.C. 175
Andrews Sisters 35
The Andy Griffith Show 80
Andy Warhol's Frankenstein 101, 147
Angels with Dirty Faces 36
Ankers, Evelyn 35
Ansara, Michael 58
Anthony, Lysette 183, 184, 185
Antonioni, Michelangelo 102
Aranda, Vicente 200
Archer, John 33
Argento, Dario 159. 181
Arkoff, Samuel Z. 69, 97
Armstrong, Michael 125
Army of Darkness 178–180
Arnaz, Desi, Jr. 125
Arnold, Jack 17, 134
Arquette Courteney Cox 194
Arquette, David 175, 189, 190 194
Arsenic and Old Lace 38, 39, 40, 41, 42, 75
Ashfield, Kate 201
Aspinall, Jennfer 146
Astin, John 170, 188, 189
Astin, Sean 189
Atkins, Tom 150
Attack of the Crab Monsters 64, 206
Attack of the Giant Leeches 114
Attack of the Helping Hand 153
Attack of the Killer Tomatoes! 112
Atwill, Lionel 27, 31, 47, 108
Aubert, Lenore 49, 52

Avalon, Frankie 125
Avco-Embassy Pictures 132
The Avengers 83, 95, 98
Axton, Hoyt 133, 169
Aykroyd, Dan 127, 128, 129, 130
Aylmer, Felix 163

Babbitt, Harry 30
Bacon, Kevin 170, 171, 172
"Bad Moon Rising" 123
Bad Taste 187, 188, 203
Badham, John 183, 186
Baker, Rick 120, 121, 122, 169
Baker, Robert S. 67
Bakshi, Ralph 155
Baldwin, Alec 156
Ballatore, Thomas 136
Bamber, Judy 61
Bank, Ashley 151
Banner, Jill 86
Baptist, Jennifer 146
Barry, Jason 200
Barrymore, Drew 189, 190
Barrymore, John 31, 32
Bartel, Paul 123, 124, 170
Barton, Benita 114
Barton, Charles T. 48
Basket Case 162, 167
Bass, Alfie 82
Bassett, Angela 186
The Bat (1926) 9, 11, 12
The Bat (1959) 59, 60
The Bat (play) 6, 7, 12
The Bat Whispers 11, 15, 16, 17
Bates, Alan 165
Bates, Ralph 89, 90, 91, 143
Batman 155, 156
Batman Returns 157
Battle of Blood Island 65
Beal, John 24
Bean, Robert 66
Bear Island 94
Bearse, Amanda 137, 138, 139
The Beast Within 137
The Beastmaster 197
Beaudine, William 37
Beauman, Phil 194
Beddoe, Don 38
Beetlejuice 155–158, 188
Beetlejuice Goes Hawaiian 158

Beginning of the End 114
Begley, Ed, Jr. 123, 124
Belaski, Belinda 170
Beltran, Robert 123, 124
Belushi, John 127
Benjamin, Richard 116, 117
Benny, Jack 28, 41
Berman, Monty 67
Bernhard, Sandra 166
Bernstein, Elmer 123, 127
Berrando, Xavier 200
Berry, Sarah 154
Best, Willie 28, 29, 30, 32, 33
The Best of Abbott and Costello Volume Four 49
Beverly Hills Cop 134
Beverly Hills Vamp 186
Beyond Re-Animator 199–201
The Bicycle Thieves 105
The Big Trail 15
Biggers, Earl Derr 125
Bill and Ted's Excellent Adventure 149
Billy the Kid 15
The Birds 114
The Birth of a Nation 6
Black, Shane 151
"The Black Cat" 69, 70
The Black Cat 34, 35
Black Sheep 203–204
The Black Torment 81
Blackmail 20
Blacula 186
Blade Runner 175, 187
The Blair Witch Project 193, 194
Blaire, Jennifer 207
Blamire, Larry 204, 205, 206, 207
Blazing Saddles 105, 107, 136
Blees, Robert 96
Bloch, Robert 3, 78, 208
Blood for Dracula 103–105, 110
Blood of the Vampire 67
Blood Simple 148
The Blood-Spattered Bride 200
Bloodbath at the House of Death 134–135
Bloodsucking Freaks 146
Bloom, Claire 177
Blow-Up 102
"Blue Moon" 123
The Blues Brothers 120
Bodden, Alonzo 196
Bogart, Humphrey 66, 112
Bond, Lilian 18, 19, 20, 21, 22
The Boogie Man Will Get You 38, 39
Boone, Pat 69
Bostwick, Barry 109, 110
Bottin, Rob 1222
Bowery Blitzkrieg 36
Bowie, David 109, 111
Boyd, Billy 192
Boyle, Danny 201
Boyle, Peter 108
Boys Don't Cry 175

Boys of the City 36
Bradbury, Ray 159
Brady, Scott 134
Brain Damage 162–163, 167
The Brain of Frankenstein 48
Braindead 187, 188, 201, 203
Bram Stoker's Dracula 137, 183, 185
Brandner, Gary 132
Brando, Marlon 111
Bray Studios 67, 68, 110
Bresslaw, Bernard 79
Briant, Shane 199
Bricker, George 23
Bride of Chucky 190–192
Bride of Frankenstein 22, 108, 172, 192
Bride of Re-Animator 172–174
The Brides of Dr. Phibes 97
The Brides of Dracula 63, 69, 110, 138
Bridge on the River Kwai 98
Brightman, Sarah 160
Brissac, Virginia 29
Brokeback Mountain 196
Broken Blossoms 6
Bronson Canyon 206
Brooks, Mel 105, 106, 107. 108, 109, 135, 183, 184, 185, 186, 195
Broughton, Bruce 151
Brown, Joe I. 73
Brown, Wally 46, 47
Browne, Coral 98, 99, 100, 101
Browning, Tod 48, 86, 183
Brownlow, Kevin 12
Bruce, Nigel 185
Bruce, Virginia 31, 32
Bubba Ho-Tep 197–199
Bubba Nosferatu: Curse of the She-Vampires 199
Buck Privates 35
Buck Privates Come Home 48
A Bucket of Blood 60–62, 64, 65, 114, 206
Buffy the Vampire Slayer 174–177
Bugs Bunny 134, 169, 170
Bull, Peter 67
Burke, Frankie 36
Burnham, Edward 95
Burroughs, Edgar Rice 118
Burton, Julian 61
Burton, Tim 115, 155, 156, 157, 158
Bury, Sean 95, 96
Busey, Jake 188, 189
Butler, David 30
Byrne, Gabriel 165

The Cabinet of Dr. Caligari 5
Caesar, Sid 107
The Caesars 89
Cahn, Edward L. 158
Calfa, Don 140, 141
Calhoun, Rory 119

Cambridge, Godfrey 34
Cameron, Ray 135
Caminnecci, Pier A. 92
Campbell, Bruce 4, 152, 153, 154, 155, 177, 178, 179, 180, 197, 198, 199, 203
Campbell, J. Kenneth 160
Campbell, Neve 189, 190, 193, 194, 195
Canby, Vincent 158
Candido, Candy 58
Candy, John 127
The Canterville Ghost 42, 43
Capaldi, Peter 166
Capote, Truman 112
Capra, Frank 38, 39, 40, 134
Carbone, Antony 66, 67
Carey, Harry, Jr. 134
Carillo, Leo 45
Carlson, Richard 28, 29, 35
Carlson, Veronica 90, 91
Carmen, Jewel 11
Carmichael, Ian 118
"Carmilla" 92
Carminati, Tulliio 11
Carney, Alan 46, 47
Carpenter, John 150, 189, 190
Carradine, David 178, 202, 203
Carradine, Ever 203
Carradine, John 40, 125, 126, 138
Carreras, James 89
Carrey, Jim 136, 137, 166
Carrie 125, 149
Carry On Cleo 78
Carry On films 67, 78, 79, 80
Carry On Screaming! 78–80
Carry On Sergeant 78
Carry On Spying 78
Carson, Jack 42
Carter, Finn 171, 172
Carter, Michael 120
Carter, Nina 120
The Case of Charles Dexter Ward 142
Casino Royale 160
"The Cask of Amontillado" 69
Cassidy, Joanna 186, 187
Castaway 166
Castle, Roy 77
Castle, William 67, 68, 69, 86, 170, 193
Castle of Blood 102
Castle of Evil 134
The Cat and the Canary 7, 11
The Cat and the Canary (1939) 24, 25, 26, 28
The Cat and the Canary (play) 11, 12
Cat People 73
Cater, John 95, 96
Cates, Phoebe 133, 169, 170
Cates, Steve 114
Catlett, Walter 44
Cavett, Dick 156
Cemetery Man 180–183

Chamberlain, Richard 165
Chan, Charlie 33, 34, 112
Chaney, Lon 9
Chaney, Lon, Jr. 45, 48, 50, 86, 87
Chaplin, Charlie 24, 84
Charlie Chan in the Secret Service 33
Chase, Charley 55
Chase, Chevy 123
The Cheap Detective 112
Cheers 119, 149
Chetwynd-Hayes, R. 118
La Chiesa 181
Child's Play 190, 191, 192
Child's Play 2 191
Child's Play 3 191
Chiodo, Charles 158, 159
Chiodo, Edward 158, 159
Chiodo, Stephen 158, 159, 207
Christie, Agatha 112
The Church 181
Cimino, Leonardo 151
The Cinema of Roman Polanski 83
Citizen Kane 165
Citizen Toxie: The Toxic Avenger IV 147
City of the Dead 69
Clampett, Robert 134, 169
"Clarimonde" 92, 93
Clark, Candy 175
Clash of the Titans 151
Class of 1984 137
Class of Nuke 'Em High 147
Cleopatra 78
Cline, Charles 17
Cline, Edward F. 44
The Cloak 78
Close Encounters of the Third Kind 134
"Close Your Eyes" 96
Coco, James 112
Coen, Ethan 148
Coen, Joel 148
Cohan, George M. 125
Cohen, Mitch 146
The Colgate Comedy Hour 55
Columbia Pictures 38, 39. 68, 128, 131, 137, 183
Columbus, Chris 132
Combs, Jeffrey, 143, 144, 145, 172, 173, 174, 188, 189
The Comedy of Terrors 73–75
Compton-Cameo 81
The Confessional 125
A Connecticut Yankee in King Arthur's Court 180
Connery, Sean 180
Connor, Kenneth 67
Connor, Kevin 118, 119
Conroy, Dan 205, 206, 207
Convy, Bert 61
Cooper, Gladys 34
Coote, Robert 98, 99

Copper Mountain 136
Coppola, Francis Ford 86, 183
Corbett, Harry H. 79
Corby, Ellen 81
Corey, Jeff 30
Corman, Gene 206
Corman, Roger 60, 62, 64–67, 69–73, 98, 114, 123, 131–133, 142, 149, 177, 178, 206, 207
Cornthwaite, Robert 81
Cortez, Stanley 35
Cosby, Bill 34
Coscarelli, Don 197, 198, 199
Costello, Lou 35, 36
Cotten, Joseph 95
Count Dracula 183
Count Yorga Vampire 138
Court, Hazel 70, 71, 72, 90, 178
Cowell, Simon 196
Cox, Courteney 189, 190
Coyote, Peter 142
Crack in the World 93
Cramer, Grant 159
Crampton, Barbara 145, 200
Craven, Wes 148, 174, 175, 186, 187, 189, 190, 193, 194
Crawford, Broderick 34
The Crawling Eye 67
Crazy House 44
Creature from the Black Lagoon 48, 171
Creature from the Haunted Sea 65–67, 114
Creber, Lewis 27
Creedence Clearwater Revival 123
Creeping Vine 77
Creepy 75
Crimes of Passion 165
Critters 147–149, 207
Cromwell, James 112
Cronenberg, David 156, 162
Cronjager, Edward 27
Crosby, Floyd 73
Crouse, Russell 38
Crowther, Bosley 29, 49, 53, 83, 84
Cruise, Tom 194, 197
Cul-de-Sac 82
Cunningham Sean S. 149
The Curse of Frankenstein 88, 110, 142
Curse of the Demon 110
Curse of the Fly 93
Cushing, Peter 63, 75, 76, 88, 89, 95, 97, 125, 126, 127, 137, 138, 142, 143, 174, 199, 200, 201
Cymbeline 98

Daffy Duck 169, 170
Dahl, Roald 132
Dale, Jim 79
Dallesandro, Joe 102, 103, 104, 105
D'Amato, Joe 181

Damon, Matt 175
Dance of the Vampires 83, 84
Danger Lights 15
The Danny Thomas Show 46
Dano, Royal 159
Dante, Joe 122, 123, 131, 132, 133, 134, 148, 168, 169, 170, 188
A Dark and Stormy NIght 207
Darkman 178
Darro, Frankie 32
Dassin, Jules 42
Davidz, Embeth 180
Davis, Geena 156, 158
Davis, Joan 35
Davis, Lucy 201
Davis, Ossie 197, 198, 199
Davis, Sammi 166
Dawn of the Dead 118, 140, 201
Dawson's Creek 189
Day, John 55
Day, Richard 27
The Day of the Triffids 110
The Day the Earth Stood Still 110
Deacon, Richard 58
Dead Alive 187. 203
Dead and Breakfast 201–202
Dead End Kids 36
"The Dead Leman" 92
Deadly Friend 175
The Dean Martin Show 107
Death Race 2000 124
De Bello, John 114, 115
Dee, Sandra 142
Deep Throat 88
Degermark, Pia 92, 93
Dekker, Fred 149, 150, 151, 152
De Laurentiis, Dino 152, 178, 179
Deliria 181
Dell, Gabriel 36, 37, 38
Dellamorte Dellamore 180, 181
De Luca, Joseph 180
De Luca, Rudy 156, 183
Demme, Jonathan 179
Deneuve, Catherine 82
Denny, Reginald 57
De Palma, Brian 111
Depp, Johnny 190
Derek, Bo 160
de Sica, Vittorio 104
Destry Rides Again 107
Devil and the Deep 20
The Devil Rides Out 110
The Devils 165
Devil's Daughter 181
Devine, Andy 45
The Dick Van Dyke Show 23
Dickerson, Beach 66
The Dickies 159
Die Monster Die! 142
Dietrich, Marlene 107
Di Lazzaro, Dalila 102
Dillon, C.J. 114
Dillon, Costa 114
Dimension Films 194, 195, 196, 197

Dinosaur Valley Girls 120
Disembodied Hand 77, 78
Disney, Walt 9, 155
Dix, Richard 125
Do You Want It Good or Tuesday? 88, 89
Doctor Blood's Coffin 69
Dr. Jekyll and Sister Hyde 89, 97
Dr. Phibes Rises Again 96–98
Dr. Terror's House of Horrors 75–78, 92, 175
Doctor X 110
Donnell, Jeff 38
Donohoe, Amanda 164, 165, 166
Dors, Diana 98
Douglas, Angela 79
Douglas, Gordon 46, 170
Douglas, Melvyn 18, 29, 20, 21, 22
Dourif, Brad 192
Downes, Terry 83
Dracula (1931) 15, 24, 183
Dracula (play) 116
Dracula AD 1972 116
Dracula: Dead and Loving It 117, 183–186
Dracula 1979 183, 186
Dragoti, Stan 116
Dreamgirls 187
Drew, Linzi 120
DuBrey, Claire 52
Dudgeon, Elspeth 18, 22, 23
Duncan, Archie 69
Dunne, Griffin 120
The Dunwich Horror 142
Durand, David 36
d'Usseau, Arnaud 93
Duvall, Shelley 155
Dwan, Allan 26, 27
Dyall, Valentine 69
"Dylan Dog" 180

E.T. 134, 148, 151, 188
Ealing Studios 201, 202
East Side Kids 36
East Side Kids 36, 37, 38
EastEnders 120
Eastwood, Clint 160, 196
Easy Does It 52
Eating Raoul 123–125, 170
Eaton, Shirley 67
Ebert, Roger 148
Eburne, Maude 38
EC Comics 119
Edeson, Arthur 20
Edison, Thomas 5
Edlund, Richard 128, 138, 139, 151
Edward Scissorhands 157
Egan, Sam 161
Eisner, Ken 207
Ekland, Britt 109
Eldredge, John 22
Electra, Carmen 197
"The Elemental" 118

Elfman, Danny 156, 180
Elmer Fudd 126
"Elmer's Tune" 96
Elvira, Mistress of the Dark 160–162
Elvira's Movie Macabre 161
The Encyclopedia of Extraterrestrial Encounters 147
English, Louise 126
English Gothic 91
Entertaining Mr. Sloan 100
Epstein, Julius J. 42
Epstein, Philip G. 42
Equinox 152
Eraserhead 86
Erickson, Hal 29
Ermey, W. Lee 188
The Evening Standard 82
Everett, Kenny 135
Everett, Rupert 181, 182, 183
Everybody Loves Raymond 108
The Evil Dead 148, 151, 202
Evil Dead 2: Dead by Dawn 152–155, 178, 179, 180
The Exorcist 125
The Exploits of Elaine 12
Eye of the Devil 82

Faber, Robert 47
The Face of Fu Manchu 93
Fahrenheit 9/11 196
Falchi, Anna 181, 182, 183
Falk, Peter 112, 113, 114
Falling Hare 134, 169
Falwell, Jerry 162
Famous Monsters of Filmland 1, 120, 131, 132, 138
A Farewell to Arms 153
Faris, Anna 195
Fast Times at Ridgemont High 133
Faustino, Michael 151
Fazenda, Louise 11
The Fearless Vampire Killers 81–86, 92, 96, 185, 186, 195
Feeney, Peter 203
Feldman, Marty 106, 107
Fellini, Federico 102
Fernandez, Julio 200
Ferris Bueller's Day Off 156
Fetchit, Stepin 32, 33
Fiander, Lewis 97
Fiddler on the Roof 83
Fielding, Fenella 67, 79
Fiend Without a Face 207
"The Fifty Worst Horror Movies Ever Made" 131
Filmways 82
Fimbrug, Hal 38
Finch, Jon 91
Finnell, Mike 132
Fisher, Terence 63, 69, 110, 183
Fitzroy, Emily 11
Flash Gordon 110
Flesh and Blood 175
The Flesh and Blood Show 125

The Flesh and the Fiends 67
Flesh for Frankenstein 101–103, 110, 147
Florey, Robert 18
Flowers in the Attic 175
The Fly (1986) 156
The Fog 150
Fonda, Bridget 180
Forbes, Louis 60
Forbidden Planet 110, 134
Ford, Allan 120
Foreman, Carl 36
Foreman, Deborah 160, 177
Fort, Garrett 18
Fox, Michael J. 188, 189
Fox, Tom 140
Fox, Wallace 36
Francis, Freddie 75, 76, 92, 93
Franco, Jesus 183
Frankenhooker 167–168
Frankenstein (1910) 5
Frankenstein (1931) 17, 18, 20, 24, 151, 155
Frankenstein (novel) 142, 165, 167
Frankenstein and the Monster from Hell 199, 200, 201
Frankenweenie 155, 156
Franz, Arthur 52, 54
Frawley, WIlliam 55
Freaks 86
Freeman, Morgan 196
Frees, Paul 96
The French Connection 108
Friday the 13th 136, 149
Friedberg, Jason 194
Fright Night 128, 137–139, 151, 183, 191
Fright Night II 139
Fritzell, James 80
Frost, Nick 201
Fry, Rick 172
Frye, Dwight 17, 102, 116, 183
Fuest, Robert 95, 96, 97, 98
Full Metal Jacket 156, 188
Fulton, John P. 31
The Funhouse 118

Gaines, William M. 78
Gale, David 145, 172, 173, 174
Galeen, Henrik 12
Gallalher, Donald 22
Galligan, Zack 133, 160, 169, 170, 177, 178
Gardner, Ava 37
Garr, Teri 107, 108
Garrett, Betty 206
Gaunt, Valerie 185
The Gautierophile 92
Geffen, David 156
Geiger, Trish 207
Gellar, Sarah Michelle 175, 190, 196
Genius at Work 37
Geoffreys, Stephen 137, 138, 139

Get Smart 107
The Ghost and Mr. Chicken 80–81
The Ghost Breaker (1914) 5
The Ghost Breaker (1922) 5, 6, 10
The Ghost Breaker (play) 5
The Ghost Breakers 28–32
Ghost Catchers 43–46
The Ghost Creeps 36, 37
Ghostbusters 127–131, 134, 188
Ghostbusters II 131
Ghosts in the Night 36
Ghosts on the Loose 37–38
The Ghoul 67
Gillespie, Dana 118
Gilligan's Island 207
Gilmore, Peter 95
Glover, Julian 120
Glut, Donald F. 120
Goddard, Paulette 24, 25, 26, 28, 29, 30
Godfrey, Derek 95
Godunov, Alexander 178
Goetz, William 47
Gogos, Basil 138
The Golden Disc 93
The Golden Voyage of Sinbad 95
Goldfinger 180
Goldsmith, Jerry 134
Goldstein, William 94
Gomez, Jose Manuel 200
The Good, the Bad and the Ugly 202
Good Will Hunting 175
Gorcey, Leo 36, 37
Gordon, Gavin 60
Gordon, Mary 31
Gordon, Stuart 142, 143, 144, 145, 172, 174, 200, 201
Gorey, Edward 157
The Gorilla (1927) 13, 14, 22
The Gorilla (1939) 26, 27
Gothic 165
Gough, Michael 67, 77, 78
Goulet, Robert 156
Gower, Andre 151
Grant, Arthur 68
Grant, Cary 39, 40, 41, 42
Grant, Hugh 163
Grant, John 35, 48, 52, 55
Grant, Kirby 46
Gray, Charles 109, 110
The Great Dictator 24
Great Expectations 47
Green, Alfred 5
Green Bush, Billy 148
Green Pastures 28
Greenbaum, Everett 80, 81
Greene, Michelle 166
Greenwood, Joan 79
Gremlins 131–134, 148, 168
Gremlins 2: The New Batch 168–170
Grenfell, Joyce 67
Greville-Bell, Anthony 99, 100
Griffith, Chuck 66

Griffith, D.W. 6, 11, 12
Griffith, Hugh 96
Gross, Michael 171
Gross, Milt 44
The Grudge 196
Guerra, Tonino 102
Guild, Nancy 54
Guinness, Alec 112
Gulager, Clu 140
Gutowski, Gene 81
Gwillim, Jack 151
Gwynn, Michael 67
Gwynne, Anne 34

Haas, Charles S. 169
Hackman, Gene 108
Hadji-Lazaro, Fancois 181
Haig, Sid 86
Haines, Donald 36
Hale, Creighton 12, 13, 14
Hall, Charles D. 20
Hall, Huntz 36, 37
Hall, Mordaunt 13, 17, 21
Hall, Regina 195, 197
Haller, Daniel 73
Halloween 11, 136, 150, 189, 190
Halop, Billy 36
Hamilton, George 115, 116, 117
Hamilton, Margaret 31, 133
Hamlet 47
Hamm, Sam 156
Hampton, Grayce 17
Happy Days 15
Hardison, Kadeem 186
Hardy, Phil 5, 17, 21, 85
Hardy, Robert 94
Harlem on the Prairie 32
Harrington, Curtis 22
Harris, Julie 178
Harry Potter 167
Harryhausen, Ray 155, 180, 206
Hauer, Rutger 175, 176
The Haunted Grande 7
The Haunted House of Horror 125
The Haunted Palace 142
The Haunting (1963) 177, 203
Hause, Jeffrey 136
Hawkins, Jack 98, 99
Hawtrey, Charles 79
Hayden, Harry 52
Haze, Jonathan 64, 65
Head 107
The Headless Horseman 8, 9
The Health Club Horror 146
Hearst, Rick 162, 163
Heavenly Creatures 188
Heggie, O.P. 108
The Hellfire Club 67
Hellman, Monte 86
Hellzapoppin 43
Hemingway, Ernest 153
Henderson, Graham 140
Hendricks, Ben, Jr. 8, 9
Hendry, Ian 98, 99, 100
Henenlotter, Frank 162, 163

Henry VI Part 1 98
Henson, Nicky 93
Hepburn, Katharine 113
Herbert, Hugh 22, 23, 24, 34
"Herbert West: Reanimator" 142, 143
Herbst, Rick 162
Herek, Stephen 147, 148, 149
Herevey, Jason 151
Herman, Pee-Wee 156, 175
Herz, Michael 147
Herzog, Werner 116, 138
Hickox, Anthony 160, 177, 178
Hickox, Douglas 99. 100, 160
Higgins, Kenneth 37
High Noon 36
Hill, Jack 86, 87
Hines, David 136
Hinwood, Peter 109
Hired Wife 31
Hirschfeld, Gerald 108
A History of the World Part One 135
Hitchcock, Alfred 53, 63, 91, 103, 114, 123, 137, 138
Hogan, Hulk 170
Hold That Ghost 35, 36, 44
Holden, Stephen 182
Holiday, Polly 133
Holland, Tom 137, 138, 139, 190, 191
Hollywood Boulevard 124, 132
Homeier, Skip 81
Homolka, Oscar 31, 32
Hooper, Tobe 118, 119, 140
Hope, Bob 24, 25, 26, 28, 29, 30, 32, 40, 52
Hopton, Russell, 18
Hornblow, Arthur, Jr. 24
Horne, Victoria 52
Horror Express 93
Horror Hotel 69
Horror of Dracula 63, 137, 138, 183, 185
The Horror of Frankenstein 88–91, 143
Horror of It All 69
The Horror Show 149
Horton, Edward Everett 42
House 149
House II: The Second Story 149
House III 149
House IV 149
House Ghosts 158
House of Dracula 49, 50, 138
House of the Long Shadows 125–127, 149
House of Usher 69
House of Wax 59, 61
House of Whipcord 125
House on Haunted Hill 50, 67, 86
How Green Was My Valley 137
How I Made a Hundred Movies in Hollywood and Never Lost a Dime 60–62, 66

Howard, Curly 181
Howard, John 31, 32
Howard, Shemp 31, 32, 35, 155
Howe, Brian 206, 207
The Howling 122, 148, 169, 170, 188
Hudson, Ernie 127
Hughes, John 156
Hull, Josephine 39, 41
Hume, Alan 75, 78, 79, 138
Hummel, Karl-Heinz 92
The Hunchback of Notre Dame (1923) 12
The Hunger 92
Hunt, Gareth 135
Hunt, Robert B. 38
Hunter, Richard 126
Hutton, Lauren 136, 137

I Know What You Did Last Summer 194
I Love Lucy 55
I Walked with a Zombie 46, 47
Ichabod and Mr. Toad 9
Ichabod Crane 3, 8, 9
If Chins Could Kill: Confessions of a B Movie Actor 179
I'm Gonna Git You Sucka 194
Imagi-Movies 143
In Cold Blood 112
In Living Color 194
In the Navy 35
The Incredible Shrinking Man 134
Independence Day 188
Indiana Jones and the Temple of Doom 131, 134
Internet Movie DataBase 1
Interview with the Vampire 137
Intolerance 6
Invasion of the Body Snatchers (1956) 207
Invasion of the Body Snatchers (1978) 175
Invasion of the Saucer Men 158
The Invisible Man 18, 30, 110
The Invisible Woman 30, 31, 32
Ireland, John 178
Irish Luck 32
Irving, Washington 3, 5, 8, 9
It 208
It! 137
It Came from Outer Space 110
It Conquered the World 64
"It May Look Like a Walnut" 23
"It's a Good Life" 107
It's a Wonderful Life 134

Jackson, Glenda 165
Jackson, Pat 67
Jackson, Michael 196
Jackson, Peter 187–189, 202
Jaffe, Robert 119
Jaffe, Steven-Charles 119
Jagger, Mick 111
James, Graham 91

James, Sydney 67
Jameson, Joyce 69, 70, 73
"The Jar" 156
Jason and the Argonauts 180
Jaws 132, 171
Jayne, Jennifer 78
Jean, Gloria 44
Jeffreys, Anne 46, 47
Jeffries, Lionel 122
Jenkins, Allen 22, 23, 24
Jeopardy! 196
The Jerry Springer Show 167
The Jim World's Greatest 197
Jodorowsky, Alejandro 111
Joe 108
John, Elton 111
Johns, Mervyn 67
Johnson, Arte 116, 117
Johnson, Buddy 194
Johnson, Chic 43, 44, 45, 46
Johnson, Michelle 160
Johnson, Noble 28, 29
Johnson, Richard 177
Jolie, Angelina 194
Jones, Chuck 134, 170
Jones, Claude 172, 173
Jones, Darby 46, 47
Jones, Freddie 199
Jones, James Earl 196
Jones, Jeffrey 156
Jones, Kevin F. 207
Jones, Norman 95
Jones, Spike 43
Jones-Moreland, Betsy 66
Jordan, Bobby 36, 37
Joseph, Jackie 64, 65, 133, 169
Journey's End 19
Jovan, Slavitza 128
Joy, Nicholas 52
Juerging, Arno 102, 103, 104
Julius Caesar 98
June, Ray 15

Kabibble, Ish 30
Kahn, Madeline 107
Kane, Bob 11, 17
Karen, James 140, 141, 206
Karloff, Boris 17–22, 30, 34, 38, 39, 48, 52, 53, 55–57, 67, 70–75, 108, 178
Katt, William 140
Katzman, Sam 36
Kaufman, Lloyd 146, 147
Kaufmann, Maurice 95, 96
Kay, Edward J. 33
Keaton, Michael 156, 157, 158
Keeslar, Matt 194
Keith, Ian 48
Keith, Woody 172
Kelly, Patsy 27
Kelly, Victoria 204
"Kelly-Hopkinsville creatures" 147, 148
Kelso, Edmond 33
Kemmer, Joachim 92

Kemp, Martin 177
Kemp, Valli 96
Kennedy, Jamie 189, 190
Kennedy, John F. 197, 198, 199
Kent, Robert E. 47
Kentucky Fried Movie 120
Kesselring, Joseph 38, 39, 42
Kevan, Jack 48
Kier, Udo 102, 103, 104, 105
Kiger, Robby 151
Kilar, Wojciech 185
Kill Bill 203
Kill Bill Volume 2 203
Killer Klowns from Outer Space 158–159
The Killing of Sister George 98
Kimble, Lawrence 47
Kind Hearts and Coronets 53, 91, 98, 201
King, Jonathan 203, 204
King, Stephen 119, 120, 152, 208
The King Is Dead: Tales of Elvis Post-Mortem 197
King Kong (1933) 112, 120, 187
King Kong (2005) 189
King of the Zombies 32, 33, 34
Kingpin 81
Kinski, Klaus 116
Kismet 15
Kiss Me Deadly 107
The Kiss of the Vampire 75, 85, 93, 138
Knife in the Water 81, 84
Knotts, Don 80, 81
Kohn, John 99, 100
Komeda, Krzysztof 85
Kopins, Karen 136, 137
Korman, Harvey 185
Kruger, Ehren 193, 194
Kubrick, Stanley 4, 156, 188
Kuzui, Fran Rubel 175, 176, 177
Kyser, Kay 30

Lackey, Skip 136
Ladd, Alan 34
The Ladykillers 201
The Lair of the White Worm 163–166
Lambert, Ryan 151
Lambton, John 163
Lamont, Charles 55, 56, 57, 58
Lanchester, Elsa 112, 113
Land of the Dead 201
Land Sharks 171
Land That Time Forgot 118
Landers, Lew 38
Landis, John 119, 120, 121, 122, 123, 131, 178, 186, 189
Lane, Charles 31
Lane, Lenita 59
Lane, Priscilla 40
Lang, Charles 29
Langella, Frank 116, 183
Lansdale, Joe R. 197
Lantz, Walter 49

La Plante, Laura 12, 13, 14
Lasky, Jesse L. 5
Lassie Come Home 137
The Last House on the Left 186, 187
Last Tango in Paris 111
The Last Woman on Earth 65
Latifah, Queen 196
Laughton, Charles 18, 19, 20, 21, 22, 42, 43
Lawrence, Marc 35
Leachman, Cloris 107, 108
Lean, David 47
Lee, Ang 196
Lee, Christopher 75, 77, 78, 85, 93, 116, 125, 126, 127, 138, 163, 166, 169, 170, 183
Lees, Robert 31, 34, 35, 48, 55
Le Fanu, L. Sheridan 92
The Legend of Hell House 134, 137
"The Legend of Sleepy Hollow" 3, 5
The Legend of the Seven Golden Vampires 116
Leighton, Margaret 118
Leni, Paul 12, 13, 14
Lenz, Kay 149
Leonard, Sheldon 46
Lethal Weapon 151
Leutwyler, Matthew 201, 202
Levy, Benn W. 18, 20
Lewis, Al 169
Lewis, Fiona 82, 84, 96
Lewis, Jerry 29, 57
Lewis, Michael J. 101
Lewis, Ted 35
Lewton, Val 46, 122
Lights Out 75
Lindsay, Howard 38
Linke, Paul 119
Little, Cleavon 136, 137
Little Miss Marker 28
The Little Shop of Horrors 64–65, 114, 133, 160
Live and Let Die 98
Lively, Gerry 160
Lively, Jason 150
Loftus, Cecilia 34
Logan's Run 122
London Cannon Films 125
The Lone Star Vigilantes 36
Looney Tunes 126, 134
Loonies on Broadway 46
Lord Byron 165
Lord of the Rings 155, 187, 188, 189
Lorenzen, Coral 147
Lorenzen, Jim 147
Lorinz, James 167, 168
Lorre, Peter 30, 33, 38, 39, 40, 41, 42, 69, 70, 71, 72, 73, 74, 75, 178
Los Angeles Herald Examiner 75
The Lost Boys 137

The Lost Skeleton of Cadavra 204–206, 207
The Lost Skeleton Returns Again 207
Louise, Anita 26, 27
Love at First Bite 115–117, 137, 185
Lovecraft, H.P. 142, 143, 144, 145, 149, 152, 153, 172, 173, 174
Lowe, Arthur 98, 99
Lowry, Jennifer 162
Loy, Myrna 112
Lubin, Arthur 35
Lucas 156
Lugosi, Bela 18, 24, 26, 27, 30, 33, 34, 36, 37, 46, 47, 48, 49, 50, 51, 52, 116, 183, 185
Lukas, Paul 28
Luke, Keye 133, 169
Lurker in the Lobby: A Guide to the Cinema of H.P. Lovecraft 142, 143, 144
Lynch, David 86
Lynch, Vernon 186
Lynskey, Melanie 187

MacBride, Donald 31
MacDonald, Gordon 162
MacGowran, Jack 82, 84
MacKay, Michael Reid 151
MacLean, Alastair 94
Macnee, Patrick 160, 177, 178
MacNicol, Peter 183, 184, 185
The Mad Magician 60
Mad Max: Beyond Thunderdome 36
Mad TV 196
Maddock, Brent 171
Madsen, Michael 197
The Magnificent Ambersons 35
Making Ghostbusters 127
Mamoulian, Rouben 57
Man of La Mancha 98
Mancini, Don 190, 191, 192
Mandel, Howie 134
Manfredini, Harry 149
The Manhattan Transfer 207
Manion, Cindy 146
Mann, Hummie 185
Mann, Stanley 99, 100
Mann, Terrence 148
La Manoir du Diable 5
The Manster 180
March, Frederic 57
Marion, Charles R. 36
Mark of the Devil 125
Mars, Kenneth 108
Mars Attacks! 158
Marsh, Terence 136
Marshall, George 28, 29
Marshall, Steve 150
Marshall, William 186
Martin, Alison 206, 207
Martin, Dean 29, 57
Martin and Lewis 203

Marty Feldman's Comedy Machine 107
Marvel Comics 147
Marx, Groucho 115, 130, 162
MASH 88
The Mask 137
Maslin, Janet 190
Mason, Danielle 204
Masque of the Red Death 73, 178
Massaccesi, Aristide 181
Massey, Raymond 18, 19, 20, 21, 22, 39, 40, 41, 42
Matheson, Richard 69, 70, 71, 73, 134
Mathews, Thom 140
The Matrix 194
Matthews, Francis 143
May, Bradford 151
May, Joe 31
Mayall, Rik 120
Mayne, Ferdy 82, 85, 92, 93
Mazin, Craig 196
McCarthy, Jenny 194, 196
McCarthy, Kevin 132, 134, 206
McClurg, Edie 162
McDowall, Roddy 137, 138, 139
McDowell, Michael 156
McEntire, Reba 171
McGann William C. 22
McGowan, Rose 189, 190
McGraw, Dr. Phil 197
McLeod, Norman Z. 43
Meat Loaf 109
Meet the Feebles 187
Meister, Nathan 203
Méliès, Georges 5
Melly, Andree 69, 84
Menzies, William Cameron 11
The Merchant of Venice 98
Meredith, Lois 8, 9
Merrie Melodies 169
Metroland 153
Metzler, Jim 178
Meyer, Russ 160, 161
MGM 82
Midnight Movies: From Margin to Mainstream 109
Migliore, Andrew 142
Mikuska, Drew 196
Miles, Art 27
Miller, David 114
Miller, Dick 61, 62, 64, 65, 132, 133, 169, 206
Million Dollar Baby 175, 196
Miner, Steve 149
Miramax Films 195
Mr. Holland's Opus 149
Mr. Washington Goes to Town 32
Mitchel, Mary 86
Mizzy, Vic 81
Moll, Richard 149
The Monkees 107
Monlaur, Yvonne 84
Monogram Pictures 32, 33, 34, 36

The Monster 9
The Monster Squad 151–152
The Monster That Challenged the World 171
Montez, Maria 31
Montgomery, Douglass 24
Monty Python 43, 112
Monty Python's Flying Circus 203
"Moondance" 123
Moore, Eva 19, 21
Moore, Michael 196
Moore, Robert 112
Moore, Roger 98
Moorehead, Agnes 59, 60
Moran, Dylan 201
Moranis, Rick 127, 128, 131
Moreland, Mantan 32, 33, 34
Morell, Andre 160
Morley, Robert 67, 98, 99, 100
Morris, Barboura 61
Morris, Chester 16, 17
Morris, John 108
Morrison, Van 123
Mortimer, Emily 194
Moss, Edward 196
Mostel, Zero 107
Motel Hell 118–119
Mowbray, Alan 52
Mrs. Doubtfire 116
Much Ado About Murder 100
Muir, Domonic 148
Muir, Gavin 54
Mullen, Patty 167, 168
The Mummy (1959) 163
The Mummy's Curse 57
The Mummy's Shroud 160
Munro, Caroline 95
The Munsters 81, 169
Murder by Death 112–114
Murders in the Zoo 31
Murnau, F.W. 84, 116
Murphy, Charles Q. 186
Murphy, Eddie 127, 186, 187
Murphy, Ralph 22
Murray, Bill 127, 129
The Music Lovers 165
Mustin, Burt 81
Mysterious Island 79
Mystery of the Wax Museum 61
Mystery Science Theatre 3000 167

Nagel, Anne 31
Nakata, Hideo 195
The Naked Gun: From the Files of Police Squad! 196
The Nanny 88
Narita, Richard 112
National Lampoon's Animal House 120
Naughton, David 121
Neal, Patricia 180
Neville, Robert 34
New Line Cinema 148
New World Pictures 149
New York State Archives 1

New York Times 158, 182, 190, 192, 193, 195
Nicholson, Jack 64, 65, 69, 70, 71, 72, 73
Nicholson, James H. 69, 97
Nielsen, Leslie 183, 184, 185, 196, 197
A Night at the Opera 115
Night Gallery 137
"Night Gaunts" 149
The Night of Anubis 139
Night of the Blood Beast 206
Night of the Comet 123
Night of the Creeps 150–151, 152
Night of the Demon 73, 110
Night of the Lepus 203
Night of the Living Dead 139, 150, 201
The Nightmare Before Christmas 158
A Nightmare on Elm Street 148, 190
Nighy, Bill 201
Niven, David 112
No Place Like Homicide 67
Noonan, Tom 151
Norris, Edward 26, 27
Norris, William J. 143
North, Virginia 95, 96
Norton, Jack 44
Nosferatu 12, 84, 116
Nosferatu the Vampyre 116, 138
Not of This Earth 60, 64
Nugent 24, 25, 26
Nugent, Frank S. 25
Nugent, J.C. 24
Nurmi, Maila 161

Oakley Court 110
O'Bannon, Dan 140, 141, 142
O'Brien, Margaret 53
O'Brien, Richard 109
The Odd Couple 112
O'Driscoll, Martha 44, 45
Of Love and Death 182
Of Mice and Men 169
O'Hara, Catherine 156
Ohmart, Carol 86
Oingo Boingo 156
O'Keefe, Miles 160
The Old Dark House 17–22
The Old Dark House (1963) 67–69, 98
Oliver, Barrett 155
Olivier, Laurence 47
Olsen, Ole 43, 44, 45, 46
Olsen and Johnson 44, 44, 45, 46
The Omen 125
Once Bitten 136–137
One Exciting Night 6, 7, 12
One Night in the Tropics 31
Orion Pictures 140
Orphans of the Storm 6
Oscar Wilde 98
O'Shea, Michael D. 185

O'Shea, Milo 98, 100
Othello 98
Our Gang 151
Ova, Paul 115
"Over the Rainbow" 96
Owen, Reginald 42
Oxenberg, Catherine 165
Oz, Frank 120

Paoli, Dennis 143
Paper Moon 107
Paragon, John 161
Paramount Pictures, 24, 25, 26, 32, 75, 186, 187
Pardon Me But Your Teeth Are in My Neck 84
Parker, Eddie 56
Parker, Edwin 58, 59
Parks, Andrew 207
Parks, Larry 38
Parrish, Helen 30
Paynter, Robert 120
Peace, J. Stephen 114
Peace, Rock 114
Peace, Steve 114
Peasgood, Julie 126
Peckinpah, Sam 88
Pee-Wee's Big Adventure 155, 156
Pee-Wee's Playhouse 175
Pegg, Simon 201, 202
Penthouse 120
The People That Time Forgot 118
The Perils of Pauline 59
Perkins, Anthony 165
Perry, Luke 176
Peter Pan 75
Peterson, Cassandra 161, 162
Petticoat Larceny 46
Phantasm 197
Phantasm IV: Oblivion 197
Phantom of the Opera (Broadway show) 169
The Phantom of the Opera (1925) 35
Phantom of the Paradise 111
Phemonena 181
Phibes Resurrectus 97
Picardo, Robert 169
Pidgeon, Walter 13, 14
Pierce, Jack 48
Pink Flamingos 111
Piranha 132
Plan 9 from Outer Space 150
Planck, Robert 15
Planet of the Apes 137
Pleasance, Donald 67
Poe, Edgar Allan 34, 69, 70, 71, 72, 73, 94, 142
Poirot, Hercule 112
Polanski, Roman 4, 81, 82, 83, 84, 85, 86, 92, 93, 105, 195
Pootie Tang 196
Pop Cinema 4
Porky Pig 170

Posey, Parker 194
Poston, Tom 67, 68, 69
Potts, Annie 130, 131
Poultrygeist: Night of the Chicken Dead 147
PRC 36
Presley, Elvis 107, 197, 198, 199
Price, Dennis 67
Price, Victoria 73
Price, Vincent 30, 31, 51, 52, 59, 60, 69, 70- 75, 94 -101, 109, 125–127, 134, 135, 155
Priestly, J.B. 17, 18
Pritchard, Robert 146
Private Parts 124
The Producers 107, 108
Professor Creeps 32
Proft, Pat 196
Prowse, David 91, 199
Pryor, Thomas M. 55
Psycho 3, 63, 64, 69, 81, 123
Psycho II 137
Psychomania 93–94
"Puberty Love" 114, 115
Punsly, Bernard 36
Purcell, Dick 33
Purcell, Gertrude 31

Quarrier, Iain 82
Quarry, Robert 96, 97
Quigley, Linnea 140
Quinn, Anthony 28

Rafkin, Alan 80
Ragsdale, William 137, 138, 139
The Railway Children 122
Raimi, Ivan 178
Raimi, Sam 148
Raimi, Ted 153
The Rainbow 166
Rains, Claude 18, 30, 31, 54
Ralston, Marcia 22
Ramis, Harold 127, 128, 129, 130
Rank, J. Arthur 47
Ransohoff, Martin 82, 84
Rasputin the Mad Monk 93
Rathbone, Basil 24, 29, 34, 73, 74, 75, 108
Ratzenberger, John 119
The Raven 69–73, 178
The Raven (1935) 70
Ray, Fred Olen 186
Raye, Martha 24
Rayns, Tony 13
Reagan, Ronald 41
The Real Ghostbusters 131
Re-Animator 142–145, 168
Rear Window 63, 138
Redding, Robert 160
Redeker, Quinn 86
Redmond, Liam 81
Reed, Oliver 165, 166
Reeves, Michael 93, 126
Regal Film Distributors 75
Regehr, Duncan 151

Reid, Beryl 93, 94, 96
Reid, Milton 97
Reiner, Carl 34, 107
Reitman, Ivan 127, 128, 129, 130, 131
Rennie, Michael 180
Renno, Vincent 52
The Reptile 110
Repulsion 82
The Return of Dracula 138
Return of the Killer Tomatoes! 115
Return of the Living Dead 3 142
Return of the Living Dead Part II 141
The Return of the Living Dead 139–142
Reubens, Paul 175
The Revenge of Frankenstein 110, 143
Revenge of the Zombies 33
Rex, Simon 195
"Rhonda the Immortal Waitress" 174, 175
Rhys-Davies, John 160
Rice, Joan 91
Rich and Famous 128
Richard III 98
Richards, Denise 196
Richardson, Natasha 165
Rieger, August 92
Rigby, Jonathan 91
Rigg, Diana 98, 99, 100, 101
Rinehart, Mary Roberts 6, 11, 69
The Ring 195
Ringu 195
Ritchie, Guy 120
Ritz Brothers, 23, 26, 27
RKO Pictures 46
Robby the Robot 134
Robin Hood: Men in Tights 183, 185
Robinson, Bernard 185
Robot Monster 4
Rock'n'Roll High School 124, 132
Rocky 146
The Rocky Horror Picture Show 109–112, 135
The Rocky Horror Show 109
Roeg, Nicolas 122, 166
Rogell, Albert S. 34
Rogers, Erica 69
Rogers, Peter 79
Rogers, Will 8, 9
Romero, George A. 102, 118, 119, 139, 140, 150, 159, 201, 202
Ronaldo, Frederic I. 31, 34, 35, 48, 55
Roseanne 174
Rosebud Releasing 153
Rosemary's Baby 83
Rosen, Phil 36
Rosenblatt, Roger 193
Rosenbloom, Max 38, 39
Rosener, George 22
Rosenman, Howard 175, 176

Ross, Shirley 24
Rossington, Norman 126
Rossito, Angelo 36
Rothwell, Talbot 79
Rubenstein, Richard P. 140
Ruggles, Charlie 31, 32
Rule, Ja 196
The Ruling Class 98
Russell, Ken 163, 164, 165, 166
Russell, Ray 69
Russell, Rosalind 31
Russo, John 140. 141
Ryan, Robert 28
Ryder, Winona 156

St. James, Susan 116, 117
Saint Joan 19
Salisbury, Mark 158
Salome's Last Dance 165
Sanders, George 93, 94
The San Francisco Examiner 182
Sangster, Jimmy 88, 89, 90, 91
Sarandon, Chris 137, 138, 139
Sarandon, Susan 108, 109, 110
The Satanic Rites of Dracula 116
Saturday Night Live 127, 135, 161, 167
Saturday Review 82
Savini, Tom 146
Saw 11
Sayles, John 132
Scaramouche 98
Scared Sheetless 158
Scared Stiff 29, 57
Scary Movie 194–197
Scary Movie 2 195
Scary Movie 3 195–196
Scary Movie 4 196–197
Schallert, William 134
Schanzer, Karl 86
Schildkaut, Joseph 43
Schlock 120
Schnarre, Monika 177
Schneider, Gary 146
Schneider, Maria 111
Schrieber, Liev 190
SciFi Channel 142
Scorsese, Martin 182
Scott, A.O. 195
Scott, Alex 95
Scott, Lizabeth 29
Scott, Ridley 159, 175
Scream 175, 189–190, 193, 194, 195
Scream 2 190, 193
Scream 3 193–194
SCTV 127, 156
See You Next Wednesday 120
Seed of Chucky 192
Sellers, Peter 112, 113, 114
Seltzer, Aaron 194
Seltzer, David 156
Selwyn, Zack 203
Serafinowica, Peter 201
Sesame Street 140

La Setta 181
The Seven Faces of Dr. Phibes 97
Seven Keys to Baldplate 125
Sh! The Octopus 22, 23, 24, 46
Shakespeare, William 98, 99, 100, 101
Shapiro, Irvin 152
Sharman, Jim 109
Sharp, Don 93, 94
Shaun of the Dead 201–202
Shaw, Reta 81
Shaw Brothers 116
Shawn, Dick 116, 117
Shay, Don 127
Sheen, Charlie 195
Shelley, Mary 107, 142, 165, 167
Sheppard, W. Morgan 161
Shimuzu, Takashi 196
Shingleton, Wilfrid 83
The Shining 135
Shivers 163
Shyamalan, M. Night 195, 196
Sidney, Sylvia 156
Signorelli, James 161
Signs 195
The Silence of the Lambs 179
Sim, Gerald 97
Simms, Ginny 30
Simon, Neil 112
Sims, Joan 79
Siodmak, Curt 31
Sir Lancelot 47
Sirtis, Marina 177
Siskel, Gene 148
The Sixth Sense 193, 194
Skaaren, Warren 156
The Skeleton Key 196
Slavin, Mary 149
Sleepy Hollow 9, 158
Slocombe, Douglas 83
Smith, Gary 114
Smith, Hal 80
Smith, Madeline 98, 199
Smith, Maggie 112
Smith, Roy Forge 185
Smith, Will 188
Snatch 120
Snyder, Howard 52, 55
Snyder, Suzanne 159
Soavi, Michele 180, 181, 182, 183
Softley, Iain 196
Something Wicked This Way Comes 159
Son of Frankenstein 24, 108
Sondergaard, Gale 24, 26, 34
Spaced 201
Speed Crazy 64
Spence, Ralph 13, 14, 27
Spider Baby 86–87
Spider-Man 154
Spiegel, Scott 153
Spielberg, Steven 132, 134, 148, 171, 188, 196
Spooks Run Wild 36, 37
The Spy Who Loved Me 95

Stage Fright 181
Staley, Joan 80
Stallone, Sylvester 146
Stanley, Eric 22
Stanley, Forrest 12, 13, 14
Steele, Barbara 102
Stephens, Bob 182
Stephenson, Pamela 135
Stern, Daniel 155
The Steve Allen Show 80
Stevens, Craig 57
Stevenson, Jessica 201
Stevenson, Robert Louis 57
Stewart, Martha 192
Stewart, Mel 172
Stone, Dee Wallace 188, 189
Storm, Howard 136
Story, Ronald D. 147
Strange, Glenn 48, 49, 50, 51
Strickfaden, Kenneth 108
Strysik, John 142
Stuart, Gloria 18, 19, 20, 21, 22
StudioCanal 201
A Study in Terror 83
Subotsky, Milton 75, 77
Sullavan, Margaret 31
Survival Quest 197
Suschitzky, Wolfgang 101
Sutherland, A. Edward 31
Sutherland, Donald 78, 175, 176, 177
Sutton, Frank 147
Sutton, John 60
Swank, Hilary 175
Swanson, Kristy 174, 175, 176, 177
"Sweeney Todd" 119
A Swingin' Affair 107

Tales from the Crypt 78
Tales of Terror 69, 70
Tamblyn, Russ 178
Tapert, Rob 152, 179, 180
Tarantino, Quentin 203
Tarantula 110, 170
Tarzan the Ape Man 160
Taste the Blood of Dracula 89
Tate, Sharon 82, 85
Taylor, Alfred 86
Taylor, Eric 34
Taylor, Sharon 114
Tea-Time of the Dead 201
Temple, Shirley 28
Tenebrae 181
Tenser, Tony 81, 82
The Terror 87
Terry-Thomas 95, 96
The Texas Chainsaw Massacre 118
That Kind of Girl 81
Theater of Blood 97–101, 160
Thesiger, Ernest 4, 19, 20, 21, 22
They Came from Denton High 109
They Came from Within 163
They Made Me a Criminal 36

Thibault, Carl 151
Thin Man 112
The Thing from Another World 81
Thirteen Ghosts 193
The 39 Steps 94
This Island Earth 48
This Sporting Life 98
Thomas, Gerald 79
Thompson, Howard 91
The Three Musketeers (1939) 27
Three Stooges 27, 55, 153, 155, 181
Thunderball 151
Thurman, Uma 203
Tigon Films 125
Tilly, Jennifer 191, 192
Tim Burton: Burton on Burton 158
Time Magazine 193
The Tingler 67, 170
Titus Andronicus 98
To Have and Have Not 66
To the Devil ... a Daughter 125
Tobey, Kenneth 132, 134, 170
Todd, Richard 126
Toler, Sidney 33
Tommy 165
Torgl, Mark 146
El Topo 111
Tourneur, Jacques 73
Towne, Robert 66
The Toxic Avenger 145–147, 167
The Toxic Avenger Part II 147
The Toxic Avenger Part III: The Last Temptation of Toxie 147
Toxic Crusaders 147
Trail of the Screaming Forehead 206–207
Transylvania 6-5000 156
Trauma 181
Trautman, Allan 140
Tremors 170–172
Tri-Star Pictures 150, 151
The Trollenberg Terror 67
Troma Entertainment 145, 146, 147
The Trouble with Harry 53
Tuchrello, Tim 119
Turner, Kathleen 165
Turner, Stephen 91
Tuttle, Lurene 81
Twain, Mark 180
Twentieth Century-Fox 109, 110
28 Days Later 201
Twilight Zone 107, 132
Twilight Zone: The Movie 132
Tyler, Brian 197
Tynan, Brandon 22

Udenio, Fabiana 172, 173
Ulmer, Edgar G. 34
Ulrich, Skeet 189, 190
The Undead 64
Underwood, Ron 170, 171, 172

The Undying Monster 31
United Artists 119
Universal-International Pictures 47–59
Universal Pictures 11–14, 17–22, 24, 30–36, 47, 108, 118, 120, 151, 170–171, 178 -179, 180, 186, 201–202
The Usual Suspects 194

Vampire 78
Vampire Circus 94
The Vampire Happening 92–93
Vampire in Brooklyn 186–187, 189
The Vampire Lovers 83
Van Buren, Ned 8, 9
Van Der Velde, Nadine 148
Van Gelder, Lawrence 192
Van Hentenryck, Kevin 163
van Vooren, Monique 102
Variety 146, 207
The Vault of Horror 78
Venturini, Edward 8, 9
Verbinski, Gore 195
Verhoeven, Paul 175
Vernon, John 158, 159
Vestron Pictures 165
Victor, Henry 33
The Village 196
Vincent 155
Vincent Price: A Daughter's Biography 73
Voodoo 77

Wain, Edward 66
Wakeman, Rick 120
Walas, Chris 134, 169
Walker, Nancy 112
Walker, Pete 125
Wallace-Stone, Dee 148
Walsh, Fran 188
Walsh, M. Emmett 148
The Walter Reade Organization 139
Wan, James 196
War of the Worlds 196
Ward, Fred 170, 171, 172
Ward, Sophie 177, 178
Warhol, Andy 101, 102, 103, 104, 123
Warner, David 160
Warner Bros 22, 126, 134156, 157, 158, 168, 169, 170
Washburn, Beverly 86

Wasteland 194
Waters, John 111, 192
Waxwork 159–160, 177
Waxwork II: Lost in Time 177–178
Waxworks 12, 13
Way Down East 6, 12
Wayans, Keenan Ivory 194, 195
Wayans, Marlon 194
Wayans, Shawn 194
Weaver, Sigourney 128
Webber, Andrew Lloyd 169
Weber, Steven 183, 184, 185
Wedlock, Hugh, Jr. 52, 55
Weinstein, Bob 195
Weinstein, Harvey 195
Weinstein Company 195
Welch, Bo 157
Welker, Frank 134
Welles, Mel 64, 65
Welles, Orson 60, 112
Wells, H.G. 31
Wendt, George 149
Werewolf 78
Werewolf of London 120
Wesley, Kassie 154
West, Mae 161
West, Roland 9, 11- 17, 59
Westcott, Helen 57
Westman, Nydia 25, 26
Westmore, Bud 48
Weta Workshop 203
Wetherell, Virginia 89
Whale, James 17, 18, 19, 20, 21, 22, 30, 54, 67, 102, 151, 172, 173, 192
What? 105
What a Carve-Up! 67, 68
Whedon, Joss 174, 175, 176, 177
When Katelbach Comes 82
When Worlds Collide 110
White, Pearl 59
White, Trevor 110
Whitlow, Jill 150
Whiton, James 94, 97
Whitten, Marguerite 33
The Who 165
Wiederhorn, Ken 141
Wiene, Robert 5
Wilbur, Crane 9, 59
The Wild Bunch 88
Wilde, Oscar 42, 195
Wilder, Gene 107, 108
Wiley, Ethan 149
Willard, John 11, 12, 25

Williams, Kenneth 79, 80
Williamson, Kevin 189, 190, 193, 194
Wills, Brember 21
Wilson, Debra 196, 197
Wilson, Larry 156
Wilson, S.S. 171
Wilson, Stephen 135
Wilton, Penelope 201
Windsor, Marie 58, 59
Winfrey, Oprah 197
Winslet, Kate 187
Winters, Roland 33, 52
Winwood, Estelle 112
Wise, Robert 177
The Wistful Widow of Wagon Gap 48
Witchfinder General 93, 126
The Wizard of Oz 110, 133
The Wolf Man 87
Women in Love 165
Wong, Victor 171
Wood, Ed 36, 150, 185
Woodbridge, George 67
Woodbury, Joan 33
Woodruff, Tom, Jr. 151
Woollcott, Alexander 6, 11
Working Title Films 201
Woronov, Mary 123, 124
Wright, Edgar 201, 202
W.W. Hodkinson Corporation 9

Yacowar, Maurice 103, 104, 105
Yarbrough, Jean 33
Yasbeck, Amy 185
York, Michael 122
"You Stepped Out of a Dream" 96
You'll Find Out 30
Young, Robert 43
Young Frankenstein 105–109, 116, 117, 183, 195
Yu, Ronny 191, 192
Yuzna, Brian 142, 143, 172, 173, 174, 199, 200, 201

Zacherle, John 162
Zane, Billy 148
Zemeckis, Robert 188
Zimet, Julian 93
Zombies on Broadway 46, 47
Zotz! 67
Zucco, George 24
Zucker, David 195, 196, 197

www.ingramcontent.com/pod-product-compliance
Ingram Content Group UK Ltd.
Pitfield, Milton Keynes, MK11 3LW, UK
UKHW050535150426
5217IPUK00026B/1940